HUMANS

HUMANS

A MONSTROUS HISTORY

SUREKHA DAVIES

UNIVERSITY OF CALIFORNIA PRESS

University of California Press
Oakland, California

Library of Congress Cataloging-in-Publication Data

Names: Davies, Surekha, author.
Title: Humans : a monstrous history / Surekha Davies.
Description: Oakland, California : University of California Press, [2025] |
    Includes bibliographical references and index.
Identifiers: LCCN 2024021626 (print) | LCCN 2024021627 (ebook) |
    ISBN 9780520388093 (cloth) | ISBN 9780520388116 (ebook)
Subjects: LCSH: Monstrosity. | Monsters—History. | Monsters—
    Social aspects.
Classification: LCC GR825 .D38 2025 (print) | LCC GR825 (ebook) |
    DDC 398.24/54—dc23/eng/20240815
LC record available at https://lccn.loc.gov/2024021626
LC ebook record available at https://lccn.loc.gov/2024021627

Manufactured in the United States of America

33   32   31   30   29   28   27   26   25   24
10   9   8   7   6   5   4   3   2   1

publication supported by a grant from
The Community Foundation for Greater New Haven
as part of the **Urban Haven Project**

For my friends

CONTENTS

Plates appear following page 186

ILLUSTRATIONS

FIGURES

PLATES

Introduction

I SPENT MY CHILDHOOD watching too much *Star Trek* and have been searching for monsters and aliens ever since. They led me through grad school. They sustained me through adventures on the road: being locked into a vault in the Vatican Library and balancing on a ladder in a Parisian basement while wrangling giant maps and directing the beam of a hot lamp, trying not to burn anything. Monsters climbed into my syllabi when I became a professor. They jostled together in my first book, on the monstrous peoples that cartographers devised for maps during the age of European exploration. But the seed for *Humans: A Monstrous History* was a chance visit to an astrobiology conference at the Library of Congress in 2014. At "Preparing for Discovery," scholars discussed how societies might prepare for the possibility of finding life beyond earth.

I was then a fellow at the Kluge Center, working on my first book in the colossal Beaux Arts–style Thomas Jefferson Library Building, across the street from the U.S. Capitol. The astrobiology conference was happening just downstairs from my office. The Kluge fellows, from anthropologists to musicologists, were invited to attend. In one of the panels, scientists discussed how societies might contain extraterrestrial pathogens and build weapons to fight hostile aliens. But it seemed to me that they were missing a trick. In the Q and A session, up went my hand. I asked, "What about preparing people on earth for dealing with the discovery that they were not alone in the universe? How would that affect people whose religious beliefs appeared not to predict life beyond earth? Wouldn't people panic? Wasn't there a risk of anarchy and looting in response to even an announcement that extraterrestrials had been found or—worse—were on earth? To prepare for alien encounters, shouldn't we be figuring out how to get along better with one another?"

As I worked through my questions, there were nods in the audience—but then the panel chair cut me off. He looked baffled and cross. My questions were not about weapons or germs, and so not something he wanted to think about. So he chose to condescend: he said that I had asked "the wrong questions," that my observations were off topic. It was then that I realized that that I was on to something. Not only did science lack some of the answers for how humanity should interact with life on earth, but it was also insufficient for thinking about the cosmos. What I had to offer came, instead, from deep in the humanities. And that something involved monsters.

MONSTERS: WHAT?

There are no monsters, but all of them are real. This is a book about monster-making: the stories societies tell about who they think isn't normal or typical—the process of defining people as something outside normal categories, as something monstrous. When people hear the word "monster," they tend to think of sinister things: vampires, zombies, and Frankenstein or sociopaths and serial killers. But there are fun monsters too, like the Muppets, and others that are somewhere between terrifying and amusing, like centaurs. What these real and fictional monsters share is a capacity to challenge or transcend ideas about typical bodies or behavior. Monsters are category breakers.

Monsters are the work of the imagination. "Monster," as I use it in this book, is a broad catchall for any term—whether it's positive, negative, or neutral—that people use to define someone who falls across or outside the categories of "normal" people or beings in the world, as far as they understand them. If people and wolves are separate categories in the understanding of the universe, then the discovery of a werewolf would be the discovery of something abnormal or monstrous. As a hybrid of two regular categories, the werewolf is a monster. This kind of monster would be alarming to meet and not simply because of its teeth. By showing that wolves and people are not entirely separate after all, a werewolf would reveal the limits of our categories and change how we thought about who, or what, humans really are.

Monsters are ideas that show us things. They reveal the edge of types of being or how far we can go before we stop being one thing and suddenly snap into another type of thing, like a light switch going from on to off, except that the monster is neither on nor off but that seesaw space in between, where the light threatens to blow a fuse as it judders between settings. My capacious definition of monsters includes anyone who becomes labeled in ways that exclude them from the definition of normal. This process of labeling—of what I call monster-making or monstrification—reveals the limits of the categories with which societies understand and organize the world and its peoples.[1]

In biology "monster" used to work as a placeholder, with characteristics and a shape that allowed people to design techniques for filling in the gaps in knowledge. Today "monster" has been replaced by phrases like "unknown species" or "newly discovered species." There was a similar phenomenon in the mathematical sciences: scientific papers and the notes of scientists were once filled with what they called "demons"—their label for unruly phenomena. This category allowed scientists to generate experiments to investigate the observations they could not yet explain.[2] Both monsters and demons were shorthands that represented real phenomena that were, as yet, imperfectly known and beyond the observers' classificatory system.

Monster-making happens when people say that someone or something is weird or does not fit, whatever that means. It's what happens when people try to organize everyone and everything into neat little boxes. Whatever the shape of the boxes, there will usually be people who don't fit in them comfortably, if they fit in them at all. We can then make new boxes, reorganize everything in the old ones, or decide that boxes are *so yesterday* and throw them out without making new ones. We can even lump together all the awkward cases in a box of their own and label it "monsters."

"Monster" itself can be a term of classification—a brusque, dismissive shorthand for "something I don't know what to do with." But monster-making is also the act of making a value judgment, a form of name-calling with great power. Communities identify groups and individuals as monstrous, as transgressing the limits of normal bodies, beliefs, or behavior, to give their abstract fears and ideas a physical form and a potential solution. Assumptions about norms and monsters lie at the heart of how societies define and classify people. This book is an alternative history of humanity, one that uses the monster as a lens to refract into view hidden assumptions that inform ideas about nature, people, and society.

Devastated by a death during childbirth? A person in sixteenth-century Europe might blame the midwife—she might be a witch. Annoyed that your workers in the Caribbean keep wandering away from the backbreaking, poorly paid work required to bring in the harvest that keeps you in luxury?

A seventeenth-century European plantation owner might lobby for a new legal category of worker: enslaved Black Africans defined as property, who belong to them and are required to do their bidding and to whom horrific punishments may be meted out lawfully should they try to escape. Monstrified individuals and groups—the monsters of the archive—reveal something about the person or communities *doing the naming*, not the person or communities they name.

Today's urgent questions about human rights, labor, wealth, health, technology, and climate justice contain traces from the preindustrial past: assumptions about who counts as a person and what counts as natural. Across arenas ranging from gymnastics to policing, monster-making has profoundly shaped how we think about science, society, and humanity. We cannot fully understand the present or avoid making the same mistakes in the future without attending to the long and volatile history of monsters. This book tells the story of how the past four millennia of monster-making created the world we live in today. Many of the examples come from the ancient Mediterranean, Europe and its empires, and the Americas and reveal an alternative history of the West through those the West defined as monsters. I see monsters as portals through which to travel through space, time, and cultures to see where humanity may be heading next. This is not so much a history of monsters as a history *through* monsters.

HISTORY THROUGH MONSTERS

Humans: A Monstrous History shows how people have defined, explained, and vilified otherness across the world through long, wild traditions of what I call "monster-making." Acts of monster-making are fundamental to understanding how people have thought about, interacted with, and classified one another. Writing history involves making tough decisions about what stories to include. Whose lives, stories, agendas, and interpretations matter? This book holds in tension the lives and stories of many individuals and peoples who were seen in their time as outside or transgressing categories. At times we can hear the voices of those who were the object of monstrification. But by and large, this book tracks not the monsters but the monster labelers: the monster inventors or name-callers.[3] It reveals the assumptions, agendas, and interpretations of those who saw others as monsters and who actively framed them as less than or threats to an imagined normal or default.

Humanity is presently hurtling toward a monster-event horizon: where people once made monsters of others, now increasing numbers of flesh-and-blood humans are losing rights to corporations or being surveilled or replaced by so-called AI. Humanity risks being pushed to the margins of the future or perhaps thrown out of an airlock. How then do we live in an age when the corporeal human being is increasingly framed as the inconvenience—the monster? We need to be prepared for meeting the strange, on earth or in outer space, with curiosity and empathy, as science writer Ed Yong puts it in his writings about animals.[4] And we also have to contend with the fact that the monster lurking in the shadows might be ourselves.

ONE

On the Ecology of Monsters

IN *FRANKENSTEIN*, MARY SHELLEY'S turn of the nineteenth-century horror novel, Victor Frankenstein's loomingly tall monster was stitched together like a sewing-class project gone fantastically wrong. The monster was nasty and ultimately (hopefully) imaginary, like Bram Stoker's blood-thirsty Dracula scowling away in his musty castle at the end of that century or the horrid thing you feared might be lurking under your bed as a child. These are the sorts of things that people often think of if you ask them what a monster is.

The horror of Frankenstein's monster lay in its in-betweenness. Like a werewolf thumping, slinking, and baying through the night, straddling the boundary between human and animal, Frankenstein's monster straddled boundaries: between dead and alive and between one body and another. Monsters like this activate our imagination. They might go on a rampage or be some sort of existential threat. The bull-headed, human-bodied Minotaur of ancient Greek mythology embodied all the attributes of the loner-threat monster. He languished in a labyrinth on the island of Crete, subsisting on a diet of takeout deliveries of bright young things sacrificed for his delectation. From creatures in ancient myths to serial killers in today's news headlines, this sense of "monster" as a one-off, a loner, and a category problem is a pow-erful form of storytelling. But that's just a small part of the story of monsters and the history of humanity.

People define what they mean by human by defining where they think "human" ends: at the monster. Monsters defined like this separate "us" (who-ever that is) from the "them" of other beings we are supposedly not: bulls, wolves, corpses. Calling in-between beings monsters reassures us that we, personally, *aren't* this weird or horrible—only monsters are like that. We,

FIGURE 1. Attributed to Lydos, Attic black-figure amphora with Minotaur, 550–540 BCE. In Greek mythology, when King Minos of Crete failed to sacrifice a bull, the gods punished him by having his wife, Pasiphae, fall in love with it. She had an artist construct a wooden cow to have sex with the bull. The Minotaur was the result. 86.AE.60. Digital image courtesy of Getty's Open Content Program.

instead, are supposedly straightforwardly ordinary humans, completely distinct from both animals and creepy things.

But the definition of human is neither straightforward nor ordinary, nor is it universal or timeless. And the category or box called "human" is not entirely separate from the categories of other beings—not even from "monsters." Depending on where you have lived and how you were raised, you may sort the beings of the world into very different boxes with no overlap—say, plant life here, humans there, and monsters (whatever they are) somewhere else. Perhaps it even seems obvious what goes where. Or you may be comfortable with the idea that a slippery slope connects human to other sorts of beings, including monsters: beings that are neither one thing nor another or are even many things at once.

If you think to be human is to be single, stable individuals or beings who end at their skin, then prepare to raise your eyebrows. I'd like us to look together at some of the ways in which people have understood the category of the human very differently: at human as a being on a continuum, capable of blending with, even into, their surroundings and other beings. Categories are conventions, and they are not universally agreed on. The boundary between human and the rest of the world and its beings—from what I'm going to call *ecology*—turns out to be blurry and permeable. Right at that edge between different categories are beings that people define (using a variety of terms) as monsters: beings that challenge those categories because they do not entirely fit any of them, because they fit multiple categories, or because they transcend them all.

In 1686, in a town in Oaxaca, southwestern Mexico, a certain Marcial de la Cruz, an Indigenous man, confessed that he had accidentally murdered his wife, Catalina María. As he told it, the couple had been out for a walk when his wife had gone on ahead while he took a dip in a river. When he scurried to catch up, he spied a jaguar, crouched in readiness to attack. After calling on the Christian God and brandishing the rosary around his neck at the jaguar, he clubbed the creature. At that moment a voice in his own language of Tíchazàa advised, "Cuckold, don't kill that woman." As the jaguar died, it morphed into his wife. After the death of his wife/the jaguar, Marcial de la Cruz fled the scene, only turning himself in for murdering his wife two years later.[1]

This act of involuntary manslaughter was not a unique predicament. Look in the inquisitorial archives of colonial Spanish America, and you'll find bundles of handwritten documents, witness statements, and reports from trials describing how a person who had injured or killed an animal turned out to have, in fact, murdered a person. Treatises about Indigenous customs describe shape-shifters and individuals whose souls could flit between bodies. The sixteenth-century Spanish Dominican friar Diego Durán described how an Indigenous person in Mexico told him that a holy man had left the area because he was being persecuted by not one but two *nahualli*, or "shapeshifters."[2]

The Mexica understood shape-shifting as part of how the cosmos worked. Beings in the visible and invisible worlds—from rocks and plants to gods—had dual natures. Competing, opposing qualities and predilections shaped their constantly shifting natures.[3] This way of thinking enlarged and blended individual types of beings and made the boundary between humans and the rest of the beings in the world porous. People could absorb the powers of things and animals. Indeed, humans, animals, plants, rocks, mountains, and stars were all somewhat *squishy:* under the right conditions, people could experience being something else. Since shape-shifting was part of the

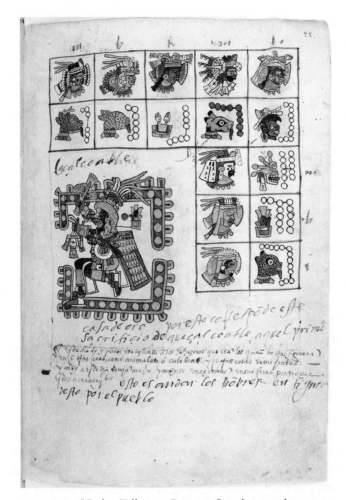

FIGURE 2. "Codex Telleriano-Remensis," mid-sixteenth century, showing a Mexica divinatory handbook or ritual calendar. The central image probably represents a priest of the god Quetzalcoatl. The squares represent different days. The Spanish annotations attempt to explain the glyphs. Département des Manuscrits, Mexicain 385, fol. 22v. Bibliothèque Nationale de France, Paris.

regular order of things, the distance between humans and ecology—the world beyond one's own body—was small.

This was not so for the seventeenth-century Catholic curate–turned-judge Hernando Ruiz de Alarcón. Raised in Taxco, also in southwest Mexico, he was posted to nearby Atenango. There he became so furious about Indigenous beliefs—as far as he understood them—that he took it into his own hands to flog Indigenous people who transgressed Catholic teachings. Becoming a one-man lynch mob was technically illegal under Spanish law, but when word of Ruiz de Alarcón's activities reached the inquisition in New Spain, he got a promotion. Around 1617 the Office of the Holy Inquisition appointed him to the role of ecclesiastical judge, responsible for informing the inquisitors of local instances of the persistence of Indigenous beliefs and practices.[4] The gnarliest problem that the Catholic Church faced was syncretism: the practice by which Indigenous people understood Catholic teachings as analogs of their existing beliefs or as add-ons that did not require them to give up Indigenous beliefs or practices.

In the course of his now-official duty as local persecutor in chief, Ruiz de Alarcón penned a scathing catalog of what he called local "heathen superstitions and customs." The *Treatise on the Heathen Superstitions and Customs That Today Live among the Indians Native to This New Spain* had issues with everything from the Indigenous way of blurring categories—"their belief that clouds are angels and gods, worthy of being adored"—to their custom of consuming mind-altering substances like tobacco and peyote (a cactus) to have visions. As for the *nahualli*, Ruiz de Alarcón concluded that the parents of such a person had made a pact with the devil, one that enabled them to wield unnatural powers in the world.[5]

A great many of today's ideas that seem like laws of the universe in one setting look arbitrary for people with different cultural or scientific frameworks. The history of how cultures have drawn the map of life—of where they placed themselves in relation to the web of ecology (beings, things, and relationships) reveals where people drew the boundary between human and "the rest," if they drew one at all.[6] The colonial-era clash of Indigenous and Catholic ideas reveals that, to understand how cultures have defined what they mean by human, we should pay attention to ideas about in-between beings—monsters. As we'll see over the course of this book, how people define where human ends and other sorts of beings begin has shaped how people interact and how they act on the world around them, for millennia. And to find the roots of the ideas that prompted Catholic missionaries and jurists to condemn Indigenous beliefs about shape-shifters, that's how far back we need to go.

Geographers and naturalists in ancient Greece and Rome identified two broad sorts of monsters. One sort was the "one-off" monstrous birth, like a two-headed calf. This type of monster could appear anywhere and was a divine sign of someone's misbehavior, a portent of doom—a sign of impending punishment sent by the gods—or an accident of nature. But there was another sort of monstrosity, one that appeared not as the one-off difference of a single individual but as a universal feature across an entire community that shared an unusual trait, like having their eyes below their shoulders or possessing an enormous lower lip. Ancient Greek and Roman thinkers interpreted confused stories about distant peoples and their practices as evidence of what they called monstrous peoples: entire communities of (to Greeks) misshapen or misbehaving individuals linked by their geography and genealogy.[7]

In ancient Mediterranean thought, people were susceptible to the environment before birth and during the course of their lives. Afro-Eurasian physicians were influenced by the teachings of the fifth-century BCE physician and naturalist Hippocrates and, later, by the third-century CE physician and surgeon Galen.[8] These thinkers understood ecology to shape people's bodies, health, and temperaments (what might today be called personalities) by affecting the four humors or essential substances that made up their bodies: blood, phlegm, black bile, and yellow bile.[9]

People's minds and bodies were apparently malleable. Their humors were altered by the environment: by airs, waters, medicaments, foodstuffs, seasons, the alignment of stars and planets, the climate in which they were born and brought up, the climates they experienced throughout their lives, and even their physical activities. Well into the seventeenth century and the disputes over shape-shifters in Spanish American colonies, scientists and medical practitioners in Europe understood the bodies, behaviors, and health of entire societies as the product of a dialogue between internal humors and ecology.[10] Humoral thinking opened up the possibility that extreme environments would contain alarming life-forms. Entire societies might be so denatured by their surroundings that they were monstrous—fundamentally different, somehow, from "normal" people.

Perhaps the most influential ancient authority on monstrous peoples was naturalist Pliny the Elder (23–79 CE), a Roman of such insatiable curiosity that he ended up getting killed by Mount Vesuvius when he went to check out

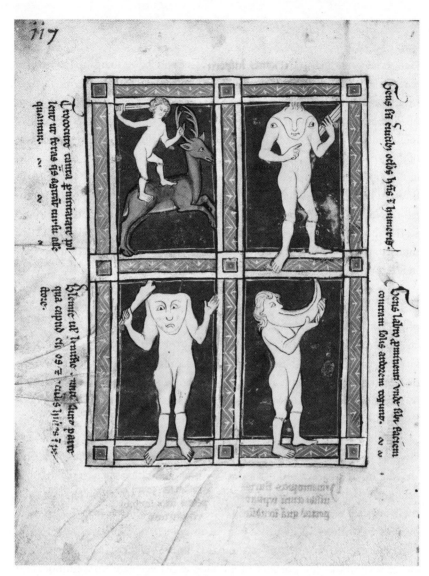

FIGURE 3. Monstrous peoples, 1277 or after. This page appears in a manuscript compendium of texts about the natural world and illustrates some of the monstrous peoples that ancient Greek and Roman authors had hypothesized as inhabiting regions distant from the Mediterranean, places where the climate was harsh enough to generate monsters. MS Ludwig XV 4. Digital image courtesy of Getty's Open Content Program, fol. 117v.

the eruption. Before his untimely end, Pliny wrote a mammoth, thirty-seven-volume treatise on the descriptive sciences, integrating the study of everything from human cultures to the earth's mineral resources. His *Natural History* served as a field guide for later geographers and naturalists in Europe for centuries, well into the era of European oceanic voyages and empires.

Pliny provided a whistle-stop tour of the peoples of Asia, Africa, and Europe—at least, of those about whom he had any intel. There are endless tidbits about local ecology, triumphs of engineering, and customs: in northwest Greece noxious fumes emanate from parts of the ground in Epirus and a thousand-foot bridge spans the Acheron River in Threspotia. In the Dead Sea "the bodies of animals do not sink in its waters, even bulls and camels floating." Here and there Pliny revealed his sources. He learned about India from Greek authors who had "stayed as guests with the Indian kings" and from writers "who accompanied Alexander the Great" on his expedition to conquer India.[11]

Pliny surmised that extreme climates and environments brought monstrous peoples into being: the most fertile regions generated peoples with exaggerated attributes, such as giants or the Panotii (beings with very large ears); desert regions caused bodies to lack things and were thus the home of pygmies (who lacked height); troglodytes found their environment so unappealing that they attempted to avoid it entirely by living in caves.[12] He featured peoples with customs he considered to be spectacular. Beyond the Ripaean Mountains, the Hyperboreans apparently lived extremely long and idyllic lives in a temperate climate. They died only when they jumped "from a certain rock into the sea" once they had had their fill of a life of luxury. By contrast, the Atlas tribe was said to "have fallen below the level of human civilization," lacking names for themselves and constantly cursing the rising and setting sun.[13]

The region most densely populated with unusual peoples was "Ethiopia," asserted Pliny.[14] It was, he surmised, not surprising that Ethiopia contained "animals and human monstrosities, considering the capacity of ... fire to mould their bodies and carve their outlines." Some of these beings supposedly had neither lips nor tongues; others communicated through gestures rather than speech. Some did not know fire. In book 7 of the *Natural History*, Pliny shifted from talking about animals to talking about people. He asserted that "India and parts of Ethiopia especially teem with marvels." By contrast, Europe (as Pliny had assured the reader earlier) not only nourished and raised "that people which has conquered all other nations" but was also "the most beauteous portion of the earth."[15] Implicitly, the farther you traveled from the eastern Mediterranean, the more monsters you were likely to meet.[16]

156.

[The manuscript folio shows medieval Latin text in two columns flanking a circular zonal diagram. The diagram labels read:]

tempata austral'
mediteraneum
ṅṙa zona habitabilis
septentrionalh frigida

FIGURE 4. Zonal map, 1277 or after. This map, oriented with south at the top, divides the world into climatic zones centered on the Mediterranean: "frigida austral[is], temp[er]ata austral[is], mediterraneum, n[ost]ra zona habitabilis, septentrionalis frigida" (cold southern, temperate southern, Mediterranean, our living zone, northern cold). MS Ludwig XV 4. Digital image courtesy of Getty's Open Content Program, fol. 156v.

A key monster-making zone for ancient Afro-Eurasian thinkers (and the medieval geographers who followed) was the equator, since they knew that the earth became hotter when they traveled south through the Northern Hemisphere. Some geographers even hypothesized that nothing could live south of the region of great heat that engirdled the equator, a region known as the torrid zone. Others told stories about extraordinary people who lived in the distant east. The far north, the regions around and south of the equator, and the distant east were thought to be so harsh in climate that there were no "normal" people. The closer life got to these places, the more deformed it became, eventually becoming monstrous just before reaching the zone where the earth became uninhabitable.

This way of thinking sprang from incorrect theories about the current habitability of parts of the earth, how much and how quickly populations adapt to environments, and the parochial, Eurocentric assumption that Europe's norms were the yardstick for everyone else. But put aside the information gaps and the prejudice for a moment and look at the underlying idea: "the greater the distance from the observer, the stranger the types of beings." There is a parallel between ancient geographic reasoning and how scientists still think about the puzzle of life on a cosmic scale. For today's astrobiologists life on other planets must look different from life on earth (the default) since it will have arisen in different gravitational fields and atmospheres.[17] For ancient Greek and Roman geographers and naturalists, the farther a climate diverged from that of the temperate Mediterranean, the greater the physical and behavioral differences between the region's people and the folks back home (the default)—and the less "normal" they were.[18] Travel far enough from the Mediterranean, and instead of regular peoples there would be monstrous ones. Apart from the scales of distance involved, is this so different— in theory and the form of reasoning—from hypothesizing that life on a distant planet might be based on silicon rather than carbon? In both cases observers noticed that life and ecology are intertwined.

For Pliny monstrous peoples at the world's edges were still *people:* at once something else yet essentially similar in kind to humanity in ways that, say, a cat, a horse, or even a monkey were not. But that, in a way, was the problem. Monstrous peoples supposedly resided only in very distant places. Yet, paradoxically, the malleability of humoral bodies as they moved through space suggested that there might be a slippery slope from the self to the monster and even to the animal. The balance of individuals' humors was known as their "complexion," a term that encompassed appearance, temperament, character, and mental aptitude. And this balance was not fixed in stone (or even in flesh). A person was fungible over space and alterations in lifestyle.[19]

Three features about monstrous peoples set them apart from one-off monstrous individuals (like the Minotaur sulking in his labyrinth) and turned them into a separate category at the edge of the human in ancient thought. Monstrous peoples lived far from the temperate climate of Europe, their bodily and behavioral variations were widespread across their communities, and they passed their distinctive characteristics down to their children.[20] Before the modern age, European and European-descended physicians' ways of understanding the human body in the world were underpinned by the theory of bodily humors. As we'll see, this alarming possibility shaped their ideas about race and nation in the fifteenth and sixteenth centuries once ships sailing under European flags undertook oceanic travel, sewing together the formerly distinct worlds of self and monster.[21]

SHAPE-SHIFTING

Ruiz de Alarcón's position on shape-shifters was typical for a seventeenth-century Christian. His treatise on Indigenous beliefs, which we encountered near the start of this chapter, opens a window onto how a faithful Catholic official saw and (mis)interpreted Nahua understandings of the world.[22] In Christian theology across many denominations, God created humans in his own image, and humans were distinct from the rest of Creation. Western theologians, naturalists, and philosophers (Christian and otherwise) spent centuries declaring that people were somehow not quite animal, not simply part of nature, but something separate and special. For these thinkers humans were flesh and blood, mammal, and mortal—yet their physical forms and mental worlds were separate from everything else in the world: humans were exceptional and a category distinct from ecology. Thus the very idea of shape-shifters was appalling to the church. Yet humoral theory had left the door open to a limited kind of shape-shifting.

Catholic missionaries and jurists who encountered Indigenous understandings of the relationship between humans and their ecology saw a cosmovision so utterly different from their own that they branded these beliefs as idolatrous, as false and dangerous errors. To these observers the Mexica way of thinking and doing was nothing less than diabolical: they had to be in league with the devil.[23] And if by any chance they *were* shape-shifting, they shouldn't, and something had to be done about it. Yet European medical thinking of the day, larded with the tenets of ancient humoral thinking, contained a competing understanding of the human in the world, one in which ecology altered minds and bodies whether they liked it or not.

Think about what's around you at this moment. Perhaps you're sitting on a chair or a bench, holding this book in your hand or listening to the audiobook using a device in your pocket. If you're outside, there may be rocks, trees, flowers, birds, mountains, or picnic snacks you can touch, smell, hear, see, or taste. If you're inside, there may be a cat on your lap or a vase of sweet peas between you and the window, wafting their perfume toward you in the breeze. To some people rocks and birds are always rocks and birds and never, ever people. To them rocks, birds, and people are separate, different categories of things or beings in the world. But in classical Mexica cosmology, and in many Indigenous cosmologies, a person might acquire rocky or avian attributes or even turn into a rock or a bird under the right conditions. Here the category of the human blended into other things: it was malleable, not fixed—and shape-shifters blurred the edges of the category of the human.

Surviving Indigenous codices or books, many of which were assembled during the early colonial period by Indigenous scribes working under Spanish authorities, lay out how the Mexica universe worked. One codex claimed that people turned into animals under the influence of natural phenomena or the day of the year (see plate 1).[24] On the day of 9 Dog, sorcerers turned into animals. If you went outdoors, you might glimpse the *nahualli*, people who could turn into animals like snakes, eagles, and jaguars, slithering, strutting, or slinking through the city. On the day of 1 Eagle, demons came out of the sky and became little girls. If you were born on this day, you would become a woman with great power. Others said that it was merely eagles who came from the sky on this day, turning into little girls, so that they could go to war, die in battle, and go to heaven.[25]

In the precolonial Americas, many Indigenous civilizations framed the animals living among them as members of their kin—closer to them than humans from rival or enemy groups.[26] Among Indigenous peoples of Brazil and the Caribbean islands in the early decades of their contact with Europeans, tamed animals and animal hunting partners were family, distinct from wild animals and people of other tribes. The main distinction was neither human/nonhuman nor noble hunting animal versus livestock. Rather, beings in the world were divided into two groups according to whether they were familiarized (part of the family or community) or were the object of predation (someone hunted).[27] While today's debates about animal rights and the attribution of the status of nonhuman personhood to animals may seem very new, in fact the question of the personhood of animals is neither new nor exclusively "Western."[28]

There's no single way to classify beings in the world. To some, like Ruiz de Alarcón, human-animal hybrids are monsters that either don't exist or are diabolical creations. For others, like many of the people on whom Ruiz de

Alarcón sat in judgment, humans and animals are overlapping categories. And for Pliny and those who read him, extreme climates created monstrous peoples. Each option makes possible certain relationships to ecology, making some phenomena clearer while obscuring others.

Communities that want to believe that human beings are separate from their ecology make different choices from those comfortable with existing on a continuum with their ecology or from those willing to imagine the world from the perspective of other species and their needs. As we'll see, how people think about the impact of ecological relationships on their selves shapes the actions they take in—and on—the world. And these actions in turn have rippling effects on human minds and bodies, which, far from being fixed and simple, are always morphing into something else.

CREATION

To best understand the past and its legacies is to think ecologically of all beings and their interrelationships, not of humans alone. For Indigenous peoples of Beringia (the Arctic region around the Bering Strait), ecology has long been a category capacious enough to contain the human. Animals, land, and peoples are bound together in the way they act on one another. They respond to one another's presence and actions, and their bodies nourish one another across space and time. Trace the sun's energy, and it will travel from plant life on land and phytoplankton in the sea, through the bodies of caribou, whales, walruses, and salmon to people and polar bears. The cycles of weather and climate and the choices, actions, and bodies of all these beings change in response to one another. If people were ever separate from their surroundings, it would be only for the briefest moment. Despite this, their lives and bodies would still depend on the web of ecology.[29]

In some Indigenous ways of thinking, understanding the origins of the known world and continuing to live in it sustainably were (and continue to be) two sides of the same coin. Neither religion nor cosmology can be separated from ecology. Indigenous peoples from the Great Lakes region of North America tell the story of Skywoman, an ancient being who brought sweetgrass from the sky. With the help of various birds and animals, Skywoman planted sweetgrass on the back of a willing turtle and thereby made life on land possible. People were junior members of ecology, who must learn from the rest of creation how to contribute to it.[30]

Stories like that of Skywoman map out a reciprocal relationship between people and nature, rather than a one-way, ultimately unsustainable process of extraction.[31] These narratives recommend different lifestyle and steward-ship decisions from stories that place humans on earth as exceptional, divinely ordained inheritors of the earth.[32] People who understand the human as a modifiable, ecological category will be more concerned about harmful changes to the world beyond their skin than those who define the human as separate from ecology. The former are more likely to appreciate that if, say, insects that pollinate plant life suffer a total die-off, they will end up with no crops to eat. Ideas about the *kinds* of things people and other beings are—their ontology—shape how people act in the world and act *on* the world.

The modern Western idea of human exceptionalism defines humans as beings who operate under different conditions and expectations from every-thing else in the world. I call this a form of monstrification, one in which self-identified monsters who broke the category of nature have declared that they are exceptional. In this form of exceptionalism, we have supposedly bro-ken the categories of animal and ecology by exceeding them, and we are sepa-rate from them. Implicit in this thinking is the premise that nothing "out there" can affect "us"—yet heat domes, Arctic vortexes, flash floods, and car-cinogenic industrial pollution make people sick and destroy their homes. The world frequently reminds us that human bodies and minds are not hermeti-cally sealed away from the rest of the world or from our effects on ecology.

SQUISHY BODIES

"She's allergic to absolutely everything," wrote Tally. . . . "Augusta mostly lives on rice and bananas, though she can eat weird things like tripe and dark chocolates with gooey centres. It's no wonder she got on the wrong train."

EVA IBBOTSON, *THE DRAGONFLY POOL*

In Eva Ibbotson's action-adventure novel, *The Dragonfly Pool*, schoolchildren connected the disorganized and forgetful manner of one of their friends with her food intolerances. To Augusta's friends both are quirky and whimsical and each seems to explain the other. I had the pleasure of reading this book a year or two after completing my PhD dissertation, during the writing of which I had immersed myself in the legacy of classical geography and humoral theory in the age of European Atlantic voyages. It was striking to see how the idea that what a person eats shapes what they are *like*, especially when they are atypical in their community, was still so widespread half a millennium later that it could make a humorous appearance in a children's book. Tripe—cow stomach—is not a popular dish in England, where the story is set, especially in the eyes of the eleven-year-old Tally. Dark chocolate's bitterness makes it an acquired taste; gooey centers that could taste of *anything*—including flavors you can't stand—also require a slightly adventurous approach to food. For Tally these whimsical, even alarming, dietary preferences explained Augusta's inability to manage ordinary life tasks, like getting on the right train.

The mind-altering possibilities of food and drink feature in fiction and in cosmic explanation, from *Dr. Jekyll and Mr. Hyde* to the curious case of Eve, the serpent, and the apple.[33] Fantasy, speculative fiction, and science fiction simulate scenarios that lean into the body's capacity for change. In C. S. Lewis's *The Lion, the Witch and the Wardrobe*, a box of enchanted, addictive Turkish Delight is the allegorical apple with which a wicked enchanter-queen ensnares a boy. White readers in the 1950s—Lewis's early readers—would have understood this potent sugary confection as an exotic, perhaps decadent, luxury, especially during the immediate aftermath of World War II, when rationing was still in effect. Lewis describes the Turkish Delight as almost impossible not to inhale: "Each piece was sweet and light to the centre and Edmund had never tasted anything more delicious."[34] Both minds and bodies are squishy in Robert Louis Stevenson's gothic horror novel, *Dr. Jekyll and Mr. Hyde*. In this tale of psychological transformation, Dr. Jekyll invents a serum that splits the violent parts of his personality off from the rest of him, only to find that the monstrous Mr. Hyde—Jekyll's alter ego—gradually takes over his body.

In J. R. R. Tolkien's *The Lord of the Rings*, a uniquely powerful ring gives its wearers magical powers and extends their lives but also corrupts their minds.[35] The ring makes its wearers meaner and cruel at times and allows them to become invisible. The ring's power, however, is channeled through and shaped by the wearers' own strengths, weaknesses, neuroses, and values. If the wearer is a hobbit, or half-sized humanoid with a penchant for eating well and living a quiet life (most of the time), relatively little of cosmic significance is likely to happen: it would be like putting the mind of twenty-two-time tennis Grand Slam champion, Rafael Nadal, into the body of a couch potato.[36] But let the wearer be Sauron, the most diabolical sorcerer ever to walk Middle Earth, and the effect of the ring is immeasurably greater.

Stories in which the power of candy or of a ring depends on who reaches for it invite us to wonder where our own nature ends and temptations, addictive substances, and mind control begin. Where people draw this line reveals another wall that societies use to define who they see as "normal"—a word defined, explicitly or otherwise, in relation to those who are allegedly abnormal: monstrous. Where's the boundary between people and their choices on the one hand and the world they inhabit on the other? Put another way, where's the boundary between a person and the world? Genes are turned on and off by physical stressors and experiences, and genetics research is beginning to reveal how to edit genes. What exactly is a human, then? We still swim in a primordial soup: our minds and bodies are still in constant dialogue with ecology and transform themselves in response. The "normal" *Homo sapiens* isn't a fixed species after all, but a shape-shifter responding to the world.

Societies frame some diseases and addictions as conditions that reveal something deeper about a person's physiology or character rather than the fault of, say, environmental pollution or of unethical companies making their cigarettes or painkillers as addictive as possible. The same societies frame other afflictions as situational and contextual. While people who suffer some afflictions receive sympathy, those struck down by others do not. Choices that societies make about how to regulate the likes of coca and alcohol create categories of obedient and transgressive (or behaviorally monstrous) citizens through legislation. Decisions to criminalize some drugs and not others have not always tracked with the amount of harm those substances were thought to cause at the time of legislation. In 1970 the Controlled Substances Act in the United States outlawed all uses of marijuana, including medical use. At the time marijuana was the soft drug of choice among hippies and African Americans. In the eyes of some commentators and historians, these decisions about how to class different recreational substances were made with an eye to punishing left-leaning and Black voters.[37]

Contagion. Pollution. Infection. These words paint the body as a besieged fortress. One might think of contagion today as being something that happens at the microscopic level—it's all about germs. But contagion has historically been a fuzzier concept than merely microbial infestation. Well into the

Abito di medico ed'altre persone, che visitano
gli appestati. Il medesimo abito, è di marrochino
di Cevante la maschera tiene gli occhi di cristallo
ed un lungo naso ripieno di profumi
Descritto dal Sig.r Manget-

FIGURE 5. Line engraving inspired by an illustration in Jean-Jacques
Manget, *Traité de la peste*, eighteenth century. In his 1721 treatise on the
plague, the physician Manget described this early version of a hazmat
suit, designed to protect the wearer from infectious diseases. The items
of this all-leather outfit of gown, garments, and boots fit together. The
beaked helmet could be stuffed with herbs; the eyeholes were covered
with glass. 10075i, Wellcome Collection, London.

eighteenth century, the idea of bad air (*miasma*) prompted plague doctors in Europe to don elaborate protective costumes, complete with headgear. These preindustrial hazmat suits had beak-shaped protrusions into which wearers could pack sweet-smelling substances that would trap *miasma*, preventing it from reaching their lungs. Centuries before germ theories of infectious disease, the idea that there might be disease-carrying agents in the air that could, in theory, be filtered out was prevalent, even if the beak-and-Zorro–mask solution wasn't quite up to the job.

In the eyes of a sixteenth-century medical practitioner in Europe, in a healthy person, the humors would be in balance. When something in the external world created an imbalance in the humors, the solution was to coax them back into equilibrium. From bloodletting to comparing a patient's urine against a color chart, Renaissance health and healing hacks and diagnostics were underpinned by humoral thinking. Practitioners understood that disease unsettled the balance of humors and that making a person healthy again involved correcting this imbalance.

Public health is a framework for thinking about humans as part of their social and biological worlds: this is the link between humanity and ecology and between the health of individuals and communities, the integrity of the mind and body, and how the world beyond our skin has the power to change who and even what we are. In nineteenth-century Japan, government officials increasingly saw the health of the state and the health of its citizens as inseparable. Commentators drew direct connections between the efforts taken by individual citizens to keep their bodies healthy and the future of the nation's wealth, power, and industry. This interest in designing current and future citizens was stimulated by Western scientific and medical literature. These works described techniques of hygiene, reproductive science, and eugenics (the discredited science of attempting to "improve" humanity by controlling who got to have children and with whom) and arguments about who was "defective" (monstrous) and who deserved to live at all.

From 1877 Japan suffered biennial cholera epidemics, killing some thirty thousand at a time. Cholera became the central public health crisis of the Meiji era (1868–1912). Establishing the source of the disease and the vectors of infection occupied many of the country's scientists and public officials. These efforts were part of a broader turn to public health measures and to an emphasis on personal cultivation of a healthy body that became prevalent in Japan from the late nineteenth century.[38] This vision of public health framed citizens whose bodies and behaviors were "normal" as contributing to the strength of the nation, while individuals with atypical bodies or lifestyles were seen as a threat to the body politic.

Where do people's bodies end? At their skin, you might say. Yet our lungs are in constant contact with the world and its stuff of life and death, from oxygen to toxins, and what we inhale affects our bodies. During the Industrial Revolution, homes and workplaces started to shape ecologies at a scale that no human or animal had ever experienced before, putting new stressors on people's minds and bodies. In Europe and North America in the eighteenth century, coal began to replace wood for home heating and to release soot and other pollutants into the air. By the nineteenth century, in London and Manchester in the United Kingdom, factories were springing up like mushrooms (or perhaps mushroom clouds). As thousands of chimneys belched smoke from coal-fired furnaces, they substituted pea soup for air, stinging eyes and lungs and griming bodies. Noxious fumes and chemicals rose from the chimneys of dyeing factories. Charles Dickens, who had spent a year of his youth dirt poor, working in a shoe-polish factory, captured in novels the misery of those who spent their waking hours entombed in diabolical temples of industry or languishing in towns and cities downwind. In *Bleak House* he wrote of "smoke lowering down from chimney-pots, making a soft black drizzle, with flakes of soot in it as big as full-grown snowflakes—gone into mourning, one might imagine, for the death of the sun."[39] There was, eventually, no pretending that bodies could handle anything that ecology—technological or "natural"—threw at them without breaking down.

Into this dystopia of pea-soup fogs and poisoned water, enter the industrial hygienist. The early twentieth century saw the coming of this new class of scientist in industrializing nations facing health crises caused by unregulated polluters. The job of the industrial hygienist was environmental-damage limitation and perhaps business-reputation laundering. To minimize sickness and premature deaths without actually outlawing chemicals or processes and thereby hampering industry, industrial hygienists adopted the idea of the threshold. This was the amount of a chemical toxin that had to be present in the environment before the substance became dangerous. This line of reasoning still assumed that the body was largely separate from its environment. For these industrial scientists, unless a person's body was flooded with enough of a chemical to drown it, that person could paddle in the stuff with no ill effects. From the 1920s the threshold interpretation led to experiments on hundreds if not thousands of chemicals in attempts to establish the point at which they poisoned the body.[40]

A challenge to threshold reasoning has come in recent years from thinking of ecology as permeable and thinking of the body as porous. This way of thinking had been sidelined by Western institutions in the wake of imperialism and industrialization. Lower but regular doses of toxins, absorbed over a long time, can build up in the body. Toxins that form in the body from a cocktail of chemicals absorbed from multiple sources cause diseases like cancer over the long term. In recent decades scientists have been facing, more directly, just how porous the body is. Public health organizations and consumer groups have come to pay greater attention to the long-term consequences of poisoning our permeable bodies.[41] And, for the general public, fears about how the stuff we eat affects our bodies peaked around genetically modified (GM) foods, vividly labeled "Franken Foods"—the stuff of monster creation.[42]

Perhaps the most ominous forms of pollution are endocrine disruptors. These substances interfere with or mimic the body's hormones (which are produced in the endocrine glands). Their effects read like the beat sheet for a slow-burning disaster movie. They reduce fertility and sperm counts and cause birth defects in people and animals. Endocrine-disruptor pollution jumps species: contaminants in water are taken up by aquatic plants eaten by smaller fish, which are gobbled by larger fish and birds; they become concentrated as they climb the food chain. Chemicals like PCBs (polychlorinated biphenyls) affect the brain and the function of the thyroid hormone, which regulates growth—especially dangerous for children. They compromise immune systems. And they contaminate breast milk. These pollutants give the lie to the idea of a safe threshold: they build up in fatty tissue of people who ingest contaminated animals, since their bodies have trouble excreting complex toxins.

In *Toxic Bodies* Nancy Langston opens her account of how hormone-disrupting chemicals affect people's bodies with the story of Maria, a woman who had grown up eating fish once a week from the Fox River in Wisconsin, fish fries being a regular menu item in restaurants in her hometown of Green Bay. But paper mills had been dumping so much waste PCBs in the river that the city poured perfume into the water to cover up the stink. By 2000 Maria, a University of Wisconsin–Madison graduate student in environmental science and a new mother, knew that her body would have absorbed and retained PCBs from fish. Breastfeeding would reduce the amount in her body, since it would end up in her milk and in her baby. Maria now faced a terrible choice. If she breastfed her child, she would transfer PCBs from her body to her infant—yet doing so would also confer the health benefits of breast milk. Once endocrine disruptors enter our air or water and are taken up by our bodies, the harm they do reaches across generations.[43]

It matters how a chemical comes to be approved for wide use. In the mid-1940s, the US Food and Drug Administration (FDA) required proof that something was safe before authorizing its use. But by 1947 the pendulum had swung the other way: now something was deemed safe until demonstrable proof was available that it wasn't. Yet, unlike sticking your hand in a campfire, the harm that pollutants do is often invisible at the moment it occurs. Some effects of endocrine disruptors don't even show up until the people who absorbed them have children, who show the symptoms only as they grow up. Individual human bodies are not just vulnerable to ecology in isolation. Our relationship to ecology is intergenerational. Environmental pollution acts like a form of time- and space-traveling radioactivity, its effects first manifesting out of sight before mushrooming into view and into people's lives and damaging their health.[44] As the influential environmentalist Rachel Carson put it half a century ago, comparing humanity to the political adversaries of the powerful noble family of the fifteenth and sixteenth centuries known for poisoning their adversaries, "We are in little better position than the guests of the Borgias."[45]

Human actions alone may drive our extinction—and in the meantime they may be monstrifying our bodies. The weeks and months following the detonation of atom bombs over the Japanese cities of Hiroshima and Nagasaki in August 1945 laid bare the cataclysmic and long-lasting consequences of human technological innovation on human bodies. Cell damage from radioactivity can be instantaneous and visible, and it can also manifest over time and generations.

The 1960s Marvel comic series *The Incredible Hulk* scaled this population-wide catastrophe down into a one-off misadventure: a laboratory accident exposes scientist Bruce Banner to gamma rays, which alter his DNA. At moments of high tension or anger, Banner's body morphs into the Hulk: green, caveman-like, his muscles bursting out of Banner's clothes.[46] Like many science fiction stories in the early decades of the atomic age, the Hulk narratives played out the possible scenarios of bodies transfigured by nuclear accidents, although this particular scenario minimizes how many people would be affected by a serious accident.

Picture an alien biologist from a distant galaxy—an exobiologist, someone who investigates the formation of life in the universe, peering at humans from the future across eons of space-time. It's 2025 on earth, but it's the distant future for the exobiologist since light takes so long to get to them from here. This exobiologist is trying to decide whether humans are a unique and discrete species. Humans possessed certain artifacts that they call art or technology and behaviors that they called culture. Some humans had come to see themselves as standing apart from the rest of life on their world. The exobiologist is writing a research paper and remains stumped: where did humans end and the rest of their world—their ecology—begin?

This was our alien exobiologist's starting point: hundreds of millions of years ago, different types of beings had emerged out of a primordial soup of protein molecules on the third planet around a pretty average star. These creatures had become increasingly complex as eons passed. Humans were just one of these creatures. They shared ancestry with other beings on the planet, had emerged out of the ecologies they inhabited, and responded to changes to their needs, desires, and environment by changing on cellular and genetic levels. Some humans thought that they had become "something else," something beyond animal. At some point, one could decide to draw a line and declare that a being called *Homo sapiens* had emerged at a particular moment. Yet human DNA continued to change, as did the DNA of other beings in their world.

For this alien exobiologist, humans as individuals and as a species would appear porous and malleable. They would note how humans ingested solids and liquids through their digestive systems and absorbed air and fumes through their respiratory tracts. All these substances transformed the humans' bodies. Indeed, without ingestion they would die. And theirs was a genealogy shared with a multitude of beings who were, in some of their cosmologies and sciences, not very different from humans.

Our alien exobiologist would conclude that people are the current end point of just one of countless threads of life that emerged out of the earth's primordial soup four billion years ago.[47] They come from earth dust but do not necessarily see themselves as *of* earth dust, as part of a volatile continuum from the earth to animals to stars to other dimensions, be they known or unknown. Yet it would be impossible to draw a line around humans in evolutionary time or between humans and the ecology that spawned them and continued to shape them.

Let's return for a moment to Frankenstein's monster, an archetypical monster in Western culture. Mary Shelley cast him sensitively even though he rampages through the world. Feeling alone in the universe, utterly unlike the humans he encounters and who scream and run the other way (when they are not trying to kill him), the monster decides to try and make himself a mate. There's a moral here for how people think about their relationship to ecology. Humanity wields transformative, annihilatory powers in the world. The stories we tell about the boundary between human and the world—where the human is in animal, plant, fungal, viral, and environmental histories—and how we relate to the earth's ecology will continue to shape the continuum across them. What human is and what "normal" means has always been in flux, but now we are putting our fingers on the morph-faster buttons. We already live on a delicately engineered precision starship hurtling through the cosmos and already encounter extraordinary beings whose own perspectives on the world we are just beginning to understand.[48] We are definitely not alone in the universe—because we are not alone on this planet.

Human or Animal?

SHE PEERS OUT EXPECTANTLY, a folded sheet in her hands, almost as if she is waiting to show us her homework (see plate 2). The vibrant pattern on her dress makes it look like a party frock: a celebration of orange-and-crimson stripes, swirls, tendrils, and tulips that echo the blooms in her hair.[1] Slashed sleeves show off a rich green fabric underneath her dress, picking up the leaves that garland her head. Antoinette Gonsalvus, or Antonietta Gonzales, born in Paris in the 1580s, was perhaps eight years old when this watercolor was copied from a recent painting. Someone, not knowing how old Antoinette was, penned the caption, "A twenty-year-old woman with a furry head resembling that of an ape and a smooth, hairless body."[2]

Antoinette's portrait appears in the massive repository of drawings, watercolors, books, manuscripts, artifacts, and objects of nature amassed by the sixteenth-century Bolognese physician, collector, and naturalist Ulisse Aldrovandi, a man who rivaled Pliny the Elder in the vastness of his interests. Aldrovandi and his assistants assembled a gigantic, encyclopedic collection, sifting acquisitions with an eye to his manifold interests, from archaeology to medicine. As I leafed through the digitized volumes of drawings now housed in the University Library in Bologna, Italy, it was difficult not to do a double-take at this portrait of little Antoinette, for her face looks decidedly furry. And this picture is in a volume largely devoted to . . . *animals*.

How would this girl in a dress have felt to find herself here: would there be surprise—or knowing? Little Antoinette is unlikely to have found animal comparisons flattering. Her condition, now termed *hypertrichosis universalis*, is extremely rare: only about fifty cases are known through surviving documentation. Antoinette was the daughter of the also-hairy Petrus Gonsalvus, or Pedro Gonzales, an Indigenous person from the eastern Atlantic Ocean archipelago now called the Canary Islands. In 1547, when Petrus was a boy, his life had been turned upside-down. He was captured by Spanish invaders of his island and taken to the French royal court. There he was schooled—in Latin, the language of the educated—and he became a courtier. He married a Frenchwoman named Catherine. The couple had six children (three daughters and three sons) who survived infancy. All the children apart from one son seem to have been unusually hairy.[3]

Petrus Gonsalvus's kidnapping and subsequent life took place against a backdrop of flotillas of ships from Europe, crossing oceans to deposit explorers, colonists, merchants, clerics, physicians, and naturalists on distant shores. From these invaders and their writings and imagery, people in Europe learned of an immense number of species that were new to them.[4] These creatures baffled and amazed newcomers and collectors back home. Where did an armadillo go on the map of life, or a bird of paradise, said to lack legs and to spend its life in the air, even while sleeping? To an observer in Europe, Petrus might have appeared to straddle the boundary between human and animal. To an observer like the naturalist Aldrovandi, perhaps Petrus was an extraordinary exception that proved the rule that humans are humans and animals are not. But if Petrus was *not* entirely human, then human and animal were not entirely separate categories. He had hairy children—like little Antoinette— with a typical human woman. What did that say about the boundary between hairy folk and humans? If Petrus and his children were not entirely human, then human and animal were overlapping categories. Perhaps it was safer to recognize them all as entirely human, just unusually hairy.[5]

Aldrovandi was clearly fascinated by parallels between humans and other animals. Questions about Antoinette Gonsalvus's relationship to humanity may have passed through his mind and through the minds of his assistants as they stuck images of people with unusual physical characteristics into volumes of animal pictures. A volume devoted primarily to birds sports diagrams of two skeletons, one human, the other avian, on the first page. A common alphabetical sequence identifies their bones. Toward the end of the volume, Team Aldrovandi inserted drawings of a number of unusual people; more are scattered across the other animal volumes.

In placing a few unusual individuals in a collection devoted to animals, Aldrovandi's workshop was not unique. The Gonsalvus family inspired numerous artists, physicians, and naturalists to think about them alongside animals. Some recorded their encounters with the hairy family in drawings, watercolors, and paintings. A watercolor album by the Flemish artist Joris Hoefnagel uses

O mni miraculo quod fit per Hominem maius miraculum est HOMO
Visibilium omnium maximus est Mundus, Invisibilium DEVS
Sed mundum esse conspicimus, Deum esse Credimus.

HOMO natus de MVLIERE, brevi vivens Tempore
Repletur multis miserys. Job 14.

FIGURE 6. Joris Hoefnagel, double portrait of Petrus and Catherine Gonsalvus, 1582, in
"Ignis: Animalia rationalia et insecta." A barren, outdoor setting complete with a straggly
shrub adds a hint of wildness to the scene and encourages viewers to interpret Petrus's unusually hairy face as evidence of wildness despite his elegant outfit. 1987.20.5.2, National Gallery
of Art, Washington, DC, fol. 1. Gift of Mrs. Lessing J. Rosenwald.

depictions of the Gonsalvus family to take viewers on an even more surprising
journey from human to animal. Hoefnagel, originally from the turreted city of
Antwerp (in present-day Belgium), settled in Munich (now in Germany) at the
court of the Bavarian duke Albrecht V around 1577. There he assembled four
albums of his watercolors of living beings under the themes of air, water, earth,
and fire. In sixteenth-century Europe, these four elements were thought to be
the building blocks of matter. The Gonsalvus family he grouped under "fire,"
along with insects, in a volume titled *Fire: Rational Animals and Insects*.[6]

The volume opens with a portrait of Petrus and Catherine. Next comes a
portrait of two of their hirsute children, dressed in matching pink. The following two pages are almost blank, but tantalizing captions announce that
Hoefnagel planned to add a "pygmy" and a "giant."[7] By combining images of
atypical individuals with insects, Hoefnagel made the Gonsalvus children,
pygmies, and giants strange, implicitly less human than typical humans, to
anyone thumbing through the album. At the very least, they were classificatory

problems: monsters that cracked open and blended categories usually understood as separate.

Like Aldrovandi and Hoefnagel, today's scientists sometimes wrestle with how to classify life-forms previously unknown to them. In 2003, on the island of Flores, Indonesia, scientists excavated fossilized bones from people averaging just 1.06 meters (3.5 feet) in height. *Homo floresiensis*, as this species would soon be called (although the nickname of "hobbit" was perhaps unavoidable), had become extinct only seventeen thousand years ago. Their presence on earth had overlapped with that of modern humans, *Homo sapiens*. So were the Flores fossils those of a late-surviving near relative of people living today, the remains of another species of great ape, or merely the bones of a few, diseased individuals?

Such debates are common in paleoanthropology. Scientists puzzled over the same issues with *Homo neandertalensis*, or Neanderthals. These conundrums share a fossil discovery that challenged understandings of human evolution. In each case scientists picked their way through three possible explanations. The first was that the fossils came from diseased but human individuals. The second was that they came from a previously unknown animal species. And the third is that these fossils revealed that paleoanthropologists needed to sit down and rewrite the story of human evolution.[8] Within a few years, the growing consensus that *Homo floresiensis* was a hominin (a near relative of today's humans) led scientists to revise the genealogy of *Homo sapiens*—people today. While scientists know what a human is in geographic space, they are far less sure what a human is across geological time.

Are humans regular animals or their own category at the limit of the category of animal? The answer depends partly on the qualities picked to define the boundary. In some ways people are becoming increasingly distinct from the rest of life on earth, denatured by their growing dependence on machines.[9] Yet, as we've explored, the boundary between the macroorganism of the human body and the world beyond it is porous. Some people place "human" on their mental map of the world on a steep, isolated mountain, far from other beings from whom they are categorically different in kind. Does this matter and, if so, for whom and why?

The boundary between humans and other beings has often seemed unclear, even absent. Some cultures, as I discussed in the last chapter, have understood beings in the world as interconnected, overlapping, and even capable of transforming from one to another. In this sort of cosmovision, the place and path of people through the cosmos is inseparable from that of animals, from the earth, and from unseen spirit worlds. At times, the lives of people like Antoinette Gonsalvus—individuals who seemed to mess up the boundary between human and animal—fascinated and disturbed people in the West not because such individuals were an exception but rather because they appeared to confirm what people had long suspected, even feared: that the boundary between human and animal might in fact be no boundary at all.[10]

In a painting by the Bolognese artist Lavinia Fontana, likely the inspiration for the watercolor sent to Aldrovandi, the sheet in Antoinette's hands is turned to face us (see plate 3). Antoinette's biography and family history are encapsulated by who "owns" them: "The wild man Don Pietro was taken from the Canary Islands, to his most serene highness King Henry of France; from whence he came to his serene highness the Duke of Parma; from whom [came] I Antonietta, and now find myself with the Lady Isabella Pallavicina, the Honorable Marchesa of Soragna."[11] And herein lies a tension: Antoinette "got" to live in palaces and have her portrait painted (her own wishes are unknown). Yet she was traded like an object, a trophy, a rare animal, or an enslaved person.

The Gonsalvus family lived much of their lives at European courts and in aristocratic villas and palaces in Paris, Parma, and Rome. Did people see the hairy members of the family as something in between human and animal or even between animal and collectible? In each setting, the family occupied an overlap between pets, exotic objects, and courtiers.[12] On the one hand, they appeared to be living the dream for the family of someone captured and kidnapped as a child: nobles commissioned their portraits and hung them next to their own—as did Aldrovandi.[13] On the other hand, individual members found themselves regularly given away by their employers as gifts, only to have to start their courtly lives anew.

Despite the fine outfits, the family's predicament paralleled that of enslaved people who were separated from family, resold, and sent away when it suited their enslavers. Indeed, some enslaved African servants were also dressed in bourgeois or courtly clothing.[14] For someone peering at Fontana's canvas in the late sixteenth century, Antoinette and her family fitted into a multifarious class of beings who could be traded and gifted. This category included pets and enslaved persons. For elites in Renaissance Europe, even if all people were people, some people were clearly more "people" than others.

Whether Antoinette wrote the words on the sheet in her hands, much less thought them, is not known. Perhaps Fontana asked her to hold the sheet when she sat for her portrait: it offered a way to integrate the biographical caption into the painting. The resulting composition brings to mind images of labeled specimens in curiosity cabinets (an early form of museum in Europe, in which unusual specimens were prized) and modern museums. And by painting Antoinette with a label in her hands, Fontana, herself marginalized by her gender, made Antoinette appear complicit in her own specimenization.

At times aristocrats and practitioners of science treated marginalized people in dehumanizing ways, perhaps more like treasured animals. Naturalists and physicians routinely interpreted unusually bodied people as being different enough to justify violating their dignity and privacy.[15] The Spanish naturalist Francisco Hernández wrote of a bearded girl, aged nine, whom he had seen in Toledo. Apparently "many saw her because they portrayed her naked."[16] These viewers got underneath the girl's human trappings to see how far her humanity extended. The physician Felix Platter did this, too. He had seen Antoinette's older brother and sister in Basel, Switzerland, in 1583. He noted that the boy's face was a little hairier than that of his sister, "whose dorsal region along the vertebra of her spine was exceedingly hairy"— something Platter could have learned only by having her undress.[17]

Aldrovandi encountered Antoinette in 1594, when she visited one of his friends as part of the Marchesa of Soragna's traveling entourage. He too described how he had examined Antoinette closely. He noted that the hair on her forehead was longest and roughest and the hair on her cheeks the softest, "softer to touch than the rest of her body." She was, apparently, "bristling with yellow hair up to the beginning of her loins."[18] Aldrovandi had pawed Antoinette—how else could he have compared the softness of hair on different parts of her face and body—and made her undress. In the absence of her own surviving testimony, the only way to do justice to her experience, emotions, perspective, and humanity is to try to put ourselves—human beings, just as she was—in her place. Did Antoinette feel confusion, fear, and shame? Or had she grown accustomed to this kind of interaction?

One of the names for the family's condition is Ambras syndrome, after Schloss Ambras, the extraordinary palace complex near Innsbruck in the Austrian Alps. Visitors can still view the full-length portraits of Antoinette Gonsalvus; her brother, Henri; and her father, Petrus, on the walls of the palace's *Wunderkammer*

FIGURE 7. Portraits of unusually embodied people, Chamber of Art and Wonders, Schloss Ambras, Innsbruck, Austria, sixteenth century. The room's contents include pictures, furniture, items of clothing, and artifacts, ranging from porcelain bowls to preserved animal parts. Photo by the author.

(cabinet of curiosities), where they have hung since the sixteenth century. On the same wall as the family portraits hangs a dual portrait of a giant and a dwarf, alongside portraits of a second dwarf, someone with congenital joint problems, a person who was gored through the eye with a lance but lived (portrayed with said lance in eye), and Vlad III Tepes, or Vlad the Impaler (the inspiration for Bram Stoker's *Dracula*). Just as Joris Hoefnagel's *Fire* album brought individuals with atypical bodies together, so did the Schloss Ambras *Wunderkammer*.

On a trip to Schloss Ambras, I saw how visitors still experience this unsettling conjunction of lives looped together (see plate 4).[19] When I stood close to the paintings, the settings that the artist chose for the Gonsalvus family came into view. Each family member stands at the mouth of a cave—a reminder, perhaps, of their origins in the Canary Islands, supposedly not a "civilized" part of the world before it was colonized by Spain. Petrus's wife, Catherine, is easily missed in the display, her cave-free portrait separated from the pictures of the unusually embodied by a large glass cabinet containing a dress.

In the eyes of Archduke Ferdinand I of Tyrol, the collector behind Schloss Ambras, dwarfs, giants, hairy people, and disabled individuals went together, just as, for the watercolorist Joris Hoefnagel, dwarfs, giants, and hairy individuals, along with insects, went in the category of "rational animals." Hoefnagel's rationale is unknown—and perhaps he changed his mind halfway through painting the album, since he did not complete the dwarf and giant pages. Yet his classificatory choices reveal the lines of inquiry that he invited his viewers to follow. Within the categories of this album, the Gonsalvus family, giants, dwarfs, and insects were all of a kind in ways that typical human individuals were not. The price for bodily difference was to be pushed out of the category of normal.

Hoefnagel's volume on fire begins with an imagined autobiographical introduction by Petrus, just as Lavinia Fontana's painting contained Antoinette's alleged self-introduction:

> Tenerife bore me, but a miraculous work of nature strewed my whole body with hairs; France, my other mother, nurtured me from a boy up to a virile age, and taught me to cast aside uncivilized manners, to embrace the natural arts, and to speak the Latin tongue. A wife of surpassing beauty befell me by a gift of God, and from our marriage bed came the most beloved children. Here you may discern the munificence of nature: those born to us resemble their mother in form and coloring, yet likewise take after their father, as they too are cloaked in hair.[20]

Hoefnagel interpreted the hairiness of Petrus and his children as an add-on, not as something that detracted from the family's humanity or their capacity for advancement or "civilization." Petrus's birth on Tenerife, in the Canary Islands, is implicitly his weakest card—he has been lucky in other regards. In Hoefnagel's romantic, almost *Beauty and the Beast* telling, Catherine completed the taming of Petrus—or did their marriage and children signify that Petrus had been a desirable husband all along?

Five of Petrus and Catharine Gonsalvus's children were hairy. One was not. A mystery! And what did it mean that they could have children together at all? Did the particularities of these children confirm the hairy family's full humanity or demonstrate that the boundary between human and animal was porous, one through which category breakers like their hairy children could pass? By painting them in an album titled *Fire: Rational Animals*, Hoefnagel, like Aldrovandi, invited his audience to invent an in-between category that straddled human and animal and to place the Gonsalvus family inside it.

Societies have felt varying amounts of unease at the idea that human and animal are overlapping categories. As we've seen, Indigenous peoples of the Americas understood beings in the world as fluid, existing in categories that entangled. The physicians, naturalists, artists, and nobles who encountered the Gonsalvus family understood them as human but also framed them as a family of peculiars. Depending on whom you asked, the family were allegedly a bit like insects or like giants and dwarfs or specimens for compendia of monsters. The monstrification of the Gonsalvus family—the storytelling in text and image that cast them as disrupting the category of normal humans—worked to assure people that the normal human and the animal were separate. People observing the hairy members of the family regularly associated them with animals. This shaped how people treated the family, the course of their lives, and how artists and naturalists recorded them in words and in pictures.

Juxtaposing some people with animals but not others became standard practice in museums of natural history in the nineteenth century. All over Europe and North America, natural history museums still include displays of artifacts made by peoples from Africa, Australasia, and the Americas, whereas artifacts from other parts of the world end up in art museums or in "Asian art" museums. While many museums have attempted to redisplay and contextualize these historical collections, the visual message persists.

These divisions reflect the racial hierarchy of humanity by which European, and later North American, white, elite, usually male scholars in the seventeenth and eighteenth centuries understood the world's peoples. This form of thinking had roots in classical antiquity. As I'll explore in the next chapter, it was this hierarchy of humanity, which placed some people closer to animals than others, that wealthy, powerful Europeans used to justify the practices of chattel slavery and settler-colonialism.

SOUL-SHIFTING

Folktales and fairy tales containing human-animal transformations and interspecies relationships ask readers to extend empathy to those who are embodied differently. They invite us to sit with our fluctuating, volatile emotional connections to shape-shifters and hybrids: as a frog becomes a prince, as a mermaid tries to live on land, as a shape-shifting clam turns into a beautiful woman after being wed to an unwilling fisher.[21] To fully experience life as "human" is to be seen for all of who one is and to be accepted for it. Folktales show how delicate and conditional empathy can be. When we encounter stories told through the eyes of frogs, mice, and mermaids, we are likely to feel empathy for beings who are, on the outside, unlike us. Who doesn't feel solidarity with Kermit the Frog as he tries to herd cats or, rather, a cavalcade of Muppets, guest stars, and photobombing maintenance rats? Yet we may feel differently about the same animals when the tale is told from the perspective of people who saw those frogs, mice, and mermaids as not quite human no matter how hard they tried.

In Chinese folklore since at least the fourth century CE, foxes had the power to shape-shift into humans—typically into women—and to seduce men. This tradition subsequently inspired Japanese folklore as well. These tales implicitly cast attractive women as cunning in ways that transgressed the category of the human: their "powers" had to have some inhuman dimension, making it more difficult for the reader to feel empathy for them. In a tale that was popular between the fifteenth and nineteenth centuries, the vulpine walking encyclopedia and femme fatale Lady Tamamo captivated emperors and destroyed empires.[22]

The idea of the soul has stakes for the relationship between people and animals. In Christian theology people have souls but animals do not, and this makes people different sorts of being from animals. By contrast, the Mesoamerican cosmovision contained transformable human bodies and souls that could jump species or even inhabit two different beings at once. In Buddhist philosophy and Hinduism, souls are reincarnated in new bodies at the point of death. When a being dies, the soul within it is reborn in another body. Depending on how virtuous or sinful a life the embodied soul had led—and the good and bad karma accrued—they might be born into a more or less fortunate dimension or social sphere or even into a higher or a lower sphere of being: a human prince who had led a selfish, dissolute life might be reborn as an insect. In this understanding of the place of the human in ecology, it is the soul that shape-shifts between human and animal, by body swapping. This process makes the boundary between human and animal an anatomical one but not perhaps an existential one. These disparate ways of thinking about the soul all pay attention to the relationship between humans and what lies beyond them, be they animals or demons.

The Japanese folktale known as *The Tale of the Mouse* explores the social consequences of transmissible souls that move between realms. During the

Muromachi era (ca. 1337–1573), when the tale appeared, people divided the world into six realms. These realms were not simply geographic spaces on the planet or even spheres of the cosmos. They were dimensions of existence inhabited by different sorts of beings. In decreasing order of appeal, these realms were heaven; the human realm; *ashura*, or the realm of vaguely humanoid warrior-gods or demons; the animal realm; the realm of hungry ghosts; and hell.[23]

The Tale of the Mouse relates the misadventures of Gonnokami, a wealthy old mouse who attempted to game the system.[24] Gonnokami declares to his retainer, Sakonnojō, that he wishes to marry a human wife, so that his descendants will not have to pay for the sins (whatever they are) that would otherwise cause them to be born as mice. Here the reader understands that Gonnokami has a transspecies agenda for wanting to marry up. If he marries a human woman, his children can hop out of the realm of animals and into the realm of humans. Sakonnojō gives this idea the thumbs-up and recommends that Gonnokami make a pilgrimage to the Kiyomizu Temple to ask the deities to grant him as a wife the daughter of a certain wealthy sake merchant. The daughter has failed to make a suitable match at peak marriageable age. Just when Gonnokami journeys to the Kiyomizu Temple, so does this unnamed young lady, with her maidservant, Jijū.

The Buddhist deity Kannon observes the symmetry of Gonnokami and the young lady's situations. Through faith and prayer, Gonnokami has elevated himself; the young lady, perhaps through past karma, has failed to make a good marriage despite much searching and effort. Kannon intervenes, Gonnokami and the lady meet, and they depart together to be married. The message implicit in this development is that the lady has come down in the world to the level of an elevated mouse. Some years later, however, the (still anonymous) lady begins to smell a rat. She remarks to Jijū, "It's horrible, like we've fallen into the realm of beasts! You know, there's something funny about the way my lord finishes his sentences." The lady and Jijū look through the slits that separate their room—which they have been instructed never to leave—from the rest of the mansion and realize that they have fallen into a world of animals. In horror and dismay, they run away, leaving their previous lives behind.

The Tale of the Mouse comes from a subgenre of Japanese folktales that scholars call interspecies (*irui-mono*) tales. On one level these tales are a Japanese version of speculative fiction or fantasy: they create worlds and scenarios beyond those of real life. But on another level, these tales work through societal anxieties through allegory. *The Tale of the Mouse* is not merely a story about interspecies romance—which likely no reader has witnessed or experienced—but also an allegory of marriage across social spheres and racial lines: the servant mice in the story speak an exaggerated eastern dialect intended to amuse the reader.[25] The plot has a charming ring that fades into a discordant jangle of caution. A young woman trying to get married is playing with fire: she knows very little about her future husband. He might well appear one way but later reveal himself to be quite different. She needs to establish what his social station really is, to avoid being dragged down by an unsuitable match. And if you are having trouble getting married (off), how low can you bear to go? In tales like this, the porous boundary that readers reckon with in their imagination is not between human and animal but across socioeconomic classes, ethnic groups, and other uneasy hierarchies through which societies organize and bestow power and status.[26]

But there is an additional message in the undertones of *The Tale of the Mouse*. If souls enter bodies according to how those souls have lived in their past lives, then souls are not created through reproduction but rather stand on the sidelines, waiting to load bodies with consciousness. Therein lies a conundrum that appears to go unanswered: people may be related to the *bodies* of their children, but their souls are something else entirely. Reproduction and fate are independent of each other; body and soul merely have a marriage of convenience. Having children is like building subway cars: builders don't get to determine who sits in the seats, and riders routinely change seats, cars, trains, and destinations. The soul, then, can slip between types of beings and even between the visible world and other spirit realms. A person's soul might be reborn in an animal in a future life—thus eating or stepping on an animal might, in theory, be tantamount to eating an old friend or crushing a deceased relative under one's heel. In cosmologies where interspecies reincarnation is possible, the distance between a human person and an animal is bridgeable as far as their souls are concerned.

HUMAN-ANIMAL HYBRIDS

The Tale of the Mouse warns that slight deviations of bodies or behavior can be signs of more fundamental differences. While soul-shifting posits a largely invisible, blended continuum between human and animal, hybrid beings with both human and animal body parts are spectacular monsters— Frankensteinian patchworks that flaunt their status. Classical mythologies

FIGURE 8. Siren and centaur in a bestiary, or book of animals, circa 1270. In Greek mythology sirens are hybrids of women and birds, believed to lure sailors to their deaths with their captivating voices. MS Ludwig XV 3. Digital image courtesy of Getty's Open Content Program, fol. 78r.

of ancient western Asia and the Mediterranean Basin contain a panoply of human-animal hybrids—beings with body parts from different species. Ancient Greek literature positively teems with examples, like centaurs who are human from the waist up and horse below and sirens who are part human and either part fish or part bird.[27] Unlike Petrus's family, many of these examples are not one-off exceptions with an alarming, not fully understood potential to interbreed with regular humans. Rather, these human-animal hybrids are their own sort of organism.

In the Middle Ages in western Europe, hybrids composed of humans and beasts of the barnyard appear in tales of the church fathers, early Christian theologians who wrote influential works that codified Christianity. Here they sometimes functioned as morality tales, giving the side-eye to contemporary failings. Human-animal hybrids prompted philosophical speculation on exactly how far the category of humanity stretched. Were human-animal hybrids like centaurs, satyrs, sirens, and cynocephali (dogheaded beings) capable of being converted to Christianity? If so, didn't that make them human? Identifying who was human—that is, Adam's descendants—also specified the community of individuals with the capacity for salvation. Beings like centaurs and satyrs were understood to be demons and immortal, as were the gods of other religions (the faiths that Christians stuck under the umbrella category of "paganism"). This removed them from the human equation.[28]

ON APES AND MEN

In Christian understandings of nature, the ape was the final creature that God created before creating Adam. These final drafts were "poor relations" of the human made in God's image. The twelfth-century philosopher Bernardus Silvestris warned that if people were to ignore the word of God, spurn spirituality, and live for the pleasures of the flesh, letting their animal impulses win over their higher levels of intellect, they would sink to the state of apes. Thus the human was only conditionally fully human: there was a spiritual contract that, if ignored, would bring about the morphing of the human soul into something bestial.[29] The ramifications were harrowing. European clerics, thinkers, and legislators frequently interpreted any resistance of Indigenous peoples to converting to Christianity as evidence that they were closer to animals on the Great Chain of Being, an ancient hierarchical ranking of beings in the world.

Saint Augustine of Hippo, a philosopher and theologian of Berber origin from the province of Numidia, now in Algeria, writing in the late fourth and early fifth centuries, offered a working definition to distinguish the "poor relations" from humans. Humans possessed reason: they were capable of thought, regardless of how weird they might look to Saint Augustine's audience. Since neither simians nor the monstrous peoples of classical texts were immortal—they were beings recorded in encyclopedic and geographic texts, not texts about gods—to determine whether or not they were human or merely humanity's "poor relations," one had to establish whether or not they possessed reason.[30]

Yet medieval Christian thinkers feared that human and animal were not entirely separate. In his popular dictionary, *Magnae derivationes*, the late twelfth-century canon (church) lawyer Huguccio of Pisa suggested, incorrectly, that the word *monstrum* came from *mastruca*, or hairy skin (furry) garments: "Who ever dresses himself in such garments is transformed into a monstrous being."[31] The thirteenth-century philosopher-naturalist Albertus Magnus wondered whether apes were beings who had once been human but then had fallen into a bestial state. He distinguished between humans, humanlike creatures, and "brutes." In the turn of the fourteenth-century manuscript known as the *Rothschild Canticles*, Adam warns his daughters against eating certain herbs that would cause them to birth dogheaded beings, apelike beings, or sciapods (a people said to possess one giant foot).[32] Humanlike creatures were understood to be effectively monstrous: they were the wedge between humans and animals, and they raised the possibility that a human could slip backward into what medieval Christians defined as a lower category of being.

The ability of apes to imitate humans has negative associations in multiple European languages. Sixteenth- and seventeenth-century dictionaries and dramatic plays make visible the overlap between "acting" and "aping"—the former a type of skilled technique, the latter, what acting looks like when it sucks.[33] To "ape" someone is to mimic them imperfectly and to show the limits of one's skill or to make fun of them through intentionally mimicking them awkwardly. Apes imitating humans performed human actions in ways that looked strange and clumsy. They drew attention to the alarming place where humanity ended and animality began.

This proximity was threatening. It suggested that apes existed along a continuum with humans, and potentially overlapped with individual people. The sliding scale was the problem: a person or their descendants might slip down the scale through errors of anatomy or behavioral choices before ending up somewhere closer to animal than to human. If the outward body was a sign of the inward soul, then not only were apes subtly nasty but any individual human person who reminded one of an ape might well be diseased in their mind or soul. This way of reasoning anticipates, and is enmeshed with, long histories of ideas about race, a theme taken up later in this book.[34]

In 1661 the English diarist and naval administrator Samuel Pepys described how he had just come face-to-face with what he called a monster from West

Africa, brought to London by a ship's captain: "It is a great baboone, but so much like a man in most things, that (though they say there is a species of them) yet I cannot believe but that it is a monster got of a man and she-baboone. I do believe that it already understands much English, and I am of the mind it might be tought to speak or make signs."[35] Pepys's central dilemma was this: you could not be certain whether something was human simply by looking at it, nor could you tell whether something you'd never seen before was normal for its own kind or a one-off accident. It was apparently far better that the baboon was merely a one-off rather than "a species," part of the regular tapestry of nature. A species of "baboones" would reduce the distance between human and animal, perhaps even turning the gap into a continuum—something way scarier than a pathology Pepys could point at in the body of a single individual. Far from being universally dreaded, a monster like this hybrid, as Pepys understood the creature, was both real and *less* of an existential threat than the alternative.

Long before anyone knew of the existence of genes or of the geologically long timeline of human origins, naturalists and theologians in Europe compared primates to humans to show how other primates were very much *not* humans. For those who believed in the Great Chain of Being, since the steps between beings arranged from the lowest rank to the highest were small, there was an overlap between the highest rank of one type and the lowest rank of the type above. Thus the most inferior humans were supposedly on a par with the most superior animals.

The seventeenth-century English anatomist Edward Tyson claimed that what he called the "orang-outang," the *Homo sylvestris*, or the pygmy was the animal closest to humans on a hierarchy of things arranged from minerals to plants to animals to humans. For Tyson the pygmy was that limit case, "coming nearest to mankind," "the nexus of the animal and rational." Unconsciously, he echoed Joris Hoefnagel's category of "rational animals," in which, as we saw earlier, Hoefnagel placed insects and unusually embodied individuals. Confusingly, the animal that Tyson called an "orang outang" or "pygmie" was not an orangutan at all. The first two engravings in the volume reveal that the creature he dissected was, in fact, a young chimpanzee that had been brought to England from Angola.[36] Tyson concluded that this creature was "no man nor yet the common ape; but a sort of animal between both."[37]

FIGURE 9. Edward Tyson, sketch of chimpanzee, 1699. Tyson dissected this young chimpanzee, which he thought was an "orang-outang" or "pygmie," to establish whether this species was closer to humans than to apes and monkeys. *Orang-outang*, fig. 1, QM21 .T93 1699. Biodiversity Heritage Library, Smithsonian Libraries, Washington, DC.

Drawing on his own dissections, Tyson laid out a forty-eight-point anatomical comparison of how "The Orang-Outang or Pygmie more resembled a Man, than Apes and Monkeys do." He followed this with a thirty-four-point list of anatomical features that revealed how the animal "differ'd from a Man, and resembled more the Ape and Monkeykind."[38] Thus, in Tyson's view, the pygmy was closer to humans than to apes or monkeys.[39] In contrast to Samuel Pepys's kneejerk response to the baboon he glimpsed at the London docks, Tyson concluded not only that his specimen was a member of a species but that it was more like a person than it was like any known animal. The "pygmie" was *not* a monster but a normal animal, and that was why it narrowed the gap between human and animal.

Almost none of the points on Tyson's comparative anatomical lists refer to mental capacities. The comparative anatomist Tyson stuck to the grisly story of his specimen's flesh, blood, and bones. He ducked the real stakes of bodily difference for Christian thinkers: what it might reveal about invisible minds and thus about how distinct humans might be from simians as souls capable of salvation. In a series of essays appended to his dissection report, Tyson defined beings that ancient and contemporary sources referred to as pygmies, cynocephali, satyrs, and sphinxes as "either apes or monkeys, and not men, as formerly pretended."[40] In Tyson's view the array of beings said to exist between the simian and the human were, definitively, animals: any being that departed from the human norm didn't sit on a blurry continuum between animal and human but rather was definitively separate from humans. His "pygmie" might be a new link in the Great Chain of Being, but he considered each link to be discrete.

Tyson argued that accounts of liminal beings that appeared to transgress the human-simian divide were in fact fakes, errors of identification, and literary inventions. Some promising specimens were merely apes that charlatans had embalmed before passing them off as humans from distant parts of the world. He surmised that the idea of the pygmy as a type of human had emerged as information about an animal became garbled when people told and retold stories about them. The "Indian or Malabar language" identified a being known as the man of the woods or wild man (*orang-outang*). The pygmies in ancient Greco-Roman texts were said to be of small stature, just like orangutans are smaller than humans. Thus European travelers mistook the former for the latter: the orang-outang, a type of ape, was mistaken for a type of human.[41]

But under Tyson's forensic detail is just the thing he denies: an interspecies relationship in which it is not so clear-cut where one category of being ends and another begins, something we might call a connected, more ecological way of thinking about beings in the world. In Indigenous modes of understanding the world as a web of relationships, what beings like humans and orangutans shared—physical bodies in the world, mortality, consciousness—made them kinfolk after a fashion.[42]

MONSTERS AND SPECIES CLASSIFICATION

At the turn of the eighteenth century, the Swedish botanist Carl Linnaeus formulated a system for identifying and naming the species of what he called the animal, vegetable, and mineral kingdoms, based on simple yes/no questions about visible physical parts. First published in 1735 in a short treatise titled *The System of Nature*, Linnaeus's binomial system became highly popular, since it did not require specialist training in biology or in Latin, the language of scholarship, to use. Plants were classified according to the parts of their flowers, quadrupeds according to their teeth, and birds according to their bills. The Linnaean system was an artificial one: it classified creatures using visible, clearly distinguishable characteristics. Yet its power was that it allowed amateurs to participate in the practice of natural history and even to contribute "new" species previously unknown to professional naturalists in Europe.

The System of Nature went through twelve editions in Linnaeus's lifetime, expanding over time as Linnaeus mapped out more and more parts of the animal, vegetable, and mineral kingdoms, and there was a thirteenth, posthumous edition. The book lays out a hierarchy of nature, proceeding from what Linnaeus termed the highest orders of beings to the lowest. The tenth edition opens with animals, of which the first subdivision is mammals, whose highest group are primates.[43] In line with his classificatory principles, Linnaeus separated humans (subdivision *Homo*) from simians (*Simia*) by dint of variations in their bodies rather than in their behavior—by characteristics of their teeth and by whether or not they had hair all over their bodies, for example.

Linnaeus subdivided humans into four types by their geography: American, European, Asian, and African. He distinguished between them using skin color (ranging through copper-colored, fair, sooty, and black); hair; eye color (Europeans apparently always have blue eyes); occasional references to other physical features (Africans are said to be known by their "skin silky; nose flat; lips tumid"); and various aspects of their temperament, behavior, and social organization.

Linnaeus adopted the theory of four bodily humors from classical antiquity, but with some crucial differences. As we've seen, in ancient humoral theory, the precise amounts of each humor in your body would vary with the local climate. If you moved locales, your humoral balance would shift—and perhaps your behavior too. Linnaeus made this relationship between humors and bodies even more significant, assigning the personality the ancients had associated with each humor to peoples from across vast swathes of the earth, thus: choleric (American), sanguine (European), melancholy (Asiatic), and phlegmatic (African).

Clothing choices were said to distinguish the American, who "paints himself with fine red lines"; the European, "covered with close vestments"; the Asian, "covered with loose garments"; and the African, who "covers himself with grease." Concerning social restraints, Americans were "regulated by customs," Europeans "governed by laws," Asians "by opinions," and Africans "by caprice." Additionally, these groups were stereotyped as having different characters. While the American was "obstinate, content," and "free," the European was "gentle, acute, inventive"; the Asiatic "haughty, covetous"; and the African "crafty, indolent, negligent." While the types of *Homo sapiens* are not arranged in the treatise in an explicit hierarchy, each point of behavioral comparison would have led a reader to see an implicit hierarchy of civilization in which Europeans sat at the top, followed by Asians, and then probably followed by Americans, with Africans near the bottom.

Cutting across these types were one-off individuals who lived in an uncivilized fashion: *Homo ferus*, or wild folk. Linnaeus provided several examples of wild individuals, mostly children, who had ended up living with animals in the long term.[44] Finally, there were peoples classed as *Homo monstrosus*: those who, by dint of the climate in which they lived or their choice of customs, were to Linnaeus atypical. These monstrous species came in types that "vary by climate or art." The Mountaineer was said to be "small, active, timid"; the Patagonian "large, indolent"; the Hottentot "less fertile"; the American "beardless"; the Chinese "head conic"; and the Canadian "head flattened." The material on the genus *Homo* fits on a single page, ending with an instruction to the reader: "The anatomical, physiological, natural, moral, civil and social histories of man, are best described by their respective writers."[45] A single turn of the page takes the reader to the next genus, *Simia*.

To what extent did Linnaeus's system cement the wall between human and animal and how did the idea of monsters shape his thinking and that of his readers? Could *Homo sapiens* and *Homo monstrosus* interbreed? This was one of the unanswered questions lurking in Linnaeus's typology. Subsequent naturalists attempted to answer such questions while grappling with an even more alarming problem: the theory of evolution.

Until about the seventeenth century, scholarly and religious thinkers in Europe dated the earth to about six thousand years ago, on the basis of the Book of Genesis. The science of geology, however, would make it increasingly difficult to imagine that the earth was not far, far older and that its form had not changed over time. Archaeological records reveal that *Homo sapiens* was using tools and abstract language forty thousand years ago.[46] While almost all scientists today take it as a given that the earth is billions of years old and that *Homo sapiens* evolved, millions of years ago, from other sorts of animals, these findings remain difficult to accept for some laypeople. Accepting the science would involve accepting that one's sacred texts were meant to be read differently (or are wrong). An ambiguous boundary between human and animal also means the loss of any unique status for humans.

In 1831 the theology graduate and amateur naturalist Charles Darwin, aged twenty-two, set sail from Plymouth, England, aboard the *Beagle*, on a survey expedition to South America. Tasked with collecting natural history specimens, Darwin would perform this duty with tremendous diligence, gathering countless specimens of animals, vegetables, and minerals, from multitudinous finches to fossilized bones of the megatherium, a giant sloth. On the *Beagle*'s return to England five years later, scientists pored over the spoils, some to identify and classify things, others to ponder what they all meant.[47]

One of the overarching patterns that would emerge from the *Beagle*'s bounty was the volatility of life-forms over space and time. Over geological eons, animals changed: long-extinct megatheriums appeared in the fossil record in locations where mini versions of them—sloths—lived today. Across the islands of the Galápagos off the coast of Ecuador, wildly different species of finches inhabited each island. The explanation—indeed, the grand theory—that Darwin would propose in his *On the Origin of Species* was that random mutations at a fundamental level of animals' physiology might enable them, in certain environmental conditions, to outcompete members of the species that lacked the mutation.

Some random mutations were beneficial, others less so, and individuals exhibiting them would be less likely to thrive. When an ecosystem or a niche within it was under stress—during a period of increased competition for dwindling food supplies, for instance—variants with mutations beneficial in the new conditions would have an advantage: they would be the fittest who would survive a period of crisis. Over time certain random mutations would be passed down through generations and eventually engender new species. At the moment when an animal varied from its parents, it was in essence a monster, or what Darwin referred to as "sports," or nature's jokes.[48] Environmental changes could also turn mutations that had once been advantageous into liabilities. The Irish elk probably died out at the end of the last ice age, around eleven thousand years ago, because its gigantic antlers (helpful for attracting mates and for dueling rivals) prevented movement through new and thickening forests that mushroomed in the wake of retreating glaciers.

Monsters were the drivers of evolution—the first respondents to ecological crises. And just as history is often written by the winners, mutations—

monsters—that win out over time become the new default against which future mutations compete and against which categories like species are defined. The history of evolution *is* the history of monsters: all life on earth was engendered, repeatedly, by monsters. Darwin's conclusions were theologically alarming. If natural forces acting on living things led to random mutations that, over time, generated new species, the boundary between "normal" and "monster" was time, chance, and context. God had been left out of the picture. The implications of Darwin's theory for understanding the human were just as disturbing: not only was humanity a malleable sort of being rather than an unchanging image of God, but at some point in the past humanity's ancestors had not been human at all.[49]

In 2005 geneticists compared the full genomes of humans and chimpanzees and learned that people share 98 percent of their genes with their nearest primate relatives. (We share almost as many with tomatoes.) Until somewhere between four and eight million years ago, humans and chimps were the same species: a being with a mix of what we now think of as "human" and "chimp" traits, along with various genes that subsequently fell out of the gene pool of both species. A simple current definition of a species is the set of beings who can mate with one another to produce fertile offspring. Thus while lions and tigers can have cubs together, their offspring—ligers and tigons—cannot, which is why lions and tigers are distinguishable as two different types of animals.

But are "species" always distinct, separated by unbridgeable reproductive boundaries? Genes suggest otherwise. Neanderthals and *Homo sapiens* evolved separately and then interbred. Everyone alive today who has some ancestry from beyond Africa has 1–5 percent Neanderthal DNA. A whopping 20 percent of the Neanderthal genome survives in the genome of modern *Homo sapiens*. Rather than going extinct, Neanderthals (like a few other hominids, such as Denisovans) merely managed to blend themselves into the very blood and bones of *Homo sapiens*, interbreeding with early hominids from Africa who made their way to Eurasia, where they became the dominant relation in humanity's lineage. One might say that Neanderthals aped humanity so well that they now *are* a part of humanity.[50]

On the scale of very deep history, species change and fissure in geological time. Medical treatments are often tested on animals before human trials begin precisely because of what they share with people (and what they are said *not* to share with us, namely "humanity," whatever that is). To our exobiologist from another galaxy, rodents, pigs, and primates would appear to be very like humans, when one got down to how bodies work and got away from size, shape, and lifestyle.

People have not only emotional, agricultural, and genetic relationships with animals but also increasingly prosthetic relationships that bind cells together. Surgical sutures made of animal substances, like silk, bridge animal, human, and technology.[51] Gene-editing techniques like CRISPR allow scientists to splice and dice DNA from one species into the genetic code of another. Such techniques allow bioengineers to grow human cells needed for transplant in fast-growing species like rats. Humans and animals intermingle in modern medicine everywhere, from the culturing of vaccines in chicken cells to the routine replacement of defective heart valves with those of pigs. In 2021 the first successful pig to human heart transplant was performed.

Transplant surgery involves solving both macro problems—the gymnastics of delicately swapping out parts of the body while keeping the patient alive—and micro ones: preventing the body's cells from seeing replacement organs as intruders and rejecting them. People can give and receive organs successfully across racial lines (which are sociocultural and biopolitical, not scientifically "real") but not necessarily across familial ones. Successful human-animal transplants are possible. Biochemically, bodily similitude and difference operate differently than how a society happens to code it using externally visible physical features.

At a biochemical level, the body recognizes similarity and difference in ways that are independent of social conventions for who or what is different or similar. Blood types A, B, AB, O, and their rhesus positive and negative variants occur across populations, albeit with some variation in frequency.[52] Blood transfusions must take these types into account. Early attempts at blood transfusions and xenotransplantations, or interspecies organ transplants, had results that could at best be described as mixed.[53] The biochemical self-other boundary is a transkinship, even transspecies, boundary with multiple doors and windows through which multiple selves can mingle safely. Apes, too, have ABO blood.

Biologists have begun to engineer chimeras, or beings composed of two or more separate genomes, for xenotransplantations.[54] In this process human stem cells are injected into pigs, sheep, and goats, thereby turning them into chimeras: genetically hybrid beings. But how chimeric are they, and what matters to us about the answer? While the proportion of human DNA in an experimental chimera like this is barely 0.001 percent of the host being, what if the injected DNA were to alter the being's nervous or reproductive systems?

Moreover, the language with which people talk about altering bodies has also begun to dehumanize the human: scientists "edit" genes just as office workers do documents. Such language implicitly gives the impression that everything that makes a person a unique, living being is knowable and known, reducible to little bricks as simple as letters typed into a computer. Techniques of genetic engineering thus promise, or perhaps threaten, to reduce the cosmic mysteries of life and heredity to engineering problems, like how to build a better bridge. As we'll see later in this book, the hype around large language models and artificial intelligence similarly strips out of the narrative everything that makes people and their experiences unique and thus capable of making distinct contributions and reduces creativity to reaching into a barrel of things people have made in the past and running copy-and-paste jobs on them.

PLANET OF THE GERMS

In the late twentieth-century movie *Men in Black*, an assortment of alien exiles has taken up residence on earth.[55] The tiniest extraterrestrials sit in people's brains, like pilots directing human bodies with the equivalent of aircraft controls. In the real world, the question of who people are as individuals is indeed bound up with tiny life-forms that control them from within their bodies: these life-forms are not extraterrestrials but rather microorganisms. On the microscopic level, it turns out that people were never 100 percent human to begin with. Our bodies and personalities are also influenced by the whims of our microbiomes. Microbial communities inhabit different areas of the human body and affect health, moods, and behavior: we are each of us a *we* made up of a macro-sized human suit brimming with microbial residents who pull our temperamental strings and feed urges for coffee and cake. Individual human bodies have their strings pulled by microbes in their gut, whose fates are controlled by what their humans choose to consume, be it yoghurt or hamburgers, and by viruses that inject DNA into human cells. To microbiologists a human individual is not a single being but rather a walking zoo: an amalgam of a body, its gut bacteria, and eons of gene editing by viruses that injected their DNA into human cells.

Viruses don't just make us sick; they make us different. People say in passing that, after a bad bout of the flu or after a terrible shock or personal tragedy, someone was "never quite the same again." What may seem like speculation or figures of speech has a genetic reality. Not all of a person's more than twenty-six thousand genes are constantly active. External stresses and stimuli can turn genes on and off. And an infectious illness can leave parts of the body permanently changed at the macro level.

The ever-mutating COVID-19 virus is an apocalyptic example of how two different species (human and virus) can effectively cross-breed at a genetic level. Biologists identify, name, and respond to particular strains of the virus according to how they act on our bodies. Viruses make clear the blurred boundary between species and the enormous difference in lived experience brought about by tiny changes in genetic structure. The severity and transmissibility of infectious diseases—how bacteria, viruses, and other microorganisms act on people—and the effects of their variants shape how scientists name and classify them and what, if anything, epidemiologists recommend societies do about them. Humans (however defined) in turn shape both other beings and their own categories for these beings.

How many versions of a person are there? Humans have as many as twenty-six thousand genes. Some get turned on and off by things external to the body: environmental triggers, foodstuffs, accidents, stress. Pollutants like lead in the fumes of vehicles running leaded gasoline or in water contaminated by industrial waste can wreak havoc at the genetic level. Genes also work together, creating a myriad of different, unpredictable effects. Like the mutants in *X-Men*, who often manifest their talents during puberty at moments of heightened stress, and the humoral bodies of ancient Afro-Eurasian medicine and geography, in the field of modern genetics, humans are plastic to their surroundings: adaptable, moldable, and able to shift their shape.[56]

Our bodies play host to fungi, bacteria, viruses, and parasites. Gut bacteria manipulate feelings and thus actions, eliding any easy division between "us" and "ecology." This opens up the question of where we as "individuals" begin and end on a molecular level. Both Indigenous cosmologies and contemporary Western science offer answers that challenge the idea that humans are discrete, one-being individuals separated by a hard boundary from the ecology they inhabit and the beings within it.[57] Yet, sometimes, people no longer seem to believe that they are an animal. Nor do some of them appear to be planning to remain an animal.

For some the best future involves leaving earth, encoding one's consciousness in everlasting microchips, or at the very least living in a metaverse, a headsetted virtual reality. Such technological wonders are pitched as workarounds for fixing stuff we broke on earth, dystopian hacks intended to replace such everyday activities as walking down the street; going into nature; growing, cooking, smelling, touching, and eating food; having physical contact with other beings in the world; and living a life that comes to an end.

Imagining human habitation on the moon or on other planets would involve figuring out how human minds and bodies might respond to environments and circumstances that are almost unimaginable. The science- and speculative fiction writer Kim Stanley Robinson has observed that many environmental and social conditions that shape beings on earth would disappear almost entirely on a starship of intergalactic colonists.[58] Colonists of the moon or of Mars would soon run out of microbes and gut bacteria. Monotonous foodstuffs would lead to nutritional deficiencies: some would be obvious and visible, while others would grind people down more slowly, without overt symptoms. The confined physical space and loss of mental stimulation through variety would have effects on the brain. Even if this colony managed to survive in isolation for decades, it would begin to face a loss of genetic diversity. If humans were ever to settle on another planet or moon, they may end up changing in ways that challenge definitions of what it means to be human.[59] By disconnecting themselves from animals, they may fall out of the category of the human who flourished on earth.

THREE

Race-Nations

IN THE 1680S THE MEXICAN INQUISITION investigated a certain Nicolasa Juana. An official report stated that she was "a white *mulata* with curly hair, because she is the daughter of a dark-skinned *mulata* and a Spaniard, and for her manner of dress she has flannel petticoats and a native blouse.... She wears shoes, and her natural and common language is not Spanish but Chocho, as she was brought up among Indians with her mother, from whom she contracted the vice of drunkenness, to which she often succumbs, as Indians do, and from whom she has also received the crime of [idolatry]."[1] Juana's physical features, dress, customs, and language were clues to her alleged doctrinal lapses. In the eyes of the inquisition and colonial officials, these lapses placed her further away from Spaniards in the multicultural racial hierarchy of colonial Mexico.

Those who weren't of entirely Spanish descent had a *casta*, a designation defined by the heritage of their parents. *Casta* was a juridical category: it determined taxation, the lawfulness of enslavement, and where someone could live. Yet a person's *casta* was also malleable. It was changed by, and observable in, everyday activities like smoking tobacco, drinking chocolate (originally consumed as a spiced beverage), and eating cassava bread and guinea pigs—practices among people with Indigenous heritage—instead of consuming raisins, almonds, wheat bread, and wine, which were items found in traditional Spanish kitchens.[2]

A half millennium earlier, and an ocean away, the eleventh-century chronicler Gerald of Wales had this to say about the English, a few generations after the Norman Conquest of southern Britain: "The English people [are] the most worthless of all peoples under heaven.... In their own land the English are slaves of the Normans, the most abject slaves. In our own land [the Welsh Marches or Welsh-English borderlands] there are none but Englishmen in the jobs of ploughman, shepherd, cobbler, skinner, artisan, and cleaner of the sewers."[3] Gerald was descended from Norman conquerors and Welsh nobility. He cast the English as fundamentally inferior, albeit essential, workers: they labored with unsavory substances, from mud to excrement. Few people today associate race with medieval Britain. Yet Gerald essentialized and dehumanized the English in ways that parallel how people define race today.

The inquisitorial report on Nicolasa Juana and the caustic chronicle penned by Gerald of Wales both show the ideas of human hierarchy intersecting with the ideas of nations and national identity. These accounts also reveal how race was not exclusively or necessarily about physical appearance or ancestry. The English, the Normans, and the Welsh did not vary in skin color or hair color to the extent that they would have varied from people living in, say, East Asia or southern Africa at the same time. But Gerald has defined the English as fundamentally different and inferior using another characteristic: their occupation. Then, as now, race was about more than skin color and hair texture.

Individuals and communities identified as almost beasts or monsters or other category problems have long populated the world's texts, images, and artifacts. While people in Europe understood some of these groups as utterly, wildly different from humans, others blurred the boundaries between types of humans: between identities like *indio* and *español*, "Norman" and "English," "American" and "alien." In such cases people identified and policed those they viewed as challenging identity categories by coining new words to identify, surveil, and constrain them. These people faced restrictions in terms of where they could live, whom they could marry, and what jobs they were allowed to do. In the colonial Americas, these were terms like New Christian, *mestizo/a*, *octoroon* (the now-derogatory term for a person with one Black great-grandparent), and *lobo* (part Black, part Indian, and supposedly therefore wolflike).

In the West people typically understand race and nation today as distinct and separate ideas. Race is a discredited theory of innate, unchanging biological differences supposedly found among people with ancestry from different parts of the world, differences that are supposedly so significant and innate that some people deserve fewer rights and resources. By contrast, people understand nation to mean a cultural category for a community with a shared history and experience or for the citizens of a nation-state (a political unit administering a particular geographic space). Yet as Nicolasa Juana's situation and Gerald of Wales's complaint show, race and nation often collapse into one another.

Today countries (nation-states) tend to define citizenship in multiple ways that often permit change or addition to one's nationality according to various criteria. But nineteenth-century Western definitions of nation-states had tied them to shared ancestry. This turned the footpath connecting statecraft to racecraft into a highway, one whose effects persist today and yet are often at odds with legal frameworks of citizenship.[4] Attempts to map race (essentialized categories bolted into systems of hierarchy) onto nations (communities based on stories about ancestry, culture, and a shared past) became messy in the face of mixed-heritage individuals like Nicolasa Juana, who straddled categories: they gave rise to fears about how stable one's identity really was.

Nation building and race-making both involve storytelling through monster-making: Both "race" and "nation" are concepts that individuals and communities create. They are shorthand for selective histories bound up with ideas about bodies, action, ancestry, and citizenship. Both concepts assume an essential "something" that gets passed down through the blood. And they both create (identity) monsters. There can be discrete peoples or races only if a community identifies and labels as illegal or as freakish individuals who straddle the border between that community and some "other" group. Otherwise these individuals would reveal, simply by existing, that the border was a space of free movement. Like checkpoints and demilitarized zones that enable two nation-states to operate separately in continuous geographic space, category disruptors (people defined as belonging in neither group, although they share characteristics of both) allow communities on either side of an imagined border to exist in cultural space without their edges colliding. Many of the worst moments in human history have at their core an urge to manage the boundaries between races and between nations.

IS IT RACE?

Race is a concept with a history that long predates the word. Today people typically define race as a category for human differentiation based on selective, often imagined, essentialized traits. It refers to the essentializing of groups whose members include individuals of all genders, abilities, and socioeconomic statuses. People with power have historically used what scholars have called race-thinking or racecraft to justify systemic, often legal, discrimination. Stuff happens, and then words play catch-up. Race-thinking predates and is distinct from any particular terminology. It does not require a single, unchanging system, and it is independent of any particular content, place, or time. In earlier forms of race-making and in forms outside Europe and its colonies, race did not necessarily appear as a word, even in hierarchical systems with the same structures. In this chapter I use race to denote not particular content but structures: the murky mishmash of laws, ideas, and practices that distribute power and positions unevenly across groups of people on the basis of their heritage. As medieval literary scholar Geraldine Heng explains, race is not substantive content but a structured relationship—not necessarily about skin color or even about bodily differences. The characteristics by which cultures confect definitions of race (or whatever they call it) are constantly changing.[5] Race sometimes intersects with other systems of power, like gender, class, and caste.[6]

But invention, or reinvention, is distinct from origin: concepts change all the time. Today, when people think of the origins of the idea of race or racism, they often think of the laws and language that Europeans devised to legitimize and control enslaved black Africans, but in fact racial thinking in Europe is many centuries older. The racism that reinvented new versions of race and that enabled and consolidated the slave trade has roots at least as far back as classical antiquity.[7] To say there is no race before the Atlantic slave trade would be like claiming that there was no science before Galileo or no medicine before the discovery of penicillin. The characteristics and structures of the idea of race, of racism, and of race-thinking—those elements currently said to define them—did not begin with the slave trade, any more than science began in the seventeenth century. Nevertheless, the transatlantic slave trade *was* highly significant—catastrophically so—in the history of the idea of race.

Heng identifies the defining element of racism that transcends time and place as being a system of ideas about innate inequality, a system that communities keep in place through structures of power, like legislation.[8] Racist thought is any system of ideas that legitimizes different rights and privileges for peoples perceived to have different ancestry from the group with the most power. People with racist views may argue that certain groups are fundamentally inferior to others in ways that continue down through the generations and that cannot be changed by external factors. And when people police the boundaries between these invented races, dehumanize people on the basis of race, and insist that some races don't belong in a nation, they are monstrifying these people by ejecting them from the category of normal, regular members of the nation.

MONSTERS OF THE NATION

Where nation is concerned, monsters come in two forms: individuals who blur the boundary between the nation and those outside it and communities who are seemingly so different from one's own that they are perhaps not even fully human. Writers and thinkers have pointed out and identified those they defined as monsters in the process of imagining their nations. Perhaps the reason mixed-heritage individuals have often been contained or erased (in administrative terms) is that they make visible how little difference there is between categories. Put another way, if there are too many Nicolasa Juanas (whom we met at the start of the chapter), are there categories at all or are we all one and the same in our singular uniqueness and thereby equal?

There are two event horizons or monster-spawning zones where a person is in danger of becoming or birthing a monster in the eyes of their community or of people in power. Monster-making, or calling people illegal or problematic, happens in response to anxieties at these points. One event horizon is the space furthest from humanity, the level of difference that asks if they are even human. These monsters are the opposite of the self, a mirror that shows you who you are by reflecting your opposite. In the ancient Mediterranean world, these were the imagined monsters in distant places: headless folks with their faces in their chests, troglodytes who huddled in caves to escape the sun, and the mysterious apple smellers who survived on a diet of smells. Today these sorts of different-from-normal monsters are the stuff of horror, sci-fi, and fantasy: zombies, cyborgs, genetically modified beings, and mutants.

The second event horizon is at the edge of one's own community, in the space between a person and an enemy, a rival, a neighbor, or even an enslaved person. Multicultural individuals who, by appearance or ancestry, are not fully one or the other of two or more communities are at risk of being called this type of monster. To those who call them monsters, these people are suspicious, alarming, and often in need of control because they challenge the identities of the peoples on either side. Visions of community and humanity cannot always sustain a clear distinction between the self and distant others. Anyone identified as too weird is in danger of being dehumanized.

Just as racism in Europe is often described as something that began with the Atlantic slave trade or Enlightenment-era science, the story of nationalism and the rise of the nation-state is often told as one beginning in the nineteenth century. In this vein Emperor Napoleon Bonaparte's imperial ambitions in Europe prompted political agitators to appeal to national feeling or to identify with those with whom they shared ancestry, cultural traits like language, and elements of shared history. Many of today's European nation-states came into being as political entities in the nineteenth and twentieth centuries. Their appearance supposedly followed the emergence of a particular form of nationalism, one based on two broad premises. One premise was that of self-definition: peoples (or at least European ones) have the right to self-determination. The other premise was that of imperial subjugation: that the territorial extent of a nation-state should overlap with the living space of a culture group that was in some way homogenous in terms of values, origin myths, ways of life, and ancestry.[9]

But nationalism has deeper roots. The idea of a people with common characteristics and a shared idea of their history extends as far back as the earliest surviving stories—so do questions about the political legitimacy of others to rule over a people or even to live alongside them. Acts of monster-making have contested and built the borders of nations for millennia, moving walls that chart the shifting contours of the idea of nation, both in the sense of a people and in the sense of a nation-state.

Today's fuzzy concept of nation draws on ideas about race and about the nation-state. One definition of nation is legal, administrative, and theoretical: it denotes one's legal citizenship or nationality, something that can be fulfilled in many ways. While race is typically seen as a classification based on embodiment (bodies and physical appearance), nationality is usually not. Citizenship is—on paper—a legal concept, closely related to the concept of a nation as a space on the map (a nation-state)—and what people usually think of today as nationality (typically meant as legal membership of a nation-state). Physical appearance, dress, or behaviors are not necessary or sufficient to identify or bestow citizenship.

Yet this legal and administrative sense of citizenship-as-paperwork is a long way from how citizenship is performed, policed, or accepted in practice.

Thus a second sense of nation is bound up in somatic difference—in visible differences in physical appearance and customs. White, undocumented people from Europe—tourists who have overstayed the maximum length for their visit, for example—can pass for US citizens, whereas Chicanx persons may be asked, on the basis of their physical appearance, to prove that they are not undocumented immigrants from across the US-Mexico border. People who look a certain way get told to "go back where you came from," while others who look different do not.

Today's nation-states define and group peoples in inconsistent ways, and official apparatuses like census-reporting forms make these ham-fisted ways of thinking glaringly obvious. Native peoples did not have a category in the US census until 1860. The "one-drop" rule introduced in 1930 decreed that anyone with African ancestry, no matter how small a fraction, was Black, not white. Until the 1960s it was the census takers rather than the individuals concerned who determined what their race was. The 2020 US census saw lower numbers of returns from "hard to count" groups. These included people of color, noncitizens, and immigrants; many feared data being used against them. This was especially the case for individuals considered to be undocumented immigrants (under current law) even though many pay taxes. Underreporting skews records used for making policy decisions about numbers of congressional seats, the drawing of districts, the distribution of budgets, and all manner of public services.[10]

People within each race differ much more in appearance than people at the edge of one race do from people at the edge of another. Witness, for instance, census disagreements about whether or not people from countries east of Greece and west of Pakistan, such as people from the Middle East, should identify themselves as white. And which ancestors "count" for determining where you are from? You might have ancestors who lived in different parts of the world and who would be identified as different peoples. Yet go back far enough, and you do not know where they were from—so there are inconsistencies in terms of the "when" of your ancestors' geography.

People imbue the concept of nation with physical traits. This sense of nation imagines an essential characteristic that existed in a people at some distant moment in the past and that is preserved in some of their descendants (but not necessarily in those whose ancestry includes enough of "other" people for them to no longer pass as citizens of a group defined by selected physical features). In this vision of nation and its knock-on effects on nationality, citizenship becomes, for some, not a state of being or identity but an action they can never complete.[11] The legal administrative notion of nation is in theory more explicit and transparent than the more fluid, cultural idea of nation as a people. But in practice the legal administrative idea is informed, even structured, by the cultural one.

In other words, there is a definition of citizenship that shapes everyday practice (and prejudice) that is built on a very different idea of the nation than that of the modern nation-state. In this way of thinking, a nation is a people with shared ancestry and history in a particular place in the world, not the inhabitants of a shape on the map within which the laws, including those of citizenship, of a particular nation-state apply. Some can pass, some cannot, and this determines what their lives are like.

I've coined the term "race-nation" to describe the continuum running from race to nation that led writers like the bicultural medieval chronicler Gerald of Wales to spill so much anxious and angry ink. Race-nation is Frankenstein's monster, the fearsome child of the citizenship paperwork of nation-states. Like the creature that Victor Frankenstein assembled out of disparate body parts from anatomy theaters and abattoirs and, through his unholy experiments, imbued with life, a nation-state's bureaucracy is built from an awkward, unsightly amalgam of past ideologies.[12] This monstrous body of paperwork perpetuates the jerky, inconsistent, often abominable journeys of these undead ideologies through time and space.

The political scientist and historian Benedict Anderson defined the nation as "an imagined political community—and imagined as both inherently limited and sovereign." In doing so he drew on the words of philosopher and social anthropologist Ernest Gellner: "Nationalism is not the awakening of nations to self-consciousness: it *invents* nations where they do not exist."[13] Ideas about communities are also made in the imagination of others, who invent inherently distinctive ethnic groups said to have come into being at a moment in the distant past. Race-nation is a concept that exists in how people act toward individuals and communities who challenge the observers' sense of their own distinctiveness. I introduce the term here to tell a history of race and nation through how communities imagine themselves by defining and policing those deemed to be monstrous because they break existing categories.

The long history of narratives about people's bodies and nations reveals the roots of numerous ideas that persist today but yet are out of step with how we officially think about race and nation. The signs and codes of race-making and nation-making are protean, constantly lived, contested, and rewritten by communities that think, live, and act alongside one another. To solve the structural problems of the present, we must first acknowledge and trace their origins.

MALLEABLE BODIES IN THE ANCIENT MEDITERRANEAN

Ancient thinkers in Afro-Eurasia divided the world into five zones of latitude, as discussed in chapter 1. The Greek geographer Strabo (ca. 64 BCE–24 CE, from Pontus, now in Turkey) defined these horizontal bands of land, from the North Pole to the South Pole, as the polar, temperate, torrid, temperate, and frigid (polar) zones. For the ancient Greeks, humans inhabited the middle position in Creation between gods at one end and animals at the other. An influential example was the naturalist and philosopher Aristotle (384–322 BCE), who proposed that only the two temperate zones were habitable and that the best sort of people were to be found in the ideal climate. This theory contributed to European racism in ways that endure into the present.[14] To Aristotle humanity itself had degrees, visible in behavior. Godlike figures with superhuman levels of virtue or heroism resided at one end of the scale, bestial individuals at the other. Everyday humans, somewhere in between, exhibited both vice and virtue.[15]

At the bottom of Aristotle's scale of humanity were barbarians, defined as people who did not speak Greek. *Barbaroi* (babblers) possessed insufficient intellectual prowess to behave like Greeks or to form a functioning civil society. Aristotle's distinction between Greeks and barbarians was essentially one between humans and nonhumans. Those who failed to learn Greek might never achieve full human capacities for reasoning, despite being anatomically human. Here a people's identity (Greekness) was bound to a behavior (speaking Greek), such that those who did not behave this way (non-Greek speakers) were deemed to be physiologically inferior—monstrous for failing to be Greek, if you will. In this way the action (speaking Greek) and its absence were signs of difference that revealed a hierarchy of humanity.[16]

But couldn't all these peoples just speak Greek? Certainly some of them did, just as many peoples in the Roman Empire would both learn Latin and "become" Roman through the process of conquest (not that this made

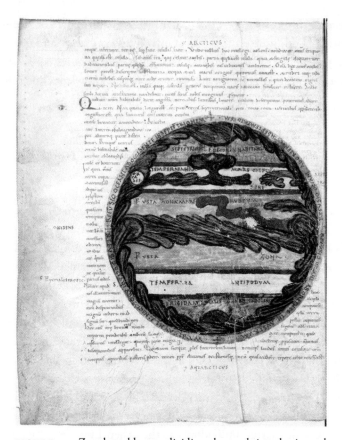

FIGURE 10. Zonal world map, dividing the earth into horizontal climatic zones, first half of the eleventh century. Ancient thinkers believed that the climate in each zone influenced the physical, intellectual, and moral characteristics of its inhabitants and that "civilized" peoples couldn't be found in places of extreme heat or cold—a theory that propped up European racism and colonialism for centuries. Département des Manuscrits, Latin 6371, Bibliothèque Nationale de France, Paris, fol. 20v.

everyone equal in practice). Yet peoples who did not occupy the ideal geographic position of the temperate Mediterranean were thought to be innately limited by the physiological effects of their location.[17] No matter how hard they tried, barbarians couldn't always change their linguistic spots—even if they wanted to.

Ancient Greeks and Romans had a variety of words for group identity based on shared culture or descent, including *gens*, *genos*, *ethnos*, *natio*, and *phylla*. Herodotus recounted how the Athenians told the Spartans that they would never betray them to the Persians, since the Spartans shared blood with the Athenians. Implicitly the Persians, with whom they did not share blood, were consequently not part of their nation (to whom they owed some sort of loyalty) on the basis of their genealogy. According to ancient thinkers, harsh climates deformed human minds and bodies. As their distance from the eastern Mediterranean grew, people became, apparently, less civilized, more barbarous, and—eventually—monstrous. Latin texts written in the Roman Empire referred to monstrous communities as *gens* (people) or *natio* (nation)—some sort of variant of humans rather than another species of animal entirely.[18]

After the fall of the western Roman Empire and during the gradual spread of Christianity through Europe from the sixth century onward, ancient ideas about bodies, behavior, and geography continued to shape how people thought about what it meant to be human. Aristotle's definition of barbarians took on a Christian hue for the faith's followers in Europe. In Christian thought in the early Middle Ages, anyone who did not convert to Christianity had demonstrated their inability to use reason properly; consequently, Christian thinkers deemed such people to be barbarians.[19] The primary characteristic for group identification and social hierarchy thus shifted from language to faith, inventing new communities, or in- and out-groups. Communities managed the boundaries between the Christian self and neighboring, suddenly hyper-visible groups by identifying and controlling those who practiced seemingly monstrous or unconventional forms of behavior.

Today people tend to think of a person's skin color as fixed—at least within parameters set by seasons, tanning beds, spray tans, and skin-whitening products—even though individuals and observers may code their race differently at different moments in their lives, according to clothing choices, hairstyles, locations, and social contexts. Yet medieval European romances described a few people whose skin color changed dramatically when they changed their faith. These extraordinary cases illustrate the idea that the body was malleable, affected even by thoughts and deeds in ways that could be seen. Such stories also point to a need to be able to *see* someone's faith and to deep anxieties that, since behavior could be faked, one needed to read the book of the body to really know.

In *The King of Tars*, a fourteenth-century English romance, the sultan of Syria converts to Christianity, turns white, and then converts back to Islam, at which point his skin darkens again. An even more dramatic shape-shift appears in a late thirteenth-century Christian chronicle, the *Cursor mundi*. Four black, excessively hairy Muslims ("sarasinis") with mouths in their chests and an eye in their foreheads, "misshapen creatures," allegedly begged King David of Israel to show them the wood that would later become the True Cross. Once the king did so, not only did their skin supposedly become as white "als [*sic*] milk," but their complexion or "hew" became that of someone with what the poet calls free blood, "fre blode," and "their shap [shape] was turned new."[20] Not only did converts' skin change color, but they apparently became free as their bodies were remade. People's faith was alarmingly invisible in their minds. Nevertheless, if it changed, signs were supposedly visible on their bodies. The distinction between monster and human could thus be seen as one of active choice, in the manner of Adam and Eve's fall from grace.

Yet many authorities feared that faith could *not* be read from the body but that faith mattered enough that people's lives should be constrained accordingly. Sometimes authorities chose to impose a visible marker on people to make sure that they were visibly "other." Since the Middle Ages, people who were Jewish were sometimes required to wear badges and to live in prescribed areas. The Fourth Lateran Council (1215) in Rome effectively turned religious difference into a racial category: the church demanded that Jews and Muslims wear visible markers of their religion.

In 1290 England expelled its Jews. This was "the first permanent expulsion in Europe."[21] For decades beforehand the English had juridically singled out Jews spatially (by passing laws stipulating exactly where Jews could live, for instance) and somatically (by mandating, in 1218, that Jews wear identifying badges on their clothing). Christians also invented the false, defamatory story that Jews committed the ritual murder of Christian children, a myth whose first known appearance dates to 1149.[22] This lie is called "blood libel." English laws about Jews were designed to ensure that a religious difference was also a visible one that could thereby be more easily contained. Numerous medieval theological, medical, and scientific writings came to argue that Jews were physiologically different from Christians. Medieval manuscript illuminations reveal stereotypes in the making.[23] And thus anti-Semitism is a form of racism.[24]

The expulsion of the Jews was not the first moment of race-nation crisis in the British Isles. The islands were far from culturally or ethnically homogenous in the Middle Ages. By the twelfth century, Britain had been colonized and reconfigured several times over. Around 43 CE Emperor Claudius began to add the dark and rainy archipelago to the Roman Empire. In the fifth century CE, the Angles arrived from present-day southern Denmark and northern Germany. In the eleventh century, the Normans, themselves ethnically diverse, came, conquered, assimilated into the local population, ruled, and stayed.

What did medieval Britons, new arrivals, and bicultural individuals say about one another? How did they write and think about individuals of mixed heritage?[25] As literary scholar Shirin Khanmohamadi puts it, "The earliest ethnography of Europe emerged from its borders, particularly as they underwent expansion in the twelfth century."[26] In twelfth-century Britain, chroniclers labeled peoples they called the Irish, the Scots, the English, and the Welsh as barbarians or even as beasts. Writers and artists who depicted customs and daily life carved attributes for each of the notional peoples in Britain into people's imaginations. Yet the intermingling of cultures and families was happening all around them; some of these early ethnographers, like Gerald of Wales, were themselves its product. These chroniclers tried to construct on parchment clear boundaries between peoples, even though these communities were constantly blending.

Gerald was as dismissive about the Irish as he was of the English: "Although [the Irish] are fully endowed with natural gifts, their external characteristics of beard and dress, and internal cultivation of the mind, are so barbarous that they cannot be said to have any culture. . . . This people are a barbarous people, literally barbarous. Judged according to modern ideas, they are uncultivated, not only in the external appearance of their dress, but also in their flowing hair and beards. All their habits are the habits of barbarians. . . . They are a wild and inhospitable people. They live on beasts only, and live like beasts."[27] Gerald extrapolated from his disapproval of Irish styles of dress to the claim that the Irish were effectively beasts: their lack of external refinement was, he argued, a sign of their mental inferiority. Elsewhere he would describe Ireland as a place inhabited by human-animal hybrids like werewolves and ox-humans.[28]

Inventing one's nation and those of one's neighbors involves calling out—and walling up—the in-betweener who reveals that these nations sit on a continuum. Monsters are category problems that have to be defanged. Characterizing individuals as monsters allows communities to marginalize them and so to some extent erase them. But these people actually exist, regardless of the fact that society minimizes or challenges their existence. There *are* individuals with multiple ancestries, caught between expectations, neither fully one thing nor another. What is *really* imaginary is what medieval literature and monster scholar Jeffrey Jerome Cohen calls "imagined or desired absolutes like 'Angle,' 'Briton,' 'English,' and 'Norman,' 'Christian,' and 'Jew.'"[29] These are theoretical constructs. Not only are all these peoples a mix of peoples, but the mixtures, identities, and stories they tell about themselves and others are constantly changing.

As scholars and cultural critics like Kwame Anthony Appiah and Afua Hirsch remind us, ethnicity is a narrative about biology that links individuals to a community imagined to be homogenous and unchanging over time.[30] Although descriptive terms assume discrete identities and communities, the normal order of things is a continuum of diversity. Medieval England was a multifaith place and a postcolonial place, where multicultural chroniclers practiced race-making by invoking bodies, behavior, and the disciplining of hybrids: individuals whose cosmopolitan ancestry threatened to bring down the walls between different "nations" within Britain. The irony is that those walls had human-sized holes in them all along.

In mainland Europe in the Middle Ages, the word *raza* (race) appeared in Romance languages, where it referred not to nations but to local familial groups: the dogs bred on a certain estate, say, or a particular noble family.[31] In this way *race* was a frame that allowed them to distinguish among noble and ordinary extended families who shared bloodlines and faith and looked similar. In the worlds of farming and animal husbandry in medieval Iberia, *raza* referred to the genealogy of animals. From here the word jumped species, as it were, to humans. Here, although the term *raza* did not yet refer to a system of human hierarchy based on selective, essentialized traits, such a system was already in place.

This framework for thinking about ancestry was complicated by the fact that thoughts were believed to affect the blood. In the fifteenth century, as the self-styled Catholic monarchs Isabella and Ferdinand sent troops to drive Muslims out of what is now southern Spain and to force Jews and Muslims to convert to Christianity, recent converts from Judaism (labeled *conversos*) and from Islam (labeled *moriscos*) were deemed to be inferior in ways that could not be undone by education or environment. There emerged a language of "purity of blood": these so-called New Christians were deemed to transmit their moral failings to their children and were subjected differently to political power and law, most spectacularly by the Spanish Inquisition, founded to root out those who practiced their former religions in secret.[32] Laws to keep New Christians separate soon followed. A key fear of the authorities was that "old" Christians would become tainted by association: the corruption in the blood of *conversos* would affect their customs, which would then allegedly contaminate the properly faithful.[33] Similarly, in the sixteenth century, the Spanish Crown banned New Christians from traveling to the Americas to prevent their beliefs from compromising missionary efforts.

The challenge of managing faith was that it was ultimately invisible. The best that one could do was attempt to see into someone's beliefs by extrapolating from their behavior: clothing, rituals, and dietary practices, like abstaining from eating meat on Fridays or not combining meat and dairy. Stereotypes about physical features show how hard people tried to make faith visible on the body—and how faith could subsequently become a convenient way of monstrifying people.

MAKING IT OKAY TO BE WILD

It all began with a book.

In 1455 a scholar in a monastery stumbled across a copy of a long-lost text: the *Germania*, a thirty-page history of Germanic peoples, written by the ancient Roman historian Cornelius Tacitus around 98 CE. For humanist scholars in Germany, who were engaged at the time in recovering lost ancient Greek and Latin texts, the *Germania* was an unprecedented opportunity to meet their ancestors. What they found, however, was the antithesis of deep learning and settled urban or agricultural life, ideals that the Romans had rolled (or flattened) out across the empire and that these scholars also prized. Ancient Germans, it turned out, had been . . . *wild*.[34] In medieval folklore wild people lived in the Alps and in northern Europe—challenging habitats that had molded the inhabitants over generations until they became the sort of people who could thrive there. Lacking metalworking skills, these people were strong enough to uproot trees with which to fend off dangerous animals. Wild men patrolled the edges of civilized regions, guarding them against outsiders; other wild men were Christian hermit saints.[35] Some were the heroic ancestors of origin myths and were a symbol for heraldic shields.[36]

The monstrifying capabilities of climate meant that the far north was a space where minds and bodies were misshapen. But where the north became a monstrifying space was relative; it varied depending on where the observers

FIGURE 11. Martin Schongauer, *Shield with Stag Held by Wild Man*, engraving, circa 1480–90. In this engraving a wild man carries a heraldic shield, perhaps symbolizing his position at the foundations of the family tree. 28.26.7, Harris Brisbane Dick Fund, 1928, Metropolitan Museum of Art, New York.

themselves lived. Scholars in medieval Britain were anxious about how far north they lived.[37] In the medieval Islamicate world, scholarly texts posited "humoral failings" in northern European bodies.[38] For people living in the Mediterranean, regions of biting cold were as uninviting as those of raging heat. To the northeast were the lands (southern Siberia) of the Scythians, who ancient Greek and Roman geographers thought were eaters of human flesh.[39] Routes northwest from Greece led to the lands of Goths, Celts, and Laplanders imagined as monsters at the edges of categories, alarming peoples to be avoided for fear of ontological mixing.

For Renaissance German scholars, discovering that their ancestors were wild necessitated raising the reputation of folkloric wild men. They needed a history that honored their ancestors and reframed behaviors that were inconsistent with their existing values, aspirations, and understandings of the distinction between civilization and barbarism (with which they associated wildness). These scholars wrote new interpretations of the ancient German

FIGURE 12. Einhard, *Vita et gesta Karoli Magni*, title page, 1521. Charlemagne, the first Holy Roman emperor, sports the clothing and personal grooming choices of a medieval wild man, while Charles V (*on the right*), Holy Roman emperor more than six centuries later, is dressed to show off wealth, power, and—implicitly— civility. Ger 435.49*, Houghton Library, Harvard University, Cambridge, MA.

past, narratives that celebrated what they had come to see as the wildness, strength, and simplicity of their ancestors before the Roman had marched in. By the sixteenth century, the reputation of ancient, wild Germans had risen so high that the first printed history of Charlemagne, the eighth-century emperor of large parts of western Europe, contained a portrait of him attired in period "wild" clothing: loose leggings and a reed crown bearing greater resemblance to a feather headdress rather than the jeweled crown he was said to have worn.

France—the kingdom populated by Frankish (i.e., Germanic) tribes in the north—claimed to have inherited Charlemagne's mantle as the defender of Christianity. French scholars and merchants in the mid-sixteenth century imagined the new king Henri II not merely as a warrior-king but also as someone on an honorable path to erudition. Wild nobility with a capacity for learning and peak civility was apparently also imaginable for the Tupinambá cannibals of Brazil. In 1550 a few were brought to Rouen, Normandy, to participate in a festival to honor the newly crowned Henri II and to confirm the rights and privileges of the city in the eyes of the new monarch. The young king was treated to scenes devised by the city's dignitaries, scenes mapping out a personal development trajectory to refinement, toward an ideal of

Figure des Brifilians.

FIGURE 13. *C'est la déduction du sumptueux ordre*, engraving, Rouen, 1551. The Brazilian tableau at the festival was staged in honor of Henri II of France's ceremonial entry into Rouen in 1550. Sig. [K.ii.v–iiir], Typ 515.51.272, Houghton Library, Harvard University, Cambridge, MA.

kingship that embraced both the sword (the traditional implement) and the pen (of learning).[40] The Tupinambá tableau was one of the scenes laying out his journey.

By writing new backstories for their genealogies, scholars in northern Europe wriggled out of the frame of the Renaissance equivalent of descended from hillbillies—or worse, from monstrous peoples—when compared to citizens of the urbane city-states of Renaissance Italy, the site of the heart of the ancient Roman Empire. But this renarrativizing would develop a sinister edge many centuries later. Tacitus had talked up the rustic German tribes to annoy his urbane Roman compatriots. He had extolled their morality and observed that they were "unmixed by intermarriage" and "pure."[41] Until the proclamation of the German Empire in 1871, Germany was an idea, not a single kingdom or state. In the nineteenth century, Tacitus's *Germania* gave voice and text to German nationalists who wanted a unified political nation for Germans (whatever that meant for a sprawling region of varied dialects and traditions). For senior figures in Hitler's National Socialist Party, the text inspired myths of German ethnic purity. In 1936 the Nazi Party's infamous Nuremberg convention even featured a "Germanic room" covered in inscriptions from Tacitus.[42]

Yet Tacitus probably never even visited the region. Germanic peoples were not hermetically sealed from everyone else. In any event ancient Romans, today's linguists, and archaeologists all define "Germanic" differently. And Tacitus's *Germanen*—Germanic tribes as Romans defined them—are not the same as Germans. Almost two millennia after Tacitus penned his *Germania*, some of his readers were weaponizing it in ways he could never have imagined.[43] And as I'll discuss in the next chapter, ancient ideas about race and nation that had cross-fertilized one another up to the fifteenth century had far-reaching consequences when people began, in great numbers, to cross oceans in ships.

————

FOUR

Race-Nations II

THE PERIOD BETWEEN the mid-fifteenth and the late eighteenth centuries was one of new and multiplying interconnections and entanglements among Africa, Asia, the Americas, and Europe; the Indian Ocean and South China Sea (in both of which long-distance coastal maritime exchange had a much longer history); and (slightly later) across the Pacific Ocean. People, beings, and things moved, willingly or under coercion, over great distances. In the eyes of a person in Europe, formerly "civilized" people were at risk of going native and becoming a "barbarian."[1] The innate fungibility of human minds and bodies threw into question any hope that the key essence of a person was fixed. Untethered from their original locales and translated across oceans, beings who had appeared perfectly stable and solid, became ... *squishy*.

The heart of the question of monstrous peoples was spatial: some places spawned monsters. Ancient notions of the relationship between geography, climate, and human difference undergirded thinking about humanity and of the monstrous. So where exactly were the monsters? And why did they exist? Biblical scripture offers some explanations. One option was that monstrous peoples were regular folks who had become degenerate through sin. Cain (who killed his brother Abel) and Ham (who laughed at Noah as he lay on his ark in a drunken stupor) were thought to have prompted God to curse their descendants. When the floodwaters subsided, Noah divided the world among his sons, Ham, Shem, and Japheth. While the scriptures do not specify who received what, surviving maps and geographic writings from the twelfth century surmised that Ham, Shem, and Japheth received Africa,

Asia, and Europe, respectively. Ham's descendants were said to have populated Africa and to continue to bear a visible mark of his sin.[2] Visible physical differences between people living in different parts of the world were thus read as clues to the moral character of their ancestors.

The Greco-Egyptian geographer Ptolemy's *Geography*, a second-century description of the known world, had a winding path of influence on the concept of the human. In the western half of the former Roman Empire, the book fell out of view sometime in the Middle Ages. Yet the book continued to influence geographic thought in the Islamicate world and in Byzantium, which was the eastern half of the former Roman Empire, centered on Constantinople, today's Istanbul. The *Geography* offered instructions for drawing maps using latitude and longitude, together with a list of coordinates of the principal cities. A world map drawn on Ptolemaic principles would show the climatological features under which different peoples lived— Ptolemy subdivided the Northern Hemisphere into latitudinal zones, for example—and offer a grid on which to map human variety and monstrosity.

The divide between the human and the monster and between the virtuous and the damned took visible form on maps. Thirteenth-century world maps made in Europe, called *mappaemundi*, overlaid classical Greek, Roman, and Near Eastern geography with biblical traditions about the world's peoples. *Mappaemundi* made visible an originary moment—Noah's division of the world among his sons—and used it to draw genealogical trees for humanity. These maps sometimes represented the world as a circle dissected into three parts by the River Nile, the Black Sea (or sometimes the River Don), and the Mediterranean Sea.

Mappaemundi integrated scripture with monster theory. Cartographers placed Jerusalem (the Holy Land) at the center and the location of Paradise at the top. The largest surviving examples are some six feet across, richly illuminated with biblical scenes, animals, plants, buildings like castles, kings, and many, many monsters. Even on the palm-sized example known as the Psalter World Map, monstrous peoples appear on the outer rim of the world, as far away as possible from Jerusalem.[3]

Inscriptions on maps reinforced the idea that distant life was monstrous. The thirteenth-century English Hereford Map notes that northeastern Asia contains the land of "exceedingly savage people who eat human flesh and drink blood, the accursed sons of Cain." In his attempts to wall off the monsters, God was said to have caused earthquakes, bringing mountains down on mountains around Gog and Magog, Cain's kin. Alexander the Great went

FIGURE 14. Psalter World Map, circa 1265. East is at the top, Jerusalem is at the center, monstrous peoples line the southern rim of the world, and in the northeast is the curved wall allegedly built by Alexander the Great to hold back the monstrous tribes of Gog and Magog. MS Add. 28681, British Library, London, UK. From the British Library Archive/ Bridgeman Images, fol. 9r.

further, purportedly blocking off the only mountain pass by getting his troops to build a wall across it. Numerous medieval world maps illustrate the walls around the monstrous tribes of Gog and Magog, who were expected to stage a breakout at the Last Judgment.[4]

Even though continents are merely human conventions of shapes on the earth, since at least the Middle Ages, European thinkers have organized their histories and identities according to these landmasses, despite the thick connections of trade, migration, and political connections across them.[5] While the Romans had referred to the Mediterranean Sea as "Our Sea" (Mare Nostrum), and maritime connections were stronger than overland ones, given the higher security of seaborne travel (pirates being easier to avoid than bandits, local travel restrictions, and tolls), interpretations of the Bible helped to cement the ancient notion of parts of the world—Africa, Asia, and Europe—into a foundation of ideas for making sense of human communities.[6]

In 1397 a physical copy of Ptolemy's *Geography* resurfaced in western Europe for the first time in centuries. A medieval manuscript version that had been preserved in Constantinople had just been carried to Florence by the Byzantine scholar Manuel Chrysoloras. The book was translated from Greek into Latin in 1406. From the mid-fifteenth century, the *Geography* began to circulate both in manuscript (handwritten) copies with maps newly drawn using Ptolemy's coordinates and also in print.[7] These maps reappeared in western Europe in precisely the decades that ships from Europe were beginning to sail in the open sea in the Atlantic. As the Ptolemaic coordinate system became the framework for world mapping in Europe, illustrated world maps made the connections between climate, human variety, and geography explicit and visual.[8]

As the literary scholar Geraldine Heng puts it, for Christians in medieval Europe, "race is what the rest of the world has."[9] Coordinate-based exploration and mapping fused ideas about monstrous peoples onto ideas about humanity in ways that were so alarming that they necessitated new ways of thinking about individuals, bodies, nations, and geography.[10] If monstrous peoples lived "over there" in the distant north, south, or east-west (east eventually meets west on a round world), wherever the climate was especially nasty, then where exactly was the boundary between human space and monster space?

Maps gave these ideas a distinct visual form. A world map from 1551 assembled by the Spanish master chart maker Sancho Gutiérrez framed the far north as a place of monsters. Since map illustrations were expected to

FIGURE 15. Sancho Gutiérrez, *Carta general*, detail showing parts of Africa and northern Eurasia, 1551. Across the four sheets of this enormous world map, most of the unusually embodied people appear in the far north. ONB/Wien K I 99.416, Austrian National Library, Vienna.

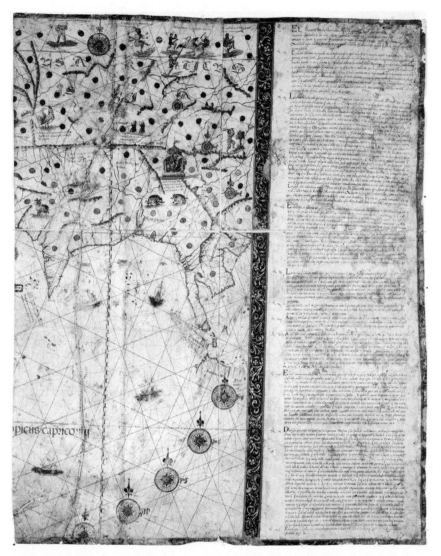

FIGURE 16. Sancho Gutiérrez, *Carta general*, detail showing northern East Asia, 1551. Illustrated sixteenth-century world maps often included depictions of rulers and of idolatry (such as the practice of worshipping the sun) in eastern Eurasia. Both appear in the center of this detail; the far north is again a region of monstrous peoples. ONB/Wien K I 99.416, Austrian National Library, Vienna.

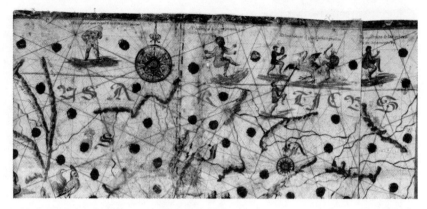

FIGURE 17. Sancho Gutiérrez, *Carta general*, detail, 1551. The monstrous peoples in the far north were all described by ancient geographers and naturalists. Across this map Gutiérrez synthesized ancient sources and firsthand accounts from recent European oceanic expeditions. ONB/Wien K I 99.416, Austrian National Library, Vienna.

emblematize things that were typical about a region, a single image of a dog-headed or one-legged being would have been interpreted at the time as signs that there were entire tribes of dog heads and one-legged monsters in this part of the world (see plate 5). And since bodies and ecologies were interconnected, these images made arguments about the effect of the environment on bodies.[11] These in turn contributed to European racism in ways that endure to the present.

Circumnavigating the earth brought monstrification to the top of concerns about nations for Europe's clerics and colonial administrators. Once ships sailing under European flags were undertaking long-distance oceanic voyages, geography created a new inflection point in the category of the human in Europe and among its settler-colonists abroad. The problem was this: people feared that minds and bodies were malleable. In theory people who had (been) moved thousands of miles might be reshaped by their environment. Settlers might even change into monsters if they spent too long in a monstrifying climate.

Something had to be figured out to manage colonists' minds and bodies, to prevent them from ceasing to be fully Christian and human in places where they were no longer eating, drinking, or doing the same things they had at home.[12] For colonists from England or France, the medical traditions from home were not necessarily suitable for understanding European bodies in the climate of the Caribbean. If tropical diseases were fundamentally different from those in the temperate zone, then one would need a new sort of medicine tailored to the tropics. European physicians in the Caribbean in the eighteenth century noticed that numerous newcomers to the region, such as enslaved Africans and English planters, became very sick on arrival and often died.[13] Yet if they survived this sickness, they would not appear to get it again. Nor did people who had lived in the region a long time or Indigenous inhabitants appear to suffer from what became known as a "seasoning sickness."[14]

European naturalists and physicians came up with a conclusion that solved some of their anxieties. They decided that a person from the temperate zone underwent only limited changes in response to time spent in the tropics. This narrative provided an added justification for racial slavery. Commentators and planters in the Caribbean argued that people from Africa were better able to withstand hard work and the tropical climate. By insisting that there was something fixed in the blood from an "originary" continent, these writers allayed fears that European bodies could ever change so much as to become "tropical."[15]

MAKING RACE-NATIONS IN LAW

In Steven Spielberg's *The Terminal* (2004), the political disappearance of Viktor Navorski's country while he is airborne makes him a stateless holder of an invalid passport, unable to leave the airport terminal at which he had landed. Monster-making is a legal process, one by which individuals and entire communities can cease to exist in the eyes of the law. The process can create new forms of legal persons and even withhold legal personhood entirely. Laws create the illusion that the categories they invent are fundamentally real and comprehensive rather than negotiated conventions, economic or political conveniences, or clumsy approximations.

A very different, epoch-defining sort of fiction disappeared the humanity of millions of people using the ink-and-paper instruments of law. In Europe's Atlantic colonies from the sixteenth to the nineteenth centuries, the lives of Africans and their descendants were gradually constrained by a succession of legal systems devoted to separating Black and white lives and experiences. To justify this difference, these laws defined "Africans" as a distinct legal category of being. Before the Atlantic slave trade, slavery in Europe and North

Africa had been a condition independent of the color of a person's skin. Since classical antiquity and well into the eighteenth century, individuals with various customs, physical features, and lands of origin were enslaved. Slavery was seen as a situational, potentially temporary condition resulting from, for example, bankruptcy or capture in wartime.

For the seventeenth-century Americas, new legal instruments called "black codes" were developed by jurists and administrators in Europe to differentiate between poor white people and people of African descent.[16] These laws turned a visible and physical difference (skin color) into an economic one. They invented a new, liminal category for Black Africans transported to the colonies: lawmakers deemed them to deserve fewer rights than white people and caused them to be legally defined as chattel property and enslaved for life. Empire's bureaucrats pushed Black people from the category of human into the category of property in legal terms. In so doing they engaged in acts of monster-making: they defined race and Africans in ways that served plantation owners, legitimized slavery, and reframed people of African descent as outside the category of the human in some respects. These changes were made in anticipation of—and eventually in response to—servant and slave rebellions against appalling conditions.

In colonial English America, elite plantation owners–turned-legislators devised a series of laws that redefined the concepts of servant, slave, Christian, white, black, and "Negro" and the relationships among servants, slaves, masters, the community, and the law. The earliest English codes were devised for the island of Barbados. Following the ways these laws defined classes of people offers a vivid example of how laws define who counts as human. From the first English settlement on the island of Barbados in 1627, indentured white servants, Africans, and Indigenous persons did most of the backbreaking work of cultivating cotton, indigo, and (eventually) sugar. By 1636 the Barbados Council had resolved that "Negroes and Indians, that came here to be sold, should serve for life, unless a contract was before made to the contrary." The English now envisioned servitude as something that would change an Indigenous or African person—but not a European person—for life. Descriptions of plantation life by travelers, clerics, and planters suggested that enslaved Africans were treated far worse than servants and that slavery was understood to be hereditary.[17]

A body of Barbadian laws from 1652 included some that laid out common conditions of servitude and slavery. Both groups were framed as chattel— living property of their masters, like livestock—that a creditor could seize.

The act "to restrain the wandring of Servants and Negro's," however, drew a distinction between servants and Africans, punishing them differently. Servants would have months added to their service. Captors of escaped Africans—who could be servants or even other slaves—were to whip their captives, return them to their plantations, and receive a reward in sugar commensurate with how far they had traveled.[18]

The 1661 Slave and Servant Acts invented "Christian servants" and "Negro slaves." They distinguished between "English" servants and other Christian servants: "children of the English nation" younger than fourteen couldn't be indentured. They defined Africans in a way that made their enslavement permanent and embodied, not temporary and situational. There was supposedly no overlap between "Christian" and "Negro." The 1661 acts broke the labor solidarity between servants and enslaved people.[19] Servants and free persons now received even greater rewards for catching and returning enslaved runaways (up from ten pounds of sugar per escorted mile to a flat rate of a hundred pounds of sugar per runaway). The laws gave "rights" to servants but dehumanized Africans, calling them "heathenish" (not Christian) and "brutish" (akin to animals). They were considered not as individuals but as an amorphous group—"an uncertain dangerous pride of people"—whose humanity was constantly questioned and undermined by the very language of the law.[20]

Many Black and servant codes prohibited enslaved African-descended women from becoming pregnant and banned or penalized sexual relationships between masters and their chattel.[21] Such laws attempted to define certain individuals as monsters (that is, to call out as criminals those who broke these rules) to wall out entire communities from spaces of power and privilege. In colonial North America, children were assigned the race and legal status of their mother, thus defining the offspring of slave owners and enslaved women as enslaved. Laws of hypodescent automatically assigned mixed-race children to the lowest racial category of their ancestry. If no one wanted to be (or to bring into the world) an in-betweener whose rights would be severely curtailed and lead to punishment, then "races" could, in theory, be kept separate in ways that supported differential access to power.

Law is an apparatus that sketches out what a state and a society consider to be unacceptable or monstrous behavior punishable by law. Sentencing laws that apply differentially across groups bring race-nations into being. The US Constitution declared all men to be equal and extended voting rights to male property owners. Enslaved Africans were now monstrified in the eyes of the law in an additional way. Not only had the law defined Black people as non-persons in black codes that defined them as property, but they were now denied the vote. Yet they counted as three-fifths of a person for the purpose of determining a state's population. Since representation in Congress was related to population, this enlarged the number of congressional representatives that landed men in plantation states would have in the federal government as well as the number of electors they received for identifying the winner of a presidential election.

After the Civil War and during the Jim Crow era, segregation laws replaced black codes. New forms of crimes were defined (such as "vagrancy" and "insulting gestures"), and laws were applied selectively on the basis of whether someone was Black or white. Once in prison, a person was defined as someone who *could* be enslaved. The Thirteenth Amendment, which had abolished slavery, still permitted it as a punishment for crime. Laws prohibited interracial marriage until the Supreme Court overturned them in 1967, yet some southern states took their time repealing state prohibitions, with Alabama's law against interracial marriage remaining on the books until 2000.[22]

While Jim Crow laws were outlawed by the late twentieth century, today a system of mass incarceration has taken its place. As Michelle Alexander has laid out in extraordinary detail in *The New Jim Crow*, the United States and the colonies from which it coalesced devised successive legal systems to treat people of African descent differently from white citizens. These legal regimes culminated in the current system of mass incarceration through the way crimes are defined, policed, and sentenced. The cycle of sustaining race-nations with different lives and opportunities in the same country thus continues through new legal instruments of racial control, instruments that allow individuals to be monstrified and thereby stripped of the rights of citizenship. As Alexander put it, "We have not ended racial caste in America; we have merely redesigned it."[23]

Being convicted of a crime has sweeping, lifelong consequences in the United States: legalized discrimination for life in the spheres of health care, housing, the workplace, education, public benefits, and jury service. Convicted felons often face the loss of voting rights in prison, and even for life, depending on the state. African Americans are convicted of crimes at far greater frequency (as a percentage of the total number of African Americans) than white people. The majority of these African Americans are convicted for nonviolent drug use, even though drug use and sales occur at similar rates among all people. Within a single country there unfold very different sorts of lives constrained by the way different laws apply according to the color of their skin.[24]

Fears about monstrous essences that deform species and nations and about monstrous beings straddling the human and the animal have long appeared in fiction: in ancient origin myths (the Greek Minotaur), medieval epics (Grendel and his mother in *Beowulf*), Renaissance drama (Caliban in Shakespeare's *The Tempest*), and eighteenth- and nineteenth-century gothic horror (*Dracula*). Modern science fiction, fantasy, and horror movies invite audiences to think about race and identity using imagined monsters. *White Zombie* (1932) and *King Kong* (1933) played to white fears about Black people; such films would be followed by their inverse, in which white people were cast as villains. George A. Romero's *Night of the Living Dead* (1968), appearing at the height of the civil rights movement in the United States, follows an epidemic of white zombiism, in which a Black man is the hero who protects a white woman. Other movies revisit age-old anxieties not to demonize the monsters but to show us that they too are human and that they are also us.

William Shakespeare's *The Tempest* questions the fixity of the human form through perhaps the most indelible of his monsters. First printed in 1611, the play opens with a shipwreck conjured up by the magician Prospero, the exiled Duke of Milan. Prospero's brother Antonio had usurped his throne and banished Prospero and his baby daughter, Miranda, twelve years previously. The pair wash up on an island, where Prospero brings under his power two of the island's existing inhabitants: Caliban and the sprite Ariel. Caliban is a creature of contested humanity, a so-called monster borne of a witch and the devil, "not honoured with a human shape" but feared to be capable of disrupting human lineage.[25] Caliban, whom Prospero announces as a "poisonous slave," had been himself dispossessed by Prospero of his rightful island domain: this island his "by Sycorax my mother, / which thou tak'st from me."[26]

Prospero describes Caliban as a "moon-calf": a misshapen, ignorant creature incapable of learning, born under the influence of the moon, a heavenly body feared for its malevolent effects on minds, bodies, and temperaments. He was, to Prospero, "a freckled whelp, hag-born": the unholy result of a

FIGURE 18. Program for *The Tempest*, Shakespeare Tercentenary Celebration, New York, 1916. The cover shows Caliban, the being allegedly born of the devil and a witch who was dispossessed, imprisoned, and enslaved by the sorcerer Prospero. Program Collection, Folger Shakespeare Library, Washington, DC.

union between a witch and the devil. Caliban had supposedly lived out his youth learning the arts of sorcery from his mother, Sycorax, happily cocooned on an island distinctly lacking in amenities conducive to cultivating a civilized mind or body. Prospero claims that Sycorax worshipped a false god, Setebos. For early audiences this betrayal of God through the most intimate fealty to Satan would have spoken to ongoing anxieties about witches in their midst.[27]

Caliban's name is an anagram of "can[n]ibal," a neologism derived from the name of an Antilles Island people, the Kanaima or Caniba, to refer to beings who were said to consume human flesh. As early as 1503, Iberian legislation began to single out tribes who were deemed to be *canibales* as those against whom someone could legally wage war. To call someone a cannibal was to justify their dispossession for the sake of their (future) victims. Caliban's very name, then, appears to justify his fate: he had shown Prospero the necessities of survival on the island only to be imprisoned on a rock—a pattern mirroring numerous dispossessions in the history of European colonization and the sorts of narratives used to legitimize dispossession. Caliban's words barely register as human speech in the ears of the sailors. Miranda recounts how, before her patient teaching, he would "gabble like / A thing most brutish." The ancient Greeks had called those who could not speak Greek but, to Greek ears, "babbled" instead *barbaroi* (barbarians). Minds being invisible, the power of a certain kind of speech was a sign of being fully human.[28]

Perhaps worst of all, Caliban was said to carry the power of polluting the bodily community of humanity. Prospero fears that Caliban and Miranda might spawn a tribe of monsters or, as Caliban boasts, that he might have "peopled . . . / This isle with Calibans." If Miranda and Caliban were capable of having (fertile) children, then how different was Caliban and his "vile race" from humanity anyway? A few decades before Shakespeare wrote this play, Petrus Gonsalvus's family, whom we met in chapter 2, were having their portraits painted—and showing that a person whom some saw as being closer to animals than was typical *could* have children with someone who looked like everyone else. According to Caliban's reasoning and Prospero's fears, the purity of humanity would appear to be nothing more than a myth. The question of mixing Caliban's and Prospero's lineage echoes a perennial colonial fear about the effects of new climates on settlers. The "hag-seed" that gave rise to Caliban was said to be resistant to all climates, signaling the power of the monster over the human.[29] Perhaps the descendants of Caliban and Miranda would be much more monster than human, aided by the degenerative powers of the island's environment.

For wealthy investors able to afford seats rather than tickets in the standing-room—only pit in London's Globe Theatre, this fear might have been very close to home. Second sons of wealthy planters were often sent to the Caribbean to manage the family plantation. There they were liable to suffer unfamiliar climates and foods and catch diseases like yellow fever, all of which might alter their bodies in ways that would cause them to die a painful death or protect them from future severe illness while making them "different" from their family back home.[30]

The Tempest suggests that beings who seem innately different might still have children together. This made visible the danger distant peoples posed for European myths about the timeless fixity of nations. Shakespeare sketched Caliban as an everything monster, the frightful analog of the everything bagel and the flesh-and-blood equivalent of an astronomical black hole: a being of contested humanity who appears to have swallowed the era's deepest fears about minds, bodies, and nature's power to shape them. But Caliban doesn't simply mess with the human-animal boundary. He also embodies core assumptions about race, nation, empire, and monsters that were circulating in early seventeenth-century England.

Two years before *The Tempest* was first performed, in a sermon encouraging Englishmen to sail to Virginia "to bring the barbarous and sauage people to a ciuill and Christian kinde of government," the preacher Robert Gray said that "these Savages have no particular proprietie in any part or parcell of that Countrey, but only a general residencie there, as wild beasts have in the forrest . . . without any law or government."[31] The Puritan travel editor Samuel Purchas later wrote that the Algonquians had "little of humanitie but shape, ignorant of civilitie, of arts, or religion; more brutish then [*sic*] the beasts they hunt."[32] And after the massacre of the Jamestown colonists in 1622, Edward Waterhouse, a firsthand witness and Virginia official, declared that conquering the Algonquians would be easier than civilizing them and recommended, among other things, "pursuing and chasing them with our horses, and blood hounds to draw after them, and mastiues to teare them, which take this naked, tanned, deformed sauages, for no other then wild beasts."[33] In the eyes of such writers, the Algonquians were simultaneously human and not human: monstrified in ways that justified their dispossession and annihilation.

In 1968 *Planet of the Apes* captivated moviegoing audiences with another racial allegory. This time it was set not on a faraway island but in the future.[34] Apes rule the world. Humans are off the edge of the civilizational map: they have neither technology nor the power of speech and are, to the apes, animals to be hunted for sport or to be eradicated as vermin—definitely not fellow apes. With their scraps of clothing, thick hair, and hunter-gatherer lifestyles, the humans bear an uncanny resemblance to waxworks in today's museum dioramas of prehistoric hominid species. A chase scene through a museum containing just such human dioramas makes this parallel explicit. While the humans are white, young, and slim—characteristics that usually put someone on the top of the social hierarchy in a Hollywood movie—here they languish at the bottom of a hierarchy headed by (golden-haired) orangutans, with (black-haired) chimpanzees occupying the middle position and gorillas just after them. Viewers follow the trials of George Taylor, played by Charlton Heston, a member of a group of twentieth-century astronauts who crash-land on earth after traveling into the future and whom the apes subject to a barrage of dehumanizing assaults and experiments.

The film and its four sequels and four prequels visualize racial difference as species difference.[35] Released between 1968 and 1973, during the era of civil rights and anti–Vietnam War protests, the films' critiques of the United States have race at their core: the conquest of land inhabited by groups said to be uncivilizable and mentally incapable of learning; enslavement; proxy wars fought overseas; police brutality; cognitive dissonance when identity myths are challenged; animal rights; systemic discrimination and social stratification by color; and medical experiments conducted without the informed consent of the subjects. At the close of the first film, the toppled remnants of the Statue of Liberty signal humanity's failure to use technology responsibly. When the apes discover that the sole surviving astronaut can speak, he is deemed to be "a freak, a monster," not a sign that humans are capable of being civilized. In much the same way that racial mixing was seen as a threat to whiteness in a segregated America, the thought of a missing link between apes and humans, in the form of a speaking human, is a fundamental challenge to the apes' identity.[36]

Another genre through which people have been speaking back to the fiction of race is horror. The director Jordan Peele's acclaimed *Us* (2019) invokes zombies to critique contemporary socioeconomic inequalities. The story opens with a wealthy Black family taking a San Diego beach vacation, only to witness the emergence of murderous doppelganger zombies who want to replace them. They gradually learn that Black and white families have to kill or be killed by these beings, who are dressed identically in prison-uniformesque jumpsuits (red ones, all the better to hide the bloodstains). Moreover, the beings are "tethered" to them: they share souls with them. And they insist that "we're . . . Americans."[37]

Peele's narrative invites viewers to wonder whether for every wealthy American there is a double—identical in hopes, dreams, abilities, character—

who performs drudgery and endures endless suffering, just out of sight: the essence of how global economic inequality operates.[38] Sometimes people may see or fall through the portals that connect these worlds, each part of the same world and yet almost entirely apart from its doppelganger world, existing in parallel with one another, overlapping, yet just in a slightly different dimension and thus almost insensible and invisible. Society and infrastructure—from housing costs to immigration controls—keep these racialized socioeconomic worlds apart. Conventional, wealthy people who can afford to be apolitical but identify as "good people" prefer not to have discussions about the people trapped in the other world. Anyone on the inside who broaches the topic will certainly face social disapproval.

This dynamic brings to my mind the novel by China Miéville, *The City and the City*, styled after the Cold War era. A fictitious, vaguely Eastern European city has been divided into two. Barring accidents and exceptional circumstances, it's illegal to cross from one to the other, an action called "breaching." Yet some parts of the cities overlap, with shared streets and buildings—these areas are "crosshatched." Entering a crosshatched zone while obeying the law involves "unseeing" the other city.[39] The world seems to sustain just such inequalities by combining an "out of sight, out of mind" philosophy with social pressure against making waves—a dynamic that Miéville's invented twin city mirrors.

Returning to Peele's *Us:* viewers are left wondering whether, sometimes, someone might manage to crawl out of the darkness—the poorer side of a country or the world—and whether that means one has merely stepped into a double's life of relative ease. Such people may even forget their earlier suffering in subterranean shadows—but they must always look over their shoulder, for their doppelganger would happily take their place in this zero-sum world of exploitation. The readiness of audiences to sympathize with the dispossessed, the monstrified, in these narratives suggests that a more empathetic way of framing difference, of unlearning historical assumptions, is possible. When and why individuals choose one narrative over another tells us who they think is really, *really*, human.

MONSTROUS DINING

Cook them? What good are tube grubs if they don't wiggle on the way down?

"HOMEFRONT," *Star Trek: Deep Space Nine*, 1996

In the TV franchise *Star Trek: Deep Space Nine*, the species known as the Ferengi are a mirror for some of the less desirable traits of present-day humans. Their dietary norms are a symbolic litmus test of the potentially unbridgeable cultural gap between Ferengi and humans. Wholly dedicated to the pursuit of profit, they do not recognize women as full citizens—two characteristics that set the Ferengi apart from twenty-fourth-century humans, but which, conveniently, turn them into a mirror of contemporary humans. Traditional Ferengi men expect their women (to whom they refer as "females," which has more agricultural overtones than "women") to chew their food for them. Ferengi like gulping down their tube grubs alive, a point of gastronomy they share with the Klingons, who also appreciate live food. These preferences bring to mind Western anthropologists' stereotypical separation of cultures that cook or process their food from those that supposedly do not.[40]

Ideas about food shape categories for community and humanity. Religious laws often include dietary restrictions. In Jewish religious texts (some of which became part of the corpus that Christians call the Old Testament), eating category-breaking animals was prohibited. In the Book of Leviticus, problem animals and animal categories define each other. Whales live in water but are not fish; bats have wings but are not birds. Dietary restrictions prevented the faithful from polluting their bodies with the flesh of such monstrous animals. Pigs had the hooves of cows yet did not share their eating practices. (Some ancient dietary rules made good sense in hot climates before the era of refrigeration.)

For soldiers, clerics, administrators, and colonists from Spain arriving in the Caribbean and Central America from the late fifteenth century, it was unclear how different Indigenous minds and bodies might be from their own. The twelve apostles of Christian theology were thought to have preached in all parts of the world, but the inhabitants of lands in the west Atlantic appeared unaware of their teachings. Had these people forgotten the apostles' teachings, or were they incapable of understanding them? Were they descended from Noah or from some antediluvian ancestor who had escaped the Flood and whose progeny had been cut off from the apostles? If these people were unable to understand the true faith or to apply reason, were they capable of learning, slaves by nature, or even fully human?[41]

Existing traditions for thinking about humans—as descended from Adam, shaped by the environment, susceptible to monstrification in harsh climates, arranged on a continuum from barbarism to civility—left open the possibility of people from Europe changing in a new environment.[42] As we've seen, Europeans were anxious about how the body was porous and squishy rather than an unchanging fortress. Where ideas of race and nation were concerned, the very legal system of Spain and its colonies was predicated on identifying and treating "New" and "Old Christians," and *españoles* and *indios*, differently.[43] Many Spaniards feared that "going native" and eating Indian foods, especially ritual substances, would change them and even turn Christians into idolaters: chocolate and tobacco had properties with the power to reshape the body, mind, and faith. As historian Rebecca Earle put it, "'Race,' in other words, was in part a question of digestion."[44]

For a Spanish cleric in colonial Latin America, if their Catholic, Spanish-descended parishioners ate too much chocolate, they might transform into *indios*. If they had to make bread out of cassava root instead of wheat and replace wine with a beverage made from fermenting local grains, perhaps transubstantiation would be impossible. Then how could Communion even work? Moving the bodies and stomachs of believers across oceans might thus jeopardize their spiritual salvation. Some dimensions of the idea of race were physiological and environmental rather than political or sociocultural. Hierarchies were attached to the effects of ingested substances on different bodies, for example. Europeans understood diet as shaping the fluid, fungible categories of people's body, humoral balance or complexion, and behavior during their lives.[45] And God was what one ate.

Dietary choices were thought to reveal moral character. Ritual substances like tobacco and chocolate in the Americas pierced the veil between the spirit world and the world of the everyday. For commentators and observers in and from Europe, the possibility of Indigenous, idolatrous practices from the Americas becoming partly normalized and consequently turning their own people into idolaters seemed like a threat. This prompted angry pamphleteering and the anxious penning of many, many missionary instructions and scientific treatises. Reports of cannibalism in distant worlds and of cannibalism at home in cases of siege warfare raised questions about how the body would rise at the Last Judgment if it had become part of someone who had eaten it.

In classical Mesoamerica tobacco's uses ranged from the medicinal to the mind-altering. During the sixteenth and seventeenth centuries, Europeans became accustomed to tobacco, and yet the substance was associated with idolaters. To get around this problem, they told a new story. Some European medical practitioners framed tobacco-the-substance as blameless and put the burden of behavior on the users and their rituals.

People are easily disgusted or unsettled by ways of relating to animals and to foods that are different from their own. Such feelings may be about self-differentiation and pride, but they are often also about fear: of losing that identity, of the transformative effect that food is thought to have on the body. Racial and national slurs and stereotypes often essentialize groups by means of diet, from the medieval Iberian epithet of *marrano* (pig) to refer to Muslim neighbors who did not eat pork; to Western horror at the idea that people could eat dogs (poor Lassie!); to intra-European jibes like Kraut (to refer to Germans and their love of pickled cabbage or sauerkraut), Frog (an English jibe at French enthusiasm for frogs' legs, an iconic delicacy), and *les rosbifs* (French for the carnivorous British and their stereotypical penchant for "meat and two veg," stereotypically roast beef, potatoes, and a boiled-to-death root vegetable). Palates and stomachs become accustomed to what they usually digest; memories and associations are wrapped up in those tastes. When individuals attempt to divide people by drawing attention to, or creating a narrative about, different dietary practices, they are drawing on carousels full of baggage about food and community.[46]

Embedded in this instinct for gustatory name-calling is fear of the ramifications of the adage "You are what you eat." By extension if you eat things that are sufficiently unorthodox, you may cease to be yourself—or at least no longer be a law-abiding or "normal" member of your community. Such a proposition was even more alarming in the past than it is today. Ancient theories about food and the body predicted that eating the food of unfamiliar climates would either kill you or turn you into the local inhabitants.

BLENDED CATEGORIES IN THE SPANISH EMPIRE

The problem with souls is that they are invisible: whether or not someone has one, and just how sentient it is, is something that numerous writers and thinkers have tried to pin down by sketching out what they thought were the visible markers of fully human souls. In mid-sixteenth-century Spain, the Great Chain of Being, the continuum from the lowliest worm to humanity sketched out by ancient thinkers, was one of the tools brought to bear by the Spanish Crown on the proper way to administer the inhabitants of "the Indies," or the Spanish imperial holdings in what came to be known as the Americas and East Asia.[47] A legal debate between Bartolomé de las Casas and Ginès de Sepúlveda turned on whether or not Indigenous peoples of the Americas were capable of grasping Christianity entirely or whether they were merely "natural slaves" or individuals capable of only limited mental processes, or what Las Casas termed "nature's children": individuals who were not yet fully human.[48]

Colonial Spanish America quickly became a place of frequent marriage between *españoles* (Spaniards—a term used in the empire to denote white people), *indios*, *negros* enslaved and free, and their mixed-race descendants. New administrative and existential problems emerged: What was the legal status of these people? How could you identify who was what? The historical archive reveals people who identified—and who were identified by the state and by individuals who saw them—as a variety of different identities at different moments of their lives. Race, *casta*, and other frameworks were attempts to classify, identify, and control people: they imagined fixed categories and attempted to shoehorn into them a rainbow of individuals who varied by genealogy, faith, lifestyle, and physical features.

Some could, through their lifestyle, position themselves and their children differently in the eyes of both law and community.[49] Eat Spanish foods, dress in the Spanish manner, and refrain from Indigenous practices, and a *mestiza* became a Spaniard.[50] Not only was it possible to "fake it till you make it," but you could "fake it till you become it" through choices and bodily efforts.[51] Some individuals—notably bigamists, who show up in the archives when they were found out—even managed to live, simultaneously, what Ben Vinson III has called plural caste lives, inhabiting the habitus of, say, *lobo* (part Black, part Indigenous, and supposedly wolflike) in one family in one town and *castizo* (three quarters Spanish, one quarter Indigenous American) in another.[52]

No one could predict the appearance of children from their parents, nor could anyone predict how they would choose to live over the course of their lives. The case of Nicolasa Juana in the last chapter is just one example in the archives. Within certain constraints *casta* was malleable. In eighteenth-century Mexico attempts to classify category-breaking, mixed-race individuals took a visual turn in the form of *casta* painting (see plate 6).[53] These canvases offered idealized images of tidy, ordered social groups easily identified through a handful of attributes that distinguished one group from another: dress, skin color, foodstuffs. The paintings suggested a fixed relationship between the *casta* of a child and the *castas* of the parents. In practice, however, lived experience suggested the opposite: *castas* were themselves malleable, ambiguous, and volatile.

During Latin American independence movements of the nineteenth century, the ways in which mixed-race individuals and communities were imag-

FIGURE 19. *Casta* painting, detail, eighteenth century. The four vignettes identify mixed-heritage children by their *casta*, or what Spanish colonial elites defined as "mixed-race ancestry." Museo Nacional del Virreinato, Tepotzotlan, Mexico/Bridgeman Images, XOS5863246.

ined underwent rapid change. Indigenous rights and protections became tied to assumptions about what counted as "modern"; access to support for Indigenous peoples has often involved remaining "traditional" in stereotypical ways, as if Indigenous people were time-travelers or Rip Van Winkles who remain unchanged despite living in the world.[54]

RACE, NATION, AND CITIZENSHIP

Twenty-first-century citizenship is ostensibly about paperwork, a contract between an individual and a body politic, one that can be fulfilled in a variety of ways: birth within the nation's borders, legal residency for a period, legal immigration, or refugee resettlement. Yet the lived experience of a naturalized citizen depends on whether or not they can pass for the mythical citizen in appearance, customs, and speech. In the United States, for instance, white English-speaking immigrants who acquire a conventional American accent are seen as normal, legitimate, and belonging in ways that an immigrant from, say, Central or South America with, say, an Iberian or Indigenous name, darker skin, or an accent identified as "an accent" will not be. This will hold even though Iberian settlers in the present-day United States predate those from Britain, and Indigenous peoples beat everyone else to the so-called New World by some ten thousand years.

At the same time, characteristics that do not mark the body—notably religious ones—have historically also been turned into race-nation markers. Nazi Germany exemplified this way of thinking. In a multipronged assault on the body politic, the Nazis classed as noncitizens, imprisoned, and murdered people who were Jewish, as well as Roma, Sinti, homosexual, and disabled people and the most outspoken critics of the regime. Jewish people were forced to wear the yellow Star of David. The Nazis also forced those they deemed to be "lazy" or "asocial" to wear an inverted Black Triangle in concentration camps. The regime applied this designation to Roma or Sinti people and to anyone the Nazis considered to be, for example, an alcoholic, prostitute, homeless person, thief, murderer, lesbian, or someone said to have broken the law forbidding sex between Jews and "Aryans," who were defined as Germans deemed to have no more than one-eighth Jewish ancestry.[55]

To protect dearly held ideas of race, nation, and citizenship, people patrol the boundaries of these categories and identify the monsters: the hybrids, the in-betweeners. Legal structures make in-betweeners either invisible (no box to tick) or hypervisible ("illegal"). In the United States, for example, paths to citizenship are often closed to agricultural laborers and others doing work that is deemed both essential and backbreaking (e.g., care work) and requires no expensive education. People who do these jobs are cast as both being lazy and taking jobs away from legitimate residents, but in fact they perform jobs that few others will do. Large numbers of people from Latin America work in the United States in essential but low-wage jobs in what are often seasonal, dangerous, or precarious industries like agriculture. The forms of paperwork that exist do not permit enough of them to do this work legally. This lack, combined with policies that create economic hardship and political instability south of the US border, created the conditions that brought the category of undocumented immigrants from south of the border into being. There are no forms of document for which these workers qualify. Yet their labor is economically beneficial and even essential.

What stories do people tell about the same actions by different people? US law enforcement officers have, historically, identified far greater threats to their person and to public order when they faced down young, multiethnic or Black protesters demanding an end to racial, climate, or economic injustice than they have when they have seen white, visibly armed or pointed-hood–wearing protesters. Punishments meted out by judges do not necessarily reflect the amount of harm caused by an action. Who decides that an action is a crime and what sort of crime in the first place?

Just as societies decide what counts as a crime, they decide how to allocate wealth in relation to work and capital. The federal minimum wage in the United States has remained at $7.25 an hour since 2009. Yet CEO pay has ballooned: in

1965 the average CEO pay was 20 times that of the average worker; in 2023 CEO pay was 399 times more than the average employee salary. In the first six months of 2023, the world's five hundred richest people became, collectively, $852 billion richer—making some $14 million a day.[56] The absence of laws that prevent such egregious wealth for executives while workers struggle to pay bills silently declares that no harm has been done—on paper. What is needed is new terms and language on a regular basis, while guarding against the real risk of new systems perpetuating old racial, gender, and class inequalities.

Similar race-nation formulations leading to unequal rights are also visible in European nation-states and their past and present colonies. In the French Caribbean islands of Martinique and Guadeloupe, the highly carcinogenic pesticide chlordecone was used for two decades after it was banned in the United States, although it was not used in mainland France; its long-term persistence in the soil means that around 90 percent of the inhabitants of these islands have the chemical in their bodies. In the United Kingdom, the Windrush scandal broke out in 2018. Elderly people of British Caribbean descent who had moved to Britain in the postwar period, invited by the British government in a period of chronic labor shortages, were threatened with removal and even deported, for lacking paperwork that they had not been required to acquire or to keep. The characteristics that communities use to define who counts as full citizens and how laws apply to them do not remain fixed.[57]

WHO GETS TO BE A CITIZEN TODAY?

In 2019 the biographer Robert A. Caro described the experiences of one David Frost, an African American who attempted to register to vote in the South in the 1950s and who, on the way into the office, saw someone in a police car shoot out the taillights of his car.[58] In the eyes of this police officer, there was presumably nothing unlawful or undemocratic about his attempt to make it more difficult for a Black person to vote. If this is what he thought, he presumably didn't consider US citizenship for an African American to be legitimate in the first place. Did the officer think that Black people were fully human? If he did, then what did it mean to define a category of humans who did not get to vote in their own country?

Some of the ongoing consequences of the monstrification machine of Atlantic slavery are voter suppression and anti-Black violence, both of which are manifest in Frost's experience. According to the Equal Justice Initiative, some four thousand people were lynched between 1873 and 1950. It took 120 years after Reconstruction for lynching to be classed as a federal crime. Southern senators had repeatedly voted as a block to reject such legislation, which had been proposed two hundred times. By drawing out this process, these senators allowed lynchings of African Americans to continue without legal consequences in southern states. What motivated this justification of the freedom to lynch was not just the denial of the humanity of African Americans. The southern senators implicitly, perhaps consciously, denied the social contract on which the rule of federal law is built. When President Joe Biden signed the Emmett Till Antilynching Act in March 2022, lynching was finally defined by law as a federal hate crime.[59]

Fluid identities and debates about who belongs persist around the world. In 2018 Mamoudou Gassama, a Malian citizen in Paris, scaled four stories of a burning building to rescue a baby. Gassama subsequently received an audience with the French president Emmanuel Macron, who rewarded him with French citizenship and a job as a firefighter. The South African comedian Trevor Noah observed that, somewhere between climbing the building and rescuing the child, Gassama had apparently become French. In Europe and in former European colonies with white majorities, the successes of Black and Brown citizens are claimed for the nation, whereas the rhetoric around poverty and crime stresses their Blackness, Brownness, and foreignness.

The medieval idea of one's faith having a physiological effect is another root of today's assumptions about culture and ethnic heritage. It lies beneath current conversations about patriotism, work ethics, faith, and the capacity for "becoming" a full citizen, from the United States to Brazil to India to France. The consequence of monster-making is thus not just the invention of nations. It is also the invention of races: biopolitical and sociocultural category groups said to be innately and permanently different and unequal.

Collective identities are not concrete things that exist in nature, to be picked up and put in pockets. Rather, they are called into being and made up, giving no more obvious clues to their ingredients than a cake resembles a grocery bag of eggs, flour, butter, and sugar. The identities and the communities that invented them also change, and some of those changes go unnoticed or are even denied. While a group may insist on an unchanged essence with the distinctiveness of the yeasty brew of a San Francisco sourdough starter, that group, like the sourdough, may be itself but is also always changing.

Speaking of Trevor Noah, his autobiography, *Born a Crime*, encapsulates in its title an act of administrative erasure. Mixed-race relationships were illegal in South Africa under apartheid; Noah, the son of a black Xhosa mother and a white Swiss father, lived out his earliest years hidden at home. Religious and secular legal regimes thus create not just monsters of hypervisibility but monsters of invisibility: individuals and communities rendered nonpersons through their legislative absence and thus exploitable or excludable in ways that are not prohibited by law. The fear of being changed or overrun by people of another heritage leads people to demonize in-betweeners: to make and stake monsters into place to offer resistance at the boundary. By declaring the very existence of mixed-race individuals as illegal, lawmakers effectively define them as monsters—something beyond regular categories that needs to be suppressed. These sorts of laws are not simply chapters in the past but part of recent history, ongoing definitions, and living memory.

Monster-making laws show how racecraft and nation building operate in exactly the same way. Race fixes explicitly the idea of innate differences of the world's peoples in a hierarchy. Nation fixes distinctive traits in local communities and allows that rhetoric of hierarchy to congeal on its own through everyday actions, speech, and writing. While modern nation building might disavow racecraft, in practice it supports the legacies of racecraft, resists their dismantling, and bakes in new processes of race-ing while disavowing it.

The myth that there were ethnically homogenous people in Europe before oceanic migrations gave rise to the idea that cultural intermingling is something new. Misapprehensions about a homogenous "Anglo-Saxon" race said to have existed in the Middle Ages fuel conspiracy theories about "white genocide" or the gradual disappearance of white people due to lower birth rates and displacement. Examining how and why Christians in medieval Europe saw monsters in Jews, Muslims, and settler-invaders from other parts of Europe makes visible the deep roots of today's debates about nationhood and citizenship. It allows us to better understand problems that are inherent, but rarely discussed, as part of civic life: a lack of attention to how nation could be imagined more productively as community relationships and not necessarily blood relationships.

Native American nations define tribal belonging in ways that vary from nation to nation. These definitions are also different from US federal definitions or blood-quantum laws. Today's notion of citizenship as a legal category that individuals can come to fulfill in a variety of ways has something in common with flexible Indigenous conceptions of belonging. Yet this is not how citizenship is typically experienced by actual individuals. In contemporary nation-states, communities often behave as if nation is about genealogy— something that, in the popular imagination, is also visible (racialized)— whereas citizen laws, at the most general level, may define nation as a legal category and, by extension, the community as capable of change. These examples of how societies think about the body in relation to race and nation remind me of volcanic lava: flowing, changing, and yet slowly congealing and hardening; malleable but with limits, the course of its flow altered by strategically placed boulders and yet—when hot enough—flowing over villages with barely a change in speed or direction. Race and nation are not fixed, however much people may want them to be.

There was and is still a lot at stake when attending to the monsters that communities make up and wall off. Lived experience does not always match documentation. Embodiment shapes the experience of people in the world, experiences that, through their inconsistencies, make earlier values and modes of monster-making visible. Monsters reveal how societies frequently apply the concepts of race, nation, and citizen inconsistently. In such regimes history textbooks and curricula in schools become separation narratives like those written by the medieval Norman Welsh writer Gerald of Wales. By dehumanizing parts of a community, these and other narratives can even be twisted into justifications for genocide.

For whom do you feel empathy? How much? Empathy is a personal geography, a map of who matters to you and thus who is most human. Is it possible to make a whole, multicultural body politic with empathy for one another, without tension? One that celebrates rampant hybridity and the transcending of categories? Perhaps this is a process and a regular exercise to be built into civic and institutional and personal life rather than a judgment that happens once and for all time. Perhaps, if people keep at it, they might begin to see that there is beauty in monstrosity.

FIVE

Gender, Sex, and Monstrous Births

IN THE DECADES AROUND 1700, James Paris du Plessis, manservant to the English diarist Samuel Pepys, compiled a monster scrapbook. Titled "A Short History of Human Prodigious and Monstrous Births," this miscellany of handwritten notes, colored drawings, and the occasional printed cutting is now housed in the Department of Manuscripts at the British Library in London. Folded into the volume are so-called monsters: a two-headed child; a "Tartar" with a horse's head; "a man with a monstrous goiter . . . being a terrour to all big bellyed women that saw him"; and a "hermaphrodite." Performing around London were a "spotted negro prince"; a "black wild man" from the East Indies, covered in hair; and a "wild and hairy Irishman."[1]

These unsettling glimpses into the lives of individuals and Du Plessis's interpretations (or perhaps, at times, fabrications) point to a question that scholars and theologians, jurists and physicians, and the general public in Europe had asked since antiquity: What are the parameters of "normal" for a human body? Du Plessis's selections shed light on how people defined where normal ended and abnormal—prodigious or monstrous—began. As we've seen, in play were thorny issues of how distinct humans might be from animals. Distant places might engender monsters—but, if so, where did "foreign" end and "monstrous" begin? In Ireland? As people in Europe understood it, there was a point between conception and birth when monstrosity might be made, even close to home. How much was this caused by the external world and how much by the monster's own parents? A so-called monstrous birth raised questions of divine punishment and warnings, and the lives of atypically embodied people who survived infancy could be fraught with social and logistical challenges. While the language of today's questions

FIGURE 20. James Paris du Plessis, *A Wild and Hairy Irishman*, in "Prodigious and Monstrous Births," a manuscript miscellany, circa 1730–33. Each example in this manuscript was an image followed by a description over one or more pages. This Irishman was apparently hairy all over except for his legs; contemporary descriptions of hairy people often mentioned where these people weren't hairy or the texture of hair on different body parts. These individuals were often seen naked or nearly so. Sloane MS 5246, British Library, London, UK. From the British Library Archive/Bridgeman Images, fol. 53r.

about the norms and limits of humanity often looks different, tactics of labeling and exclusion remain.

Du Plessis's sustained interest in monsters may have been prompted by an alarming incident that took place in 1680 in Pithiviers, France, when he was around fifteen years old, and with which the miscellany opens. As he recalled it, a heavily pregnant woman had come to live in his maternal home to be close to a minister and to medical assistance. The woman had been an admirer of a two-headed monster in an almanac (a calendar and weather manual) at the time of her conception. Her husband, "taking notice of it, took the Almanach from her, and burnt it, but she procured herself another, and so a third, which he also took from her; this lasted till her longing was over and the mischief was done." The mischief here was understood to be the images. It was commonly believed that looking at alarming pictures while conceiving or being pregnant could lead to a "monstrous birth" (as it was called then).[2] Her husband feared the worst, and it came to pass. The woman gave birth to a stillborn, two-headed boy. "This accident was kept very secret, and the child being a monster and not having been cristned [christened]." The infant was buried with equal secrecy, in Du Plessis's own bit of the garden, where, as he put it, he "accidentally" dug it up:

> All this was kept very secret from me, though I was very inquisitive and whatchfull but having received a great slap on the face I was foursed to leave off my curiosity. A few dayes after being busy a digging in my little garden, I discovered a little box in which I found this little mounster, which I buried again and by it I discovered part of the misery which I also keept a secret. A little while after I found Dr Martels closet open, and I found in it the foresaid Almanack with the Relation as I give it hear.[3]

How much of this really happened? It's hard to say whether the fifteen-year-old boy had been a reliable witness and whether the adult Du Plessis was remembering a full and accurate account of events. The young Du Plessis appears to protest too much: Is he making excuses for his nosiness or illuminating his investigative energy? Many years later Du Plessis would try to sell his monster compendium to the gentleman physician, collector, and naturalist Sir Hans Sloane, one of the founders of the British Museum and president of the Royal Society, the foremost scientific organization in England. Du Plessis may well have had a nose for the financial possibilities of monster anecdotes and testimony, living as he did in an era when monsterly reading matter, from illustrated maps to broadsheets describing unusual births, sold well.

Whatever it was that Du Plessis saw and whatever his motivations were for writing, the details of this anecdote reveal something about the anxieties surrounding gender, reproduction, and monsters. Regardless of the story's accuracy, the account illuminates a widespread interpretation of unusual births: a woman's insatiable attraction for a deviant creature—even in the form of an image—could generate a child who was in some fundamental way not her husband's. Her repeated exposure to—or what Du Plessis considers her consumption of—monstrous information and imagery seemed to have consequences for her offspring. People like this pregnant gentlewoman raised questions about the category of the human for their communities and for those who read or heard about their atypical embodiment. If a priest could and should baptize or christen a "mounster," that implied that they were capable of and deserving of receiving the sacraments, of participating in religious life and community, and of salvation.

Individual monstrous births posed social, political, legal, theological, and medical challenges in the millennia before genetic testing—so too did gender expectations and definitions of biological sex, themes that people often discussed alongside monstrosity. Yet ancient assumptions and values, rather than being cast out in the light of new technologies, still lurk in a reservoir of ideas for thinking about gender, embodiment, and disability today. Individuals who transgressed physical or behavioral expectations of gender and sex were often described as monsters or as in-between individuals who failed to meet the criteria to count as what society deemed desirable or normal. People whose relatives, neighbors, or religious or legal institutions labeled them this way had their power, liberty, legal protections, and even safety constrained. Monsters were the results of the mysterious processes of generation and reproduction. Who knew what they might reveal about the limits of what it meant to be human?

NATURE'S ERRORS AND THE MATERNAL IMAGINATION

As we saw in chapter 1, for ancient Greek and Roman naturalists and philosophers, there were three broad types of explanations for atypically embodied people. One was that they were divine portents of doom: warnings of imminent punishment or punishments in themselves. Another was that they were simply one-off accidents or even jokes played by nature. The third was that extreme climates engendered monsters in distant regions. For the naturalist and philosopher Aristotle, many monsters were the occasional consequence of nature attempting to work the brute and resisting stuff of matter, efforts not always entirely successful. Individuals with too many fingers might fall into this category, for example. While Aristotle's theories were partly forgotten in Europe after the fall of the Roman Empire, his treatise *Generation of Animals* from the mid-fourth century BCE was reintroduced into Europe in the thirteenth century through Latin translations from Arabic manuscripts. Detailing not just animal reproduction but also human births and bodies, this treatise influenced subsequent thinking about law, medicine, sex, and gender.[4]

No one in this period had any idea what actually went on inside human reproductive organs. Reproduction was shrouded in mystery: its processes happened out of sight, and the results could be explained only through speculation after the fact. Since monsters did not appear with tags explaining their causes, one had to observe them in the hope that study would reveal what kind of a monster they were. Was a two-headed baby, for example, a sign that someone had angered the gods, that the mother had the misfortune to see a picture in a book while pregnant, or that she had been daydreaming about monsters while having sex? Each interpretation offered a different explanation of strange outcomes to the process of reproduction.[5]

Unusual outcomes of the mysterious processes of generation and reproduction were also considered monstrous or uncanny among the Nahua of classical Mexico: pregnant women and children were believed to be malleable, their rapidly changing bodies at risk of being transformed by celestial bodies in fundamental, unwelcome ways. Traditional warnings included one about eclipses, during which pregnant women were urged to stay indoors or risk their child being transformed into a mouse. Midwives and physicians advised pregnant women to beware of what they looked at, for an unborn child could change its form to mirror objects of the mother's gaze. Moreover, a mother's actions or experiences could also shape the physical appearance of her child.[6] Before the nineteenth century, a widespread belief in Europe was that a mother's thoughts, deeds, and character—and especially the maternal imagination—shaped children in the womb, a theory that mirrored Nahua understanding. Hence Du Plessis's remark that a man with a goiter was a terror to "all big bellied"—pregnant—women. If a pregnant woman saw such a person and created this shape in her mind, it might shape the child in her body.

Still worse was the idea that simply thinking about a particular person or animal had the potential to influence the unborn child's development. According to Du Plessis, the imagination of his own mother-in-law had managed to achieve this effect. The woman had been captivated by the sight of a "very large lobster" at London's Leadenhall Market but had failed to acquire it on being "asked one exorbitant price." She returned home and took an ill turn. On confessing her longing to her husband, he returned to the market, acquired said lobster, and surprised her with it. "At the sight of which she fainted, and when recovered she could not endure the sight of it"; consequently, she gave birth to a lobster-shaped infant.[7]

Du Plessis's extended family seems to have encountered or lived among monsters at almost every turn. Some were not just strange but challenged the idea that humans were entirely separate from animals. Of the "child in the form of a lobster," Du Plessis wrote that he had drawn the accompanying illustration from the mother's description.[8] The watercolor today, however, looks all lobster and no child. But it does give a sense of how pervasive fears about monstrosity were in seventeenth-century England and how close to home the objects of those fears could be.

Questions of gender, reproduction, and monsters created anxieties about the power of women. Since paternity could not be proved before genetic testing, constraining a woman's behavior and social sphere was the only strategy available to protect family lineage—excepting very occasional inherited features like the so-called Habsburg jaw, characteristic of the inbred imperial Habsburg dynasty in western and central Europe, which at least narrowed down paternity to blood relations. On a married woman's children, the sacrament of marriage conferred her husband as their father, even though no one could really know who their father was. In this way paternity was necessarily socially constructed rather than known as a biological fact.[9]

Monstrous births filled sixteenth- and seventeenth-century European news pamphlets, medical texts, and encyclopedias dedicated to monsters.[10] Medical-advice manuals provided glimpses of monster-avoidance techniques. Pregnant women were encouraged to avoid frights and to refrain from looking at unsavory animals like apes, lest they give birth to a misformed child. These stories illuminate anxieties about unknowable things: female imaginative desire, paternity, and the fragility of the category of the human. If all it took was a cat picture hung in front of the marital bed or a "boo!" moment at a fairground to induce a woman to give birth to an animal-shaped child, then the category of the human was about as stable as a scoop of Jell-O.

Children who didn't look like their father might even be a sign of adultery, be it through physical acts or imagined ones.

In sixteenth- and seventeenth-century Europe, monstrous births were almost a meme. As moveable-type printed books (introduced in China and Korea centuries earlier) became increasingly available and affordable, and with the establishment of printing houses everywhere from Lisbon to Prague, monstrous births spawned new genres of books and images. Eye-catching single-sheet broadsheets or text-rich posters hung prominently at printer's stalls. Even those who could not afford to buy a book on monsters might well have seen printed illustrations—early modern clickbait—at a street market or broadsheets on a tavern wall.

Early modern writings about monsters contained numerous examples of individuals with a difference of sexual development, sometimes called "intersex." Some appeared in scientific and religious treatises about monsters.[11] Others featured in monster miscellanies that omnivorous readers assembled. The title of Du Plessis's monster miscellany includes "hermaphrodites." An announcement about an intersex person from Angola appears in a monster miscellany belonging to the Irish physician, naturalist, collector, and Royal Society president Sir Hans Sloane (1660–1753). The advertisement reveals that there were popular and educated audiences for monsters. The first part is in English and ends thus: "The private parts are equally masculine and faeminine [sic], and so perfect in each sex, that 'tis hard for the curious examiner to distinguish which has the superiority." The text then degenerates—or evolves?—into Latin and describes the elements of these "private parts" in explicit detail. Printing the anatomical section only in Latin restricted this graphic information to highly educated individuals, most of them men. The advertisement then returns to English to end by framing this person as a monstrous commodity: "This creature to be seen at the golden-cross, near Charing-Cross, price 2s. 6d."[12]

How different did individuals have to be from a rubric before someone defined them as a monster? And how could anyone know whether the monster was an accident or a warning? The sixteenth-century German Protestant scholar Conrad Peucer suggested that, to tell a prodigy (a divine sign) from a misbirth or natural accident, a person should pay attention to their emotions at the moment of seeing it. As Peucer put it, monsters that show something "have always terrified human minds, overcome by presages of sad and calamitous events, and affected them with wonder and fear."[13] In other words, how someone felt about a monster would supposedly reveal something fundamental about the monster. This way of thinking opened numerous cans of worms, causing great harm to those whom other people found alarming. (There are echoes of this reasoning in the present, when white people shoot—and often kill—unarmed Black people and claim that they were defending themselves. The language of the perpetrators' defense narratives dehumanizes their victims, claiming they were enormously tall, strong, and fearsome—even if they were children. The unease the shooters may have felt became a proof of something about the other person.)

In 1650, in a mean-spirited treatise titled *Anthropometamorphosis*, the English physician and natural philosopher John Bulwer even proposed the maternal imagination as a reason for the blackness of a person's skin: since many nations considered the devil to be white, people probably wished to be darker to assert their alterity from the diabolical, and they used cosmetics to bring this about. Then the combination of the effect of maternal imagination on the process of generation and the cosmetic alteration of the skin led to an inherited trait: "For thus perhaps this which at the beginning of this complexion, was an artificial device, and thence induced by imagination; having once impregnated the seed, found afterwards concurrent productions, which were continued by climes, whose constitution advantaged the artificial into a natural impression."[14] Bulwer's diatribe against painting skin black was part of a broader critique of vanity, fashion, and cosmetics.

The question of where Blackness came from continued to occupy scientists and philosophers in eighteenth-century Europe. In 1741 the Academie des Sciences in Bordeaux, France, even ran an essay competition around the following question: "What is the physical cause of the Negro's color, the quality of [the Negro's] hair, and the degeneration of both [Negro hair and skin]?" The larger questions behind the question and the longer exposition of what the jury was looking for were, Who is Black? And why? The third question was more far-reaching: What did being Black signify? Among the entries was the conjecture that by thinking of a Black man while pregnant, a white woman could produce a Black baby.[15]

The language with which people talk about category-breaking so-called pathologies changed in the nineteenth and twentieth centuries. Yet medicalized monster thinking continued, circulated, and multiplied. In Japan monster traditions date back many millennia. In the nineteenth century, these traditions absorbed, transformed, and responded to the influx of European medical writing by generating new categories of monsters and explanations of why they mattered. Attempts to avoid monstrous births then became

FIGURE 21. John Bulwer, *Anthropometamorphosis*, title page from the 1653 edition. Bulwer's sulfurous treatise railed against cosmetics and fashions, which, in his eyes, deformed bodies that had been made in God's image. In this image Nature, enthroned under the tent and flanked by Adam and Eve, judges the uses and abuses of the body perpetrated by the people in the foreground. B5461, Folger Shakespeare Library, Washington, DC.

entangled with ideas about the health of the nation and thus became the subject of public health regulations. In Imperial Japan theories of medicine and bodily improvement were informed by ideas about hygiene, reproduction, and the deeply unethical and now discredited field of eugenics: the theory that one could and should improve the human species by controlling breeding in an attempt to select for characteristics deemed to be most desirable, while deselecting for others.[16]

Nazi Germany's infamous genocidal activities extended beyond people who were Jewish to encompass the Nazis' political opponents and Roma and Sinti traveler communities. They also encompassed gender-fluid individuals and individuals whom they identified as disabled. The world's first transgender clinic, the Institute for Sexual Research, founded in Berlin in 1921, was an early casualty of the Nazi regime. In May 1933 Nazi troops attacked the building, made off with some twenty thousand books, and burned them in the street. The clinic's founder, Magnus Hirschfeld, had pioneered treatments and fostered a community of care. Queer and Jewish, Hirschfeld's likeness would appear on Nazi propaganda as an emblem of the antithesis of Nazi ideals.[17]

WOMEN AS MONSTERS

What were women capable of? As we've seen, people in premodern Europe believed that women could create monstrous births simply by thinking. Certain psychological maladies, like "hysteria," were also associated with women's bodies. This particular ailment was mentioned in ancient Egyptian medical treatises and imagined as a mental illness starting in a person's womb and characterized by excessive emotion and lack of discipline.[18] Such language is still pervasive. Women are stereotyped as being irrational and emotional, a framing that appears to exclude anger as an emotion and to preclude bar brawls from counting as evidence.

In his *Generation of Animals*, Aristotle also pronounced that any offspring that did not resemble its parents—and especially its father—was an error of sorts: a monster. Meanwhile, while women were necessary for life to continue, he ceded, they too fell into the category of monster, in essence, for having failed to have been born as men: the woman's seed had defeated that of the man and birthed another woman. Women, to Aristotle, were both monstrous (after a fashion) and potential monster incubators.

From religious authorities, civic laws, and customs, late medieval Europe inherited a default setting of women being led rather than leading. Where women's behavior was concerned, women who entered spaces not meant for them were monstrous, even pathologically diseased individuals who disrupted society. While numerous women flouted these conventions, and while there were spaces in which women had authority over their own lives, instances in which women held high office were rare enough that a woman performing the duties of a ruler (rather than merely being a consort or wife of a monarch) was a cause for concern. Inheritance laws typically ruled that a title or a crown passed to the eldest son. In the absence of a son, it would pass to the oldest daughter, who, once married, might well find that her husband muscled in on her authority. Moreover, a female heir—whom men in Europe would have considered a weak monarch—was a temptation to lobby for the monarch-in-waiting's hand in marriage, to make political demands, or even to invade the kingdom when she ascended the throne.

In mid-sixteenth-century France and England, the era of religious Reformation saw the rise of two ruling queens at confessional odds with the majority of their subjects. The Florentine Catherine de Medici, widow of Francis I of France and an ardent Catholic, ruled as regent when her infant sons became king of France in succession. France was in the grip of a religious civil war between Protestant followers of John Calvin and those who had remained loyal to the Catholic Church. In England the Catholic Mary Tudor, daughter of Henry VIII, ascended to the throne as Mary I in 1553. Yet many of her subjects had become Anglican, a new denomination that Henry VIII had established, with himself as its head, when the pope had refused his request for an annulment of his marriage to Catherine of Aragon.

Both Catherine de Medici and Mary I became subjects of polemical pamphlets, in which their failings were literally ascribed to their monstrosity.[19] The Scottish reformer John Knox, exiled from London for his inflammatory preaching, published angry screeds against Mary I. The most famous of these was *The First Blast of the Trumpet against the Monstrous Regiment of Women*, published anonymously in Edinburgh, Scotland, in 1558. What tipped Knox over the edge at this point was an unholy trinity of Marys: three Catholic queens jostling on the island of Britain. Mary Stuart had become queen at one week of age, on the death of her father, James V, king of Scotland (although Mary did not actually govern while still in diapers) in 1542. In 1554 Mary's mother, the French Catholic aristocrat Mary of Guise, had decamped from France to Scotland to rule as her daughter's

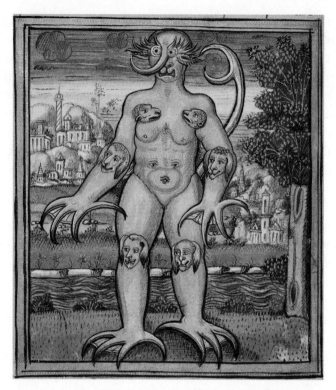

FIGURE 22. Pierre Boaistuau (1517–1566), the "monster of Kraków," in *Histoires prodigieuses*, a compendium of remarkable births and events, 1559. This image features a child allegedly born with barking dogs for kneecaps, who lived for just four hours. This page is from the illustrated manuscript exemplar that Boaistuau presented to Elizabeth I of England. MS 136, Public Domain Mark, Wellcome Collection, London, [fol. 29v].

regent, following palace intrigue. And in 1558 Mary Tudor had become Mary I of England. In Knox's view "the empire or rule of a wicked woman" was "abominable"; "a woman promoted to sit in the seat of God (that is, to teach, to judge, or to reign above man) is a monster in nature . . . a thing most repugnant to his [God's] will and ordinance. . . . He judges it a monster in nature that a woman shall exercise weapons [and] must judge it to be a monster of monsters that a woman shall be exalted above a whole realm and nature."[20]

Knox attempted to conjure for the viewer an actual physical monster in the place of a woman queen: "For who would not judge that body to be a monster, where there was no head eminent above the rest, but that the eyes were in the hands, the tongue and the mouth beneath the belly, and the ears in the feet? Men, I say, should not only pronounce this body to be a monster, but assuredly they might conclude that such a body could not long endure." Here Knox leveraged the everyday experiences that people would have had with infants with severe birth defects—disabilities severe enough that the child would not survive long after birth—or seen in pamphlets and broadsheets. Knox's description, sprinkled with epithets like "monstriferous horror," may have prompted readers to remember pamphlets they had seen of sensorially challenging or augmented monsters.[21] One such example was the monster of Kraków, Poland, who featured in widely circulated printed accounts and whose unusual features included an extra pair of eyes above his navel. He appeared in a lavish manuscript monster miscellany that the Huguenot (French Protestant) scholar Pierre Boaistuau dedicated to Queen Elizabeth I of England in 1559 and first published in 1560.[22]

Knox's reference to a headless body invokes the ancient idea of a monstrous race of *blemmys*, or individuals with no heads, who had their faces in their chests. In other words, having a woman on the throne was equivalent to the state lacking a head and mirrored the physical headlessness of those who were, in European eyes, an abominably shaped people who lived in distant, harsh climes. The monstrousness of the monarch was a problem for the entire kingdom: "And no less monstrous is the body of that commonwealth where a woman bears empire; for either it does lack a lawful head (as in very deed it does) or else there is an idol exalted in the place of the true head." The reader could read the present state of England in one of two ways: either the kingdom had no head, making it a monstrous, headless commonwealth, or it was headed by an idol—a fake imitation of God. Either way the situation could not be left unchallenged:

> The duty . . . of the people . . . [is] to remove from honour and authority that monster in nature. . . . [Through their inaction] the nobility both of England and Scotland [are] inferior to brute beasts, for that they do to women, which no male amongst the common sort of beasts can be proved to do to their females: that is, they reverence them, and quake at their presence, they obey their commandments, and that against God. . . . I judge them not only subjects to women, but slaves of Satan, and servants of iniquity.

Knox urged people to stop being "subjects to women." But Mary I died before the pamphlet was published, and the Protestant Elizabeth I succeeded her. Knox's attempt to leverage misogyny for his religious agenda backfired.[23]

Such paper trolling dehumanized the queens and undid the traditional emotional bond between monarchs and their subjects. Instead of being a divinely ordained monarch, to be obeyed without question, second only to God, the queen had become someone it was legitimate—even necessary—to plot against. Actions like bearing arms against her, or even contemplating regicide, could be viewed as honorable rather than treasonous. The effectiveness of polemical pamphlets lay in their power to convince readers that these queens were not people but rather category problems: women in places they should not be, who were monstrous and who sowed moral disorder at the very heart of the state. The intersection of gender and an ongoing religious crisis created conditions in which these pamphlets were published and translated widely and consumed voraciously.

Such virulent responses to the place of women and to the range of activities and sociopolitical commitments permissible for women persisted. In the nineteenth and twentieth centuries, women in Europe and the United States were often confined, against their will, to hospitals, sanatoriums, and psychiatric institutions for behaving in ways that would have been acceptable for men but were deemed significant breaches of norms for women. Reasons individuals were incarcerated included reading books, wearing trousers, and riding bicycles. Despite the expansion of women's opportunities around the world through voting and abortion rights in the twentieth century, the early twenty-first century has seen their erosion in multiple countries. Humanity has yet to fully throw off the prejudices of the likes of Aristotle, for whom men were the default, the only ones fully human.

GENDER FLUIDITY

People today sometimes imagine that fluid gender identities are twentieth-century developments. Yet there were many individuals across time and place whose identities, appearance, and lifestyles transcended the binary male/female expectations of their societies.[24] A range of sexualities was the norm across the ancient world. And, for many cultures, the heteronormative gender binary was not the default mode for bodies, feelings, or behaviors related to what we now refer to as sex or sexuality. There were, in other words, LGBTQIA+ individuals everywhere from the ancient Mediterranean to preconquest Mesoamerica.

The terminology for talking about sex, gender, and sexuality today is constantly changing and varies across the globe and among individual members of LGBTQIA+ communities and activists. "Gender fluidity" and "transgender," for example, are terms that implicitly presume the existence of fixed and discrete binary categories for sexes and genders, which some individuals fail to meet.[25] By contrast, in a framework of language built around the idea of a continuum of human diversity, there would be nothing to transgress, since one way of being would lead into another. It is possible to glimpse such frameworks in certain past moments and places. They offer ways to imagine more inclusive futures.

How individuals experience the world today is deeply shaped by the idea of a male/female binary constituting the only regular options and by how societies view bodies and behavior in relation to these categories. The difference between the terminology of the present and that of the past poses an added difficulty when talking about historical settings. Since the central thread of this chapter is the concept of monstrosity (with or without the exact word) as people used it to describe human bodies and behavior, understanding each context involves understanding its own terms. Relating these terms to today's language can help to explicate the distinctiveness of past contexts while showing continuities, resonances, and influences that reach into the present.

In highland Mexico, before the arrival of Spanish conquistadors, people expressed a wide range of what are now referred to as gender identities. In a number of Indigenous societies, people understood that gender was sometimes ambiguous. More broadly, they recognized that the body was mutable. The body changed in response to hallucinogenic substances, rituals, and unusual natural phenomena like eclipses. Gender ambiguity played a part in certain rituals. Both gender and age could function as social categories that shaped an individual's responsibilities and position in society, from their participation in rituals to their clothing and accessories. By regulating how people could behave, what they could wear, and how they were permitted to speak, some societies made visible, transparent, stable, and unambiguous things that were in practice changeable or that did not fit easily into permitted categories like binary gender roles. If, as was the case in some parts of ancient Mesoamerica, gender was neither straightforwardly visible nor fixed in relation to individual bodies or types of physical traits—if what passed for appropriate male and female gender roles, appearance, and behavior varied—

one way of assigning social roles and power was to invent hierarchically arranged identities according to visible characteristics, regardless of how they might map onto the desires or identities of individuals.[26]

Clerics and administrators of the past two millennia often attempted to impose their particular visions of Christian morality wherever they went. By demonizing practices that were not their own, they shored up their own moral authority and justified their political and economic power. In Europe individuals who transgressed physical and behavioral expectations of gender and sex were often described as monsters, their behavior pathologized—even criminalized—as homosexuality (often termed sodomy or bestiality) or other supposed errors of thought, action, or anatomy. The assumptions behind these actions were ancient. During the centuries of European imperial hegemony, enslavement, and colonization, European clerics, traders, settlers, and administrators transported these ideas around the world, where they cross-fertilized local ways of thinking about gender, sex, and reproduction. The results of these encounters were unpredictable and far from inevitable, but their consequences persist.

NONBINARY THINKING AND CHRISTIANITY IN THE LATE ROMAN EMPIRE AND THE MIDDLE AGES

Between late antiquity and the end of the Middle Ages (ca. 200–1400 CE), Christian scholars, theologians, jurists, and medical practitioners frequently drew on the Bible to think and write about nonbinary individuals. At stake was figuring out the limits of who counted as human—and, by extension, who got to go to heaven (sins permitting). The Book of Genesis contains a potential nonbinary individual at the start of human history: Adam. God was said to have created Adam and then created Eve. According to some early versions of Genesis, God split Adam in half, using one of his sides to make Eve. In a translated version that became widespread, Eve was created from Adam's rib (and was therefore, by implication, inferior to Adam). Either way, for some early Christian thinkers, Adam may have begun as a unified whole transcending the male/female division. Medieval science and gender historian Leah DeVun and other scholars of early Christianity call this idea "primal androgyny."[27]

Adam's potential androgyny raised troubling questions for adherents of gender binaries in the here and now: Was the original "natural" state of humans androgyny (the absence of sex), or did human history begin at some point after that, once Eve was created and once Adam and Eve had distinct bodies and sexual preferences? What was the perfect physical form and sexual behavior of the human, whom God was said to have created, in his own image, when he made Adam? Was sexuality inherent in the perfect human or something that manifested after the Fall from Paradise? Was Eve an equal part of that perfection, or not? Much hinged on a pronoun: whether or not God had made a single individual (him) containing male and female features or two individuals (them). Medieval scholars spilled lakes of ink attempting to write their way to an answer while probing the Bible for clues.

Since the Bible was an authority in the Christianizing Roman Empire and, after its dissolution, in subsequent Christian kingdoms, the reflections of these commentators had ramifications for understanding and policing the here and now. The church had a hand in redefining social customs and writing laws about sexual practices, gender roles, marriage, and the category of the human in relation to animals and to monsters (whatever they were). Uncertainties raised by the idea of primal androgyny also had a knock-on effect on power structures beyond the home. Framing the relationship between Adam and Eve as one of legitimate inequality, in which Eve showed obedience to Adam, justified the institution of marriage. By extension this justified the patriarchy and the authority of rulers. Thus any reframing of Adam and Eve had the potential to delegitimize religious and secular authorities.

In the lands of the Roman Empire, theologians and physicians developed several contrasting explanations of nonbinarism out of attempts to understand human creation. One possibility was that the original human or humans combined male and female attributes until these humans were divided in two. This worked out in Greek, Jewish, and Christian scholarly traditions in slightly different ways. In Greek philosophy these originary beings were incorporeal; in a Jewish midrashic tradition (a tradition of interpreting religious texts), Adam had a single, two-faced body with two sets of genitals; in the Christian tradition, Adam was fully male and female until Eve was removed from him.

A very different, second possibility was that the original human predated gender and was (confusingly) *both and neither* male and female. According to the Greek-speaking Jewish philosopher Philo, the original spiritual human was a masculine-leaning androgyne, whom God would later parse out into corporeal male and female individuals. In a third strand of thinking (the Gnostic tradition, which promised access to secrets about the divine), God embodied both male and female.

In a fourth twist, the original humans lacked both sex and physical bodies. Proponents of this view included the fifth-century theologian the bishop Gregory of Nyssa. For Gregory Adam and Eve began as perfect, angelic humans of the same, ungendered form. It was only their fall into sin (after snacking on the apple) that activated latent gender differences and sexuality. More important, these imperfections would be left behind upon resurrection at the Last Judgment, at the end of time. This implied that all sexed individuals were flawed.[28]

In late antiquity (fourth and fifth centuries), in the lands of the crumbling Roman Empire, new interpretations that legitimated the gender binary began to circulate in learned circles. Saint Augustine of Hippo (354–430) posited that humans had been embodied and sexual even during their innocence in Paradise. Saint Augustine went so far as to describe as "monstrous" the idea of what we now call intersex, or the condition of a single individual possessing a combination of male and female organs. Saint Augustine dismissed both versions of the primal androgyne, the angelic incorporeal version and the embodied version. During the consolidation of Christianity as an official state religion in the Roman Empire in the fifth century, Saint Augustine's interpretation was influential. It helped to justify the institution of marriage and the subordination of women to men at the cost of alternative social relations that biblical authorities and early Christians had suggested. Christians, newly empowered and emboldened, used their authority to mandate only one kind of sexual relationship, beginning two millennia of disapproval and downright oppression.

This convention brought the gender-experimental possibilities that earlier writers had drawn out of the Bible into line with how the majority of men organized their domestic and legal lives. The notion of monogamous marriage was an idea that was thought up, established as law, and then policed. There was nothing inevitable about it, either in ancient texts; in the Bible (insofar as its early readers could tell, for multiple readings were possible); or in the ways in which people had lived for as long as anyone remembered. Yet by writing laws in which the only permitted sexual activity happened within monogamous, heterosexual marriage, legislators had effectively ruled that all other practices were abnormal. Additional laws decreeing that same-sex relationships were a "sin against nature" would follow. These ruled that individuals who practiced them were monstrous—something other than human.

Extensive surviving writings, instructions, and warnings from the European Middle Ages about how people should and should not behave suggest that binary thinking and marriage were not no-brainers to which everyone subscribed. Medieval scholarly texts reveal that the idea of the primal androgyne continued to be debated for centuries. Not everyone agreed on whether two-sexed individuals—people we now refer to as intersex or as having a difference of sexual development (DSD) and often termed "hermaphrodites" in the past—were monstrous or not. At the same time, few clues survive to shed light on how people who did not write—or whose writings were not preserved—thought and acted. Individuals oppressed or marginalized by secular or religious authorities were rarely allowed or even able to record their own interpretations of their humanity, experiences of the world, or thoughts on practices of monstrification. A person who was enslaved, poor, female, or nonconforming in some way or who was an Indigenous person who had been displaced or dispossessed under settler-colonialism was someone whose voice and experiences were not typically seen by white Christian men as worth preserving. Consequently, what one could think and know about the past had gaps that fell unevenly across individuals and communities. But, at times, there are still traces of the life choices individuals made and of how they regrouped in the face of other people's reactions. These traces offer a glimpse of life under and resistance to society's monstrification of one's actions or embodiment.

The binary categories of male and female did not simply refer to two individuals who were necessary for reproduction. These categories were also framed as "active" and "passive": a giver and a receiver, a decision maker and an implementer. This social relationship between two unequal individuals was a microcosm for the functioning of society, divided at every level into those who decided and those who had to follow. The social and legal ramifications of binarism were wide-ranging. In many European kingdoms, only men were allowed to inherit titles, function as witnesses at trials, choose their heirs, or become priests. Whom someone was allowed to marry depended on whether they were assigned the gender of man or of woman. For intersex people, relating to society thus involved assimilating into one or the other category of male or female.

What of intersex individuals in everyday life? What was their nature and status, and what—if anything—did authorities think needed to be done about them? To answer these questions, Christian thinkers and rulers turned to the Bible's predictions about the *end* of history: the resurrection. According to the Bible, at the end of time, all individuals would be reborn in the most perfect versions of their bodies. Those who had lost limbs during their lives would regain them. Other dimensions of perfection were unclear, such as the age of one's resurrected body and whether or not individuals identified as hermaphrodites would be reborn in the same form as they had lived on earth. An even greater transformation would be the loss of sex altogether from everyone. If perfection was androgynous, perhaps resurrection would render everyone sexless?

In the here and now, theoretical musings like this affect how intersex individuals are treated on the ground. They determine whether or not people view intersex individuals' bodies or behavior as crossing a line between normal (even better than normal) and monstrous and what sort of societal threat (if any) is imagined to emanate from intersex individuals. According to medieval naturalists, theologians, and legal theorists, what a resurrected body would look like—and whether someone would be resurrected at all—would depend on whether the current body and behavior were fully human.

In his *Generation of Animals*, the ancient Greek naturalist Aristotle had pronounced that all humans were either male or female. Any person with both male and female organs merely had redundant body parts brought about by excess amounts of matter. Only in lower-order animals were hermaphrodites part of the normal course of things. Affirming that normal humans were one of two kinds, male or female, was not simply a way of policing human society. This line of thinking also served to affirm humanity's discreteness as a category from the categories of plant and animal.

In the late twelfth century, ancient Greek texts that had survived only in Arabic translations or in Greek manuscripts in Byzantium (the Greek-speaking eastern half of the former Roman Empire) began to be translated into Latin. These translations circulated in western Europe. Thirteenth-century scholars in Europe also received previously inaccessible texts from the Islamicate world. As ideas from these texts circulated, they changed the ways in which educated people in Europe thought about gender.

In the mid-thirteenth century in Latin Europe, the view of physicians, scholars, and theologians on the anatomy of human sex moved from seeing a continuum from male to female, with a number of sexes in between, to a binary understanding of sex. Some naturalists argued that nonbinary sex, or anatomical variation beyond a certain constellation of physical features defined as male and female, was not a normal feature of humans. For these thinkers, as with Aristotle, nonbinarism was merely a condition sometimes found in lower-order animals and plants. Anyone who exhibited both male and female sexual organs was flawed on the outside but ultimately either male or female on the inside. In other words, all individuals could and should be assigned male or female.

Authors recommended a panoply of contradictory ways of identifying people's sex: the anatomy of their genitals; their sexual behavior; their own choice of how they want to be identified; how well they fit social conventions of male or female; or even the overarching balance of their humors (the balance of blood, black bile, yellow bile, and phlegm). At stake were not merely the social lives of nonbinary individuals but also their juridical lives: men had significantly more legal rights and power than women, so the assignation of male rather than female conferred on an individual a higher place in society.

From the eighth century, the 'Abbāsid caliphate ruled, from Baghdad, an empire that stretched from the eastern Mediterranean to what is now known as the Middle East, encompassing North Africa and stretching north and east through central Asia. The learned world of the 'Abbāsids was one of translation: works from regions such as Persia, the kingdoms of what is now known as the Indian subcontinent, and the Greek-speaking world were translated into Arabic. Scholars reading across these traditions cross-fertilized material and generated innovative new works in the fields we now call the biological and physical sciences, mathematics, philosophy, and medicine. With the Muslim conquest of large parts of what is now Spain in the early eighth century, Arab centers of learning emerged in such cities as Toledo and Granada, cities where Spain's Moorish legacy is visible in breathtaking medieval architecture. In these centers of learning, Jewish, Christian, and Muslim scholars translated, read, and thought with one another and their scholarly traditions.

For the influential Muslim physician, naturalist, and philosopher Ibn Sīnā (980–1037, who became known in the Latin West as Avicenna), male and female existed as two discrete categories, as did several intersex categories with distinct genital combinations: two sets of functioning genitals; one set of functional, dominant genitals; or no functioning genitals at all. Other Islamic writings blurred the categories of male and female, leaving room for feminine males and masculine females. Importantly, these authors did not view these categories as failings, errors, or monstrous—in contrast to, say,

Aristotle. Yet the very capaciousness of medieval Islamic thought, drawing as it did from a multitude of traditions, including Greek thought, meant that it contained contradictions. These sustained ongoing debates on the nature of the human in relation to anatomy, demonstrated reproductive ability, personal preference, and societal understandings of how individuals of a gender looked and acted.[29] Medieval surgery manuals from Europe show attempts to change the anatomy of individuals whether or not they wished it.[30] By pathologizing bodies that they did not consider to be normal, these practitioners effectively identified and defined these individuals as monsters.

RACE, GENDER, AND SEXUALITY MONSTRIFIED

European theories about monsters, gender, and sexuality frequently intersected with ideas about race. In the ancient Roman naturalist Pliny the Elder's *Natural History*, monstrous peoples Pliny hypothesized to live in regions distant from the Mediterranean included "hermaphrodites," said to be male on one side of their bodies and female on the other. Pliny's writings influenced subsequent commentators in the ancient world and across medieval Europe. Surviving thirteenth-century world maps contain textual descriptions and illustrations of monstrous peoples said to live in those parts of the world most distant from the Holy Land, a number of which transcended the male/female binary.[31]

Ideas about sexuality and theories concerning the monstrous alterity of distant peoples reinforced and even generated one another in medieval Latin Europe. Secular and religious authorities' negative judgments of the moral standing of nonbinary individuals were thus entangled with ideas about the inferiority of distant peoples. One of the ways in which people in medieval Europe distinguished themselves from others was through lifestyle. How sex worked, happened, and with whom were foundational distinguishing features.

Categories of gender communicate how a society expects human bodies and behaviors to make visible how people relate to the labor of reproduction. Surviving records from the tenth century BCE onward reveal the presence of eunuchs at imperial courts across the regions of the modern Middle East, Greece, Iran, and China. Eunuchs had distinctive jobs and social spaces permitted to them that were defined by their castration: educating princes, guarding courtly women, being companions for elite men, and—since they could be trusted not to have dynastic ambitions toward their own (nonexistent) offspring—acting as trusted political aides.

Literary scholar Abdulhamit Arvas has shown how, at the Ottoman court in the sixteenth and seventeenth centuries, eunuchs were enslaved individuals with elite status by way of their access to restricted spaces, notably to the enclosure of the sultan's harem. Yet castration was not the only embodied characteristic that defined their gender and social status. Exactly what sort of eunuch someone was and the range of spaces they could enter also depended on how Ottoman courtiers and officials identified them in terms of local, dynamic categories of race.[32]

East African boys purchased by the court had already been fully castrated (with penis and testicles removed) regardless of the boys' wishes, but white boy servants from central Asia were sometimes given the option whether or not to be castrated, and when they were had only their testicles removed. In Ottoman writing and in social life at court, Black eunuchs from Africa were placed at the bottom of the social hierarchy. Similarly, elite Ottoman men and those who ran their households gave African women servants more physically demanding work than white women servants. They assigned African eunuchs work that brought them closer to women in the sultan's harem than any other men. Not only did Ottoman households purchase eunuchs fully castrated, but they had also selected them for traits of appearance deemed in Ottoman circles to be least attractive.

Thus Ottoman elites selected African eunuchs to fit what was effectively a third gender that was not simply about being eunuchs—castrated individuals with high voices and beardless faces—but also about lacking a physical appearance that women were thought to find attractive. Ottoman treatises and European travelogues detailed this strategy. In the disturbing words of the Frenchman Michel Baudier, the sultan's women are served by "black eunuchs, from whom they have taken all. . . . Their perfection consists in their deformity, for the most hideous are the fairest." They were possessed of a "Moorish deformity" and had "flat noses, wide mouths, thick lips, eyes almost out of their heads, great ears, their hair curled like wool, and their face fearfully black." This, then, was a two-pronged strategy for policing women's desires and the sultan's lineage. The perfect guards and servants of the sultan's harem were deemed to be both physically emasculated and devoid of attractive features. Yet, for some, this might have been something they would have chosen, just as some white boys chose to become eunuchs. Separating choice, pressure, and coercion in the lives of individuals with little or no power is almost impossible. Yet what is clear is that gender as lived experience at the Ottoman court expanded beyond the binary of male/female, that gender had a racial component, and that gender was fluid and, at times, chosen.

Eunuchs and stories about them knitted together a cultural connection between the Ottoman Empire and Europe. Eunuchs appeared in literary works and travelogues, including the plays of Shakespeare.[33] Yet their presence also signaled, for European readers, a different approach to sex and gender. Just as theories about hermaphroditic tribes had done in the Middle Ages, stories about eunuchs at the Ottoman court signaled how the Ottomans were different from people in Europe.

Colonial clerics, administrators, and settlers from Europe thought about, interacted with, wrote about, and disciplined local sexuality in the Americas, Asia, Africa, and the Pacific world in colonial settings. In early Spanish America, imperial administrators, jurists, inquisitors, and clerics opined on Indigenous and African-descent populations' sexual customs and gendered behavior. In colonial New Spain (roughly present-day Mexico and environs), a host of sexual transgressions including homosexuality were lumped together in official records under the category of bestiality, "the nefarious sin," or "sins against nature." Colonial officials' choices of whether to categorize stories of sexual practices as "sins against nature" or not depended on the race and social status of those accused of crimes. Defendants who were priests, white, or of a higher social status were less likely to receive harsh punishment for behaviors recorded in the archive as "sodomy" or "bestiality."[34]

Between the late fifteenth and nineteenth centuries, the Atlantic Middle Passage didn't merely sustain the kidnapping and forced migration of Black women, men, and children but also transformed how their enslavers gendered them in legal and social terms.[35] In 1662 a new Virginia law decreed that children of an enslaved woman and a free man would inherit the status of their mother rather than their father. This rendered the children of enslavers and of enslaved women as enslaved under law, not people but property. The law severed the traditional link to rights and privileges that accrue via patrilineal descent. Instead of inheriting property from their fathers, these infants inherited the condition of enslavement from their mothers and were *defined* as property. Colonial law framed these children not as the kin of white children born to the wives of their fathers but rather as heritable possessions.[36]

This way of thinking is in stark contrast to paternity anxieties in Europe concerning the vagaries of the maternal imagination (where fathers feared the possibility that their wives' offspring were not theirs). By defining, in practice, enslaved women as producers of more property rather than as individuals who might become pregnant with their children, enslavers used slave codes to narrow the category of woman to exclude enslaved women (and, in related ways, enslaved men).

WHO COUNTS AS NORMAL TODAY?

"Gender is social, but sex is biological" is a popular soundbite, but in fact both gender and sex are social, for both are ideas that vary with time and place. While sex is supposedly about physical characteristics, precisely which characteristics "count" as typical for men and for women and how to describe and understand the continuum of physical variety in between these are decisions that societies make through actions, laws, and customs.

Aristotle's opinion that women were merely failed men may seem fanciful today. Yet the bias against seeing women as regular humans in medicine shows how Aristotelian thinking persisted well into the twentieth century. Women's symptoms and pain are more likely to be dismissed. The long-standing convention of excluding women (who were and still are deemed too volatile and various) from drug trials has only recently been called into question. Clinical trials used to be performed only on men. This was both to protect anyone who might be pregnant and because women's hormonal cycles added an extra level of complexity to evaluating the results. Yet drugs and treatments developed from them are administered to everyone, at dosages set according to a limited demographic of the population: men. And then there's the extensive and, in some countries, as I write, increasingly punitive legislation around pregnancy and parenthood that discriminates against those who identify as women and those who are able to become pregnant and denies them the power to make their own reproductive health choices in consultation with their doctors.

If the only categories for people are "male" and "female," then those categories monstrify everyone who doesn't identify as either. They also monstrify everyone who society decides is muddling or falling outside these categories. In professional sports, hormones have become the new gender-policing mechanism, confirming whether someone is "male" or "female" to ensure that men do not compete in women's competitions. But who decides what upper level of testosterone is "normal" for a woman? How do testosterone levels vary with ancestry? And who is more likely to be challenged on their "normality" in the first place? As we'll see in the next chapter, by using white norms to define who is a woman, professional-sports organizations penalize women with racial backgrounds in which typical hormone levels are different. As traditions of monstrosity—of gender, race, and ability—intersect, who is or is not considered to be normal becomes increasingly unpredictable.

_____

SIX

Monstrous Performance and Display

IN THE ATLANTIC PORT CITY of La Rochelle, France, diligent tourists might find their way to the gently decaying, albeit under renovation, rue Fleuriau. The mansion at number 10 has a courtyard containing a sculpture by the Senegalese artist Osmane Sow of François-Dominique Toussaint L'Ouverture, the eighteenth-century Black revolutionary leader of Haiti. The statue was installed in 2015 to memorialize the abolition of slavery. The mansion, once the property of the Fleuriau family, is now the site of the Musée du Nouveau Monde, a museum dedicated to the history of France's relationship with the Americas—what Europeans called the "New World." The Fleuriau family had made their fortune through plantations worked by enslaved people.

The most arresting artifact in the museum is perhaps the painting known as *La Mascarade nuptiale* (loosely, "The wedding procession"). Eight individuals from the household of Queen Maria I of Portugal meet our eyes in this group portrait painted by the Portuguese court painter José Conrado Roza in 1788 (see plate 7). A second version of the painting, preserved in a private collection, contains an inscription announcing that it was made for Queen Maria I of Portugal and that it "comprises the true portraits and colors which represent not only the physiognomy and colors but also the height and breadth of each of the following persons, for all of which all precise measurements were taken." The portraits are life-sized and apparently lifelike, especially where the subjects' heads and faces—their physiognomy—are concerned.

To stand in the room with this enormous canvas is an uncanny experience. The painting's eighteenth-century viewers might well have imagined that these individuals were just as wondrous to behold in real life. The modern viewer gazing on the painting is, perhaps, in a small way, complicit in enfreakment: the ongoing spectacularizing of these people's bodies that

FIGURE 23. José Conrado Roza, *La mascarade nuptiale*, gallery view in the Musée du Nouveau Monde, La Rochelle, France, 1788. This enormous group portrait depicts the individuals, many of them dwarfs, sent to Portugal from various parts of its empire to attend the wedding of Dona Roza (*second row, left*), said to be Queen Maria I's favorite dwarf. Photo by the author.

began a quarter of a millennium ago.[1] This painting encapsulates how atypical people were treated as objects of spectacle in Europe from at least the fifteenth to the early twentieth centuries.[2]

The portrait commemorates the wedding of Dona Roza, Maria I's favorite "dwarf" (as extremely short adults were designated then) to a certain Dom Pedro; the couple occupy the panel's center rung. Each of the eight figures bears a description on their costume that tells their story.[3] The eighteen-year-old Dona Roza and Dom Pedro, aged between thirty and forty, had been sent to the queen by the governor of Angola. Dona Roza was apparently "greatly admired for her face which combines vivacity, wisdom, and grace which makes her greatly esteemed." Her dainty pink lace-trimmed dress is accessorized with matching shoes and a fan. Dom Pedro sports an embroidered crimson three-piece suit, tricornered hat, cane, and black stockings and buckled shoes to match his suit. He was said to be identifiable by his "strange

FIGURE 24. José Conrado Roza, *La mascarade nuptiale*, detail, 1788. A brief biography of each figure in this painting is written somewhere on their clothing or accoutrements. In this detail these texts appear on one of the tambourine cymbals, the sash, and the shorts. Musée du Nouveau Monde, La Rochelle, France. Photo © Photo Josse/Bridgeman Images.

face," but what it was about his face that the viewer was supposed to find strange is unclear.

The couple's titles (Dona and Dom) were reserved for nobility—yet they were "sent" to Portugal. They were probably enslaved. Could they have been free people who came of their own volition? If so, it is unlikely that they would have gotten away with saying no. So how elevated could their status have actually been—and how likely was it that they had been ennobled by the Portuguese Crown? In the front row, Dona Anna, aged seventeen, and Sebastiaō, aged thirty-one, both sent from Mozambique, carry musical instruments; one of the functions of courtiers, servants, and enslaved persons at court was to provide entertainment. The remaining figures were sent from Brazil. The fourteen-year-old Martinho de Mello e Castro, perched at the top of the carriage in a bishop's costume, underscores the fantastic, staged nature of the scene. In the front row, Marcelino de Tapuia, aged twenty-six, dressed in featherwork headdress, skirt, and arm and leg ornaments and brandishing a bow and arrow, models the attributes with which Europeans had associated "New World" inhabitants since the late fifteenth century. At the center of that row is Dom Jozé, aged thirty, sent by none other than the viceroy of Brazil.

Also in the front row is twelve-year-old Siriaco, painted almost naked, revealing the pattern of his skin pigmentation. His shorts appear to be composed out of a checkered harlequin or clown costume—a sign that the viewer was supposed to question his common sense or view him entirely for entertainment. This choice also implied that he was not civilized enough (in European terms) to dress properly. As with pictures of Antoinette Gonsalvus,

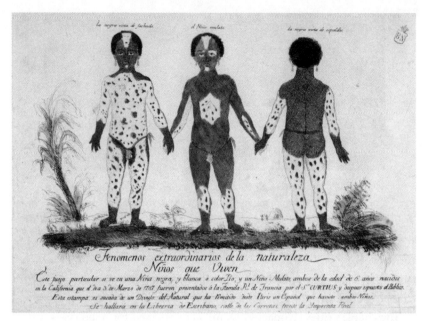

FIGURE 25. *Fenomenos extraordinarios de la naturaleza*, Madrid, 1787. Two six-year-olds from California were presented to the royal family of France and then shown to the public. Their skin pigmentation appears to have made them curiosities in the eyes of European spectators. INVENT/14815. From the collections of the Biblioteca Nacional de España, Madrid.

an element in the painting provides the medium for his biography. Scholars saw individuals with vitiligo, who were sometimes referred to as albinos, as holding the key to the category of the human.[4] They were often exhibited, studied by physicians, and illustrated.

These eight people represented some of Portugal's imperial possessions. Trophy courtiers, they stand in for the administrators who sent them to Lisbon. During the 1780s the governors of Brazil sent people to the Portuguese court for what one might call a human cabinet of curiosities.[5] The painting memorializes their presence and captures their likely experience at court of being displayed or being performers, by virtue of their embodiment, whether they wanted to be or not.

SHOWS, FAIRS, AND FESTIVALS

An oasis of calm welcomes visitors to London who step from the bustling frenzy of Euston Road into the Wellcome Library. If they swipe past the security barriers, twirl up a glass staircase, and enter the Rare Books Reading Room, they might consult a voluminous set of binders of ephemera: pamphlets, newspaper cuttings, postcards, photographs, and handbills. Each of the five binders is encased in a stiff-sided archival box. On a sticker on the spine of each box, the cataloger summarized the contents with a single pithy, disturbing word: "Freaks."[6] These binders full of people framed as monsters reveal dehumanizing classificatory systems at work. As pamphlet after pamphlet and cutting after cutting reveal, these individuals were category breakers in the eyes of many who saw them. Sometimes these people leveraged their distinctiveness into a life in show business, after a fashion: they let people gaze, for a fee, at their unusual anatomies—or endured it, under duress.

Leafing through the binders, I was struck by the familiar London street names and iconic venues at which events once called "freak shows" had taken place for decades, even centuries.[7] There was the Egyptian Hall in Piccadilly, the site of misadventures in Edith Nesbit's early twentieth-century children's books. Another locale was 94 Pall Mall, an address that evokes the Monopoly boardgame. In 1829, and again in 1869, Chang and Eng Bunker, the original Siamese twins joined at the hip, appeared here. The Criterion Theatre still has a restaurant decorated with Byzantine and ancient Egypt-themed decor. It was founded in 1873. The building at 22 New Bond Street is now a Burberry store. Saartje Baartman was put on display at 225 Piccadilly, on Piccadilly Circus "near the top of Hay-Market," steps from the Criterion Theatre and next to Soho and Leicester Square, where street performers still draw crowds.[8]

On the days immediately following Christmas Day, visitors to Alexandra Palace could view an array of performers, from a circus to "the wonderful Jackley Troupe" to the cryptic "monster Christmas tree and decorations." "Adonis, the Marvellous African Dwarf," was another person on whom an impresario had bestowed an ironic, mocking name. The Adonis of Greek mythology had been the lover of the goddesses Aphrodite and Persephone and had embodied the "perfect" male body. Entry to the palace cost a shilling—about half a day's labor for a skilled tradesperson in 1873, the year the theater opened. To encourage visits out into a cold, wet, possibly snowy or icy London, in which midwinter nights still begin around four in the afternoon, "the entire palace [was] thoroughly heated and illuminated until 9pm," and it was "accessible under cover" from many parts of London. There were special, extra trains laid on from King's Cross Station to make the journey easier.[9] Advertisements like this sold the idea that colluding in the enfreakment of these people by going to see them was wholesome holiday entertainment for the family.

Fairs in Europe had centuries-long traditions of performances by individuals with atypical bodies or purportedly hailing from some far-flung part of the globe, who posed or went about their supposed daily activities in front of audiences.[10] People who were very tall or very small or had a different number of limbs than the usual complement made regular appearances.[11] People from Africa, Asia, and the Americas were often objects of spectacle against their will (as far as their will can be determined or imagined). A family from southern Africa exhibited at the Egyptian Hall in Piccadilly around 1847, labeled "Bosjemen" or "Bush People" on a cutting from a newspaper or handbill, apparently averaged a little over four feet tall. The unpleasant, dismissive poster encouraged anyone interested in comparative human physiology and culture to visit. A backhanded modicum of empathy embedded in the advertisement provides a glimpse into the lives these people led on display: "We can readily excuse the sullenness said to be sometimes indulged in by our wild yellow skinned friends, for called upon so often as they are to gratify the curiosity their appearance in London has excited, it would require more philosophy than a savage could well acquire in his desert home, to receive with the smiles and graces of a courtier the successive audiences that throng the exhibition."[12]

An array of performers appeared in an early eighteenth-century monster compendium assembled by James Paris du Plessis, Samuel Pepys's manservant who appears in chapter 5. One was a "black wild man" from the East Indies, "covered all over the body and arms and hands with very thick long black hair, could never larn to speak, read nor rite" and "was sold to a company of rope dancers." Another was a "Negro prince" from Guinea, who had been kidnapped at the age of eight and taken to Virginia, where he escaped when the ship transporting him arrived at the coast. A certain Colonel Taylor is said to have "entartained" the prince and taken him in—in what capacity Du Plessis does not say, although he did learn "to speak pritty good English." In any event the boy "was sold in London and show'd publickly at the age of 10 years in 1690," when Du Plessis saw him, seeing him again in 1725. His show-worthy characteristic appears to have been vitiligo: his body, according to the writer, was "of a Jeet Black intermixt with a clear and beautifull white, spotted all over."[13] Du Plessis implies here that white skin is beautiful but black skin is not—defining white as the default for human skin.

Du Plessis's compendium also included a "wild and hairy Irishman" and a "Wild East Indian from Bengall."[14] "Wildness" was a characteristic that tens of thousands of Europeans (and later, Americans) would pay to see in fairs every year. According to ancient authorities, wild individuals were closer to animals than regular ones. This view reduced the barrier to taking people's rights away: they were supposedly childlike and irrational. The charge of wildness has been used against entire peoples: early English settlers in New England wrote that Indigenous peoples were wild and uncultivated, lacking agriculture—a technological "performance," if you will. In fact, these peoples did tend to and live in dynamic relationships with plant life, animals, and the land. Their activities were merely invisible to the English, who were looking for monocultural crop plantings.[15]

Du Plessis also wrote of a "monstrous Tartar," said to have been captured in Hungary in 1664 by a certain Count Serini. This person had "spent all his arrows in fight against the Christians"—an invented narrative about a crack horseman that reframes the Tartars' terrific archery skills and horsemanship as the acts of a human-horse hybrid, as if he were truly a monstrous centaur.[16] Centuries before Charles Darwin's *Origin of Species* and the debate over a potential missing link between humans and apes, people were drawn to fairs and shows to marvel at mysterious instances where human and animal seemed to collapse in on each other.

Other performers monetized the fact that their height turned heads. Advertisements paired people so that they magnified each other's contrasting stature. Thus were the "Amezen Queen" and "General Mite Tiny" on shows together. In the Royal College of Surgeons, the skeletons of Mlle Crachani, "a Sicilian dwarf," and of Patrick O'Brien, "the Irish giant," were displayed together. Henri Cot, "the French Giant," appeared on a postcard with Prince Colibri, "the Midget." Some advertisements crushed together a bewildering range of human performers-cum-prisoners. Mr. Smith's exhibition, a bargain at just one penny, boasted "the Norfolk Giant," Tom Thumb, "the celebrated dwarf," a two-headed child, and "the African Lady! In her Native Costume": "This beautiful creature, in addition to possessing exquisite beauty and elegance of form and feature, speaks all the Ancient and Modern Languages, with the greatest ease and facility."[17] In Mr. Smith's curatorial telling, the edge of humanity was a place of both atypical births and prodigious excellence.

People captured abroad weren't the only ones coerced into performing. A seventeenth-century letter preserved in the Royal Society in London tells the story of a pair of conjoined twins from a very poor family. People were eager to see the twins. For their parents, deciding to show their children might have been the most reliable way to keep them and the rest of the family alive. Around 1714 sixteen- or seventeen-year-old Constant or Constantia was apprenticed to a quilter. According to a paper that the Scottish physician and anatomist James Douglas read at a Royal Society meeting, the quilter, "observing something extraordinary about her lower parts had her examined by some old women who immediately pronounced her an hermaphrodite" and "her mistriss [*sic*] designing to make a penny of her exposed her as a wonderfull prodigy of nature's first in Smithfield about halfe a year ago."[18]

Other letters preserved in the Royal Society indicate that not everyone with an unusual embodiment or medical difficulty cared to be poked and prodded. One Nathanial Fairfax, writing in about a monstrous birth at Framlington in Suffolk, England, wrote, "The instance, methinks, would be something apart to instruct us, how oddely nature bestirrs herselfe in her closet worke, when unluckiely put by her haunts, especially if the mother were more free to gratifye the curiosity of an inquirer."[19] The child's mother apparently had no desire that they become objects of curiosity and resisted attempts to specimenize their bodies and invade their privacy.

Charles Byrne, another figure known as the "Irish giant," earned his living by performing his wondrously monstrous height—almost eight feet of it—at London's fairs in the 1780s. Being renowned did not protect him. His sorry story provides a rare glimpse of a performer's feelings, mixed, at best, about being the object of an audience's gaze: Byrne left instructions that he should not be displayed after his death, even leaving money to some fishers to give him a sea burial. Yet, when Byrne died in his late twenties, his body was sold to the surgeon John Hunter, who had bribed the fishers to renege on their prior agreement.[20]

Hunter had Byrne's skeleton rendered by boiling his body in a kettle, later donated to the British Medical Association. Byrne's remains also ended up on display, at the Hunterian Museum in London, where I came upon his skeleton in a case in 2014. The accompanying label summarized Byrne's life and wishes, including his desire not to be on posthumous display.[21] In that instant, I too was implicated in the ongoing dismissal of Byrne's wishes. Happily, Byrne's skeleton came off display a couple of years later. In May 2023, when the Hunterian reopened after a long renovation closure, Byrne's remains were no longer on display (I went and checked). His bones have not, however, been given the sea burial for which he had asked and paid. The museum's official statement is that the skeleton "will be retained as it is an integral part of the Hunterian Collection and will be available for bona fide research into the conditions of acromegaly and gigantism."[22]

What was it about Byrne that made it acceptable to ignore his wishes for privacy in death—and for his wish for a sea burial to continue to be thwarted? How tall (or short) does someone have to be before others feel so little empathy toward them that they are no longer seen primarily as a person but an example of a pathology—a monster—who could, without reservation, be displayed in the interests of "science"? Byrne's life and the aftermath of his death suggest that people recognize full humanity on a case-by-case basis. Individuals who seem sufficiently unlike the community in which they find themselves may well have their distinctiveness weaponized against them in both life and death.

The lives of individuals who performed their "monstrous" bodies were fraught with prejudice and uncertainty. One John Worrenberg, "the Swiss dwarf," met his end in 1695 in Rotterdam, in what is now the Netherlands, "being carried in his box, over a plank from a quay on board of a ship—the plank breaking, the porter and he fell into a river; and being enclosed in his box, was drowned."[23] At the other end of the scale, the man known as "the modern Goliath" and also, ironically, as "Little Frank Winkelmeier," who died in 1887, struggled with discrimination and with the logistics of everyday life. Asked in an interview, "Are you always treated with equal consideration wherever you go?" he replied, "No, I cannot say I am. For instance, when I was showing myself at the Folie Bergères, in Paris, the people were most insulting, and made me feel very wretched and uncomfortable." The announcement of his death, officially of tuberculosis, appeared in the *Globe*, where it included an anatomical description that veered into the vegetal: "The huge shambling body had no better principle of cohesion than a clothes horse. The legs seemed to be protesting against the weight of the trunk, and to be painfully divided against themselves as to their angles of injunction in the upper and lower portions. Poor Winkelmeyer, in fact, was physically a kind of human weed, and his sole distinction was in being a weed nine feet high." He was only twenty years of age.[24]

One of the most poignant accounts in the Wellcome Library's "Freaks" Ephemera Collection is the simple typed advertisement for a certain John Grimes, three feet, eight inches high and fifty-seven years old:

> At the age of between 30 and 40 years, [he] would lift up from the ground upon his two hands two full-grown men at once; but his drunkenness disabled and weakened him at or after the age of 40 years. He was as broad as long, from hand to hand stretched.... He sold himself to a surgeon some years

before his death for six pence per week, to be dissected after his death. . . . He was born at Newcastle upon Tyne, in the County of Northumberland. He married one wife, by whom he had four children. . . . Grimes died in 1736, and was dissected, and his skeleton made by a surgeon over against the Fountain Tavern in the Strand.[25]

Perhaps Grimes got around the indignity of being peered at for a living in life by selling himself in advance of his death. Yet this sum was a pittance—less than half a day's labour for a skilled tradesperson at the time. This announcement made an impression on the monster anecdote compiler James Paris du Plessis. He copied it into his monster miscellany and appended a watercolor devised from his own viewing of Grimes.[26]

More disturbing is the case of Mary Toft, who suffered a miscarriage in 1726. Toft appears to have been coerced, by the organ-grinder's wife, who was present at this tragedy, to pretend to give birth to live rabbits on a regular basis. The woman would provide Toft with a supply of rabbits whenever a doctor came to examine her. When Toft finally confessed, she was so distressed that she declared that she wanted to hang herself—a line that appears in noted anatomist and male midwife James Douglas's transcription of her confession but is crossed out in the fair copy. She went on to also implicate her mother-in-law and the surgeon John Howard.[27] The story entered the news cycle.[28] Toft was willing to capitalize on her misfortune, at least for a while—but seemingly not for as long as those around her wanted her to do so. What con artists choose as their con can reveal something about what average people who were their marks might believe. It is difficult to imagine medical professionals being taken in by this stunt. Were they in on the con too? Was this a collective creation of fake news by a combination of opportunists and individuals not terribly invested in unmasking the con?

Long before Charles Byrne's disturbing end and Mary Toft's rabbit stunts, fairs and shows had been venues at which every slice of European society, from the general public with limited education to scholars, naturalists, and the aristocracy, went to see individuals who looked so different that they appeared to have crossed a line into the category of the marvelous, the monstrous, or the freakish, all terms that crop up regularly in advertising pamphlets and commentaries on the performers. In Shakespeare's *The Tempest*, which we examined in chapter 4, the shipwrecked Trinculo encounters a sleeping Caliban, a being he cannot classify ("man or fish?") and observes, "Were I in England now . . . and had but this fish painted, not a holiday fool there but would give a piece of silver: there would this monster make a man: any strange beast there makes a man: when they will not give a doit to relieve a lame beggar, they will lay out ten to see a dead Indian."[29] Showing an unclassifiable monster, person, or animal, captivating the imagination of every mark on vacation—every "holiday fool"—was the way to make a fortune at shows and fairs.

One such fair was Bartholomew Fair in West Smithfield, London. First chartered in 1133, it ran, amazingly, until 1855. This three-day summer fair attracted all manner of marvelous and bizarre exhibits. A pamphlet from 1641 noted the fair's popularity among "people of all sorts, high and low, rich and poore, from cities, townes, and countrys, of all sects . . . and of all conditions, good and bad, vertuous and vitious, knaves and fooles, cuckolds and cuckhold-makers."[30] In 1802 the poet William Wordsworth wrote of Bartholomew Fair's

> albinos, painted Indians, dwarfs,
> The horse of knowledge, and the learned pig,
> The stone-eater, the man that swallows fire,
> Giants, ventriloquists, the invisible girl . . .
> All freaks of Nature, all Promethean thoughts
> Of man his dulness, madness, and their feats
> All jumbled up together to make up
> This parliament of monsters.[31]

For Wordsworth a fairground buzzing with unusually embodied individuals, prodigious animals, talented performers, and people from faraway places was a mirror universe in which reality was inverted—a "parliament of monsters." Venues like this contributed to what literature and bioethics scholar Rosemarie Garland-Thomson terms "processes of enfreakment": storytelling that defines some people as so abnormal or pathological that their humanity and person-hood is erased, and the "freak" object is all that society perceives.[32]

All walks of society could gaze on those whom fairground hustlers called "freaks." An admission ticket to view a one-hundred-pound child, billed as "wonderful phenomena of nature" (presumably for the unusual size) had two price brackets: "Ladies and Gentlemen" and "Mechanics, Servants, and Children." The prices were not printed, but there were blank spaces into which the impresario in charge of the viewing could write in the day's prices. Another advertisement bolstered the intellectual credibility and social respectability of a performance: it noted that the performer, "a little wild man, born in St. David's Streights," had been viewed twice by royalty and by Sir Hans Sloane, the president of London's scientific hub, the Royal Society.[33]

There were also more exclusive ways to peer at those with unusual bodies. Wealthy punters could pay for performers to entertain them and their select friends in the privacy of their homes. Elizabeth Armitage performed her muscular beauty at the Cosmorama on Regent Street in London and also at "Evening Parties of the Nobility attended if required."[34] James Paris du Plessis's monster compendium describes an intersex person who "was publickly seen in London in the Year 1702" and "seemed to be a Perfect Partaker of boath sexes." According to Du Plessis, "its viril Plerge did Erect by Provocation." This blunt sentence of commentary is accompanied by a drawing, complete with a liftable flap on the page to allow the viewer to lift up the figure's clothing and observe the range of genitals.[35]

Scholars and physicians attended such exhibitions. These included naturalist John Evelyn, diarist Samuel Pepys, and microscopist Robert Hooke, members of the Royal Society's first scientific society.[36] Learned journals and meeting minutes reveal practitioners of anatomy, ethnology, and medicine viewing and even examining bearded ladies, piebald individuals, and people from overseas. An intersex African exhibited in London in the 1740s was, according to the poster announcing their presence, described and illustrated in treatises on anatomy and on "hermaphrodites"; viewings cost a shilling. In a sickening twist to the typical performance, visitors could carry away a souvenir of an engraving of the African in "a new engraved figure of the parts in their present state."[37] In a sense the Royal Society reframed certain individuals whom enslavers and impresarios marketed as "freaks" as crossover acts: at once entertainment for the masses and respectable and pedagogical, even the stuff of new scientific discovery.[38] For showmen the Royal Society's interest in anyone classed as a monster was marketable.

At the height of European imperial dominance in the nineteenth and early twentieth centuries, peoples from Tierra del Fuego, sub-Saharan Africa, Australia, and similarly distant corners of Europe's empires were transported to such cities as London and Paris and forced to perform their lives on public display at exhibitions and fairs.[39] The language of their exhibitors made clear that they viewed these people as the lowest rung of humanity, as almost bestial, incapable of receiving God's grace.

In 1853 a brother and sister pair named Maximo and Bartola made a stop in London as part of an international tour. Originally from El Salvador and born with microcephaly, a condition that impaired their cognitive abilities, they appear to have been sold by their mother to a man who promised to care for and exhibit them. Perhaps coerced into performing, the two young people were ushered to Buckingham Palace to meet Queen Victoria and members of the royal family.[40] The handbill text announcing the visitors' appearance is at once frightful and illuminating:

> The most marvellous of all Human Beings ever seen by White people were discovered in the hitherto unexplored City of IXAMAYA, in Central America, 1849. They are totally unlike anything deemed Human—their Heads being formed like the head of an Eagle—Their Hair growing erect on the head, in form and dimensions of a huge grenadier's cap. Their frames are beautifully symmetrical, yet almost Lilliputian in size—eyes black and liquid—silky skin, of a deep olive colour—affectionate—amiable—intelligent—and pleasing in manner. THIS EXTRAORDINARY LIVING MAN and WOMAN constitute, according to the most scientific authority, the MOST MARVELLOUS EXISTING HUMAN PHENOMENA! They were formerly used by the Mayaboon Indians as living idols.... They will be exhibited Daily at this Place, from 10 a.m. till 11 p.m.[41]

The bill frames the "Aztecs" as living outside of time—perhaps even primitive—their small proportions supposedly so extraordinary that an Indigenous group used to venerate them as "living idols." Yet they were only "discovered in . . . 1849," just four years before this announcement. Viewers of Bartola and Maximo's performance would be part of an exclusive club with access to "the most marvellous existing human phenomena." Whether they are fully human or not is left to the viewer's discernment. In addition pamphleteers and commentators used the siblings' lives to tell a cautionary tale: that these siblings were the last, inbred, aristocratic members of a formerly great empire in the last stages of degeneration, a process that some suggested had been set in motion by the intermixing of European and Indigenous peoples.[42] For London audiences Bartola and Maximo had the potential to challenge their understanding of what it meant to be human anatomically, temporally, and geopolitically cut off from "modernity."

The British debut of Bartola and Maximo had been preceded by a US show that began in the late 1840s. A playbill announcing Bartola and

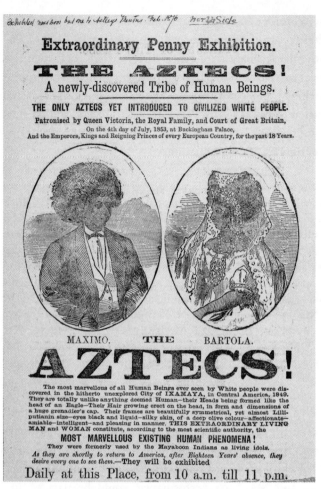

FIGURE 26. Handbill advertising an exhibition of Maximo and Bartola, the "Aztec Lilliputians" from Iximaya in Central America, circa 1878. Such exhibitions were attended by everyone from servants and children to royalty, who often paid for private viewings at court. EPH 499A:18, Public Domain Mark, Wellcome Collection.

Maximo's appearance in Philadelphia in 1852 called them "fairy-like," idols to those who supported them "with superstitious veneration," "employed as mimes and bacchanals in Pagan ceremonies and worship." It even argued that the couple are "not dwarves"—atypically short human beings—but rather "a new and absolutely Unique Race of Mankind, whose distinctive peculiarities constitute the most Extraordinary and Inexplicable phenomena that the history of the human races has yet produced."[43]

The pitch framed Maximo and Bartola as another race entirely, one even more different from white viewers than Indigenous Americans. Yet the viewers of this playbill, and perhaps some of the members of Maximo and Bartola's audiences, may well have been Black, Brown, or of mixed heritage. There may have been enslaved people in the audiences. The reactions of such individuals were likely to have been more ambiguous, and more hostile, to shows in which Black, Brown, and Indigenous people were shown for their bodily difference than those of white viewers.

The advertising rhetoric of these sensationalist advertisements also hints at the breadth of popular interest in the sciences of human genealogy. In the decade before the 1859 edition of Charles Darwin's *The Origin of Species*, a work in which life on earth involved one species morphing into another through monstrous singularities, the question of just how different a person had to be before being "something else" had already captured the popular imagination in Europe and North America. Science had become the handmaiden of sensation.

In the 1880s a girl known as Krao, abducted from Laos, in Southeast Asia, was exhibited at the Royal Aquarium in London. Emblazoned on the handbills promoting her appearances were the words "'Krao' the 'missing link,' a living proof of Darwin's theory of the descent of man." The explorer Carl Bock had "captured" Krao and her parents, all of whom were unusually hairy. Krao's father then died from cholera, and the government detained her mother in Bangkok. Bock took Krao to England.[44]

Some descriptions of Krao focus on the intrepid efforts required to "collect" her. There is something of the Indiana Jones adventure about some of these framings. A handbill depicting Krao against a jungle backdrop shows her seemingly mid-climb, with one foot on a tree stump and arms curled around an imaginary tree, in front of tall ferns and banana fronds.[45] Other aspects of the language cast her almost as a pet and certainly as a specimen for gaping at. The reverse of the two handbills illustrated here printed extracts from such publications as the *Times*, the *Daily Telegraph*, *People*, and *Nature*. These quotations bandy around phrases like "strange hairy little creature," "not a monster," "enveloped in a natural soft fur," "human monkey," and "nothing repulsive about her appearance." According to the linguist and anthropologist Augustus Henry Keane, who published his notes from a "private interview" with Krao in *Nature* in 1883, she was "living proof of the presence of a hairy race in Further India."[46]

"KRAO"

THE "MISSING LINK,"

A Living Proof of Darwin's Theory of the Descent of Man.

SPECIAL LECTURES, 2.30, 5.30 & 9.30.

SPECIAL LECTURES, 2.30, 5.30 & 9.30.

THE WONDER OF WONDERS.

The usual argument against the Darwinian theory, that man and monkey had a common origin, has always been that no animal has hitherto been discovered in the transmission state between monkey and man.

"KRAO,"

a perfect specimen of the step between man and monkey, discovered in Laos by that distinguished traveller, Carl Bock, will be on Exhibition in the New Lecture Room, during the Afternoon and Evening.

ALL SHOULD SEE HER.

SEE OPINIONS OF THE PRESS ON THE OTHER SIDE.

Aquarium Westminster March 31 1887

FIGURE 27. *"Krao," the "Missing Link,"* handbill showing a seated child, Krao, who was being exhibited at the Royal Aquarium, London, 1887. Darwin's *The Origin of Species* was perhaps the best thing to happen to impresarios who showed people: it allowed them to spin their voyeuristic events as educational lessons and even as contributions to science. EPH 499A:104, Public Domain Mark, Wellcome Collection.

The Canadian showman who exhibited her, G. A. Farini, or Guillermo Antonio Farini (the stage name of one William Leonard Hunt), would eventually adopt her and then exhibit her successful conversion to "civilization," fully dressed. Once Krao was past puberty and in her twenties, Aquarium visitors found her adult body threatening, as if it fell outside the category of

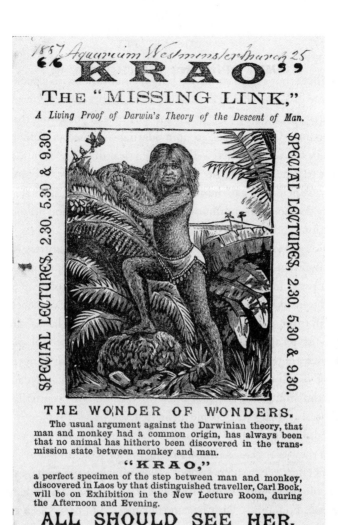

FIGURE 28. *"Krao," the "Missing Link,"* handbill showing Krao against foliage, announcing her appearance at the Royal Aquarium, London, 1887. She is posed as if she were in the jungle. EPH 499A:105, Public Domain Mark, Wellcome Collection.

human: they objected to witnessing what they interpreted as the offspring of a woman and an animal.[47] The invasion of Krao's life, privacy, and dignity was just one example of a larger pattern of Western scientific curiosity and the desire to experiment being used to justify violating the lives and bodies of others.[48]

Dis/ability is not a fixed condition but one that varies with a person's age and fortune (e.g., losing an arm in a fishing accident, developing chronic postviral fatigue, or succumbing to osteoporosis due to lead poisoning from polluted water mains). Questions of accommodating—in the built environment as well as in the technosphere—the full physical diversity of humanity relate not just to gender and height but also to physical ability and mobility more broadly. Where "typical" human variation ends and "disability" begins is a category decision that communities make through laws and person-to-person interactions and empathy (or lack thereof).

A widespread disability accommodation in some countries is affordable corrective eyeglasses: research and technological developments undertaken over centuries make it possible for hundreds of millions of people to see well enough to read, drive, work, and live fuller lives because of pieces of glass or plastic in front of their eyes. In these settings "needing glasses" does not register as atypical (beyond, perhaps, the elementary school playground). Eyeglasses are thus a life-changing accommodation that is not universally available or affordable yet clearly transformative and inclusive in ways that benefit individuals and their societies. Most adults will eventually need reading glasses, as their eyes become farsighted.

Words like "disability" and "impairment" aren't applied to people simply because they wear glasses. The availability of an accommodation in the form of lenses effectively renders various vision impairments manageable, almost to the point of invisibility. In a similar way, after the SARS epidemic of 2003, face masks on public transit became normalized in parts of East Asia. And just as glasses also function as fashion accessories, perhaps face masks might, too, along with hats and scarves.

TALENT

Get too good at something too early, and you might end up being labeled a "child prodigy." On one level the label is a mark of admiration, something that recognizes how good a child is at something. But on the playground, where sticking out of the crowd can get you noticed by the wrong people, charges of virtuosity and of monstrosity are joined at the hip. "Prodigy" has a long history of negative connotations. In ancient Greece and Rome, and in

Europe for centuries afterward, the term "prodigy" signified an omen, a sign from God—something outside the ordinary course of nature.[49] Embedded in this etymology is the possibility that people could be so good at something—so gifted—that they are, somehow, separate from the rest of humanity.

The eighteenth-century musician Wolfgang Amadeus Mozart was regarded by patrons, musicians, and concertgoers in his own time as a child prodigy. He played the piano in public when he was barely more than a toddler and composed music before he was double digits old. During his short life, he expanded the horizons of possibility for orchestral music. Today his compositions continue to form a key plank of the standard repertoire of Western classical music. Mozart's prodigious talent cannot be separated from his highly atypical musical education. Mozart's father was a music teacher who was determined to turn his children into excellent musicians through a carefully devised training regimen. Mozart had an older sister, Anna Maria Mozart, who was herself a highly accomplished musician. The experience of teaching Anna Maria enabled Mozart senior to fine-tune his pedagogy for his son, who, moreover, had the model of an older sibling to show him what was possible, to stretch him, and thus to catapult him even further. Intense, deliberate training and an experienced role model who can double as a sparring partner create the conditions that can sometimes make the extraordinary possible for a young person in the performing arts.

Examples can be found outside in sports, as well. The luminous tennis careers of Venus and Serena Williams illuminate individual talent and grit. They also demonstrate the sisters' stretching effect on each other within the highly effective, deliberate, and holistic training program devised by their father. Their talents and achievements are *superlative*, but that does not imply that they or other Black athletes who reach the top of their sports are in some way abnormal. As I discuss later in this chapter, there is a racial politics to whose talent and hard work are celebrated by white-dominated media as talent and hard work rather than as signs of enfreakment.

Cultural values and identity conventions also shape ideas about what a sport's players "should" look like. Does the archetype of a tennis player look like Rafael Nadal or Roger Federer? Serena Williams or Maria Sharapova? Such debates are not just about whether a player's technique is effective on the court or not. Aesthetics—how the look of something makes people feel—is part of how viewers respond to athletic performance. How much of a usually desired physical characteristic (like height) or talent (like intelligence) does someone need before society defines it as a pathology, as something that is wrong with a person, perhaps even as a threat to society? Excellence some-times appears so dangerous that societies consider that those who possess it should not be permitted the same freedoms as others. Where the line between a mutation of concern and everyday variation lies is a matter of opinion, not a law of nature.

Marvel Comics' *X-Men* franchise makes visible society's deep suspicion of excellence: there comes a point at which being smart, fast, or strong crosses the line from seeming desirable to being vilified as pathological. In the first movie, *X-Men*, societies fear that mutants have sufficient intelligence and bionic abili-ties (like setting things on fire) to outsmart and out-tech people: to take them over, to replace them, perhaps even to annihilate them. There is a "school for the gifted," in which individuals with unusual powers—individuals that soci-ety calls "mutants"—live and learn in secret to preserve their safety. There is talk of "mutant registration," perhaps because "nobody even knows how many exist." This throughline parallels the Holocaust, of which one of the characters, Magneto, is a survivor. The registration of Jewish residents across Europe as countries were overrun by Nazi Germany was a step along the path to genocide. *X-Men*'s creator, Stan Lee—also the creator of Spider-Man and the Hulk—was an American of Romanian Jewish ancestry. Jewish characters and themes appear regularly in his work, in which those othered by circumstance or society are central, heroic characters. In effect, Lee's body of work offers an accessible counternarrative to anti-Semitism and to monstrifying narratives in general.

Until the mid-nineteenth century, the star roles of Cleopatra and Othello in Shakespeare's plays were performed by white artists. Until the twenty-first century, stage lighting conventions did not typically take into account the different lighting needs of darker skin.[50] In 2019 Halle Bailey was cast in the lead role of Ariel for a Disney live action remake of *The Little Mermaid*. A backlash from some white viewers ensued. How, they said, could a Black woman be a credible mermaid? As it happens, female water spirits have been part of African and African Atlantic diasporic mythology for centuries.[51] In 2022 there was a similar outcry from some viewers about a Black hobbit in Amazon Prime's *The Rings of Power*. But in a work of fantasy, there is no history that requires "historical accuracy." Whether there "really were" Black hobbits or Black mermaids or whether there weren't doesn't come into it.

Such criticisms have a history, one that is about gender as well as race. When US screenwriter Gene Roddenberry was casting the original series of

Star Trek in the 1960s, he wanted a woman to play the captain's second-in-command. Studio executives wouldn't have it—it wasn't believable to them. Roddenberry insisted: in the future women would be in roles like this. The studio compromised: he could have a woman somewhere on the bridge. Roddenberry took the opportunity to cast a Black woman as a bridge officer, a role that went to Nichelle Nichols.

During an episode that aired in 1968, her character, Uhura, and Captain Kirk (played by William Shatner) kissed, one of the first onscreen interracial kisses. When NBC studio executives heard about it, they wanted the scene reshot, even though its transgressiveness was diluted by the fact that the crewmembers' minds had been temporarily altered. The executives feared pushback from viewers in the US South and didn't want the actors to actually kiss. But Nichols and Shatner messed up each take in which they didn't kiss, and the original version aired. In the event audience responses were overwhelmingly positive.

Be it casting for astronauts or hobbits or mermaids, a society's resistance to seeing people of all embodiments in works of fiction reflects deep assumptions about what normal, leadership, beauty, or heroes look like. When a story is already fantastic, requiring viewers to suspend disbelief with regard to mermaids, a half-sized species, or interplanetary warp drive, what does it mean that some people find that having a Black person on the screen is what makes a world unbelievable—or unwatchable?

Historical conventions in Western dance also created categories of ideal bodies. If a woman is too tall, that may disqualify her from becoming a ballerina, as she may be too heavy for the types of male bodies preferred for ballet to lift her safely. Ballet was historically a white European art form; Black and Brown performers in white-majority countries face discrimination because casting directors judge that audiences would not find, say, a Black swan princess believable.

And are grace and masculinity mutually exclusive? It depends on who you ask—and when. In some parts of the world, ballet is not at odds with traditional ideas about masculinity. Public funding and the legacies of historical and contemporary icons—like the Polish Vaslav Nijinsky (1889/90–1950), who came to fame dancing with the Ballet Russes in imperial Russia, and the Cuban British Carlos Acosta (1973–)—are part of the reason ballet can be a socially convincing demonstration of masculinity for men in some countries.

No matter what the dancer's gender, no one who watches a few minutes of professional ballet can miss how many almost unimaginably strong and well-trained muscles it takes to dance. Yet an eight-year-old boy interested in ballet in, say, the United Kingdom might choose to be discreet about this particular after-school hobby or burgeoning professional aspiration, which many of his peers might read as effeminate, the sign of a boy who likes the "wrong" things.

ART AND "CIVILIZATION"

What do monsters have to do with art? Quite a lot, as it happens. Western art appreciation today is bound up with eighteenth-century assumptions about what constituted fine form and great beauty. The traditional grand narrative of "Art" with a capital A has been a circular story. It took as a given certain technical choices as "best" and judged art of all places and times accordingly. By that yardstick the art of classical Greek antiquity and its imitators in the Italian Renaissance constituted the pinnacles.

Yet, even for viewers holding that particular Eurocentric rubric, wondrous, seemingly monstrous artifacts that combined novelty, strangeness, danger, and desire had also long been fashionable. In the sixteenth century, Europeans placed artifacts like Mexica masks and obsidian mirrors in a category that prompted frissons of excitement, somewhere between art, science, and civility on the one hand and ugliness, idolatry, and barbarity on the other. Spanish invaders burned the vast majority of Mesoamerican codices, fearing they were manuals for summoning the devil; the handful of examples that survived the early decades of colonization were those collected and shipped to Europe for collectors to display in their curiosity cabinets.[52] Museum visitors in Europe have encountered African metalwork from the kingdom of Benin (looted from the Royal Court by the British army in 1897) and ancient Egyptian canopic jars containing the internal organs of pharaohs or their feline companions (sometimes carried off under cover of darkness to be sold to European institutions like the British Museum).[53] By challenging conventional definitions of beauty by their power to evoke emotions of awe, admiration, and pleasure, works made by peoples whom Europeans viewed as inferior challenged Eurocentric understandings of who counted as the ideals of humanity.

In the early twentieth century, new artistic movements like cubism drew heavily on Indigenous arts of Africa, the Americas, and the Pacific. The works of artists like Picasso owe a deep debt to Indigenous artworks, which began filling art dealers' showrooms and museums from the early twentieth century. Yet until recently, the arts of Africa, the Americas, and the Pacific were—some might say often still are—identified as "art" for the art market and simultaneously disavowed as such. In the nineteenth and twentieth centuries, art critics and dealers invented the category of "primitive art."[54] If one laid cultures out on a map based on their similarity to the West, primitive art was to be found at the "edges" of the earth.

The art dealers' advertisements that open the July–August 2019 issue of *Apollo Magazine*, a preeminent art magazine for connoisseurs, reveal that there is still a geography to deciding what counts as art as opposed to something that is not quite art. The pages illustrate such artifacts as an anthropomorphic Marquesas Islands statue or *tiki*, a "fetish skull" from Africa or Oceania, and a mask from "pre-Columbian Mesoamerica." Thomas Murray of Mill Valley, California, advertised a new catalog: "Rarities from the Himalayas to Polynesia." Galerie Flak of Paris showcased "Ferocious Poetry: Ancient Arts of New Ireland."[55] What makes something a fetish, a rarity, or a ferocious work? Does it have something to do with aesthetics, technique, artistic transmission, or something else?

"Fetish" and its cognates in European languages is a term borne out of European colonial activities in Africa. Indicating a malevolent force or object, the word was a dog whistle for accusing someone of practicing sorcery.[56] "Rarities" is also a potent word: in the age of European exploration and colonization, a rarity was an expensive, exotic, and desirable object, animal, or even people, like the Gonsalvus family we met in chapter 2. The Himalayas and Polynesia advertise Thomas Murray's reach and contacts in the twenty-first century. They are not random foreign places but two iconic locales of great distance for people in the West, locales that required money, expertise, connections, and sheer luck to reach and survive. Today people carry oxygen in their attempts to reach the roof of the world. The Polynesian islands in the middle of the world's largest ocean were the sort of place where eighteenth-century sailors washed up, ridden with scurvy, after interminable weeks at sea. Both are lands at the two extremes of sensory distance from the West. And as for calling the arts of New Ireland—an island in Papua New Guinea in Southeast Asia—"ferocious poetry": that is pure exoticism, activating the reputation of the inhabitants of Guinea as cannibals. Gazing at these adverts in sequence, I was struck by the marketing of objects in imperial, racist, monstrifying terms that called into question their status as works that exhibit thought and skill. Geographic inaccessibility would appear to engender monstrous objects, the kind of story that harks back to ancient Greek theories of civilization diminishing the farther one traveled from Greece.

BUT IS IT MUSIC?

When the Russian composer Igor Stravinsky's ballet *The Rite of Spring* premiered in May 1913 on the boards of the Théâtre des Champs-Élysées in Paris, it played with the idea of the primitive and thereby broke a number of upper-class European conventions for what counted as "art." The ballet's subject was slightly risqué: a prehistoric pagan fertility rite in which a community sacrifices a woman who dances herself to death to ensure the passage of the seasons.[57] But Paris was also an imperial metropolitan center with a long-standing appetite for the exotic, for consuming that which was edgy. Since at least the Champollion expedition to Egypt in the 1820s, when French archaeologists shipped boatloads of booty from ancient tombs to France and around Europe, Paris had been attuned to ancient pagan ritual and aesthetics from distant parts of the world as a pleasurable spectacle. *The Rite of Spring* was not simply a back-to-the-peasants folk reconstruction intended to preserve traditional Russian culture but rather, as the musicologist Annegret Fauser has argued, a work devised in Paris for the Parisian scene, one in which exotic, pre-Christian, and folkloric themes were not new.[58] Yet the ballet is infamous for prompting extreme reactions from the audience, many of whom detested the performance. So what went wrong?

In essence *The Rite of Spring* was a category problem. As Fauser describes in an essay on the ballet, the press reportage on the morning of the premiere contained "mixed messages and missing signposts" that left the audience at a loss as they tried to categorize what they saw and heard.[59] But the problem had perhaps less to do with mixed messages from the press and more to do with the genuinely category-breaking nature of the piece. *The Rite of Spring* was at once an avant-garde artwork performed by a classically trained orchestra and an elite cadre of dancers and capable of suggesting unsettling rituals and values from the deep past. The ballet was a hybrid—a monster.

Part of the challenge for the audience at the premiere was the decidedly pagan feel and sound of the spectacle. The choreography, the work of acclaimed dancer Vaslav Nijinsky, contained unprecedentedly jerky, jagged movements

NIJINSKY'S REVOLUTION IN CHOREOGRAPHY : THE POST-IMPRESSIONISTIC AND PREHISTORIC DANCE, "SACRE DU PRINTEMPS."

FIGURE 29. Dancers for Igor Stravinsky's premiere of *The Rite of Spring*, Paris, 1913, in a review in *Sketch Supplement*, July 23, 1913. Their traditional folk costumes and heavy, jerky movements divided audiences at the premiere. XLE3760267, Lebrecht Music Arts/ Bridgeman Images.

that conveyed the dancers' tension and the otherworldliness of the story. The dancers' heavy, tense pacing was a far cry from the lithe, elegant, tippy-toed pointe work more typical of nineteenth-century balletic traditions. Any members of the audience who had seen the human exhibitions at the Expositions Universelles (1889 and 1900) or at subsequent fairs may have wondered whether they were peering at what they considered to be the margins of Europe through a time machine bolted onto a mirror. The dancers' costumes were as unsettling as their movements. Designer Nicholas Roerich's loose-fitting, concealing peasant costumes and wigs trailing long plaits were light-years away from the tights, tutus, and severe hair buns of typical balletic outfits.

And then there was the music—or diabolic cacophony, to some eardrums. Stravinsky's score vibrated with dissonant, unsettling chords that cried out to be resolved into something milder and simpler. It bristled with staccato jabs like sonic daggers that propelled the action and quickened the heartbeats of the audience. The *Rite* turned out to be audiovisual Marmite: the future of music for some, the dulcet tones of cats being gutted for others. The audience, divided between the entranced and the appalled, began arguing so vehemently about the merits (or lack thereof) of the performance that they drowned out the orchestra, leaving the dancers unable to follow musical cues until Nijinsky climbed up on a chair and began yelling prompts. The bunfight deteriorated into a riot. A three-way spat between a hissing man, the woman who had slapped him, and her escort led to the declaration of a duel, to take place the following day. A number of audience members were arrested, and the performance was halted.[60]

Stravinsky was part of a Russian classical musical movement that sought to find inspiration in Russian folk traditions—to build a national classical musical style rather than simply to mimic the aesthetic traditions of western Europe. (This was something akin to remixes in haute cuisine in recent years. These moves, spearheaded by the likes of chef Ferran Adrià in Catalonia, Spain, reinvent peasant and popular dishes as something elite and refined.) Composers like Stravinsky and Prokofiev had introduced traditional melodies they heard in villages and adopted folktales collected by ethnographers. In a similar vein, between 1930 and 1945, the Brazilian composer Heitor Villa-Lobos composed his *Bachianas Brasileiras*, an orchestral suite that infused classical form with the Indigenous, African, and Portuguese folk rhythms and melodies of popular Brazilian culture—a "New World" Bach redux, as it were.[61]

Stravinsky's sources of inspiration, like those of a number of his contemporaries, were ancient. Yet the way he turned folk music into lines for orchestral instruments sounds novel and futuristic, even today. He made instruments play at the edges of their registers—the deep bassoon playing high, reedy, almost squeaking lines, for instance. For early audiences the result was deeply unfamiliar and a little off—uncanny. As conductor Michael Tilson Thomas puts it, "Stravinsky had gone too far forward in trying to go back."[62] For some the spectacle must have seemed like an undead version of a European past, one that the great and the good of Parisian society had never expected to see revivified before their eyes. Even worse, the ancient, the contemporary, and the future were blended into one—it was impossible to separate the urbane, sophisticated world of classical music from the rural, spirit-driven, presumably pitchfork-ridden universe of prehistoric Russia.

A decade later, in the aftermath of World War I, the self-styled bastions of high culture would offer similar, if less spectacular, criticism of a new musical genre that came into being on the other side of the Atlantic: jazz. Once again harmonies that transgressed Western classical music's major and minor scales and off-the-beat beats that raised one's adrenaline levels were held up by white parents as reasons why jazz—a genre created by African Americans—was corrupting the young. By the 1950s the jazz vanguard took a turn away from danceable music to music for its own sake, inventing a new subgenre along the way: bebop. A conscious disavowal of the minstrelsy tradition of white performers in blackface makeup pretending to be African American entertainers, bebop was for the musicians: the audience could take it or leave it.

The idea that "art" could be challenging rather than simply pleasant or entertaining is one that, at times, audiences continue to challenge. Yet for artists art is also a form of communication—and can be a form of resistance. What one wants to say with one's art may not be comfortable for those who watch, read, or listen to it. This is as much the case with the performing arts as it is the visual arts. Discomfort around color-conscious casting of theater and film, like the discomfort around blending an imagined traditional classical European music with other forms of music, signals the work that art invites societies to do on themselves: to examine whom they define as normal, who gets pushed out of the category of normal, and why.

SPORTS

Who gets to decide on the rules of sports? Who sits on the arbitration committees? While international decision-making bodies in sports and the assumptions behind them continue to default to participants and to ways of organizing the world from the Global North, they cannot be said to represent all of humanity. Debates about beauty, strangeness, excellence, disability, and belonging share one thing in common: conventional, even arbitrary, long-standing, often racially charged assumptions about the boundaries of normal.

Between 1967 and 1976, the National Basketball Association (NBA) banned players in the National Collegiate Athletic Association (NCAA) and in high school sports from using the slam dunk, a technique in which players jump high enough to put the ball through the hoop with their hands rather than releasing the ball in the air and throwing it in, making the shot much harder to deflect. The ban was widely interpreted as one aimed at curbing the unprecedented scoring power of Kareem Abdul-Jabbar (known as Lew Alcindor in high school and college), the seven-foot, one-inch college basketball player. Others suspected a broader racially motivated reason: Abdul-Jabbar was Black, as were most of the players who used the dunk.

Sports is an arena in which human physical norms and technical abilities are regularly invented and policed by officials and by viewers. Some rule changes are ostensibly related to the necessity of a professional sport remaining entertaining enough to be profitable, as techniques, technology, and serendipitous anatomical alignments lift individual athletes into leagues of their own. In the 2000s the grass at the All England Tennis Club in Wimbledon, South London, was gradually resowed to make the ball bounce slightly higher, giving returners an extra tenth of a second to hit the ball. This was the age of Pete Sampras's almost unreturnable serve, the colossus among giant serves that had, for a time, turned the long rallies of 1980s men's tennis, with its tiny rackets and even tinier shorts, into a TV memory. Big servers' games had felt, at times, like serving exhibitions rather than tennis matches.

Other rule changes are couched as safety protocols to prevent athletes from attempting the most dangerous routines. Yet for the outstanding athletes who develop and perform such routines safely, the wording of rule changes can dismiss their excellence. In 2019 the African American gymnast Simone Biles successfully executed a particularly complicated dismount from the vault: a double-twisting double back, or two twists plus two flips. This combination had never been performed on the vault before, and, while it had entered the repertoire of routines on the floor in 1988, it remained rare to see it there. Competition judges got in a huddle to score Biles's extraordinary achievement. Vault scores include a difficulty tariff: the higher the difficulty of the moves in the projected vault, the higher the tariff and the higher the score. The judges awarded Biles's unprecedented dismount a tiny difficulty tariff, ostensibly to dissuade other athletes from attempting such a dangerous dismount.

There were other ways in which the judges could have addressed safety besides lowballing Biles's talents and achievements. The quality of a vault's execution was already part of the scoring system. The judges could have defined the vault as one that came with both a high difficulty tariff and high points deductions for flaws in execution. This would have dissuaded gymnasts for whom what came to be known as the Biles dismount was possible only by the skin of their teeth, clumsily, and with great risk of injury.[63] But by deciding otherwise, the judges framed Biles as outside of human athletic norms. Prodigious excellence, like disability, is social—a category created and imposed by people, in concert with their definition of normal. Both are invented and configured by rules, scoring, and accommodations—matters that lawyers, administrators, members of competition juries, and sports federation councils sit down and hash out, inventing individuals into the category of "monster" as they define the limits of normal.

For Wesley Morris, critic at large at the *New York Times*, the tennis superstars and sisters Venus and Serena Williams were "human Rorschach tests": spectators revealed their assumptions and prejudices through how they responded to the Williams sisters. One could say the same about tennis umpires and linespeople. The poet, playwright, and essayist Claudia Rankine wrote movingly about Serena Williams's experiences of racism on the tennis court and how the strength it took to be Serena seemed possible only in fiction. She endured dubious line calls at critical match moments over the years before snapping, at which point she became the media's sports villain. Stories and committee judgments told this way strip away the context that gives meaning to a person's actions.[64]

Protocol for polite behavior and professional conduct often requires judgment calls from umpires. Did someone mutter a rude word on the tennis court or not? Did they argue for too long over a line call? Comparing the on-court behavior of tennis players John McEnroe and Serena Williams suggests that point and game deductions for code violations (for arguing, swearing, and racquet abuse) have been unevenly applied to the two athletes. Their long careers overlapped only briefly. Nevertheless, patterns of debate about what is or isn't acceptable—success, confidence, clothing, discourse—for women athletes, Black and Brown athletes, and in particular Black women athletes reveal that tennis authorities don't apply the same standards of "normal" or "acceptable" to all tennis players. How—and if—they apply rules depends on, and draws power and legitimacy from, their values and assumptions. Societal conventions, laws, and privileges apply unevenly to athletes depending on the color of their skin, as does courtesy—or lack thereof—from spectators. Black football players in Europe still sometimes suffer the indignity of having bananas hurled at the pitch when they play.

Visual stereotypes of people of African descent have been part of the Western landscape for centuries: medieval maps dividing Africa's peoples between enthroned kings and monsters; advertising posters depicting even the unwashable Ethiopian's Blackness coming off under the power of Sunlight soap; blackface performances in the United States in the nineteenth century; and the Netherlands depicting Santa's helper as Zwarte Piet, or Black Pete. In this context the Australian newspaper *Herald Sun*'s 2018 cartoon rendition of Serena Williams destroying her racquet activates deep reservoirs of dehumanizing, racist imagery and assumptions, reservoirs whose contents bubble up to society's surface at regular intervals.[65] The scene in the newspaper cartoon shows Williams floating in midair, midjump, hovering over a broken racquet. An infant's pacifier lies on the ground nearby, implying that Williams is behaving childishly. This formulation was baked into the racial categories that European intellectuals crafted during the age of Atlantic slavery: one of the justifications of slavery and of discriminatory practices in its aftermath was the claim that African peoples—and many other colonized peoples—had the mental capacities of children.

Perhaps in no sport is artistic style more entangled with athletic ability than it is in gymnastics. A 2021 lead story in the sports section of the *Houston Chronicle* activated another dehumanizing motif that Europe and its white-majority former colonies have long leveled at Black people: the trope of the animal. The headline announces that "[Simone] Biles finds beauty in beastly athleticism."[66] According to correspondent David Barron, one has only to ask Biles how the world of gymnastics rates her artistry to "darken her day." According to Biles, "They don't want to talk about my artistry. They already say it's horrible." Biles's own judgment of her performance is that she brings "power and elegance in power." The headline writer's own, perhaps unconscious, position and certainly his tin ear for context, history, and language are betrayed by the contrast between "beauty" and "beastly athleticism." Barron himself leverages the word "darken" to mean something negative.[67] These word choices undercut Biles, who had asserted that strength and beauty are not mutually exclusive. They also implicitly question whether Black can be beautiful.

In 2009 eighteen-year-old South African runner Caster Semenya prepared for the World Championships in Berlin. Before traveling, she was sent for what she thought were routine drugs tests. They turned out to be invasive gender tests. The day before the 800 meter final, she was summoned and subjected to more tests. The International Association of Athletics Federations (IAAF, now World Athletics) leaked the results to the press before communicating them to Semenya. This is how she learned that she had a difference in sexual development, on the day she won a gold medal. Semenya felt dehumanized by the ensuing press treatment and public reactions: "It was as if the entirety of humanity had discovered some kind of alien that looked like them but wasn't them had been living amongst them." For some she fell outside the category of the human. It felt like "being wiped off the map of humanity."[68]

The IAAF decided that, since Semenya's body produced more testosterone than they considered normal for a woman, for her to continue to compete in women's events she had to have a gonadectomy: surgery to remove the organs that produce testosterone. Semenya's lawyers negotiated a less horrific, but still horrible, alternative: Semenya would take drugs to reduce her testosterone levels, despite the unpleasant and potentially long-term side effects. Semenya took the drugs, endured the side effects for years, and kept running. In 2011 the IAAF finally announced an official number for testosterone levels for women's events. Years of arbitration and lawsuits around athletes' gender tests and medical interventions ensued.[69]

In 2018 the IAAF announced new, even more stringent testosterone regulations, rules that would apply only to athletes with DSD competing in three middle-distance events. The IAAF had officially defined the category of women by one number—one that mattered so much that it apparently applied only for the events in which Semenya competed. And the IAAF hadn't proved that the way elite athletes' bodies responded to testosterone gave them an unfair advantage. In 2019 a sports arbitration court ruled that the IAAF could continue to use testosterone levels to limit participation in women's events.[70]

Some critics of the ruling argue that this number was devised using testosterone levels in white women, thus removing the majority of the world's women from the equation, delegitimizing them from the start. Others observed that a person's sex cannot be determined by a number and that conventional categories of sex are socially agreed-on conventions with a history. The conventions in international athletics were created by white men for whom whiteness and the difference between "men" and "women" were default lenses through which they saw the world—their subjective viewpoint—and through which they had selected and interpreted evidence. Individuals who are intersex—who have a combination of attributes commonly associated with women as well as those commonly associated with men—do not fit neatly into a rigid binary division of sex.[71]

Semenya argued that if someone spent her life growing up as a girl, identifying and living as a woman, then it is as a woman that she should be allowed to compete, without medical intervention. She observed that no one pushes drugs or surgery on the likes of swimming legend Michael Phelps or Usain Bolt, whose physiological differences contributed to their success.[72] Evidently for men, the sky—or the divine—is the limit, whereas women athletes, especially Black and Brown women, are policed or crushed into a narrow vision of embodiment and achievement, at greater risk of anonymous allegations to the IAAF that they are supposedly too fast, too strong, and too masculine, triggering investigations. Semenya was not the first athlete to have her life turned upside-down this way.

Gender policing disproportionately rules against athletes from ethnicities where women's typical testosterone levels are higher than those of white women. Being internationally competitive in sports is about far more than testosterone and encompasses economic advantages that make it possible to train from a young age and that shape the environment in which an athlete lives, works, and grows.[73] Pathologizing athletes with DSD today is part of a larger pattern of monstrifying individuals who appear different from local norms. As we've seen in this book, people judged as having too much hair or too much or too little height or being in various ways unusually embodied have often had their privacy and personhood trampled. And the recent uptick in gender policing stereotypes all women, creating conditions for investigating, harassing, and excluding anyone who identifies as a woman but who does not look or act like the stereotypical white damsel with long straight hair like Rapunzel in the fairy tale.

When people label individuals or groups as category problems for failing to fit into a box, those finger pointers are in fact pointing at fears in their own imaginations: at the thought that the category of the human is malleable, that their own bodies are squishy rather than fixed, that there is no simple line between "normal" and "abnormal," and that—who knows—in another life, in a parallel universe, at some point in the future, society might label the labelers themselves as category problems.

SEVEN

Gods, Magic, and the Supernatural

RELIGIONS, COSMOLOGIES, AND EXPLANATIONS of the observable world have framed a wide range of individuals and practices as atypical or singular. One quality that some of them shared was the apparent capacity to traverse the murky conduit between visible and invisible or intangible worlds that cannot be accessed at will. Sometimes cultures considered those who crossed this threshold as threats or anomalies. In other cases, perhaps confusingly, they viewed monstrosity as a regular aspect of their cosmology, even of their gods.

GODS AND ORIGIN STORIES

The history of how people have understood what "human" means is bound up with how people have defined the divine. One is almost the monster of the other—very like them but across a divide that is generally, but not always, unbridgeable, like the humans purportedly made in God's image in Christianity. Epics and origin stories from ancient central Eurasia, in the region roughly east of present-day Greece and west of India, often pitted a human (usually a man) against a monster. The most famous example today is *The Epic of Gilgamesh*, the oldest written work containing a monster and perhaps the oldest extended piece of literature that still survives. The earliest surviving versions date around the late second millennium BCE. *Gilgamesh* was written in Sumerian, one of the languages of ancient Mesopotamia, in what is now southern Iraq. Scribes pressed the characteristic bird-print wedges of cuneiform script onto clay tablets. The epic's relationship to historical rulers remains unclear.[1] Narratives like *Gilgamesh* provided source material for many ancient Greek myths, those sweeping accounts of galactically ancient deeds of the gods and of the dawn of the cosmos. They formed part of a much broader and deeper pattern of influence of western Asian culture and science in ancient Greece.[2]

King Gilgamesh, made by the gods, was said to be perfect: one part human and two parts divine. He conquered the city of Uruk, in present-day southern Iraq, but then ruled as a tyrant. His despairing subjects begged the gods for help; they created Gilgamesh's polar opposite as his adversary: Enkidu, a wild man who grew up with animals. He had hair "thick as grain," in some accounts, that covered his body like that of an animal and bestial lifeways like eating grass and living in the forest rather than with people.[3] But the plot is foiled. A series of peculiar events activated Enkidu's human brain, and he was led to Uruk. Here Enkidu was entranced by Gilgamesh, whom he viewed as a worthy adversary—and the city a worthy prize to wrest from him in battle. But their battle ended in a draw, and the two became friends, a story arc that recurs regularly in modern superhero stories. The two superhumans later set out together to kill a monster, Humbaba. Many shenanigans later the gods punished Enkidu's actions against them by killing him. Gilgamesh grieved for his friend by going on a quest for personal immortality. He failed and returned to Uruk, where he came to terms with the city as his legacy.

In the *Gilgamesh* epic, the boundaries between god, human, and animal are porous. Gilgamesh begins as part divine, yet, faced with his friend's death, desires nothing more than to break another barrier, between human and immortal. Enkidu has a wild, almost animal side, yet it is through his influence that Gilgamesh becomes a better ruler. The larger moral is the value of tempering "civilized" predilections (like tyranny) with nature (in the form of the wild, simpler life Enkidu once led) and the human desire to control how change unfolds, even though our power is limited.

Gods are beings who bring beings into being, particularly the beings calling them gods. Many cultures have understood the origins of humanity as involving making humans out of other beings and substances. The beings doing the making are, by definition, referred to as gods. Creation is by definition an act of monster-making—of making something unprecedented, a type of being beyond existing categories of beings. The very idea of an origin includes the idea of breaking categories: something unprecedented is going to be brought into being. In that sense, divinity and humanity are each other's monsters. Gods sometimes made humans by breaking open the category of god. At times communities demonize individuals or groups for being too different. Yet category breakers are part of the consequences of having a classificatory system at all. The leveling up and down across the categories of god and human puts pressure on conventions about where human skill and power end.

The gods of classical Eurasian antiquity created monsters, humans, hybrids, and the very stuff of the universe. What might today be called cosmic time—eons marked by the different states of matter in the universe and by the level of coalescence of heavenly bodies—was marked by epic moments of genesis and battle. Astronomically significant entities like Gaia (the earth) birthed new sorts of beings; quasi-humanoid and monstrous gods fought intergenerational struggles for cosmic supremacy, killing or (in the case of Cronos, who was Gaia's son) even eating their own offspring in their attempts to prevent being ousted.

In the eighth-century BCE epic poem *Theogony* (or *Origin of the Gods*), attributed to the poet Hesiod, many of the earliest entities in the void of the universe were gross prototypes—less-than-ideal first drafts of Ruin and Death. Gaia mated with Ouranos, the sky, to produce entities both human in form and monstrous: the Titans (giants in some versions of the story), the Cyclopes (one-eyed giants), and the baffling Hecatoncheires (monsters who sported fifty heads and a hundred hands). The twelve Titans mated with Gaia to produce the next generation that, in turn, tried to kill off its forebears. Zeus, one of the Titans' offspring, defeated them altogether.[4] Greek gods who mated with mortals gave birth to new forms of beings—demigods— unlike themselves. Demigods were monsters in the sense outlined by the ancient Greek philosopher Aristotle: they were children fundamentally different in kind from their parents. In this framework for the universe, god and human were porous categories.

In Mesoamerican cosmologies it was not one-off individuals who were descended from gods but all beings, after a fashion. In these worldviews beings were composed of divine essences: the gods had put a certain something of themselves into all their creations. Understanding the cosmos encouraged treating physical things—"living" or not—with respect: everything had a sentient, divine essence. Even plants and animals consumed for food deserved to be acknowledged for giving up their forms so that others might continue to thrive.[5] Thus a number of origin stories from Mesoamerica detail how the gods required human sacrifice in exchange for the existence and continuation of human life on earth. In Quiché Maya cosmology, the gods raised land out of the sea, created animals, and then attempted to make beings who could speak. Their initial attempts failed, and the gods destroyed their creations, apart from a few who escaped—monkeys. Finally, they made humans out of maize. These gods, likewise, expected the originary humans to sustain them through worship and human sacrifice.[6]

In some Aztec cosmologies, the gods sacrificed themselves to create the sun and the world. In turn the gods needed to be fed, via human sacrifice, to repay this debt and to sustain the cycle. In one account Quetzalcoatl, among others, had created humans by combining blood from their penises with ground bones of previous generations of humans.[7] Aztec gods were often protean: some had multiple settings as types of beings with different shapes or had split personalities. Many gods took human form but had animal counterparts (see plate 1). Aztec sculptors and painters attempted to capture both the visible elements of beings in the world and their occult spiritual qualities and animal counterparts.[8] Elsewhere in Mesoamerica Mixtec gods took human form when they appeared in the material world.[9]

The Aztecs said that their ancestors had come from Aztlan, a place north of present-day Mexico City, and had conquered the peoples in the Central Valley, around what became the city of Tenochtitlan, present-day Mexico City.[10] The god Huitzilopochtli had guided the Aztecs' original migration, in the twelfth century, to Lake Texcoco, where they had founded the twin cities of Tenochtitlan and Tlalelolco around 1325 and 1338.[11] The Aztecs' arrival at the "right" place was apparently signaled by multiple category transmutations. The god Huitzilopochtli had spoken to one of the Aztecs' leaders in a dream, urging the Aztecs to perambulate through the world until they saw an eagle sitting on a nopal, or a prickly pear cactus. In one surviving version of the account, when the Aztecs reached Lake Texcoco, they saw an eagle consuming a snake while sitting atop a nopal; in another version the eagle eats a bird. The cactus had sprung out of the ground in the middle of a lake, where the Aztecs had flung the heart of an enemy after battle.[12] This lake was where the Aztecs settled and founded the city of Tenochtitlan.[13] Embedded in this explanation is the cycle of nourishment between the bodies of enemies—just as the cactus seemingly grew from an enemy's heart, warriors and, in turn, communities absorbed something of the strength and attributes of those they vanquished.

In Jewish, Christian, and Islamic religious texts, monsters also appear in descriptions of the end of the world. And sometimes they appear at moments

FIGURE 30. Diego Durán, illustration of an eagle eating a snake on a cactus, in *Historia de las Indias*, 1579. In one cosmology the god Huitzilopochtli told an Aztec leader in a dream that this omen would appear where the Aztecs should settle. Vitr/26/11. From the collections of the Biblioteca Nacional de España, Madrid, fol. 14v.

where human history and myth collide, sewing together origin stories with more recent events. The misadventures of the monstrous tribes known as Gog and Magog did both. Gog and Magog, examined in chapter 4, were said to be descended from Japheth, one of Noah's three sons. That meant they were related to humanity by blood. For Christian writers they were enemies expected to destroy the world at the end times. In a monster-blending move, from around the twelfth century, medieval maps began conflating Gog and Magog with Jews, who were then facing restrictions and expulsion.[14]

The tribes appear in accounts of the military expeditions into India of Alexander the Great (356–323 BCE) of Macedon (now a region in the northeastern Mediterranean). Herodotus, a historian who tagged along on the general's campaigns, chronicled the expedition, describing how Alexander directed the building of a wall to imprison the monstrous tribes. In Herodotus's telling Gog and Magog would spend their days attempting to break through the wall; each night God would mend it. The monsters were expected to multiply until they consumed all the water in neighboring regions and, at the Last Judgment, or the end of time, to finally break out from beyond Alexander's wall and embark on a killing spree, to be stopped by God only when they attacked the sky.[15] Accounts of how Alexander's men imprisoned Gog and Magog appear in Islamic texts including the Qu'ran, as well as in Jewish and Christian texts like the Book of Genesis.

The twelfth-century Arab Persian geographer Zakariya Al-Qazwini's geographic and cosmographic treatise, *Marvels of Things* (*'Ajâ'ib al-Makhlûqât*), details a variety of beings who stretched across the boundary between human and "something else": beings with human bodies and animal heads, humanoid eaters of human flesh. Many of the monsters in Al-Qazwini's cosmography parallel accounts in ancient Greek and Roman texts and illuminate millennia of cultural cross-fertilization across ancient Afro-Eurasia.[16]

A nineteenth-century Persian manuscript illustrates a vivid action scene. Alexander the Great and his troops wait in front of the wall he had built to contain the monstrous side of Noah's extended family (see plate 8).[17] The edifice appears not to have been high enough; a naked female giant with flowing hair, presumably a member of one of the monstrous peoples, scales it. Another giant has escaped as well, as he stands thigh-high in the water, facing Alexander and his troops. Perhaps the Gog and Magog tribes included beings who could swim and tunnel below the wall's foundations. Alexander and his elegantly dressed retinue point at their own mouths and eyes as if rendered speechless as they witness their wall-building efforts turned to naught. Just as the wall has proved to be an imperfect physical barrier, perhaps it is also an imperfect cultural and genealogical barrier. The dark-skinned giant in the water sports a rich blue skirt decorated with almost the same patterning as the tunic worn by one of Alexander's men. The woman atop the wall has the same skin tone as the troops gazing on her.[18]

Gods in origin stories from Eurasia and Central America show how these cultures built the idea of monstrosity—the bending and breaking of categories of beings—into their understanding of the world, the divine sphere, even the lineage of humanity itself. Human, god, monster, and animal were overlapping, elastic, and porous categories: one could be more than one at once and transform from one to the other.

SOULS

Not only have human bodies been cast by epics, religion, and cosmologies as malleable and potentially monstrous, but so have human souls. Many religions have understood a human as having a physical body and an incorporeal spirit or spirits, soul, or life force. In East Asian cosmologies, the soul is not even tethered to a single earthly species, as we saw in the alarming tale of the human-mouse wedding in chapter 2. Humans are like a jar into which their soul would no longer fit if they behave too badly, and they might end up being reincarnated as a beast. Conversely, beings in the spirit world can be elevated into the human world through faithfulness.[19]

In cosmologies in which souls can both enter and leave the body, exactly where an individual being begins and ends is unclear. Passing from life to death with the consequent translation of the soul to somewhere else makes the category of the human more fluid than a solidly in-this-universe, only-flesh-and-biochemistry understanding of the human would. The body might die, yet the soul can endure. For the ancient Greek philosopher Aristotle, souls had multiple parts: the vegetative and appetitive parts were irrational; the intellective part was rational, and only humans possessed it. Souls had multiple levels, and only humans possessed the highest level. In Christianity the human soul is immortal and expected to be reunited with its body at the end of time. In Hinduism souls migrate from body to body as one body dies and another is born.

In Nahua cosmology the souls of the dead might choose to commune with the living by meeting them soul-to-soul in another, normally invisible dimension. This way of framing the effect of the dead on the living expands the category of the human beyond the corporeal being who is limited to action only while its body persists. Today's experiments in storing the brain's biochemical impulses attempt to preserve human consciousness outside the body and to mimic brain function through brain-on-a-chip technology. They may even suggest a theoretical way of gaining access to a "soul" whose body is no longer living.[20] The idea of the soul, an immaterial driver of the body, presupposes the existence of an invisible, intangible world that most people cannot access at will. It builds supernatural encounters into the "normal" of humans. It suggests that the body and soul can go about their business separately. As we'll see, fears about this separation fueled anxiety about where human ended and other, sinister beings began.

As discussed at this book's beginning, shape-shifters were part of the natural order for the Nahua people (of which the Aztecs were a tribe). The very gods disguised themselves as snakes, eagles, jaguars, and hummingbirds when it suited them.[21] Ritual specialists (popularly known in the West as shamans) could control animals, have an animal analog or doppelganger, or even take on the attributes of animals by wearing their pelts. The Nahua identified an enormous range of ritual specialists, each with distinctive powers.[22] The *tla-*

catecolotl compresses victims' hearts and "turns himself into a dog, a bird, into a chicuatli, a chichtli, a teculotl owl."[23] In the colonial period, missionaries and scholars attempting to make sense of these beliefs came to understand that ritual specialists, *nahualli*, really could take the form of animals like owls, whose eerie calls could kill those who believed in them.[24] They understood *nahualli* to control aspects of the natural world and the health of their communities.[25]

A person's *tonalli* was one of the three types of life force in Aztec belief, and it could migrate to their companion animal (also called a *nahual*). But it could also be in human bodies and, simultaneously, in their *nahual*. People and their *nahual* would then have the same sensations—and the same fate as in the case of an injury done to animals, prompting an injury to people who were somewhere else entirely, minding their own business. Most people could not control their shape-shifting. But *nahualli* could disguise themselves as animals at will and seemingly turn other people and things into animals and natural phenomena.[26] Hallucinogens, intoxicants, and a person's psychological state could also prompt transformation, as could the workings of a *nahualli*. Drink too much alcohol or pulque, and you risked becoming a rabbit.[27]

What came after death might be uncertain, even terrifying. In medieval Christianity options for the soul in the afterlife were heaven, hell, or purgatory. Actions of contrition and repentance for sins (or lack of it) during life had helped to determine where souls ended up in death.[28] An early sixteenth-century Portuguese panel painting of hell depicts a group of people who have, apparently, failed to be good enough to get into heaven (see plate 9). Some languish in an infernal cauldron; others face bodily torment from monsters wielding alarming tools and weapons. The monsters combine human and animal attributes like wings and "wrong" body parts, like the three-eyed figure in the back left-hand portion. Some of the figures in the cauldron are tonsured—the tops of their heads shaven—revealing that they are men from Christian religious orders. So, too, is one of the demons in the left-hand corner, a winged figure with a woman's breasts who stuffs what looks like a thick coin into someone's mouth. This painting probably hung in a monastery, where many of its viewers would themselves have been tonsured.

Some seventy years after the start of Portuguese voyages down the west coast of Africa, and barely three decades after the first Portuguese expeditions to land in the Americas, the painter's go-to visuals for hell included

FIGURE 31. Painting of hell, detail, Museu Nacional de Arte Antiga, Lisbon, circa 1510–20. The winged, skull-faced devil sports the feather costume and headdress that European viewers associated with the inhabitants of the Caribbean. By the late fifteenth century, elephant-ivory hunting horns, or oliphants, made by West African artisans were circulating in Europe. Museu Nacional de Arte Antiga, Lisbon, Portugal/Bridgeman Images, XIR173185.

motifs from Africa and the Americas. The devil enthroned at the top of the painting brandishes an oliphant, a type of ivory hunting horn made in West Africa, and carries a small bag on a string. He is dressed in a feather costume and headdress, items that Europeans had associated with Indigenous peoples of the Caribbean region since the late fifteenth century. By implying that Africans and Indigenous inhabitants of the Americas were devils (or at least colluded with the devil), the painter has dehumanized them—just as they were being dehumanized geopolitically and militarily by being dispossessed (in the case of the peoples of the Americas), dehumanized by enslavement (Africans and peoples of the Americas), and dehumanized spiritually (both groups faced forcible baptism, the destruction of their sacred objects, and acts of cultural genocide).

Visual images in colonial Latin America explored the afterlife in scenes that drew from Indigenous and Christian cosmology and visual traditions. In the Andes, murals of the roads to heaven and hell prepared viewers for the creatures they would meet en route. Particularly vivid examples are the

FIGURE 32. Paths to heaven and hell, Church of San Pedro Apóstol de Andahuaylillas, Peru, circa 1620s. This fresco appears at the entrance of a Jesuit church, built between 1570 and 1606 on top of an Indigenous ceremonial space. A devil on the hell side of the scene pulls on a rope attached to a man on the path to heaven, on the other side. Through the labeled biblical themes, parishioners leaving the building received visual reminders of the contrasting futures that their actions would create. Photo © Pilar Rau.

murals of the paths to heaven and to hell, circa 1620s, in the Church of San Pedro Apóstol de Andahuaylillas. The richly decorated interior earned the church the title of the "Sistine Chapel of the Americas" over a century ago. Various points on the paths are labeled with letters, and an alphabetical key describes the scenes (see plate 10).[29] The route to heaven, lined with angels, transports the soul to a paradisiacal dining table. The route to hell, guarded by monsters and demons, takes souls to a fiery end.

Souls, or consciousness, are a category for parts of sentient beings that make them truly "them," even more so than their bodies. For cultures that speak of them, souls are anchors, only they are anchored not in that which is solid but in that which is invisible, making them uncanny and strange, made from not entirely straightforward material. By making humans volatile and changeable, souls have the potential to make humans monstrous: deeply varied and multifarious rather than straightforwardly and unambiguously fixed.

Souls could function as mediators that connected the fleshy, physical world one can touch to dimensions that exist beyond the senses. By entering particular states of consciousness, humans might choose to cross the line from the material universe to the spiritual realm and function as intermediaries between worlds. Such translations across dimensions appear in a variety of ancient religions. Many are related to certain obligations of humans toward their gods.

RITUALS OF POWER AND THE HUMAN-DIVINE CONNECTION

A vase in the Museum of Fine Arts in Boston records and depicts an ancient Maya ruler—Yajawte' K'inich, divine ruler of the Ik' polity—and two attendants performing a vision-quest dance and a ritual blood sacrifice. An inscription records the date of the event: 7 Ok 13 Xul, or May 25, 749 BCE. This may have been the date on which Yajawte' K'inich underwent one of the rituals that transformed an ordinary individual into a divinely ordained ruler. The performers wear costumes that depict animal hybrids: jaguar-crustacean, jaguar-centipede, and jaguar-eagle, which may represent the dancers' companion animals.[30] For peoples of Mesoamerica and Greater Amazonia, wearing durable parts of animal bodies—teeth, pelts, feathers— was a way of absorbing the animals' powers.[31]

The immaterial world is a source of power and authority in many cosmologies. People who seem to have access to spirits or gods have long been revered, even feared. Charlemagne, the first Holy Roman emperor, was crowned by Pope Leo III in Rome on Christmas Day, in the year 800. Starting around the seventh century, Christian monarchs in Europe argued for the legitimacy of their rule "by the grace of God." Their coronations also became religious rituals and were framed as moments when a royal person became a divinely ordained, quasi-divine, crowned monarch.

The process of coronation is, in my view, a ritual process of monstrification: the monarch is supposedly no longer straightforwardly a mortal human but rather one possessed with what historian Ernst Kantorowicz memorably described as "the king's two bodies." One body is mortal and physical, the other mystical and spiritual. This doubling parallels how members of certain Christian denominations understand Christ himself in a binary fashion, with a mortal body and a universal institutional presence on earth in the form of the church (not to mention his trinitarian existence as part of the Son, Father, and Holy Ghost).[32] In France and England, kings—and, on the very few occasions that they inherited the throne when their kingly father

FIGURE 33. The path to heaven, Church of San Pedro Apóstol de Andahuaylillas, Peru, circa 1620s. The sheeted figure in the foreground experiences both diabolical temptation (the rope pulling him toward hell's maw) and a vision of the Holy Trinity in the form of the three identical men on the balcony. Photo © Pilar Rau.

had no sons, queens—ruled by divine order. The monarch was the head of each kingdom's church, albeit under agreement from the pope, until King Henry VIII declared himself head of the Church of England. Upon coronation these monarchs were imbued with an element of divinity that both legitimated their rule and set them apart from their subjects.

FIGURE 34. Diego Durán, illustration of a sacrificial ritual, in *Historia de las Indias*, 1579. The priest in the center wears the pelt of an apex predator. Vitr/26/11. From the collections of the Biblioteca Nacional de España, Madrid, fol. 103v.

Between the Middle Ages and the eighteenth century, monarchs were believed to possess a superpower known as the "royal touch." Simply by laying their hands on a sick person—typically someone with scrofula (a painful disease of the lymph nodes now known as tubercular adenitis), leprosy, or a disabled limb—monarchs could heal them. Some sufferers were so ill that they could not walk and had to be carried.[33] During the ceremony of the royal touch, monarchs would touch each sick person, acting in this sense like a magical healer, their actions reminiscent of accounts of Jesus Christ healing the sick.[34] The royal-touch ceremony was purportedly a medical miracle made possible by divine will, which had anointed God's legitimate political representatives on earth purportedly through their coronation—another sacred ritual. Successful performance (and many did think themselves to be improved after experiencing the royal touch) was demonstrative proof of monarchical legitimacy.

Forming medieval European kingdoms involved building relationships based on socially accepted stories about different kinds of beings. The king was purportedly a different sort of being from his nobles, who in turn were different from the peasants on their lands. Questioning the distinct rights, privileges, obligations, and responsibilities of each group was consequently a big deal and not for the fainthearted. By performing ceremonies that only monarchs were capable of executing, kings (or the occasional queen) placed themselves closer to the divine in the eyes of their subjects.

Things that some would describe as inanimate objects were (and still are) believed to connect the visible world to divine, diabolical, and supernatural forces. Sometimes it is physical bodies or body parts that become identified as uncanny—as weird in ways that suggest mysterious forces. Observers or religious authorities might end up identifying these objects as relics: things imbued with miraculous qualities or magical powers, often by virtue of the saint or religious leader from whose body they arose or touched. In the Catholic Church, a relic is either a part of a person or an item that is significant, such as Mary's veil, and that is capable of interceding with God. Some relics comprised the bodies or body parts of saints or martyrs, such as a tortured limb, bones, teeth, or hair. The sick and the dying would line up for the chance to touch or even see relics, for they were said to have miraculous healing powers.[35]

Christian relics were and still are often stored in ornate receptacles—reliquaries—made of precious materials. Reliquaries sometimes take the form of the relic within them—an arm-shaped box to store an arm bone, for example—becoming almost a prosthetic for the relic itself, whose physical appearance is often underwhelming without knowledge of its story. Denuded of its awe-inspiring container and ritualistic setting, the average relic would be unrecognizable as a miraculous object.[36] In a church relics of multiple individuals might be stored together in a crypt. This is the case in the Basilique Saint-Sernin in Toulouse, France, where visitors can still view dozens of reliquaries in their damp, winding, subterranean resting place.

In the late eighth century, the Frankish emperor Charlemagne donated relics to the basilica, which then became a popular stop on the pilgrimage route to Santiago de Compostela in Spain. For believers objects that had come into contact with a divine or saintly figure could be imbued with supernatural powers.[37] Famous among these are the Passion relics, most of which were objects associated with Christ's torture and death, like the Turin Shroud, said to be the cloth in which Christ was wrapped after his deposition, and the cross and nails with which he was crucified. A thorn purported to have come from Christ's Crown of Thorns has been at Saint-Sernin since the thirteenth century; also preserved there is a relic deemed to have come from the True Cross. The body of the Spanish missionary Francis Xavier, who preached in Goa, India, apparently remained incorrupt after his death, as if by some miracle. Xavier's enduring body was one of the reasons why the Catholic Church declared him a saint.[38]

Bodies may be corporeal, but relics are social. People decide that some artifact or body part is a "relic." The number of exemplars of the same relic could be far greater than the amount of substance in the "original" body. Relics, like superheroes, can emerge seemingly out of nowhere when they are needed and fall out of fashion over time. Societies determine when a body part transcends the usual destiny of such things (decomposition) and when to declare that it straddles the boundary between this world and other worlds or heaven.[39] The bread and wine of the Catholic and Anglican ceremony of the Eucharist—in which what outwardly still looks like bread and wine is believed to have become the blood and body of Christ—is another example. Disagreement over transubstantiation—the miracle by which this is said to happen—was just one of the causes of the series of sixteenth-century religious schisms known as the Reformation, a movement that sprouted fears of all manner of monsters.

From the fifteenth century, Christian thinkers had begun to view as dangerous a variety of forms of difference that they had tolerated in the past. During the Reformation communities turned against themselves and families split apart. People monstrified one another on the grounds of their variant understandings of Christianity. Members of each new Christian denomination saw adherents of its rivals as monstrous by virtue (or vice) of their abhorrent beliefs and practices.[40] Christians were also appalled at the violence communities and armies enacted on one another in the name of religion. In the words of the scholar Cornelius Gemma, writing in the sixteenth century, "Fauns, Satyrs, . . . Cyclops, Centaurs, Pygmies, Giants, . . . Anthropophagi, and others of such kind . . . there is no need to travel as far as the New Islands. . . . [They] and beings more hideous still [exist] among us, now that the rules of justice are trampled underfoot, all humanity flouted, and all religion torn to bits."[41] For Gemma the violence and terror of the Reformation, when people attacked, killed, and hacked up their own neighbors, was as monstrous as anything in explorers' tales.

In the sixteenth and seventeenth centuries, around five thousand people were executed in Europe for holding religious beliefs that, in the eyes of religious and secular authorities where they lived, pushed them so far outside the flock of the redeemable as to be capital offenses. Yet for those who shared the views of the executed—perhaps one city-state over, in a place with a different official branch of accepted Christianity—these victims were martyrs or saints, not heretics or enemies of the church or state.

SUPERNATURAL OBJECTS AND FOODS

In some cultures material objects could have supernatural powers that reconfigured the essence of a person. Eating things could be a way of crossing dimensions, and enchanted foodstuffs could pierce the integrity of the body. In African and Indigenous American cultures, divine intervention in the condition of human bodies could form part of healing practices.[42] The Aztecs conceived of the universe as a series of spheres subdivided into planes. The highest level, Topan, was that of the heavens and comprised nine planes. The middle sphere, Tlalticpac, comprised the earth, including the sea, observable atmospheric effects, observable celestial bodies, and the beings on and in the earth. The lowest sphere, Mictlan, was subterranean and comprised the nine planes of the underworld.[43] People could consume, on purpose, things that shifted their shape or cracked the wall between earthly space and the divine world. Consuming substances like chocolate, tobacco, certain mushrooms, alcohol, and peyote resided at the core of rituals that pierced the gauze between the visible world and the spirit world. Hallucinogens produced visions and allowed their consumers to communicate effectively with gods.[44]

The potential efficacy of ritual practices carried out using materials or ingested substances from a new setting were a cause for concern for both enslaved Africans and Christian missionaries in the Americas.[45] Would objects of power continue to work after crossing an ocean? Would relationships with beings in the invisible world, such as gods and spirits, change? If key pieces in a certain ritual varied—if, say, making the bread and wine for mass had to happen without wheat or grapes—how would that affect the resonance of that performance? Experiencing material things of spiritual significance—regalia, objects of power, foodstuffs—shaped enduring ideas about beings in the world, from gold and wood to maize and chocolate.

In colonial Latin America, Catholic authorities worried that Indigenous and African foodstuffs and practices that Christians labeled as witchcraft would cause illness and worse in people who ate their foods. For anxious clerics those who prepared food—typically women or enslaved persons—

could potentially enchant what they or their parishioners ate to influence, or even to poison, them. In colonial Guatemala ordinary people categorized some illnesses as supernatural ones, caused by the practice of witchcraft. Indigenous, Black, and mixed-race individuals, along with women, were disproportionately more likely to be suspected of such practices. Folk healers and midwives, operating outside the regulated medical administration of the empire, appear in the archives of the Spanish Inquisition as well as in civil cases, accused of such crimes as poisoning people and causing them to fall in love with the "wrong" person.[46]

In 1550 the *cabildo*, or town council, of Tlaxcala (in central Mexico today) issued a decree in Nahuatl, titled "Against Dancing with Feathers Around the Crucifix." The decree declared that "it is to be ordered that no one take away, take down, or dance with the precious feathers and other kinds of feathers that are attached to all the church properties, the litter, and the case for covering the cross." Anyone who disobeyed would be fined the sum of eighty pesos. The fact that the *cabildo* issued this decree in Nahuatl reveals the *cabildo*'s central targets: people who were sufficiently Indigenous to understand Nahuatl.[47]

Such syncretic practices, blending Christian and Indigenous understand-ings of the supernatural and conventions for rituals, show up in documents about what not to do—like decrees prohibiting certain activities—and in inquisitorial witchcraft trials. Culturally mixed activities alarmed colonial religious administrators by confusing and subverting what they saw as proper forms of veneration. Implicitly, these variations were also a sign of the limited effect of Spanish spiritual teachings and colonial power and perhaps a sign of Indigenous resistance to political and cultural oppression.

In classical Mexico and Guatemala, for the Nahua (including the Aztecs) and Maya, chocolate was a drink and a potent ritual substance for millennia before the arrival of colonial settlers from Europe. Consuming chocolate with the appropriate ceremony brought about an altered state that suppos-edly permitted those who drank it to communicate with the gods.[48] In colo-nial New Spain, chocolate met much suspicion. The inquisition frequently tried, convicted, and burned at the stake Indigenous women accused of using cacao for the practice of witchcraft. In seventeenth-century Guatemala, women were accused of mixing ingredients of enchantment into chocolate drinks, which would mask the flavor of poisons, love potions, and concoctions to alter a person's temperament—that of a violent husband, for example.[49] Yet chocolate parties were all the rage in eighteenth-century Valencia, Spain. It was not entirely the substance that was the problem but rather who was consuming it and how.

Food, race, religion, and the body were entangled in the Spanish Empire.[50] For Indigenous peoples chocolate was a suitable substance to give to the gods, a practice that, in Christian eyes, amounted to idolatry. A key fear of Christian clerics in the Americas was that substances like chocolate, tobacco, coca, and peyote had mind-altering properties and transformative powers on the body and could turn white colonists and Christians into idolatrous *indios*.[51]

THE EARLY MODERN WITCH HUNT

In 1486 the soon-to-be-infamous witch-hunting manual, *Hammer of Witches*, began rolling off the presses in the German city of Speyer. Penned by the theologian and inquisitor Heinrich Kramer, the treatise would go through almost forty printings by 1670.[52] Kramer insisted that witches—individuals with unnatural powers procured by working for the devil—existed. And although there were also male witches—those learned in magic from books were called sorcerers—he contended that the majority of witches were women. Kramer invoked religious scriptures that cast aspersions on women and characterized them as "credulous," "naturally more impressionable," "intellectually like children," and morally dubious. He claimed that women had voracious sexual desires, practicing "many carnal abominations." He concluded that women were easily turned away from service to God and toward serving the devil. By using religious texts to intellectualize misogyny, Kramer defined women as a category of person innately sinful and most likely to practice witchcraft.[53]

Between the late fifteenth and eighteenth centuries, Europe and its overseas colonies experienced a spectacular and horrific form of monster-making: the early modern witch hunt.[54] It was, in part, a response to the fissuring of Christianity, a runaway train unleashed by the fracturing of religious communities over what "real" Christianity was and which practices were a perversion of the true religion. Treatises like Kramer's *Hammer of Witches* discussed the existence of witches, the threats they posed, and how to hunt them out and prosecute them.[55]

Magic had not always been seen as a major existential threat. Between about the fifth and late fifteenth centuries, various folk practices that Christian authorities considered as supernatural had been ignored by state and religious authorities. Indeed, the medical knowledge of women midwives and healers—skills that appeared mysterious to others— had been core societal contributions for centuries. Yet from the late fifteenth century forward, these spheres of activity were increasingly viewed by state officials, religious figures, and the general public as signs that people, and especially women, were consorting with the devil. In an era of centralizing state institutions and professionalizing medicine, rogue practitioners who promised alternative solutions threatened elite power. Whereas neighborly grumbles about someone cursing a cow would have previously been ignored by the authorities, anyone who had or claimed to have powers independent of the church and state was now a person of juridical interest.

In the early decades of the witch hunt, the majority of individuals accused of witchcraft were older women, sometimes healers or midwives. Older women who were no longer able to bear children—and especially women who had never married or had children of their own—were deemed by their friends and neighbors to be jealous of young, fertile women and thus easily tempted into using their powers to harm newborns or their mothers.[56] In this way the idea of the "normal" woman was tied to being under the control of a man and having the ability to bear children; postmenopausal women of independent means, whether they were rich or merely eking out a living as a midwife or healer, disrupted these norms.

The mysteries of generation and childbirth have always stirred a mixture of wonder, apprehension, and, especially if things began to go awry, fear. In the event of the death or illness of a newborn or a new mother, grief-stricken attempts to understand misfortune led some bereaved parents and relatives to accuse the midwife. Faced with medical mysteries and misfortunes they did not understand, demonizing midwives and healers—those who seemed to hold power over life and death—was a way to make sense of loss.

A witchcraft accusation could also be a weapon against women, particularly against older women. Women were accused of poisoning children, causing male impotence, injuring animals, and making entire fields of crops wither away.[57] Targets who were independently wealthy were viewed with suspicion for breaking the social norms of dependence on a father or a husband. Poor women faced resentment for the strain they might put on a community's resources in times of hardship.

In the fifteenth century, the question of how women acquired unusual powers over nature became loaded with fears of diabolism, or the worshipping of the devil rather than of God. Witches were believed to have sex with the devil, who then acted on the world to make the witches' spells work.[58] The signs of a witch were that their bodies and behavior were inversions of norms. A late fifteenth-century engraving by Albrecht Dürer captures this sense: a naked, somewhat wrinkled, muscular woman rides backward on a goat. Making someone ride backward on an animal was a common punishment for people believed to have transgressed gender roles and moral conventions. The woman's clutch on the goat's horn and the distaff, or spinning tool, heighten the sense of sexual transgression.[59]

Between the sixteenth and eighteenth centuries, women were far more likely to be accused of consorting with the devil or performing evil magic than men. The Salem witch trials in colonial New England are an infamous example. Women were also targets of witchcraft accusations in colonial Latin America, where they were generally suspected of subverting religious and social norms. In the 1690s the head of Guatemala's inquisition went so far as to complain that there were so many "shameless women" that there were insufficient jails to contain them.[60]

Witchcraft trials were storyboarding events: inquisitors (for cases tried in religious courts, lawyers (for those tried in secular courts), witnesses, accusers, and their victims collaborated—willingly or not—in cocreating explanations that erupted with monstrous, diabolical acts for everything from biblical floods to everyday life and its misfortunes.[61] At the height of the panic, no one was safe from being storyboarded as a witch. In the 1720s parents in the city of Augsburg in the southern German province of Bavaria got it into their heads that their children were performing obscene and brutal acts under diabolical direction. Some twenty children, most of them aged between six and ten, were suspected. Their own parents asked the city council to imprison them.[62]

Accounts of what witches got up to came out of testimony and confessions obtained under torture. These are notoriously unreliable: people will say whatever they think will stop the torture. Surviving records reveal great numbers of trials in which people protested their innocence and then, under torture, admitted to guilt, gradually expanding on their tales until the

FIGURE 35 *(left)*. Albrecht Dürer, *Witch Riding Backwards on a Goat*, engraving, circa 1500. Motifs like the gender of the witch and her wrinkled, aged body and transgressive behavior—riding backward, naked, and holding onto a goat's horn—constituted the stereotype of the witch in sixteenth-century European culture. 19.73.75, Metropolitan Museum of Art, New York. Fletcher Fund, 1919.

FIGURE 36 *(right)*. Hans Baldung Grien, *The Witches*, chiaroscuro woodcut, circa 1510. This scene encapsulates sixteenth-century fears about witches: they gathered in secret, at night, to bewitch food-stuffs and perform rituals. 41.1.201, Metropolitan Museum of Art, New York. Gift of Felix M. Warburg and his family, 1941.

torture ceased. Their confessions, drawing on common beliefs about witches, were speckled with descriptions of flying through the air, encounters with the devil that included sex and beatings, and poisoning and killing people and animals.[63]

Printed images populated viewers' imaginations with witches in action. Hans Baldung Grien's early sixteenth-century woodcut of a witches' sabbath shows a naked witch flying backward to an assignation. Three equally naked witches sit around a cauldron. They signal women's control over the food they cook but also invert its nourishing function. The skulls of a child and a horse suggest the residue of diabolical feasting. The roasting sausages echo popular myths about witches' power to make men impotent. Noxious clouds billow from the cauldron, and its pseudo-Hebrew lettering activates anti-Semitic myths of sacrificial rituals.[64]

Moreover, a trial confession was not penned by the defendant, who might well have been illiterate, anyway, but by an inquisitor or court recorder. All this does not mean that inquisitorial witchcraft trial sources are useless, however. Rather, it is a question of thinking through precisely *what* it is that they tell us.[65] People who suspected that their very neighbors were witches feared that individuals with superhuman, diabolical powers were acting against them. In 1628 witchcraft denunciations in Bamberg, Germany, rose through the social and political ranks of the city to reach its mayor, Johannes Junius, who was interrogated and tortured.

The trial records detail how Junius began by protesting his innocence. Once torture in the form of thumbscrews, leg screws, and *strappado* (tying him to a pulley) was applied, he confessed to having become a witch after having sex with a strange woman, who then transformed into a goat and threatened to kill him unless he renounced God and gave his service to the devil. A letter that Junius wrote to his daughter during his incarceration provides a firsthand window into the experience of torture for the alleged crime of witchcraft. Junius noted that each of the six people who had denounced him had told him they'd been forced to make false accusations, going on to beg him for forgiveness as they went to their executions. Of his own doings, he noted, "Innocent I have come to prison, innocent have I been tortured, innocent must I die. For whosoever comes into the witch prison must become a witch or be tortured until he invents something out of this head.... And so I made my confession as follows, but it was all a lie."[66]

One of the ways in which witch hunts die out is that they spread so widely and lead to so many people denounced that they lose all credibility. The cracks in European witch hunt reasoning appeared when extremely powerful individuals, high-ranking men, and children were denounced as witches and, at times, went to trial and worse. Once there were too many witches and a constant rain of ever more accusations, the legal apparatus—the courts—began to shut down, and prosecutions ceased. When the accusations cut so deeply and broadly through society, they framed so many people as monstrous that the only way out of the crisis was to decide that, in fact, no one was monstrous.

In a number of West African and African diasporic religions, like Haitian vodun, spirit possession was believed to be possible: by performing particular rituals one could supposedly enable communication with spirits.[67] Embedded in these worldviews was the idea that a shaman could steal people's spirits and control their bodies. The Haitian practice of vodun mediated between the material and invisible worlds by turning embodied souls into entrapped ones. White plantation owners believed that witch doctors created beings called zombies, individuals in an in-between state of undeadness.

European observers and commentators framed vodun as a sign of things gone wrong, of the diabolical actions of African and Afro-Caribbean ritual practitioners who harnessed the power of the devil.[68] But zombiism was only a small part of a much larger set of practices, beliefs, and understandings of nature. Vodun and African and Afro-diasporic religions cut across modern Western categories of science, religion, medicine, and magic. This meant that, for example, African healing practices might be categorized by enslavers and religious inquisitors as idolatry.[69]

The Vatican archives contain a number of *bolsas de mandinga*, or medicine bundles, that African-descended people made, bought, exchanged, and wore in the era of Atlantic slavery. These *bolsas* typically comprised a combination of African ritual substances and European artifacts like paper containing writing (another form of magic to those who could not write, although the written word was also part of magical rituals of those who could, as in the case of Jewish magic). A number of surviving examples are attached to inquisition documents about alleged practices of vodun. Their original purpose was to guard the wearer from physical harm or from feeling pain.[70]

In the age of Atlantic slavery, European and US colonists and observers developed their own ideas about the otherworldly powers they feared enslaved Africans possessed.[71] Colonial ideas about zombies and zombiism were distinct from African and Afro-Caribbean beliefs and practices. When talking about zombies, it is important to specify whose ideas, testimony, or actions are legible in the sources at hand. In the eyes of outsiders, the Haitian religion of vodun was emblematized by zombiism.[72]

For enslaved Africans in the Americas, slavery was an institution that attempted to strip from them their past, future, language, culture, kin, and legal recognition of personhood, an institution that proclaimed they were bare labor, a line in an account book, worth only what they might make with their toil.[73] But while enslaved Africans' bodies may have been controlled, to an extent, by someone else, their minds were not. And minds could find ways to free bodies. Fear of what an enslaved population might do—rebel and kill their masters, for example—fueled white narratives about vodun, stereotyping it around spirit possession or zombiism.

One form of absolute rebellion for enslaved people was suicide, an act that permanently withheld their labor from enslavers and that would enable their soul to return home. But a fear that plantation owners made sure to circulate among enslaved communities was that suicide prevented a soul from leaving the world, keeping it, instead, disembodied, where the body had died—a soul without a body. European responses to African spirituality in the age of Atlantic slavery were part of multiple larger stories, including fears of slave rebellions and the narrowing of forms of accepted Christian beliefs and behaviors during and in the aftermath of the Reformation, the breakdown of the authority of the church under the pope, and the creation of Protestant denominations and the Anglican Church. American responses to accounts of zombiism in Haiti in the twentieth century were another cluster of stories that invented zombies.

The most recent phase of the invention of the zombie began in the twentieth century, when US writers and filmmakers sensationalized Haiti through a garbled and selected array of practices. In the 1920s and 1930s, the reporter William Seabrook's *The Magic Island* began a long and commercially lucrative history of US characterizations of Haiti through zombiism, and zombie horror movies like *White Zombie* played on white racial fears of being turned into zombies.[74] Today's zombies have come to the workplace, as dehumanizing labor practices threaten to turn people into soulless worker automatons.

MAKING SENSE OF THE WEIRD

In Japanese culture, yōkai is a multidimensional term for the preternatural: for strange phenomena, supernatural entities that generate mysterious phenomena, and visual images of such phenomena or beings.[75] Yōkai are the imagined embodiments of experiences that cannot be fully explained using knowledge of how the visible world operates. Naming and defining yōkai is a way of having a shorthand, visual summary for a category-breaking experience. Yōkai, constantly multiplying and coming into being in new situations, reveal a culture observing, describing, and classifying the things in the world and their effects.

Yōkai function in similar ways to many folk beings: they offer vivid stories and characterizations that are memorable how-to guides for managing life in the world through, for example, proper behavior and the avoidance of dangerous foods. Similarly, scientists in European traditions have long talked about gremlins and demons. For them a "demon" was a shorthand for a gap in understanding that scientists hoped to fill over time, what historian of science Jimena Canales calls a "placeholder for the unknown."[76]

In the ancient Mediterranean and western Asia, people believed that gods created portents: signs, strange occurrences such as the appearance of monsters, coded messages to be unpacked. These messages might tell of impending punishments or take the form of a divine finger pointing at sinful individuals or groups so that communities could take appropriate action. Divine messages pointing to religious beliefs (or the lack thereof) could take the form of monsters.[77] If one-off monsters were signs from God, then how could an observer read them? During the Protestant Reformation of the sixteenth century, religious thinkers weaponized instances of monstrous births by interpreting them as visual metaphors sent from God to illustrate the corruption of the church under the pope and his agents, the priests.

Theologians and reformers like Martin Luther and Philipp Melanchthon leveraged accounts of monstrous births by reading the elements of monstrous bodies in ways that substantiated the reformers' claims that the established church had become decadent. Religion (or the lack thereof) became something that was read as taking the form of monsters. The reformers grasped that the information technology of the printed book, pamphlet, and broadsheet enabled them to circulate their interpretations to broad audiences. Artists and printers devised vividly illustrated polemical texts in which they claimed that instances of monstrous births in present-day Europe demonstrated the corruption of the Catholic Church.[78]

Two monstrous births, the Papal Ass and the Monk Calf, achieved notoriety after reformers interpreted them as signs of the rot in the Catholic Church. In December 1495 the Tiber River in Rome burst its banks, unleashing an apocalyptic flood. The so-called Papal Ass was said to have appeared after the waters receded. Before the century was out, there were printed, symbolic engravings that read the monster as divine retribution and a critique of papal political power.[79] In 1523 Martin Luther and Philipp Melanchthon, university professors–turned-architects of the Protestant Reformation,

FIGURE 37 *(left)*. Lucas Cranach, *Of Two Vvoonderful Popish Monsters . . . a Popish Asse*, woodcut, 1579. This image of the so-called Papal Ass first appeared in a German-language pamphlet in 1523. According to an array of contemporary texts and images, the body of this monster had appeared after the Tiber River in Rome flooded in 1495. Philipp Melanchthon, a professor and Martin Luther's co-agitator, read the creature's horrifying medley of body parts as signs of corruption in the church. STC 17797, Folger Shakespeare Library, Washington, DC.

FIGURE 38 *(right)*. Lucas Cranach, *Of Two Vvoonderful Popish Monsters . . . a Monkish Calfe*, woodcut, 1579. This image of the so-called Monk Calf first appeared in a German-language pamphlet in 1523. The professor and religious reformer Martin Luther read the features of the Monk Calf as signs of monastic and papal failings. STC 17797, Folger Shakespeare Library, Washington, DC.

assembled and published a slim pamphlet combining accounts of these monstrous births. Luther would describe the Monk-Calf as a monstrous calf born in Freiburg, Saxony, in 1522 that, like the Papal Ass, was going viral in print. Luther's co-agitator, Melancthon, wrote a description of the Papal Ass. The renowned artist Lucas Cranach devised fresh illustrations of the monsters.

The pamphlet's Papal Ass sported the head of an ass, an elephant's foot instead of a right hand, a hoof and claw in the place of feet, and the head of an old, bearded man on its posterior, complete with a tail that ended in a raptor's head with a barbed tongue. Melanchthon described how the creature's griffon's claw signaled the grasping nature of religious canons who had appropriated Christendom's wealth and sent it to the pope; its female breast and belly emblematized the depraved appetites of churchmen for excessive eating, drinking, and sex.

In the paired tract, Luther described a monstrous calf born in Freiburg, Saxony, in 1522 from head to hoof using biblical scripture as a road map. He declared that this Monk Calf had the head of a monk, identifiable from his markings resembling a monk's tonsure. Such critics of the established church urged the faithful to read monstrous births as signs of God's displeasure over papal excesses and as a warning that the end of days was imminent. By playing on the viewer's fear of mixed categories—monsters—commentators justified and intensified their criticisms.[80]

With the dawn of the Industrial Age, novels like *Frankenstein* ran simulations of worst-case scenarios for human-machine interactions. There emerged also a renewed interest in what European thinkers called the supernatural. Whereas seventeenth- and eighteenth-century natural philosophers (loosely, practitioners of the physical and mathematical sciences) had distinguished themselves from "primitive" cultures by their fetish for the observable world over invisible agents, the Victorians in Britain and their counterparts in the United States and in France created new societies dedicated to investigating the supernatural in the nineteenth and early twentieth centuries. The extraordinary wonders of electricity had torn open the imaginative barrier between "real" and "superstition" and even between alive and dead.[81]

Some uncanny bodies became associated with curses and misfortune. In the early twentieth century, British journalists and the general public began to tell new stories about ancient Egyptian mummies, in which a "mummy-curse" was visited on all those involved in opening and looting tombs. Preserved mummies had long been familiar in Europe, where they were misidentified as the source of *mummia*, the Persian word for bitumen, a gumlike substance with medical uses. During the sixteenth century, European apothecaries offered mummy cures, fake or the real deal, in powdered and chopped preparations.[82] Ironically, European missionaries, jurists, and colonists accused peoples in other parts of the world, like Brazil, the Caribbean, and Southeast Asia, of being cannibals and justified their enslavement and dispossession on this basis.

There were in fact no curse stories associated with mummies in ancient Egypt. Rather, as literary critic Roger Luckhurst has shown, the curse stories were explanations created in Britain, a psychological response to the feeling

PLATE I. Calendrical page, "Codex Telleriano-Remensis," mid-sixteenth century, from a Mexica (popularly called Aztec) divinatory handbook or ritual calendar. The calendrical patron Tepeyollotl has taken the human-jaguar guise of the divine sorcerer Smoking Mirror (Tezcatlipoca). The squares represent days like 9 Dog (a dog and nine balls). The annotations in Spanish, in three different hands, attempt to explain the Nahuatl glyphs, such as what to do and expect on different days. Département des Manuscrits, Mexicain 385, fol. 9v. Bibliothèque Nationale de France, Paris.

Mulier uiginti annorum hirsuto capite Simiam imitante reliquo corpore glubro.

PLATE 2. Watercolor of Antoinette Gonsalvus, late sixteenth century or early seventeenth century, in a volume of images devoted to animals, assembled by the Bolognese physician, collector, and naturalist Ulisse Aldrovandi and his assistants. Biblioteca Universitaria di Bologna, Ms. Aldrovandi, Tavole di animali, vol. 1, c. 132r. © Alma Mater Studiorum Università di Bologna–Biblioteca Universitaria di Bologna–Further reproduction or duplication by any means is expressly prohibited.

PLATE 3. Lavinia Fontana, portrait of Antoinette Gonsalvus, late sixteenth century. Antoinette Gonsalvus holds up a sheet of paper that outlines how her father, a "wild man," was abducted from the Canary Islands and taken to France and how she ended up in a noble household in Italy. Private Collection, Photo © Bonhams, London, UK/Bridgeman Images, PFA51958.

PLATE 4. Portraits including a man with joint problems; a dwarf; a man gored by a lance; Vlad III Tepes ("the Impaler"), the inspiration for Count Dracula; Petrus Gonsalvus; and Petrus's daughter, Maddalena, in the Chamber of Art and Wonders, Schloss Ambras, Innsbruck, Austria, sixteenth century. In the oldest European curiosity cabinet still surviving in its original location, portraits of these unusually embodied people take up part of a wall. Photo by the author.

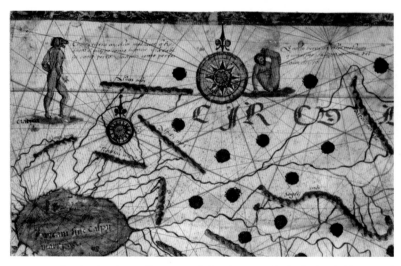

PLATE 5. Sancho Gutiérrez, *Carta general*, detail, 1551. Both the dogheaded being and the figure with a single, giant foot that serves as a sunshade are examples of monstrous peoples that, according to ancient Mediterranean geographers, inhabited regions with extreme climates. ONB/Wien K I 99.416, Austrian National Library, Vienna.

PLATE 6. *Casta* painting, eighteenth century. This genre of paintings invented stereo-typical everyday scenes that named and supposedly illustrated mixed-heritage children and their parents. These canvases implied that there was a fixed relationship between the appearance and characteristics of children and the heritage of their parents. Museo Nacional del Virreinato, Tepotzotlan, Mexico/Bridgeman Images, XOS5863246.

PLATE 7. José Conrado Roza, *La mascarade nuptiale*, 1788. This group portrait brought together individuals whom colonial administrators had dispatched from Brazil and from parts of Africa to Portugal to attend the wedding of Dona Roza (*second row, left*), said to be Queen Maria I's favorite dwarf. Musée du Nouveau Monde, La Rochelle, France. Photo © Photo Josse/Bridgeman Images.

PLATE 8. Zakariya Al-Qazwini, *'Ajâ'ib al-Makhlûqât* (*Marvels of Things*),
Iran, 1822. Alexander the Great's troops face off against two members of the
tribes of Gog and Magog, monstrous beings whom, according to the ancient
Greek historian and geographer Herodotus, Alexander had attempted to wall
off from the rest of the world. MSS or., Supplement Persan 1148, Bibliothèque
Nationale de France, Paris, fol. 75.

PLATE 9. Painting of hell, circa 1510–20. This array of people who failed to get into heaven includes monks, identifiable by their tonsured heads emerging from the cauldron. The devil's clothing and accoutrements were modeled on West African and Caribbean artifacts, thus associating Africans and Indigenous peoples of the Americas with infernal horrors. Museu Nacional de Arte Antiga, Lisbon, Portugal/Bridgeman Images, XIR173185.

PLATE 10. The path to hell, Church of San Pedro Apóstol de Andahuaylillas, Peru, circa 1620s. Finely dressed figures walk a raised path over water toward a building. Most parishioners would have been illiterate; visual imagery served didactic and mnemonic ends: priests could point out scenes during sermons. Photo © Pilar Rau.

that grave robbing the pharaohs was wrong.[83] Power across space and time lay at the center of mummy curses, a late nineteenth- and early twentieth-century narrative genre. Mummies came to be viewed as uncanny objects capable of punishing those who disturbed them. Curse stories were counter-narratives, critiques of colonial violence and of the looting of ancient artifacts. In this way they were inversions of stories about the efficacy of miraculous relics.

The very idea of an origin includes the idea of breaking categories: something unprecedented is going to be brought into being. In that sense divinity and humanity are each other's monsters. Gods sometimes made humans by breaking open the category of god. At times communities demonize individuals or groups for being too different. Yet category breakers are part of the order of having a classificatory system at all. The leveling up and down across the categories of god and human puts pressure on conventions about where human skill and power end. What do our gods expect of us now? Who even are our gods in an era of rising secularism and rising religious fundamentalism? For a start people are being sacrificed at the altars of the economy and globalization, by weapons like algorithms and data-scraping bots. These sacrifices may not be as spectacular as those depicted in Aztec codices. But they are sacrifices nonetheless, and they are constant and widespread, as we'll see.

EIGHT

———

Machines

IT'S 2019. I'M IN A BAR in Providence, Rhode Island, chatting with graduate students and researchers with PhDs. One of them, who holds a PhD in
Latin American literature, observed approvingly that programmers were
now teaching robots how to write poetry. But this struck me as a total waste
of time. Why would anyone bother making robots who could write poetry,
except to advance the field of robotics? His answer: it was worth building
robots who could write poetry "so that people won't have to." What would
we do instead, and why would anyone want to read robot poetry, anyway? He
replied that we would do nothing at all; "we could watch movies." Despite
the rest of the group arguing with and (mostly) disagreeing with him for half
the evening, my colleague stuck to his guns: it would be handy to have robots
writing poetry for people.

In that moment we were at odds about the essence of humanity. I was
baffled and disturbed by his position. It was one thing to design robots to
clean up nuclear waste or to perform boring, repetitive tasks so that—at least
in theory—people could do more intellectually or creatively rewarding work,
including (I imagine) building robots and writing poetry.[1] But to get robots
to write poetry "so that we don't have to" seemed a toe dip into a new pool of
dangerous waters—waters that might dissolve what "human" means entirely.

Did poets want robots or so-called AI (artificial intelligence) "saving" them
the effort of writing poetry? Forms of creative expression like writing poetry,
painting, making music, or dancing are things people do because they want to
be building something with their own minds and bodies. There is something
inside them they want to say, with ink, paint, notes, or twirls. Creative people
are driven to experience the often difficult, dangerous, tear-storm-filled, and,
basically, epic journey of figuring out their message and how to say it, growing

with the effort, and becoming someone a little different by the end. For poets like this, "stopping writing" (as my colleague put it) isn't going to cut it.

The arts are activities that people engage in *for fun*. Whether they write murder mysteries set at the office or play the accordion in an amateur band, they make things to be in the world and to make sense of it, to feel themselves growing, to connect with other humans, to chase that elusive flow state of being in the zone, making something, however weird or imperfect it may turn out to be. Would they stop because they didn't "need" to (whatever that means) anymore? I doubt it. They are already doing something they don't "need" to do.

Then there are people who read poetry (or look at paintings or enjoy music or novels). Would I want to live in a world in which machines wrote all the poetry? No. When I read a poem or listen to a jazz trio, I'm connecting directly with people. And there's enough poetry and music out there in the world already—no machines are necessary for me to not run out of entertainment. When I follow the work of a contemporary writer, artist, or musician, it is to experience what a human is making in the world right now—not what a predictive text algorithm might plagiarize out of text in its database. To aim to replace future artworks with AI-generated knockoffs is to misunderstand people who make art as well as those who want to spend time with art.

But at the heart of my colleague's provocative position was a utopian ideal: of a future in which technology was advanced enough to "do everything," even write poetry, so that no one needed to work. Yet this position wasn't convincing either. His utopia sounded more than a little dull, and nobody wants to be bored out of their minds. To *not* do anything requiring physical or mental effort, ever, sounded like the dystopian future of Pixar's *Wall-E* (short for Waste Allocation Load Lifter: Earth Class), where humans have become lumpen starship-dwellers who do, basically, nothing. They spend their waking hours watching screens, sipping drinks through straws, permanently living at the movies, their muscles atrophied from sitting for too long in lounge chairs. These people have become passive consumers and nothing else: technology does almost everything for them.

To be sure, it would be great to live in a world where people didn't have to do or make anything in order not to starve to death. But the reason people are starving today isn't because there aren't enough machines to do work. In fact, the ballooning of tech companies in the twenty-first century has coincided with a meteoric rise in income inequality to levels last seen in the United States with the Gilded Age robber barons of the nineteenth century.[2] It's social and political, not technological, change that's needed to save millions from long hours of poorly paid, precarious, or backbreaking work in service of corporations posting gigantic profits. And writing poetry isn't something that its practitioners do to make much money (except for the luckiest few), but because they *want* to make things and to do things. But by misunderstanding the full palette of the human, advocates of "so that people won't have to" tech goals also misunderstand what a utopian or simply better future for all might look like.

Back in 2019 it already seemed urgent to write something about human relationships with machines: robots, neural networks, and artificial intelligence. To me the extraordinary and undertapped creative potential of flesh-and-blood people was one of the reasons why we matter. Creativity defines humanity. One of us is unique and distinctive no matter how many extraterrestrial life-forms may exist. The idea that machines could or should take over making art or writing diminishes the work of teachers, of human-authored books about how to make art and to write, and the fact that people can *learn stuff*. Yet even a scholar of literature (my Providence colleague) could envision a life of idleness consuming algorithm-generated content as progress. What did that say about the value people placed on appreciating things made by humans rather than by machines? Were human experience and creativity going to become redundant, and, if so, who would we even be? By deciding what robots are for, we are defining what humans are.

Fast-forward to 2024. Stories about generative AI are everywhere. Human labor is increasingly framed as an obstacle to corporate profits. Authors, artists, and their guilds are suing companies like OpenAI that are using the "fair use" clause in copyright law—a law devised to enable human beings to quote one another briefly, giving due credit to the author they're quoting, without the trouble and expense of paying for permission to reproduce other people's work—to feed copyrighted works into their LLMs (large language models).[3]

The goal of comprehensive automation dismisses the uniqueness of each of us. It monstrifies us by making our essence something that is no longer seen as typical or even as normal. Suddenly, humans are framed as the problem—as redundant. Tech companies are framing those aspects of humanity that machines can mimic as the only forms of action or content with value in the future. But if everything that makes us irreducible to algorithms, everything that is too complex to turn into numbers on spreadsheets, is dismissed and ignored—humanity will be over, dehumanized by society, even if there are still humans on earth. Insidiously dehumanizing narratives warp how people define the human, framing us as inconveniences to the march toward maximum profits for a select few.

Dehumanization is a form of monstrification. It's not about saying someone is a different species, although dehumanizing language can include slurs like that. The kind of economic dehumanization I'm talking about here is where someone deems that people are nothing more than the products of their labor and where they don't get to have needs any more than a toaster gets to have needs. It's the sort of narrative that claims that workers don't need anything beyond what it takes to drag them into the office and, maybe, to not get hauled off the street for being homeless in a place where what little they are paid barely allows them to afford shelter.

The world of creators is just one arena in which machines are reconfiguring definitions of the human, as we'll see. The rhetoric from Silicon Valley is of "saving humanity." But far from saving anyone, creating and "training" LLMs has become another way to exploit people. These companies are hiring, for a pittance, remote gig workers in the Global South as content moderators to "train" racial bias and harmful language out of LLMs, exposing workers to horrific racist and sexist content in the process. In 2023 moderators based in Kenya called for a government investigation into the trauma caused by moderating OpenAI's ChatGPT content.[4]

To be sure, there are global problems that are so urgent and severe that we should explore every avenue, including AI, to solve them. Key among them is the climate emergency. And in medicine there are things that AI (with proper guardrails) can do to extend and enhance the work of people and to save or improve lives.[5] But how we think about and legislate corporations that develop AI and claim to own our data will determine the future of the idea of "human" and what "human rights" will mean.

ROBOTS

Long before technology invaded our virtual worlds, machines had been clunking around in the physical world. Today wealthier homes are littered with innovations, from Roombas (robot vacuum cleaners) to Siri (Apple's digital assistant).[6] These products blur the boundaries between natural and artificial and between human and machine. Robots are as much a part of how societies imagine the future as they are already ordinary in the present. "Robot" conjures up disembodied metal arms in factories, apocalyptic machines like *Doctor Who*'s Daleks (blenders on wheels determined to "Exterminate! Exterminate!" people), or perhaps the alarming robot dogs designed by companies like Boston Dynamics. People instinctively fear a robot in action. In fact, current robots are delicate, easily fooled, and even more easily disabled with low-tech hacks like a bucket of water.[7]

What have machines got to do with monsters? In the history of monsters, machines are everywhere. Machines that simulate or augment human bodies span an unsettling continuum from technology to humanity: robots, androids (robots designed to resemble humans, as far as possible), geminoids (androids designed to resemble women), cyborgs, Roombas, holograms. For today's nonroboticist "robotic" carries a sense of clumsy hunks of clanking metal. But some machines in science fiction are almost indistinguishable from human beings. People fantasize about building machines that are monstrous: that reduce the gap between humanity and machinery. Some sci-fi "machines" contain human body parts or began as human beings (like some sci-fi cyborgs). They challenge the categories of human and machine by being both and neither: monsters. Other contraptions have little more autonomy than a basic toaster (although even some toasters now have "smart" capabilities).

We can tell humans from robots because robots are built, not born.[8] Still, just as definitions of "human" and "animal" affect each other, so do definitions of "human" and "machine" and concepts like "AI." After all, how can something that doesn't have a mind and isn't alive be intelligent? For roboticists a robot fulfills four criteria: they have a physical form; they can sense the world; they can analyze sensory data and make evaluations; and they can act on their findings. "Robot" is a general term encompassing everything from a sensor-controlled vacuum cleaner to androids.

The word "robot" in English dates back to the 1920s, to a play by the Czech writer Karel Čapek called *R. U. R., or Rossum's Universal Robots. Robota* is the Czech word for a person forced to perform labor. The play, translated into multiple European languages within two years of its publication, features artificial beings created to work in factories. Novels, comics, and short stories soon established "robot" in English to mean a fully artificial, mechanical being devoid of flesh and blood, moving, sensing, thinking, and doing and yet somehow also lacking a mind—*robotic*.[9]

While a robot is an independently moving decision-making machine, it doesn't have to have a convincing body, voice, or set of movements. The most basic robots lack the typical human body-part complement of two arms, two legs, a head, and a torso. Such beings might include Roombas, R2-D2 from *Star Wars*, and perhaps the Tin Man from *The Wizard of Oz*, who has the standard number of limbs for a human but is clearly a clunking hulk of, well, tin.

An android (or geminoid) is a closer mimic of human form, voice, movement, and behavior, perhaps even covered in imitation skin. So while *Star Wars'* R2-D2 is a rudimentary robot (it looks and acts like a beeping vacuum cleaner), the human-sized, human-shaped, human-(albeit British)-voiced C-3PO is an android. *Star Trek: The Next Generation's* Lieutenant Commander Data is also an android. Arnold Schwarzenegger's character in *The Terminator* is an android, and *Blade Runner* features androids who are virtually indistinguishable from flesh-and-blood people. These androids are distinctly different from one another, and perhaps some would call them robots rather than androids on their personal scale from clanking lump of tin to human being. Whatever they're called, real and science fiction autonomous(ish) machines exist on a continuum with humans in terms of their (science fiction) appearance, movements, talents, and mannerisms. One step closer to us in appearance than androids are cyborgs. This is where things start feeling *really* creepy. Cyborgs are organic beings with added robot parts. Like some androids, they can be indistinguishable from a fully organic human. *Battlestar Galactica* is one of the many science fiction entertainments awash with beings that can be called cyborgs.[10]

This is not a hard and fast terminology. Some machines may not fit my ersatz taxonomy, or yours. C-3PO in *Star Wars* is physically the archetypal robot: a tin man with jerky (albeit charming) movements. Yet in speech and interactions he is indistinguishable from a pompous, highly educated, nervous human. With dialogue and mannerisms that mirror the Niles Crane character of the comedy franchise *Frasier* a couple of decades later, C-3PO is surely an android rather than a mere robot. In *Star Wars* both C-3PO and R2-D2 are called "droids." Each of us will classify them a little differently. What interests me is what happens next: What does thinking about androids—or cyborgs or robots—do to how people think about humans and monsters?

TO FRANKENSTEIN AND BEYOND

Ancient writings about robots reveal how people have tried to make sense of what exactly life is and whether or not it can be built rather than born. Automata in ancient literature are entities that are neither conjured into existence by gods nor created using magic.[11] In Byzantium and the Islamicate world in the Middle Ages, there was a long and continuous tradition of mechanical rather than magical models to explain the world and the human body. There are also mechanical devices that we might call robots today: what historian of science Elly Truitt defines as "self-moving or self-sustaining manufactured objects." There were robots in the medieval Mongol Empire. In western Europe automata first appeared as gifts from farther afield, beginning with a ninth-century automaton from Baghdad. The word "automaton" appeared in the sixteenth century, and its first recorded use is in scholar and novelist François Rabelais's *Gargantua and Pantagruel*, which contains "little automated machines" that "move by themselves."[12]

How does someone decide whether something is magic—an instance of breaking nature's rules using a supernatural power—or just a science they don't possess? Speculative writing since classical antiquity has grappled with this question.[13] In preindustrial Europe thinkers and practitioners sometimes disagreed over whether mechanical devices that appeared to go against nature were products of sorcery and diabolism or merely pleasurable mechanical marvels such as ingenious devices or engines.[14] That fear of reaching beyond human ability and breaking a social or spiritual contract reverberates through writings past and present.

Fiction and films have cautioned that imbuing the nonliving with the power to act can go very wrong. In Mary Shelley's classic monster novel, *Frankenstein*, the scientist Victor Frankenstein devises a being out of body parts from corpses, imbuing them with life and sentience using electricity. The result, predictably, is horrific and tragic. In the early 1980s, the movies *The Terminator* and *Blade Runner* did for androids what Shelley did for reanimated corpses: provide a cautionary tale about how much could go wrong. *The Terminator* movie, the first of a long franchise, is set in the Los Angeles of 1984, into which a terminator android from a postapocalyptic future was sent back in time. Skynet, an AI "Global Digital Defense Network," had decided that humans were the problem and had begun a nuclear war. In *Blade Runner*, inspired by Philip K. Dick's 1968 novel, *Do Androids Dream of Electric Sheep?*, viewers follow a bounty hunter across a Los Angeles of 2019 (then far in the future) as he tracks fugitive synthetic beings he has orders to kill or "retire." These scenarios share a concern for the safety of humanity in the wake of a rival species on earth. (To be sure, humanity already has plenty of rival species on earth, most of them microscopic. But still.)

Cut to 2023 and the real world. Malfunctioning robotaxis in San Francisco and a writers' and actors' strike in Hollywood are just two of the AI stories making headlines in California. Screenwriters faced the threat of job losses, as LLMs, trained on human writing, without authors' consent, enable predictive text to create plausible content drafts. After months of strikes and negotiations, the final contract contained a provision that enables the manipulation of an actor's digital likeness, opening the door to synthetic performances by a few big-name actors and fewer jobs for other actors and production crews.[15] An AI-generated doppelganger of Tom Hanks, created without his consent, has already appeared on the internet. Hanks is one of several celebrities whose voice or likeness have been duplicated. The concerns of Hollywood's writers and actors were part of a larger set of grievances about how studio and streaming-platform executives have chosen to distribute profits from the labor of workers. As I type these words in 2024, the news industry is hemorrhaging jobs on newspapers and magazines, as search engines like Google have decided not to distinguish between real content and AI-generated content on Google News. Advertising revenue is driven by clicks.

Our data is being packaged and sold, and groups who have historically faced the greatest exploitation are being exploited the most, in a phenomenon that two scholars have called a "data grab." "Algorithms of oppression" compound the legacies of sexism and slavery by building human prejudices into their data and algorithms, proprietary black boxes that receive no oversight, or "weapons of math destruction."[16] The present and the future as they are currently unfolding seem as bad as, if different from, the apocalyptic scenarios of science fiction. The category of the human is under threat from stories about how machines are better. The question we need to be asking is, Better for *whom?*

AUTOMATION AND ITS DISCONTENTS

Laborious drudgery runs through robot history. The first robots in Western writings were built by the ancient Greek smith-god of fire and artisans, Hephaestus. He devised mechanical servers: self-propelled tripods, mounted on wheels, all the better for whooshing around Mount Olympus as servants to the gods.[17] In Homer's epic the *Iliad*, the sea goddess Thetis visits Hephaestus's forge and encounters his self-propelled, thinking automata made in the form of women. These "Golden Maidens" were his workshop assistants, and he had endowed them with all the knowledge of the gods.

The nineteenth-century British thinker Thomas H. Huxley suggested that both humans and animals had something of the automaton about them.

Commentators on automation in the workplace, from computational machine inventor Charles Babbage to Karl Marx, used the unsettling metaphor of the machine to describe the experience of being a person in a factory.[18] Office work is its own form of drudgery. Writing about T. S. Eliot's poem *The Waste Land* a month after it was published, in 1922, the critic Edmund Wilson suggested that the poem described the plight of a "whole civilization"—for people "grinding at barren office routines in the cells of gigantic cities, drying up their souls in eternal toil whose products never bring them profit."[19]

Karel Čapek's *R. U. R.* describes a robot takeover of the world. Once "mindless" robots are given the capacity to feel, this formerly compliant workforce develops needs and demands.[20] Čapek's 1920s play invited audiences to empathize with robots trapped in a system that had . . . dehumanized them. The parallel with downtrodden human factory workers was clear: society did not recognize them as having minds with needs, emotions, motives, and experiences. First performed in a decade noted for its labor movements, the play did what science fiction does best: it uses an unfamiliar, imagined, futuristic technological setting to throw contemporary societal problems into sharper relief. It evokes empathy for people who are typically written out of full civic humanity—in this case, factory workers.[21] Movies about humanlike androids laboring at boring, repetitive, or dangerous tasks for little reward is real life for many people, as writers like Naomi Klein and Matthew Desmond have shown us in heartrending detail.[22] And surely very few have managed to live free of periods of drudgery for employers and organizations that failed to recognize their individuality and their needs as flesh-and-blood people.[23]

In the early twentieth century, drudgery was built into the US engineer Frederick Winslow Taylor's proposal for a maximum-efficiency factory floor. Taylor recommended distilling each worker's tasks into simple, concrete steps and assigning a single type of task to each worker. He suggested that factory managers could reduce errors by providing checklists and routines. Today, for anyone who has conceded that multitasking is the new smoking ("should I close those one million tabs on my browser?"), factories where individual workers have narrowly defined tasks may seem sensible. But overoptimize such steps and the work will provide no creative or intellectual satisfaction and perhaps even bore workers to death. Work like this reduces workers to automata—opening the door to replacing them with machines.[24] Implicitly, these practices assume that every task that matters can be automated.

How people define, organize, and justify working arrangements for robots and for people are interrelated. There are indirect, often unseen or latent costs in thinking reductively about the work a person does, in not recognizing the adaptability and infinite possibilities of people, seven billion (and counting) unique individuals whose full meaning and value cannot be reduced to rote actions. Organizing work for people in ways that even robots could do it monstrifies human beings. Technology has already compromised our privacy, autonomy, quality of life, and quality of work—all in the service of convenience for some, exploitation of most of us (directly or through our data), and inordinate wealth for corporations, their shareholders, and senior executives.

There are two contrasting aims through which people think about what robots and machines might do in the future. At one extreme is the aim of robots as a replacement of human labor entirely—something like the thinking of the literature scholar in that Providence bar. This aim undergirds today's fears about corporations cutting people out of the economy and society. It also leads to reductive thinking about simple robots, like robotic arms in factories: What's cheaper, human or machine? At the other extreme is the aim of having robots that allow people to extend their reach and skills. Robots have been used in mining and to study volcanoes for decades. Their use in dangerous spaces saves people from risking their lives and safety—they can control the robots remotely, from outside the mine or away from the volcano.

Technology can also create time and mental space in which people can grow and extend their potential. By functioning as an assistant that takes care of automatable or highly monotonous, time-consuming tasks, it can free up the headspace that creative, adaptable, endlessly fertile human minds need to make new things and think fresh thoughts. Machines might in theory take over rote tasks entirely to leave humanity free to fulfill their as yet barely tapped creative and analytical potential. This brighter, alternative future would make room for people to do deep and meaningful things for more of their lives. Each person's brain has a breadth and versatility that is unmatched by robots and by AI: machines can compute things quickly and accurately but fail at most things that people find easy. Today's robots would be inept at juggling kettles, teapots, tea leaves or teabags, and cups and saucers to make tea well (although my fellow Brits may disagree on just how many people can brew a proper cup of tea).[25] Why bother trying to make a machine to do what people can do far better? Yet, in practice, technological innovation and rollout is akin to the Wild West—little, late, and weak legislation; chaotic and inconsistent structures; gangsters profiting at the expense of the vast majority of individuals; and a lot of bodies on the ground. According to law professor Frank Pasquale, to prevent robots from dehumanizing people, we need what the sociologist Alondra Nelson, writing about epidemics in the early months of the COVID-19 pandemic, called "anticipatory social research."[26]

The potential dangers of robots inspired science fiction writer Isaac Asimov to devise his Three Laws of Robotics. In the 1940s Asimov created a long-running series of novels about robots, undergirded by laws that were supposed to guide how robots operated in human society: (1) no robots may injure humans or, through their inaction, allow humans to be harmed; (2) robots must obey humans in all cases, except where to obey them would be to contravene the first law; and (3) robots must protect themselves so long as they are able to do so without contravening the first or second laws.[27] Asimov's novels reveal, time and again, how these deceptively simple laws are in fact impossible to obey in practice.[28]

For Asimov the central danger was death by robot. Eight decades later the existential risks that technology poses are more varied and less concrete. Law professor Frank Pasquale recently devised a new set of four laws for robotics and AI systems: that they "should complement professionals, not replace them"; that they "should not counterfeit humanity"; that they "should not intensify zero-sum arms races"; and that they "must always indicate the identity of their creator(s), controller(s), and owners(s)."[29]

FEELING FOR ROBOTS

Whose lives do people care about? Could you empathize with a motorized bucket? If the bucket acts like a human, then the answer may be yes. In Pixar's *Wall-E*, mentioned earlier in this chapter, a trash-compactor robot in the twenty-ninth century builds skyscrapers of refuse cubes on an earth devoid of plant life. Humans have left earth for an endless cruise on starships, where practically all essential tasks are performed by technology. Initially planned as a five-year exile from a polluted planet, the cruise is now centuries old. The movie's protagonist, a robot named Wall-E, is more human in form than *Star Wars'* R2-D2: he has a recognizable head (that looks and moves like a pair of binoculars); neck (with an expressive range of movement); and hands (pincer-like, each with two flat fingers and a thumb). Yet Wall-E also has trailer-track wheels rather than legs and speaks in blurps and whistles. For a rust-buckety, rudimentary robot, Wall-E garners great empathy through his tastes, actions, and mannerisms.

To be sure, cinematic devices don't have the same effect on everyone, everywhere, for all time—nor do fictional robots. One person's robot is another's toaster. But what artistic choices *can* tell us is how creators, editors, and studio executives strategize to reach their target audience. Wall-E's character mirrors, even caricatures, a particular vision of what it means to be human. Wall-E mimics the hand-holding he sees in an old movie he watches on a videotape, echoing the behavior of children, and of the alien in *E.T.*, who behaves a bit like a pet crossed with a human child. Viewers empathize with Wall-E more than they do with an elegant, technologically sophisticated, newer robot he will meet and even more than with the people in the movie.

People anthropomorphize beings of both the "living" and "manufactured" kinds: cats, religious icons, boats, teddy bears. We seem to be wired to notice—or to assemble—faces.[30] The instinct to scan the world and identify the beings may be an evolutionarily wired trait. It's easier to anthropomorphize a machine with visible moving parts (not the washing machine) and when the parts make their own decisions about when to start and stop and how to respond to their environment. That's why people have less of an emotional connection to a refrigerator than to a battery-operated bunny or Transformer robot. A blender is not a robot to most of us. Nor is it one for roboticists, since the blender does not make decisions.

Even if you're someone who names kitchen appliances, you likely feel a relatively limited amount of empathy toward them and "demote" them in your mind when they irritate you. Witness the expression "frakkin' toaster," an insult that humans hurl at the Cylons, synthetic beings in *Battlestar Galactica*. It draws attention to the Cylons' machineness: they contain metallic components despite being indistinguishable from humans on the outside. The insult works like a racial epithet: designed to hurt beings who are self-aware, to diminish them as persons, and to push the reading on the empathy meter below the range for "real" people.

How robots move shapes how we feel about them. A Japanese factory has employees start the day with upper-body exercises and has the factory's robots—rudimentary stick figures that resemble clusters of golf clubs—doing the exercises alongside them. This is an effort to encourage employees to feel in community with the robots mirroring their actions. Autonomy also suggests sentience. A handheld vacuum cleaner is just a machine, whereas a

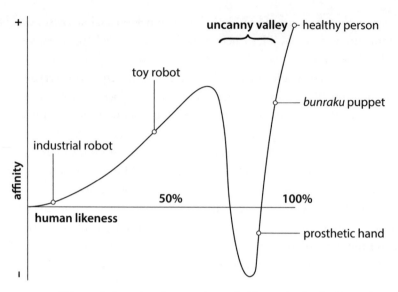

FIGURE 39. This graph shows how human viewers feel increasing levels of empathy and comfort as an object approaches human likeness and then sharply decreasing levels when the object is almost, but not quite, human. Affinity levels rise again as the object appears less and less human. Masahiro Mori, "Uncanny Valley," figure 1. © Karl F. MacDorman

Roomba elicits anthropomorphism. Despite looking about as alive as a wheel, 80 percent of Roombas have been given names by their owners.[31] The empathy someone might feel toward robots doesn't increase steadily as they look and act increasingly human. The relationship between resemblance and empathy or comfort is nonlinear: somewhere between "human" and "clearly not human" is a twilight zone that feels creepy and monstrous.

In 1906 the German psychiatrist Ernst Jentsch proposed that something could be both very ordinary and deeply creepy—unsettling or uncanny, as in the manner of a lifelike mechanical doll.[32] In 1970 the Japanese roboticist Masahiro Mori expanded on this idea. Mori surmised that an artificial being that closely resembled a human but was not quite identical to one would generate far less empathy and feelings of comfort—less "affinity"—than one that was obviously a mechanical object. Mori devised a graph and plotted human likeness against affinity for a variety of beings and things: various robots, a stuffed animal, artificial hands, a corpse, a zombie, dolls and puppets, and even an ill person. He found that human viewers felt greater affinity as likeness increases—but only up to a point. Mori's subjects felt increasingly

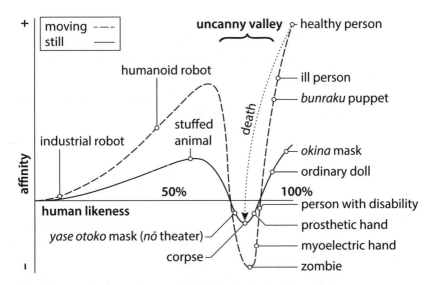

FIGURE 40. This graph demonstrates that affinity, as a function of how similar something is to a healthy person, has two curves: one for stationary objects, the other for moving ones. The dip into the "uncanny valley"—where viewers feel weirded out by an object—is much more pronounced for moving objects. Masahiro Mori, "Uncanny Valley," figure 2. © Karl F. MacDorman

weirded out by entities that were very close to but not entirely like a healthy person. A prosthetic hand was uncanny, but a toy robot, something that was less humanoid than a prosthetic hand, was relatively pleasing. If the entity was moving, that feeling was stronger; a zombie was terrifying, whereas an ordinary doll prompted mildly positive feelings. Mori called the affinity trough (or dip) toward the right-hand end of the graph's human-likeness scale the "uncanny valley."[33]

Mori's research suggests that the category of what we might call "feels like a person"—beings toward whom we feel empathy—doesn't entirely map onto "looks like a human." Viewers' emotions determine what "feels like a person" to them—just like how "feels like a monster" is an emotional category. Both reactions reveal not a monster per se but a feeling. Beings that suggest that a continuum exists from healthy people to puppets blur the boundaries between the self and very different entities. Beings like this are uncanny—we might even say monstrous.

In Ridley Scott's 1979 movie *Alien*, science officer Bishop is indistinguishable from an organic person until he is outed as both an android and company spy. It is Bishop's very similitude to "regular" humans that creeps out the crew. Viewers becomes hyperattentive to Bishop's speech, look, and mannerisms. (Was *that* a sign? Or that? Were there clues all this time?) Once discovered, Bishop sits at the lowest point of Mori's Uncanny Valley, the moment of extreme unsettledness, when something is almost but not quite human. Yet Bishop is still the same being on the outside: it's what people now know and think about him that has monstrified him.

RIGHTS AND LIMITATIONS

Androids' rights and limitations reveal how people have defined living humans and distinguished them from machines. In *Star Trek: The Next Generation*, the beloved android Lieutenant Commander Data emblematizes imagined limits to artificial life. Data is a wondrously sophisticated technological marvel, initially one of a kind, though he will turn out to have a long-lost twin. He is the brainchild of a cyberneticist whose innovations no one has been able to replicate. Thoughtful and compassionate, Data mirrors humanity's best qualities.

Data's appearance makes it clear that he is an android: bright-yellow eyes; a golden, metallic sheen to his skin; and a careful, slightly canned voice all signal that he was built, not born. Despite his extraordinary strength and computing prowess, Data's fondest wish is to continue to learn and develop into an individual who is as close to human as he can possibly be. Some skills, like tap dancing, he masters in minutes. He has mixed results with feats like playing the violin that require technical skill and creative expression to make deep connections with people. Other talents, like painting and writing poetry, elude him: his art is kind of awful. Data hunts for a spark of originality but ultimately lacks the human capacity to make something that emerges from but also exceeds the sum of its parts. There is nothing uncanny about Data's mimicry of human form or behavior because he's still clearly an android. By striving to become more like us, he underlines how extraordinary we are. Data does not blur the boundary between human and machine; rather, he confirms it.

By contrast, Data's evil older brother, Lore, is decidedly uncanny. Lore is a much better mimic of human speech and behavior. He uses verbal contractions, deploys slang naturally, and his personality, mannerisms, and speech patterns are flamboyant and suave. He's also ambitious, selfish, bitter, and evil. Data lacks these traits, excepting a desire for self-improvement. Lore was created first, but the community in which he lived found his similarity so unsettling that his creator disassembled him and built Data: a less convincing simulacrum and far more likeable for that reason. The story arc (and this viewer's feelings) map very well onto Mori's Uncanny Valley hypothesis. And "close to but not quite" being a threat is very much what "monster" often means.

In 2017 the kingdom of Saudi Arabia granted honorary citizenship to an android called Sophia, the brainchild of Hong Kong–based Hanson Robotics. Sophia looks human from the front and, furthering the illusion, can utter steams of text in response to particular words. Sophia's path through the international jet set was confirmed by an interview on *The Tonight Show Starring Jimmy Fallon*. She even crossed paths with the highest levels of government, "meeting" Angela Merkel, attending a meeting of the UN General Assembly, and appearing at the Munich Security Conference.[34]

It's not clear whether Sophia received rights or privileges along with her honorary citizenship. What exactly does citizenship mean for a mechanical being who (presumably) does not travel alone or decide what to do? Sophia the "social robot," as this type is called, has almost no skills compared to a person: a wonder of technology yet utterly limited. What larger questions does Sophia's citizenship pose when contrasted with how nations treat the millions of displaced and sometimes stateless people around the world, many of whom are prevented from working? How does she compare with the millions more who, because of geopolitical and economic structures, lack paths to citizenship where they live and work and where their labor is essential and generates profits for their employers while they are monstrified with labels like "illegal"? Humanity is very good at dehumanizing people and at humanizing nonhumans.

PROPERTY

Episodes of *Star Trek* often explore social issues, legacies of humanity's past, and the threats that may face us in the future. The success of the *Star Trek: The Next Generation* episode "Measure of a Man" depends on the viewer's ability to humanize and empathize with nonhuman characters and turns that empathy back toward humanity itself.³⁵ The starship *Enterprise* is visited by a cyberneticist, Bruce Maddox, who is introduced to the bridge crew (including Data) as someone who "is here to work on your android." The battle lines are drawn: the possessive "your" and the erasure of Data's name dehumanizes the android whom the crew regards as a friend and comrade, different but equal. Maddox wishes to disassemble Data, to better understand his brain and thereby learn how to build more androids just like him. Yet it is unclear whether Maddox's understanding is robust enough to disassemble and reassemble Data without losing, as Data put it, "that ineffable quality" that makes him a unique entity. Data refuses to submit to the dangerous process. His captain and crew support him.

Maddox had anticipated this response and has arrived equipped with official orders transferring Data from the *Enterprise* to his lab. Maddox dismisses the crew's objections: "You're endowing Data with human characteristics. If it were a box on wheels I would not be facing this opposition." Data chooses to resign his commission rather than allow Maddox to dismantle him. Yet Maddox denies that Data has the autonomy to resign, for "it," as Maddox repeatedly mispronouns him, is merely a machine, not a sentient being. This reasoning appalls Capt. Jean-Luc Picard, who declares that "you cannot simply seize people." Maddox disagrees: "Data is a machine. He has no rights."

Questions underlying robot ontology (what kind of "thing" robots are) and ethics thread through this episode. Are we capable of building something that acquires sentience, and, if so, would this change its status from property to individual with the same rights as a human being? How can one prove that any being is sentient rather than parroting words and aping behaviors associated with sentience? Embedded in verbs like "to parrot" and "to ape" is wiggle room to declare that something that walks and talks like a human is not human. Such arguments were the bread and butter of white imperialists wishing to perpetuate systems of slavery and servitude that exploited peoples of Africa, Asia, and the Americas. Could a machine have a soul? A judge brought in to adjudicate on Data's future determines that she does not know but that he should have the freedom to explore that for himself, as a person, not as property.

People in the real world are as unsure and divided as to what a human soul is, whether souls exist, and how much they matter. To reduce humanity to actions that can be automated is to ignore that ineffable quality that makes us human. Yet AI corporation executives that insist that they be allowed to mine our creative works for free depend on and require that ineffable quality. Artworks, literature, and music generated by microchips miss the point of art, diminishing what "human" means by separating souls, hearts, and minds from the labor of making things.

In the movie *The Matrix*, the world is a web from environment to mind to body to machine.[36] Events in people's imagination have effects in the physical world. The world is run by sentient machines to whom people are merely biofuel. Humans have been plugged into a virtual reality world, their mental energy powering the world of the machines. Humans have been dehumanized by "superior" technology: humanity is at risk of bringing about its own extinction, killed, like the ancient Greek Oedipus, by its own creation. The machines view themselves as the earth's rightful inheritors. In the words of Agent Smith, one of their humanoid avatars in the virtual world, humans are a "virus," "a disease, a cancer of this planet," for which the machines are the cure. Humanity, in Smith's view, will disappear "like the dinosaurs." Preposterously unlikely? Perhaps not, if you ignore the slick outfits, even slicker shades, and the subterranean spaceships.

Today's world is full of virtual entities with legal personhood. Corporations have been around for centuries. Laws create and dissolve who counts as a person in the eyes of those with power: governments, law enforcement, institutions, and even citizens. And they permit companies to extract and own the data we create going about our lives and to monetize and sell it. As I write this, corporate legal teams are rewriting terms-of-service agreements—the novella-length documents we sign to use apps and programs—to define our data as corporate property.[37]

CYBORGS

In the TV series *Battlestar Galactica*, cyborgs called Cylons contain so many organic components that they seem to be beings with a consciousness indistinguishable from biological humans. The corollary of this scenario is, How many prosthetics would it take to turn a person into a cyborg? Artificial limbs have been around for centuries.[38] Pacemakers and even artificial heart transplants are no longer mere science fiction. Could a person become a monstrous human-machine hybrid? Engineers build machines; might genetic engineering and cybernetics turn us into machines? These are questions of definition rather than substance. Whether or not people acquiring prosthetics become something else in the eyes of the law or their society is not about them but about the stories people tell about them.

Perhaps the danger of becoming a cyborg has been here for some time: it doesn't require soldering metal implants to our bodies but rather losing parts of our humanity, a shred at a time. Costs and benefits for corporations are different from those for workers and consumers. The neoliberal rhetoric of efficiency for the good of corporations has led to the loss of benefits and the basic necessities of living for their workers. In *Star Trek: The Next Generation*, the terrifying machine-organic cyborgs known as the Borg burst into people's living rooms in the 1990s. As I see them now, they offer not just a worst-case-scenario alien first-contact situation but also an unsettling parallel for what people lose once "efficiency," defined too narrowly, runs amok.

The Borg Collective—known simply as the Borg—is a bipedal, composite species whose sinister, greenish, cubic ships troll the galaxy in search of intelligent species. When they find species with knowledge and distinctiveness they wish to acquire, they assimilate the species. Borg drones (individuals of previously assimilated species) inject the captives with nanoprobes (microscopic robotic devices), transfiguring them from the inside, and implant them with cybernetic parts. These prosthetics allow instant communication across the collective and give the new drones superhuman strength and built-in armaments. An arm is extended with a prosthetic that can end in various tools; an ocular implant sits on a biological eye; nanoprobes coursing through a drone's blood repair their cybernetic implants; and a cortical node in the brain controls all the implants. In the wake of a Borg visitation, a planet's intelligent life is blended into the collective, leaving nothing behind.

Borg drones are genocidal and monstrous, transforming other "normal" species into more drones. As the nanoprobes enter the bodies of the victims, blood and color drain out of their skin, leaving behind a skeletal pallor. Hulking metal implants and armaments cover large parts of their faces and bodies, and they become Borg drones. Drones move awkwardly and robotically, kill indiscriminately, and appear to have no emotions or empathy. Their only goal is to continue to develop technologically by integrating the biological distinctiveness and scientific expertise of others into their collective. The Borg have one hive mind that can hear and process all the voices on a particular Borg ship—or cube—at once. It is controlled by the Borg Queen, whose desire to continue absorbing civilizations until the end of time is the single purpose being served.

For unassimilated species imperfectly bumbling through the universe is preferable to losing individuality for greater collective knowledge and technological efficiency. No one wants to join the Borg Collective; they must be assimilated by force. Upon assimilation there is no private consciousness or agency; over time Borg drones' individual desires, memories, and personalities are suppressed. They have been abducted, physically and mentally transformed, and turned into little more than automatons serving their leader's ambition. These one-time individuals will spend the rest of their lives committing collective acts of genocide and forced assimilation.

Monstrifying, excluding, and annihilating communities by deciding they don't deserve any rights doesn't require cyborgs. Societies decide that differences are irreconcilable all the time and see the loss of other people's quality of life, human rights, and even their lives as justifiable in service of a dominant or invading society's ambitions.

ALGORITHMS

A tech-world joke runs like this: AI is anything that a computer can't do—yet. Once it can, that becomes merely machine learning. AI doesn't mean being sentient or superintelligent or being better than humans at any one thing. Machines have been able to perform calculations with large numbers faster than humans since the abacus. To think about AI-related social forces and assumptions that affect who gets to be seen as fully human, we need a narrower definition (with a higher bar) for AI than, say, being unbeatable at chess. A useful definition of artificial intelligence might look like this: AI is software that can learn and can act more or less autonomously.[39]

Technology embodies and exaggerates the values and biases of its builders and the people who implement it. Humans are dangerous designers, their goals often misaligned with those of other humans and even with their own long-term interests. The current socioeconomic environment of neoliberalism and neofascism rewards sexism, racism, ableism, and greed. Technology built without breaking these monstrifying, dehumanizing values will not promote human flourishing. Algorithms have biases baked into them One philosopher has called AI tools "bias optimizers." Unless there are guardrails set up by people independent of tech companies and their lobbyists, increasingly sophisticated and embedded AI will magnify humanity's worst elements for the profits of a few at the price of suffering for the many.[40]

Algorithms and neural networks urge us to think about whose agendas they advance and who is harmed by opaque, simplified, proxy indicators.

Who gets to offer feedback on algorithms and who gets listened to? An arrest predictor is not a crime predictor. Computer engineers are disproportionately cishet white men, yet the AI they create affects everyone.[41] The idea of misaligned intelligence is helpful, but it is important to always ask with *whom* it is misaligned. Humanity is not a homogenous group of people with exactly the same needs, values, embodiments, or goals. Sometimes a terrible technology is not unfit for purpose; rather, it is functioning just as its makers and designers intended, which is to harm people (just not their makers).

Misaligned artificial intelligence is already part of many people's lives, in everything from social media advertising to the setting of insurance premium rates to the tracking of "failing" schools. AI in law enforcement generates evaluations that affect people's lives in the eyes of the law, like the amount of money they need to front to make bail after arrest or the length of a prison sentence.[42] AI lacks the empathy, knowledge, and imagination required to even begin to make ethical decisions because the people doing the programming aren't encouraged to incorporate those values into their work.

Machines don't need to be smarter than us to harm us: they just need their goals or those of humans who direct them to be opposed to those of people. This is why it is not enough to try to improve general artificial intelligence. We must address human decisions to harm others to improve their own lives. A utopian technological future will require fixing humanity's software before building smarter machines. Unless societies create conditions for people to fulfill their full potential—including basic humanitarian conditions like access to food, water, shelter, education, and safety—those societies will continue to disavow the full capacity of humanity and to squander potential while causing harm.

LET THEM EAT ROCKS

With the rising triumphalism around AI, fairy tales about what machines can do and false narratives about human potential seem to be everywhere. LLMs feed into creators' insecurities about whether they are fast enough or good enough to do what they are trying to do. Yet it's the fear, effort, and sorrow of making things that changes makers in ways that help them create something that moves people. If writers' book outlines come from a click of the button, they miss out on the connections and insights that come from making effort with their own mind, insights that couldn't have come from anyone else.

And then there's the little detail of LLMs hallucinating, lying, and making up citations. ChatGPT, in response to human prompts, fabricates evidence and sources when it provides answers. If fewer people have knowledge and expertise, fewer people will be able to tell whether AI-generated content is even true. If lying has already been hardwired into software, whatever claims its human engineers may make about democratizing information or saving labor, their product has failed.

Nor is AI "saving humanity." OpenAI servers consume gobsmacking amounts of water and energy. According to Microsoft's own internal energy audit, the company's water consumption jumped by 34 percent between 2020 and 2022, an amount that a 2023 *Forbes* article described as equivalent "to nearly 1.7 billion gallons, or more than 2,500 Olympic-sized swimming pools." Engineering and computer science professor Shaolei Ren connected this increase to Microsoft's AI development. In the same period, Google's reported water use jumped by 20 percent.[43] In Council Bluffs, Iowa, and Las Vegas, Nevada, where OpenAI and Google computing hubs guzzle water as a coolant, their water consumption rose.

The drive to automation has made it easer to commit fraud and generate misinformation. Google's AI overviews have recommended using glue to secure pizza toppings and eating rocks to stay healthy. Amazon stocked mushroom foraging guides that look like unedited chatbot burblings; users risk picking poisonous or endangered varieties.[44] AI-generated text, images, music, and video exacerbate economic, social, and climate injustice just to make company executives, owners, and shareholders richer. By blurring the boundary between real and fake, GenAI has become an existential risk to representative democracy.

PRESERVING HUMANITY IN THE AGE OF AI

Machines don't need to do everything. Living out eternity in a cage, however gilded it may be, would diminish humans to creatures that just take up space. This waste of space rhetoric is already implicit and explicit in how workers and the poor (workers or not) are criminalized and marginalized. Their individuality and existence as minds with thoughts, needs, feelings, experiences, and potential are often denied by corporations wanting to pay people less and politicians looking for scapegoats on whom to pin voters' grievances. Systems that legalize the theft of labor and monstrify people are not new. The especially brutal, widespread, and systematic case of chattel slavery, which unfolded over centuries, led to the largest involuntary movement of people in the history of humanity and the worst genocide. In the early twentieth century, a new machine with side effects appeared: the automobile. Car lobbies encouraged pulling up railways and public transit instead of simply adding cars as an option. Consequently, the United States is full of towns and cities with no sidewalks and little or no public transit, forcing people to use cars so as to not die walking on the road, while their health becomes worse from air pollution and the lack of exercise, and the planet becomes warmer.

Other industries have spent decades crafting stories that minimize the damage of their products. The tobacco and opioid company spokespeople lie about the harm caused by their products to maximize their own profits. Lawsuits have (finally) begun to follow. Lawsuits against fossil fuel companies are being filed, alleging, among other things, eroding human rights and telling lies about the environmental impact of their businesses. Lawsuits against generative AI companies are also in progress. Extrapolating from rock-eating tips and mushroom poisoning to the risk of an AI tool fabricating technical manuals, these companies knowingly allow potentially lethal information to circulate in the world.

Is there a better future? What would people choose to do with their time if robots freed them from economic constraints and things they didn't want to do? To answer that one has to determine what it is people don't want to do. There are various possible levels of robot delegation—spheres of effort that societies might choose to work toward as they legislate and expand robotics in the future. The most obvious and least controversial is the level of robots existing to do dangerous or boring work. Perhaps the most ethically fraught level would be to assign robots to perform emotional labor, managing the comfort and emotion of humans. A more sweeping choice would be to have robots to do everything that requires willpower (work and tasks that make our hearts sink), to create infinite time for leisure. The most all-encompassing level would be to have robots perform every action that requires any mental or physical training or effort, including making artworks intended to stimulate human minds. This was the ideal level of robot delegation that the literature colleague who believed robot poetry was the way of the future envisaged.

How people imagine what humanity would choose to do if robots and technology removed the need to work to enjoy a good quality of life tells us something about how they define what it means to be human. Writer Gene Roddenberry's vision of the future is a compelling utopian example. *Star Trek* replicators are capable of turning energy into most forms of matter, including food. The United Federation of Planets has done away with money, since their technology can replicate goods and materials. This does not, however, mean that federation citizens spend their lives on deck chairs sipping drinks bestrewn with paper umbrellas. Rather, they strive to better themselves, to create art, to advance scientific and medical knowledge, to exercise the hell out of their muscles on the holodeck (the virtual reality deck on starships), and to explore the galaxy. Poetry, far from being something that people delegate to artificial life-forms or algorithms to produce, is the sort of mental workout that people choose out of their own free will. Indeed, in a classic episode that is a remix of the *Gilgamesh* epic, Captain Picard's grounding in "old Earth" literature enables him to learn how to communicate with a species that speaks only through metaphors and allusions drawn from an ancient epic.

TOMORROW'S HUMAN-MACHINE RELATIONSHIPS

We need to investigate who benefits and who loses from the decisions that AI and neural networks make. Since technology magnifies the bias of designers and datasets, groups who have historically faced discrimination pay an even higher price for the failures of technology. Evading these questions is a technopathology of the contemporary world. Corporations tell us that any technology that lowers costs for institutions or for business owners is automatically beneficial; imply that there are no other communities or institutions that matter to the cost-benefit analysis of a technological innovation; and that anything that cannot be counted does not count.

For many tech corporations, people exist to provide data about themselves to power the lives of a few—an uncanny parallel with *The Matrix*.[45] Advances in AI and robotics threaten to make flesh and blood an optional extra of personhood or even an inconvenient aberration within a larger category of legal persons. As corporations acquire rights and privileges of personhood, corporeal persons become the monster. If machines are beings who do what they are told and have little or no agency over their own futures, then where is the human-machine boundary in late-stage capitalism?

How do we want to spend our days: are we doers or are we like the globular humans in *Wall-E* who live in lounge chairs, remote controls in hand, out of practice turning their minds to make anything or solve problems, even unable to use their atrophied muscles? Wall-E is more human than the people in his world. If people in the future were to give over that much to machines, it will be the machines who are human. The price will be that humans will have become monsters to us.

Who knows what humanity could do if machines did lift everyone into secure, rewarding work and living situations. The barriers to getting there—or to even getting closer—are the political, economic, and legal structures through which governments and individuals dehumanize people. Many corporations view people as nothing more than economic resources lying around and waiting to be exploited: as workers, as customers, or as market research data. Large corporations frequently behave as if they don't see employees as deserving of human rights.[46] This sort of political economy is not new. Most infamously, enslaved people in the era of the Atlantic slave trade were framed by enslavers as property. After depersoning came the laws that stripped people of their rights. Implicit in the way people treated the enslaved was the loss of their right to exist at all. In the most apocalyptic version of this hypothetical scenario, humanity survives in a mere handful of ultrarich people and their machines.

The vastest amount of human potential is lost, since the great majority of people, rich or poor, do not spend much of their time living as their deepest, most creative selves. If the point of machines is to improve human lives, then attending to solving basic human problems—like providing safe, clean, and efficient energy; sufficient food and water; and a habitable climate—is the most worthwhile assignment for computer scientists. But if very few individual people count as humans and if machines themselves get to have their own agendas regardless of their effects on human people, the future of the present may look even more like the world of *The Matrix* than it does today.

NINE

Extraterrestrials

FOR GEOGRAPHERS IN EUROPE before the late fifteenth century, "extraterrestrial" space began on earth. As I described earlier, ancient Greek and Roman geographers expected the earth to become uninhabitable around the equator. Opinion was divided on whether it was possible to cross that zone of great heat, or what they called the Torrid Zone. How many landmasses might be on the other side? And who or what might live there? The inhabitants might be antipodes—people with their feet on backward—a category from whence the geographic term "antipodean" comes. They might do stuff that seemed deeply weird, like living in caves or eating one another. Most unsettling, just visiting these places might change the body of the traveler.[1]

Since at least the late fourteenth century, "alien" in English meant a "foreign-born natural resident."[2] For the seventeenth-century aristocrat Lady Margaret Cavendish, Duchess of Newcastle-upon-Tyne in northern England, alienation began at home. A considerable student of nature and a writer of fiction, she attracted gossip and ridicule despite her high social status. Writers and thinkers, both men and women, couldn't understand her writing on science and called her "Mad Madge." The diarist Samuel Pepys described her as a "mad, conceited, ridiculous woman and her husband an asse to suffer [i.e., let] her to write what she writes to him and of him."[3]

Considering the treatment Cavendish received on this earth from her peers, it's not surprising that she imagined a planet where she gained respect, power, and acknowledgment—a place where, perhaps, she *could* feel at home as an intellectual and a woman. In her speculative fiction romance *The Blazing World*, a woman travels to the North Pole, where she discovers that this earth touches another. She crosses into this other world and finds it populated by speaking mammals who treat her like a great sage. The mammals take her to their court where she, perhaps predictably, marries the emperor. There she becomes a patron of learning.

In real life Lady Margaret had been the first woman to attend meetings at the Royal Society in London, founded in 1667, which functioned as the kingdom's premier setting for experimental science. In her novel the empress founds schools and scientific societies. In a move unsettlingly prescient of *The Muppet Show*, her court is made up of human-animal hybrids: bear-men practice experimental philosophy, bird-men astronomy, ape-men chemistry; the fox-men are—of course—politicians; the giants are the obvious choice for architects; and various bird-men are orators. The empress spends her time becoming an expert in illusion, which allows her to change the outcome of a world war and liberate her new nation—truly the imagined life of a superheroine and surely the life Lady Margaret felt herself equal to living had her society let her do so.

THROUGH THE LOOKING GLASS AND THE CLOSET

In the age of rockets, "extraterrestrial" conjures up space travel to planets and moons beyond the earth's atmosphere. But thinkers and writers have also long imagined ways of slipping into other dimensions that are not exactly supernatural but rather both like and unlike this world. In Lewis Carroll's *Alice's Adventures in Wonderland*, reason itself is turned on its head if one passes through the looking glass. In C. S. Lewis's allegorical *Chronicles of Narnia* novels, a transdimensional thread connects humans on earth—the blood of Adam and Eve—to a land in a parallel world in which magic is real. It is the scene for a multigenerational epic, with a form that loosely resembles the biblical story from Creation to the Last Judgment. In Ursula K. Le Guin's *The Left Hand of Darkness*, an anthropologist from earth on a mission to a planet where everyone is ambisexual is treated like an aberration, a monster. Setting a work of fiction in an alternate world offers an opportunity to prototype what society would be like if its members were ontologically different. At the same time, these alternate worlds are most powerful when they refract into view things about this world that people usually brush under the carpet.

One of the scenarios that exobiologists are preparing for is an encounter with extraterrestrial life that is capable of affecting human bodies. While this may bring alien plagues to mind, a nonpathogenic way in which beings affect one another is through empathy: by imagining what another feels and coming to feel that way oneself in the process. Connection across species animates *E.T.*, the archetypal alien-encounter movie of the subgenre in which humans don't get eaten. The 1982 movie opens with a heartrending scene: eight minutes in, an alien is inadvertently left behind in a forest on earth as the mother ship leaves. The alien stumbles his way out of the forest and into a close encounter with humanity. Even though everybody screams when they first meet E.T. (the extraterrestrial), he rapidly becomes the movie's most sympathetic character.[4]

Soon E.T. and Elliott, one of the children who first encounters him, develop a symbiotic psychic and physiological connection. When E.T., comfy in Elliott's home, finds his way into a beer can, Elliott, who is at school, loses his inhibitions. Sitting in biology class looking at frogs, he decides to free them. When E.T. watches television, Elliott acts out the on-screen narrative. *E.T.* invites viewers to consider just how mind- and form-changing empathy might be. How different is it from telepathy? Elliott, feeling the loss of an absent father, connects with E.T. across species. In that act is a utopian possibility: perhaps humanity, separated by language but not by species, might be capable of connecting across divisions that seem intractable.

If you travel in the other direction, one of the imagined perils of space is that you may run into something that changes you forever. Ridley Scott's dystopian sci-fi horror classic *Alien* works through this possibility in a way that upends everything viewers thought they understood about how bodies relate to their environment and how species interact with one another.[5] The action opens on a commercial space vessel returning to earth, its crew in stasis. On receiving a transmission from a moon, the ship's computer awakens the crew. Several members investigate and find an abandoned alien spacecraft that contains a chamber full of giant eggs. When a crewmember touches one, a monstrous, tentacled creature erupts from it and attaches itself to his face. The landing party stumbles back to their own ship, where a senior officer insists that the creature and its victim be brought aboard, quarantine regulations be damned. The alien and the human eventually separate, and the monster is found dead.

The alien turns out to incubate its young inside humans, to be born via a spontaneous caesarean—the iconic, horrific fate that befalls the first victim. Perhaps the creature can breathe through human faces too. The crew members gradually learn that the alien can change its cellular composition in response to its environment. On the ship it replaces its cells with polarized silicon. The creature's "blood" is an acid that eats through the ship's hull. The alien takes control of the ship and of the narrative: humans become prey on their own ship. The monstrous alien, designed by Hans Ruedi Giger and Carlo Rambaldi, features a fearsome insectoid head with another, smaller head inside it, leaving us wondering how deep the horror goes. The monster consumes the crew and keeps some of them alive in its lair.

Alien distills apocalyptic fears about gender, extraterrestrials, environmental adaptation, and technology through the life cycle of the iconic alien—and it grounds our fears in something "real": a heartless corporation. Its front end is a computer interface called "Mother." In an unexpected plot twist, the science officer who had overridden quarantine regulations to allow the original alien onto the ship turns out to be a robot expressly instructed by Mother to do so. Mother had deemed the crew expendable in the pursuit of science and profit and orders him to ensure that the crew return with the alien. In a long and disastrous hunting scene, in which multiple parts of the ship are damaged, Ellen Ripley (played by Sigourney Weaver) manages to shoot the alien into outer space by decompressing the ship. The movie ends with the spacecraft's decompression, although questions remain: Is the monster dead and gone for good? Or did it lay an egg somewhere?

Another human-alien connection undergirds the sci-fi-meets-racial-slavery story that is the South African film *District 9*, released in 2009.[6] Here humanity is so porous that individuals can be transformed through contact with extraterrestrial DNA. The movie is an allegory of certain events that took place in Johannesburg's District 6 in 1966, when the South African government declared that the ward was now a "whites only" neighborhood and forcibly removed some sixty thousand Black residents, resettling them some fifteen miles away. The film is set in 1982, when a (fictional) space vessel full of ill, malnourished aliens resembling giant insects arrives in Johannesburg. Here they are subjected to apartheid—detained in a camp called District 9. The Afrikaners coin the slur "prawns" for them.

Years later a minor bureaucrat, Wikus van de Merwe, is tasked with moving the aliens to a new camp. Wikus manages to spray alien fuel onto himself—and starts to mutate into an alien. When researchers discover his transformation, they learn that his injured arm, which has morphed into an insect claw, can operate the aliens' weapons technology. The head of the research institute declares that Wikus has to be dissected so that humans can harness and exploit alien technology. Wikus manages to escape. As his transformation into insect-alien continues, he becomes increasingly humane.

The boundary between human and alien in *District 9* is essential for the human characters in Johannesburg, for whom the "prawns" are the opposite of civilizable or human. Yet the boundary turns out to be porous—a spectacular rendition of the fiction of race, which presumes a fundamental difference between people who look different. As Wikus turns into a monstrous mélange of alien and human, he no longer receives empathy from his compatriots. The movie's harrowing presentation of how security officers and scientists talk about and treat the aliens is a damning critique of racism and apartheid. When viewers empathize with the aliens and with Wikus after his transformation, they effectively look with these characters' eyes, with their perspective, not just at an imagined plotline on a screen but at racist and xenophobic policies around the world today. While the premise of the movie is fictional, the central biological narrative about the process of horizontal gene transfer—the transfer of genes across species—is something that already happens. Genes from microbes enter mammalian DNA on a regular basis.[7] But the point of the movie isn't the science. It's the lens the story points at racism, discrimination, and apartheid.

COLLAPSING THE DIVINE

People have imagined aliens and their alien gods and used fiction to talk about religion and ideas about the divine. In *Star Trek: Deep Space Nine*, a space station orbiting a planet near a wormhole is a setting in which one species' prophets, said to reside in a celestial temple, are another species' wormhole aliens. The potential for individual beings to level up and down between god and human, across myths, origin stories, and contemporary popular culture, puts pressure on the notion of a fixed range of human forms and abilities. In the *Star Trek* franchise, the Q continuum is able to strip members of their powers as punishment and even, on one occasion, upon request. In *Star*

Trek: Deep Space Nine, a shape-shifting species called the Dominion, which prefers to exist in liquid rather than solid form, takes the power to shape-shift away from a member as punishment, turning him into a human. Punishments that change the very form of beings transform people's bodies to memorialize how a society has judged their actions. In this sense, when communities push individuals out of their normal embodiment, they are rejecting them so profoundly that they are redrawing the boundaries around the very category of the human (or of the god) to exclude the offending person.

Just because beings are omnipotent—godlike in powers and thus worshipped by cultures as gods—doesn't mean that they are necessarily good and honorable role models. In *Star Trek: The Next Generation*, the character of Q is a seemingly far superior being, a member of the Q Continuum, a pantheon of beings capable of traveling through space and time, possessing almost infinite powers over the universe. Q calls himself an omnipotent god. But the *Enterprise* crew frequently eyeroll his claim (and thus adopt Christian, Eurocentric assumptions of what gods are supposed to be like). The crew find Q to be arrogant, irritating, inconsiderate, and reckless, with a penchant for terrible puns and gags. Vain, dishonest, and unreliable, he devotes himself almost exclusively to his own amusement. Q's mercurial nature—somewhere between prankster and teenager—poses questions about what gods, if they exist, might actually deserve from humans. *Star Trek*'s Klingons have no illusions about their gods. As Lieutenant Commander Worf puts it, "Our gods are dead. We slew them millennia ago. They were more trouble than they were worth."[8] These modern fictional examples play on ambiguous, sometimes contested feelings that cultures have long had about their gods.

The promise or threat of life on other planets creates dilemmas around salvation for the pope's official astronomer. In 2014, at an astrobiology conference at the Library of Congress in Washington, DC, I heard the pope's astronomer, Dr. Guy Consolmagno, give a presentation on his work at the Vatican. The Vatican City—the walled city-state nested inside the city of Rome—is the official domain and residence of the pope. One of the more unexpected roles in his entourage is that of his astronomer.

Consolmagno described how people loved to ask him, "Would you baptize E.T.?" Different people would use pretty much the same words but mean different things. Some would ask the question accusingly: Was he so inclusive that he would even baptize E.T.? In other cases people were curious but not worried or angry. But what all versions of the question share is an underlying question about who counts as a person in the Catholic faith: Is E.T. capable of receiving the word of God? As I listened to Consolmagno's presentation, I realized that this question was a thread woven through the history of Christianity's cross-cultural interactions.

The question of being mentally capable of becoming Christian lay at the heart of a pivotal sixteenth-century debate, in which Spanish theologians and jurists argued over whether or not the peoples of the Americas were fully human on the basis of conflicting evidence about the success of missionaries in converting them to Christianity. Whatever terms they used to describe other cultures, Christians of this period saw full humanity only in those who were Christian or who were prepared to convert. By using such an exclusionary definition of humanity, these Christians defined everyone else as monstrous.

In some ways the sixteenth-century European view that it was only white people who were really people never left Catholic cosmology and worsened over time. The Mount Graham International Observatory in Arizona, which is run by the Vatican Observatory, is a symptom. The observatory was built on a peak more than ten thousand feet high, called Dził Nchaa Si An (Big Seated Mountain, in Apache), but listed as Mount Graham on most maps. The mountain is the largest peak in the "Sky Islands," which rise more than two miles above the surrounding desert. It's a region of rich biodiversity due to the mountain's many microclimates—places brimming with worlds of their own, even if the telescopic lenses on the mountain point away from them.[9]

The observatory was built on land that is sacred to members of the Western Apache tribes and had been initially turned into reservations. When settlers complained of the loss of their access to natural resources, the region's Apache were dispossessed of their land in 1873.[10] In 1902 the mountain became one of the first regions to become part of the US National Forest. In 1984 the mountain was chosen by the University of Arizona and the Vatican as the site of a new telescope complex, with no regard for the land's sacred value.[11]

The Apache dispute the placement of the observatory and argue that the site should be protected from scientific incursion and resource exploitation.[12] Its presence has damaged the environment and disrupted their spiritual activities. Most of Consolmagno's research data comes from the site's telescope: the Pope Scope. And he defended the building of Mount Graham Observatory, which he would later direct.[13] The question of baptizing E.T. that so many put to Consolmagno might have been better phrased as a different question entirely: If you are unable to put the Apaches' beliefs, values, and rights to land above your scientific curiosity, why should you and your church be humanity's first contact with E.T.? Perhaps people and individuals who monstrify other groups do not make the best representatives for humanity.

TEN

Monstrofuturism

We who hobnob with hobbits and tell tall tales about little green
men are quite used to being dismissed as mere entertainers, or
sternly disapproved of as escapists. . . . At this point, realism is
perhaps the least adequate means of understanding or portraying
the incredible realities of our existence.

URSULA K. LE GUIN,
"National Book Award Acceptance Speech," 1973

PEOPLE WHO DON'T FIT INTO boxes don't have to be feared, loathed, or
excluded. Yet monstrifying people is so widespread today that it often feels as
if fiction is the best place in which to find alternatives. Just as science fiction
and speculative fiction distill and reveal the "incredible realities of our existence" precisely because of the alternate worlds in which they unfold, they
offer space in which to think through better ways for being in this world. As
Ursula Le Guin observes, imaginative fiction reveals some truths about the
real more effectively than realism.

Jim Henson's weekly program *The Muppet Show* modeled for late twentieth-
century television viewers (ostensibly children) an anarchic, utopian world in
which everyone was a monster, and so no one was (really) a monster. In the
late 1970s and 1980s, the Muppets—anthropomorphic animal-cum-monster
puppets—had cult status, and the puppeteers were invited to all the A-list
parties. Category-breakers were cool. The show's action unfolded at a theater,
in which a troupe of puppets and people in monster suits performed a weekly
variety show. Each week the show had a human guest star, whose body of work
informed the theme. After the ballet icon Rudolf Nureyev appeared on the
show's second season, dancing with a performer in a life-size Miss Piggy costume, celebrities reportedly began lining up to appear alongside the Muppets.
The show's other guests included singers Julie Andrews, Harry Belafonte, Joan
Baez, Alice Cooper, Elton John, Liza Minnelli, and Diana Ross. Appearances
by actors like Vincent Price (known for roles in horror movies) and Christopher

Reeve (who played Superman) inspired the show's writers and puppeteers to take their stories about humans and monsters further.

Jokes frequently revolved around the cognitive dissonance of the characters—a frog, a pig, a bear, a purple turkey-like monster—going about theatrical life as if they were human. As if that were not fantastical enough, one of the occasional acts at the theater involved sending the pigs into space, in a spoof of the original *Star Trek* series. Each sketch, song, and backstage drama threatened to bring the theater crashing down around the players' ears—or to cause an irate audience to storm the curtains—but things always worked themselves out in the end.

As a child who read out of *The Muppet Show* the rubric for how the universe *should* work, I knew the show's utopian anarchy was a far cry from the (frankly) carceral space of school, in a universe in which grownups said they were always right. Looking back on the show now, I see how striking it was that the human guests were constantly entranced by the Muppets, their worldview, their choices—and their celebration of life. To throw this joyful anarchy into even sharper relief there was prissy Sam the Eagle. Coloring within the metaphorical lines, he evoked a sense of dread that even the resident theater critics Statler and Waldorf, with their gallows humor and choleric anarchy, could not match. What becomes possible when we celebrate all our different ways of being?

WERE THEY REALLY MONSTERS TO BEGIN WITH?

How monstrous the monsters are depends on who's telling the story. This is powerfully clear when we look at translations of *Beowulf*, the Old English saga written between the mid-seventh and late tenth centuries. The saga is famous as an epic battle between good and evil. A ferocious monster, Grendel, has been making nightly raids at a Scandinavian castle in the kingdom of Hrothgar, eating and dismembering those who come within his reach. Beowulf and his warriors take the fight to the monstrous Grendel and his even more monstrous mother. But look a little closer, and that story gets a little funky.

The oldest surviving version of *Beowulf* is in a manuscript dated circa 975–1025 and was penned by two scribes, with different handwriting and their own patterns of making mistakes. We don't know how much the story changed before this version and how many versions of the story circulated. The *Beowulf* manuscript is part of the Cotton Collection, the founding British Museum manuscript collection (now at the British Library), heavily damaged by fire in 1731. The charred, jagged-edged pages mounted in modern paper frames betray the epic life it led in England. It lurched from Cotton House (which fell into ruin) to Essex House (which was deemed a fire risk) to Ashburnham House (where it and other peripatetic Cotton manuscripts survived an inferno). The manuscript's singed edges would crumble away. Someone rebound the manuscript in the nineteenth century, obscuring the lettering along the binding. And worms snacked their way through the volume—another occupational hazard for an old manuscript. As for the words that escaped fire, fixing, and verminous foodification, some had more than one possible translation. There is the issue of translating meter, for *Beowulf* is a poem: there are rhyming and alliterative passages and patterns for pauses and where the stresses fall on syllables. And then later scribes added their own edits to the original manuscript.[1]

Novelist and *Beowulf* translator Maria Dahvana Headley puts it beautifully when she calls *Beowulf* "a living text in a dead language." To capture the sense, feel, and emotional effects of a poem for readers who are meeting it in a different language, place, and time, translators sometimes swap out the "original" slang and expressions for ones that the poem's new audience will understand. Headley opens her translation, published in 2020, with "Bro! Tell me we still know how to speak of kings!" In doing so she brings to the minds of readers familiar with contemporary US slang a sense of some guy getting ready to boast while also feigning camaraderie within his circle of bros.[2]

Headley was drawn to the poem—and I, as a scholar of monsters, was drawn to her translation—by its chief villain, Grendel's mother. The *Beowulf* poet left her nameless: she is merely "Grendel's mother." At her first appearance, the poet describes her as an "avenger" biding her time before wreaking vengeance on those who killed her son. In Headley's translation, "Grendel's mother, warrior-woman, outlaw, meditated on misery." Translating *Beowulf* as a white woman in the second decade of the twenty-first century, Headley looked back over the decisions earlier translators had made about Grendel's mother, noticing how she "is almost always depicted in translation as an obvious monster rather than as a human woman—and her monstrosity doesn't typically allow even for partial humanity, though the poem itself shows us that she lives in a hall, uses weapons, is trained in combat, and follows blood-feud rules."[3]

The poet said little about Grendel's mother's appearance, besides the fact that she looks like a tall woman. Yet many translators have chosen to translate her fingers (*fingrum*) as "claws." And the very fact that Grendel's mother is a capable warrior appears to have encouraged the poem's male translators in a later era to frame her as breaking the category of human. As Headley observes, women have often been "mistaken for monstrous when one is only doing as men do: providing for and defending oneself." Earlier translators, then, had often cast Grendel's mother as more monstrous than she is in the original Beowulf text. They took the fact that she is an accomplished warrior as a sign of her monstrosity. A 1922 glossary by the philologist Frederick Klaeber rendered *aglaec-wif*—a descriptor for Grendel's mother—as "wretch, or monster, of a woman" and "monster, demon, fiend." Yet Klaeber also translated *aglaeca* (the masculine form of the word) as "hero" when it describes Beowulf, betraying his view that strong women were monstrous. Headley argues that where the word appears in other Old English texts, it is more likely to mean "formidable."[4]

Epic narratives are usually told from the perspectives of the hero and the humans, not from the worldview of those they call monsters. In the novel *Grendel*, the author John Gardner flips the perspective on the *Beowulf* poem by retelling the story from Grendel's viewpoint, in his imagined voice. Gardner asked why Grendel might have begun raiding Hrothgar in the first place—a question the *Beowulf* poet does not pose. We follow the story through the eyes of an older Grendel, looking back on his youth. He has internalized the taunts and insults that have come his way. He sees himself through the eyes of his enemies, their words ringing in his mind as his own: "pointless, ridiculous monster crouched in the shadows, stinking of dead men, murdered children, martyred cows."[5]

In the bloody feud between Grendel and the Danish lords of King Hrothgar, it is the men who strike first. A band of nobles discovers a young Grendel with his leg stuck between two tree trunks, pinioned in midair. They cannot understand his cries, although he can mostly understand their speech. The men decide to attack, with King Hrothgar, as Grendel later learns him to be, striking the first blow. Grendel's cries bring his mother on the scene, and at the sound of her fury the men flee.[6] We follow Grendel through the years as he watches bands of men and women cutting trees, building settlements, tending animals, and marauding one another's mead halls. He watches Hrothgar's power and reach grow, and he gets angry at the resulting ecocide, with its fearful animals and razed forests.

As monstrous and alien as Grendel and the Danes are to each other, Grendel becomes captivated by a blind harpist and singer, the Shaper, who comes to Hrothgar's hall. Monster he may be, but Grendel feels as much as a person. By eavesdropping on the Shaper's storytelling, Grendel learns of the creation of the world and of two ancient brothers, presumably Cain and

Abel, who fought: one each on the sides of good and evil. From this Grendel gleans that he must be of the cursed race of evil, and in his grief he runs into the hall to try to get the harpist to stop. The merrymakers see a monster and begin the cycle of nightly violence that the *Beowulf* poem recounts. Grendel will slowly turn against the Shaper: on his next visit to eavesdrop, he hears the Shaper storifying Grendel's blundering into the mead hall and realizes that the singer has taken control of Grendel's story.

If Grendel has little voice in the *Beowulf* poem, his nameless mother who has forgotten how to speak has even less. For the African American novelist Toni Morrison, the binary framing of Beowulf as straightforwardly good and Grendel and his mother as utterly bad was unsatisfying for modern readers. In an essay titled "Grendel and His Mother," Morrison also retells the story, this time with an eye to the perspectives of both Grendel and his mother. Morrison notes that "what never seemed to trouble or worry" the nobles and warriors whom Grendel attacked "was who was Grendel and why had he placed them on his menu?" She suggested that no one asked because "evil has no father." Evil for the *Beowulf* poet (and scribes) and their readers was innate in Grendel: "It is preternatural and exists without explanation." Grendel's is "the nature of an alien mind—an inhuman drift."[7]

The *Beowulf* poet casts Grendel as the quintessential adversary, "the ultimate monster: mindless without intelligible speech." After the warrior Beowulf gives Grendel a mortal wound (pulling off his arm), Grendel returns to his mother, who has neither speech nor a name. Grendel's mother seeks revenge, attacking, in her turn, the mead hall. This prompts Beowulf and his men to go out hunting for her. When Beowulf engages Grendel's mother and beheads her, her blood melts his sword. Was this yet another way in which she was allegedly monstrous? "The conventional reading is that the fiends' blood is so foul that it melts steel." But Morrison argues that there's another possible interpretation. Perhaps, instead, we might read this scene as one that shows how "violence against violence . . . is itself so foul that sword of vengeance collapses in exhaustion or shame."[8] The blade that killed Grendel's mother has ceased to exist. Its portfolio of deeds, heroic, monstrous, or otherwise, has turned to stone.

Those who translated the past for the present have shaped how people understand all manner of ancient writings. "For hundreds of years," in the memorable words of classics professor Emily Wilson, "the study of ancient Greece and Rome was largely the domain of elite white men and their bored sons." Many translations for women's experiences in classical texts were, consequently, the choices of these men, working in institutions where neither women nor people of color were considered to be of equal status to men, if they were even permitted to enter. Writing in 2017, the year she became the first woman to publish an English translation of Homer's *The Odyssey*, Wilson observed that "the legacy of male domination is still with us" in the academic field of classics and in how the general public encounters the history and literature of the ancient world.[9] This affects how we perceive who counts as normal and even as human.

Translation is not the simple one-to-one of words that a casual (or time-pressed) Google Translate user might imagine, although the ease with which computer translations and so-called AI software willingly offer up gibberish should make people pause more often (and resist calling this tech intelligent). Words often mean many different things, and they don't mean the same different things in every language. Translators decide how to render a word in another tongue, which may not have a remotely equivalent term. Even if it does, it may not carry the same associations, aesthetic feel, or emotional baggage. Translation for sense, for emotion, and for literal, word-for-word fidelity are competing aims. A translator's work is one of personal, human engagement with and mediation of another person's words for new readers—a project that requires empathy, ethics, imagination, and fine judgment.

Translation depends on and varies with the place, time, and values of the translator. As women have begun getting their own translations and retellings of classical narratives into print, the bias against women among earlier, male translators has become clear. Emily Wilson notes that Robert Fagles's widely read translation of *The Odyssey*, published in 1996, was praised by critic Gary Wills in the *New Yorker* "for being 'politically correct'" and for its "'sympathetic' treatment of female characters." Yet his translation of the passage where Odysseus's son, Telemachus, hanged the enslaved women who had sex with the suitors of the uninterested Penelope (Odysseus's wife, holding a candle for his return) belies Wills's praise. Fagles translates Telemachus's term for the enslaved women as "sluts" and as "the suitors' whores." Other translators use similar phrases. One translator dehumanizes these women to the point of calling them "creatures." For Wilson there is no such moral disapproval in Homer's original. In her translation, "Telemachus says that the women 'lay beside the suitors.'"[10] As a more diverse array of thinkers has revisited and retranslated ancient texts, we've become able to see them in new ways. Instead of adding layers of monstrification to the text, extra pairs of eyes and new perspectives have revealed that some of the monster-making in ancient texts happened centuries after the stories were first told.

THE POLITICS OF THE ARCHIVE

The practice of history is the practice of storytelling to observe, compare, analyze, interpret, and make sense of the surviving traces of the past. Scholars trained in examining the sources of the past, be they handwritten documents, plays, or paintings, ask questions of their sources. The questions they ask and their relevance for the present vary. This is why scholars repeatedly contribute new insights, perspectives, and interpretations even on texts people have examined regularly for centuries. Works of history are thus an array of evidence-based explanations that emerge in response to questions about how and why people engaged in particular opportunities and problems in the past and what that means for our understanding of the past and even the present.

In a pathbreaking essay, the US literary scholar and cultural historian Saidiya Hartman describes the challenges of trying to write about enslaved girls who experienced the Middle Passage (kidnapping and forced relocation from Africa to the Americas). She asks, "How can narrative embody life in words and at the same time respect what we cannot know?" The architecture of enslavement—its forts, the barracoon—was not just physical carceral spaces for people but was and is also a prison limiting the horizons of knowledge. That, together with what Hartman terms "the silence in the archive," has limited the range of questions that scholars have traditionally posed about the slave trade. As Hartman puts it, writing stories can be seen "as a form of compensation or even as reparations, perhaps the only kind we will ever receive."[11]

Hartman's words have inspired my efforts to experiment with modes of doing and writing history in this book, and they have also informed my decisions to talk about what we cannot know, why that is, and how that shapes how we understand the past and its legacies. Hartman's writings have invited me to ask, What are the possibilities and limits of restoring to history-the-discipline and history-as-collective-memory the perspectives and personhood of monstrified individuals and groups who rarely got to leave us their own views? An ethics of care is needed here, for without care, history becomes an act of violence or of complicity to past violence and its ongoing legacies.

Some might argue that history is about things that can be "proven" with a piece of evidence that still survives. But the idea that history is something told through written texts—as the written word being what counts as evidence—is itself a scholarly convention with its own history and politics (in the sense of having an impact on who has power over what and whom, who gets to speak, and who doesn't). And some people's pieces of paper were destroyed, on purpose, so that their voices and perspectives could not survive. Spanish conquistadors, for instance, destroyed the majority of Indigenous books in Mesoamerica in the early sixteenth century.

Where enslaved, poor, or marginalized individuals are concerned, scholars have often had little by way of written sources besides the words of those who stood in judgment of the people the scholars were trying to write about.[12] In some cases a person's words seemingly survive in the transcripts of court cases: interrogators asked individuals accused of witchcraft questions, and court recorders penned their answers. But those words are not entirely the words of those who spoke them either. Scribes and translators added, compressed, omitted, changed, or simply did not understand elements of speakers' testimony. Even if recorders were working to the best of their ability, their own assumptions, values, and prejudices shaped what they wrote down.

And then the questions themselves and the circumstances in which they were posed limited the horizons of possibility for what someone got to say. Take the case of someone accused of witchcraft, standing trial. They didn't choose the questions; they had to work within the script their interrogator had laid out, and they didn't usually end up writing about their experiences themselves. If they confessed—and there were people tasked with performing torture to compel defendants to confess—their confession needed to convince their listeners and thus contained many of the usual elements (flying, consorting with the devil, accusing other people of witchcraft).[13]

Defendants regularly told one story before torture and a more expansive one afterward. For instance, in 1617 one Collette du Mont was tried and convicted on the Isle of Guernsey, alongside two other women. They were questioned about their accomplices. Collette did not wish to detail her activities, but when she was taken to the torture chamber, "she confessed that . . . the Devil, in the form of a cat, appeared to her" and took her to avenge her neighbors. As she told it, she then rubbed herself with an ointment he had given her and flew to join sixteen or seventeen other witches for the Sabbath.[14] Thus monsters that interrogators expected could enter the records as defendants' testimony.

Around 1797 a girl was born in upstate New York to parents enslaved by Dutch settlers. By age nine Isabella Baumfree, as she was called, had been sold by her enslavers and separated from her family. Isabella was sold away a total of three times before escaping with her youngest child in 1826, the year before a new law in New York State freeing all enslaved people within its borders went into effect. Her life had been harrowing, filled with the racist violence, family separation, and heartbreak all too common among enslaved Africans.

In 1843 Baumfree converted to Methodism and changed her name to Sojourner Truth. She then devoted her life to fighting oppression and working toward women's rights and the abolition of slavery, a movement focused on Black men at the time. She traveled around the country giving speeches. As she journeyed to women's rights meetings, she was struck by how Black women were invisible to the movement. Indeed, white speakers compared the plight of (implicitly white) women to that of enslaved people to give the fight for (implicitly white) women's rights greater urgency.[15]

In May 1851 the Ohio Women's Rights Convention met in Akron. Again Truth noticed speakers who spoke before her agitate for women's rights, using the argument that their current status and situation was as dire as that of enslaved people. Here Truth would give what was perhaps the most famous of her speeches: the one passed down to us with the ringing phrase, "Ain't I a woman?" Truth called out an unpleasant truth about both the feminist and the abolitionist movements in the nineteenth-century United States. Neither white women nor Black men imagined Black women as people for whose rights they were also working. Instead, Black women fell through the cracks.[16] Truth contended that she was both a woman and a worker, a person capable of feeling, even though, to white society, no one thought about Black women when they argued either for women's rights or for the abolition of slavery.

Truth recognized a phenomenon to which the law professor and civil rights activist Kimberlé Crenshaw would give a name more than a century later: intersectionality. The theory of intersectionality is founded on the evidence-based argument that the discrimination meted out by the US justice system on people who are both Black *and* women is not merely greater than the discrimination faced by people who are *either* Black *or* women, but is of a different kind and greater magnitude altogether. It is not a simple math of prejudices about Black men and white women "added together." This plays out in the life experiences of Black women and in narratives and stereotypes that monstrify them as a category of their own.[17] Intersectionality theory predicts that people who fall into multiple or intersecting social groups that face oppression on the basis of race, class, gender, sexual orientation, or economic status experience not just greater discrimination but new, dehumanizing narratives that storify them as, for example, capable of less and deserving less than other people.

The central argument of Truth's speech—that she, too, was a woman, one who could think and feel, one who worked, one who loved her children—are the words of someone arguing that they, too, are human. Krao, whom we met in chapter 6, might have thought and felt something like this, too. Originally from Southeast Asia, she was exhibited around Europe by a Canadian showman who called her a "missing link" between human and animal.[18] As Krao, who was unusually hairy, grew up, audiences objected to having to view someone who, in their eyes, looked like a hybrid of human and animal. Once Krao was past puberty, white exhibition visitors were troubled. They interpreted the intersection of her gender, skin color, place of origin, and appearance as an adult woman to mean that she couldn't possibly be fully human.

In an ironic turn of events, the Akron convention's Publishing Committee failed to publish Truth's speech in the event's official proceedings, demonstrating the truth of Truth's observation that people failed to grasp that Black women were women too. Truth's words come down to us not exactly in her own hand: she could neither read nor write, skills that enslaved people were often barred from acquiring. Instead, her iconic speech survives in two published versions. The first printed version of the speech appeared in the spring of 1851, a month after the event. Two abolitionists, Marius and Emily Robinson, had heard Truth's speech and published it in the *Antislavery Bugle* (which one of them edited; the other was the paper's publishing agent).[19]

In 1863 another version appeared. In this version Truth's speech was rendered as if it had been given in a southern dialect—which is unlikely to have been how she spoke, since she was in fact from upstate New York and had a Dutch accent from speaking Dutch before she had learned English. Yet this is the version that became best known—and it is the version containing the iconic line in southern speech, "Ain't I a woman?" For white people in the northern states, a Sojourner Truth story in which she was from the South allowed the North to be on the "right" side of history. By subtly suggesting that Truth's experiences were the fault of people in the South, this editorial choice likely made it easier for northerners to ally themselves to Truth's cause. The differences between the two speeches reveal how her allies saw her and strategically told—and subtly changed—her story.

Sojourner Truth was not the first enslaved or formerly enslaved African to argue for their humanity. In the decades that followed, African Americans and people of African descent elsewhere in the Americas and the Caribbean published libraries' worth of history, biography, literature, and cultural criticism. These writers argued for their humanity and critiqued the worldview that created the category of Blackness and, out of and through that act of creation, built modernity on the backs of those it called Black. How does a Black person exist in a present infused with the history of that category? As Cameroonian sociologist Achille Mbembe puts it, Black people "take something they did not originally create, and make it their own."[20]

AFROFUTURISM

Difference doesn't have to mean mapping people onto a hierarchy of who is or isn't entitled to flourish, who is or isn't capable of certain jobs, or who is or isn't beautiful, ethical, intelligent, or human. Individuals and groups who have been marginalized by their societies have not just spoken back against their monstrification but have also told stories about themselves and the world in their own terms, centering their experiences. The creative sensibility now called Afrofuturism is an approach through which writers, musicians, and artists have spoken back to history and held space for those whose interior lives remain unknowable to us.

In a 1994 essay, the writer and cultural critic Mark Dery wondered why more African Americans weren't writing science fiction. After all, he explained, African American history was the stuff of the genre's plots. African Americans had experienced alien abduction (the slave trade); life as "the descendants of alien abductees"; assault by abductors using technology for bodily alteration (branding) and genetic control (forced sterilization); and medical experimentation under false pretenses (the Tuskegee experiment that unfolded between the 1930s and the 1970s).[21]

But there were already some major science fiction authors who were African American. Dery identified four Black novelists—Octavia E. Butler, Samuel R. Delany, Steve Barnes, and Charles Saunders—who "ha[d] chosen to write within the genre conventions of science fiction." In Butler's time-travel novel *Kindred*, a Black woman makes involuntary journeys into a past in which she has to protect one of her enslaver ancestors if she is to continue to exist in her own timeline, exploring how the legacy of slavery includes both the lived experience and the family heritage of present-day African Americans. Butler's *Parable of the Sower* is a postapocalyptic novel set in the second decade of the twenty-first century, in which there is widespread breakdown of civil society (including the supply of basic utilities). The story follows a young Black woman who leads a small group of survivors, on foot, from the violence-ridden cities of Southern California to the isolated region of the north, all while imagining a very different future. Dery coined the term "Afrofuturism" for this distinctively African American approach to science fiction.[22]

Afrofuturism, broadly speaking, is "a cultural phenomenon emerging from the relationship between African Americans and Western technology," literature, music, and art. Afrofuturist works explore the relationship "between science, technology, and race" and often engage "SF's themes of abduction, displacement, and alienation," themes also prevalent in African American history.[23] In this way Afrofuturism uses the hack of placing stories in the future and showing the reader a new reality to shine a light on the past and the present. At times Afrofuturist works imagine a future in which Black people are no longer spending their energies addressing the legacies of slavery but rather are thriving in a world in which their dreams, talents, and perspectives are the focus.

Afrofuturism teaches audiences how to imagine a world that doesn't cast Black people as monstrous, capable of and deserving of less than white people. This definition is expansive enough to make spaceships and time travel optional rather than essential. The literary scholar Isiah Lavender III defines Afrofuturism as a genre with a long genealogy. He argues that it emerged during the era of chattel slavery, and he has analyzed canonical works by African Americans before the nineteenth century as works of science fiction. As he puts it, "Black experience in America and around the world has *always* been an experience of spatial and temporal dislocation and disorientation, not unlike the events experienced by the protagonists of genre SF."[24] The essence of Afrofuturism is that it imagines another way of being than as enslaved persons or as people still held back by the trauma and legacy of enslavement. And this brings within its purview not just works of science fiction with rockets and time travel and not just works written since the twentieth century but also all manner of African American writing since enslaved Africans were first kidnapped and taken across the Atlantic.

In the mid-sixteenth century, a child born to an enslaved Muslim mother and her Christian enslaver and given the name Elena was given their freedom. By 1587, when they were arrested by the Castilian Inquisition on suspicion of "sodomy," they went by the name Eleno de Céspedes.[25] According to the trial records, they had married a certain Cristóbal Lombardo, been abandoned while pregnant, left their baby with friends, and then traveled through Spain. They dressed mostly as a man, took jobs restricted to men, and had relationships with various women. They called themselves Elena when wearing women's clothing, Eleno when dressed as a man. In 1586 they remarried, this time to a woman, María del Caño.[26]

Elenx, as we may call them today in recognition of their gender fluidity, was on trial because they were suspected of being a woman and thus committing sodomy (loosely, illegal sex acts with, for example, the "wrong" gender) by having sex with their cis wife. The bar for a sodomy conviction at the inquisitorial court for a woman was high. Not only did there need to be "penetration with the use of an object," but there needed to be witness testimony to that effect. First, however, the court had to be assured that Elenx was a woman (for if they were a man then his sex with a woman was not classed as sodomy). Examination satisfied the court that Elenx had no penis.[27]

But since Elenx said they had been married before, there was another problem: they might be a bigamist. They claimed that their husband had died sometime after leaving them, but whether this was true was an open question. And then there was the problem of their multiple gender presentations: Was there a chance that they were a sorcerer who could trick people into believing they were male? Whoever informed the inquisition that Elenx was guilty of sodomy had deemed that their lived gender did not match their genitals. The charge of sodomy, when brought against someone accused of having sex with another person (as opposed to with an animal) was a claim about someone's sex and gender.[28]

As Elenx recounted their story to the inquisition, they revealed that the vicar who had married her to María del Caño had also queried her gender and required a physical examination before he would let them marry. Several men looked at her from the front and declared that she hadn't been castrated. The vicar was unconvinced and ordered a second examination. This time ten (ten!) men came to perform it. Elenx, who had once been a surgeon's apprentice, used that expertise to "close my woman's part" before the examination.

The examiners felt what Elenx said was a knot caused by cauterizing a hemorrhoid. The men all declared to the mayor that Elenx "didn't have a woman's part and . . . did have a male member." The vicar, still unconvinced, had two surgeons from the royal court examine her next, and they too confirmed the earlier findings.[29]

From what can be gleaned from the trial records, Elenx was what we would today call intersex. Elenx argued that they had in fact been behaving naturally—that no sodomy had occurred. In their narrative their body changed after childbirth, their genitals always matched the gender they presented on the outside, and both their marriages were heterosexual. The question for the inquisitors was whether to believe their story or decide that Elenx was a sorcerer weaving a huge deception. The inquisition found Elenx guilty of masquerading as a man. Their illusion (as they saw it) was so extensive that it must have required sorcery. Still, the curiously lenient sentence—"corporal punishment and ten years of unpaid labor at a hospital"—suggested that the inquisitors viewed Elenx with some compassion or, at least, that the existential threat they might pose to the body politic and the body spiritual was limited.

How can we know whether someone in the past was trans or not if they did not leave words in their own hand to say that they did not identify with the gender they were assigned at birth? Things do not need a word to describe them in order to exist, so excluding people from "counting" in trans history simply because they lived before the word "trans" was in use isn't justified. Words change over time, and new words are coined. To understand the experiences among people who lived centuries ago or of people who live somewhere different from the places whose worldviews we have absorbed, we have to examine the surviving evidence on its own terms: to look for what people did, how they did it, and, in the case of written sources, for what words seem to mean in the contexts in which people used them.

Sometimes past scholars have missed seeing trans lives even when they appear in written sources. Documentary evidence from Europe during the Middle Ages and following centuries that discusses gender, sex, and sexuality reveals that religious and juridical elites framed gender as binary. They used the word "sodomy" to describe the behavior of individuals who departed from the definitions of the binary in terms of their gender in dress, behavior, or genitalia. As we can see in the case of Elenx, in medieval and early modern Spain and its overseas colonies, for instance, inquisitorial trial documents (among other sources) used the word "sodomy" to refer to an array of sexual practices, preferences, and gender expressions. The alleged practices to which "sodomy" referred include some that would be termed very differently today, such as queerness or transness.[30]

Consequently, when scholars of trans history look in the archives, they don't simply look for whether or not the word "trans" appears in documents (or whatever the word is in the contemporary lexicon of the language they are reading). The editors of a recent book of essays on trans lives between the Middle Ages and the eighteenth century, Greta LaFleur, Masha Raskolnikov, and Anna Kłosowska, observe that "there was a simply enormous range of terms that signified different aspects of gender presentation and perform-ance"—including terms like "sodomy" and "monster." And they do not look simply at what people in the past said but also at what they did. Writing trans histories is vital for countering the "assertions of the putative 'newness' of transgender experience," assertions that transphobic people use to delegiti-mize trans rights, lives, and experiences.[31] Gender crossings predate both modern language about transness and medical science.

Some people who appear in surviving written sources, like Elenx de Céspedes, lived as different genders at various points in their lives. Elenx described themselves as a "hermaphrodite," a term that used to denote some-one who exhibited aspects of male and female genders.[32] They lived, at times, as a gender different from the one to which they were (to use modern lan-guage) assigned at birth. Thus they were what, in today's language, is known as "trans" (people who identify as trans today may or may not have transi-tioned medically and may or may not wish to). Elenx's choices fall within this spectrum.

Long-standing methods of Western scholarship have hidden trans histo-ries from view. The writer, academic, trans awareness trainer, and heritage practitioner Kit Heyam puts it this way: "The discipline of history *is* set up to erase queer lives, and particularly trans lives." The (usually unspoken) norms of the discipline are to assume that people in the archive are cisgender, to gender them according to the pronoun they were assigned at birth (as far as that can be figured out), and to require enormous amounts of evidence before using a pronoun that better reflects the ways people chose to live. People's choices are separated from their identities with "phrases like 'cross-dresser' or 'impersonator.'" Heyam, who is both trans and an academic historian, puts on their scholarly hat to argue that "it's not the job of the communities we've hurt to give us the benefit of the doubt: it's *our* job to convince them that historians can be different."[33]

MONSTROFUTURISM?

What might a monster-centered ethics look like? It would take those ways of thinking that create monsters—that exclude people—and turn those assumptions on their heads to welcome in the so-called monsters. It would mean understanding that when a person does not fit a system, the system is failing, not the person. Fiction is as helpful as history for imagining different, better possibilities. As Ursula K. Le Guin understood, stories of imagined beings like hobbits and extraterrestrials (the proverbial "little green men") can distill society and human values until they are unmissable. The clarity that fantasy and science fiction can provide help us to imagine a future in which societies welcome and celebrate those whom they cast as monsters.[34]

I'm struck by how strands in Afrofuturism imagine a Black future that is no longer reacting to or in the shadow of the Atlantic slave trade. From Afrofuturism I've coined the word "monstrofuturism" for the work of imagining a future in which difference is celebrated rather than shunned. Making space for variation requires being comfortable with how our own bodies and behavior aren't fixed and not fearing people who are different because they show how our own ways of being aren't the only possible futures. In the end people (those identified as monsters and those who aren't) choose—by default, consensus, or a lurching set of events—whether they live in some version of *The Muppet Show* or in *The Matrix*.

Pixar's *Monsters, Inc.* (2001) turns viewers into the Grendel of a heroic adventure story told from the perspective of our monsters.[35] We enter the city of Monstropolis, which exists in a dimension inhabited entirely by monsters. The monsters are mortally scared of human children, who they believe are deadly dangerous and toxic. Yet these children are also essential for monster society, since Monstropolis runs on their bottled screams. Monsters who work at the city's power plant, Monsters Incorporated, must travel to the human world in the dead of night via special portals (children's closet doors), frighten kids in their bedrooms, and capture the power of their screams. When a particularly enterprising and fearless toddler accidentally wanders into Monstropolis, there is mass panic and all hell breaks loose.

The child—whom the monsters name Boo, her most common word—is a hardened toddler. Viewers see her through the eyes of the pint-sized, one-eyed green blob-with-limbs, Mike, and his giant, blue, bearlike best friend, Sully. For Mike and Sully, Boo in her pink nightie, mauve leggings, and socks (one of which she quickly loses) is the archetypical creature of nightmares. Her language is not quite regular speech; the monsters fear her germs, the potentially poisonous touch of her hands, and even her alleged laser vision. To feed her Sully throws Cheerios into the air for Boo to catch in her mouth, like a seal, while she draws with crayons. To settle her to sleep for the night, Sully makes a Cheerios trail from the living room to a corner of his bedroom, where he has made a bed of newspapers. Boo will have none of it and commandeers his bed, leaving him the floor.

Monster society is, for the purposes of the movie, deeply "normal." It's a *Through the Looking-Glass* mirror of an American city that looks and sounds suspiciously like a cartoon version of New York City. A close-up of the cover of a local Monstropolis newspaper reveals how the lives, hopes, and dreams of its citizens might parallel those of humans: "child born with three heads; parents thrilled." Viewers see the world from the panicked perspective of the monsters dealing with the child let loose in their city before witnessing the payoff, an ode to letting go of the stereotypes we might be carrying about those who are different from ourselves. Would we still be ourselves if we thought or acted differently in relation to sex, gender, or reproduction? And what might being ourselves even mean across space, time, and experiences? If every one of us is a monster—a wondrous person full of possibility and variety—then no one is monstrous. And wouldn't that be a kinder, safer, more joyous sort of world?

Epilogue

THE CATEGORY OF THE HUMAN appears to be shrinking. Far Right activists and politicians around the world are defining their nations in flat, limited ways that cast multiple groups as threats to the majority body politic. Categories are cultural and political, not absolute or universal. Yet they do powerful work in the world, informing everything from health care and legal infrastructure to definitions of beauty. Definitions of sex and gender and attempts to control people who are not white cishet men are being written up as monster narratives and used to gain political power.

Following the sudden and global rise in support for the Black Lives Matter movement after the murder of George Floyd in 2020, which prompted deeper and broader attempts to reckon with legacies of racism, discrimination, and exclusion, a backlash against inclusive ways of understanding humanity is well underway. Numerous US state legislatures have come after DEI (diversity, equity, and inclusion) initiatives, particularly those in universities, arguing that anything that is not race-blind (as they understand it) is racist. They picked an obscure theory in university-level legal studies called critical race theory (CRT) and declared that it was an existential threat. Conservative agitators monstrified CRT just as they had monstrified the word "woke." Anything that humanized Black and Brown people was supposedly the urgent problem of the decade. In January 2024 eighteen states had banned the teaching of CRT in schools, with another nine with proposed bills or school policies in progress.[1] Yet CRT was never school curricula content. Politicians and school boards have weaponized the phrase to ban books that address Black history, slavery, and settler-colonialism, as well as children's books that have Black, Brown, or queer characters. Implicit in this censorship is a monstrifying argument: that the lives, thoughts, feelings, and perspectives of people and their descendants have no place in how we understand the experience of being human.

In a number of countries, including the United States, hard-won reproductive rights are also now at risk. Abortion, contraception, and IVF treatments have become issues that Republican politicians are framing as "pro-life" but are actually "pro-control" and "anti-life." In 2024 the Alabama Supreme Court ruled that frozen human embryos were "children for the purpose of wrongful death suits." (This immediately led some Alabama clinics to halt IVF treatment altogether.)[2] Another, seemingly opposite, strategy from anti-abortion groups has been to question whether IVF should be offered at all; one of their arguments is that many embryos are discarded or destroyed along the way.[3] What both positions share is that they are "pro-control" and "anti-life." These actions come at the expense of the lives, health, and choices of pregnant people. While talking the talk of life, "pro-life" activists are meting out dehumanization and death.[4] The personhood of women and of people who can become pregnant is being erased; the personal freedom of living people is being eroded, and everyone's bodily autonomy is at risk.[5]

LGBTQIA+ rights, especially trans rights, are being curtailed in many countries. Since 2022 a number of US states have passed laws against teaching public school children about sexual orientation and gender or even providing sex education. These include Florida's 2022 Parental Rights in Education Act, known as the "Don't Say Gay" law. Bills in various states have also restricted state funding to university and college departments and programs on theoretical approaches to race and gender. Rising transphobia is costing even more lives than before. In state after state in the United States, trans people are being denied gender-affirming medical care.[6]

The power and reach of social media have enabled many Far Right activists to engage in stochastic terrorism: persistently using dehumanizing language and inflammatory rhetoric against individuals or groups, thereby inspiring listeners to commit violent acts. In 2023 three teenage girls bashed sixteen-year-old Nex Benedict's head repeatedly on the floor of a high school bathroom in Oklahoma. Benedict, who died in the hospital the next day, was two-spirit, trans, and gender nonconforming.[7] In the United Kingdom, the "gender-critical" movement has pitted women's rights against trans rights.[8] In Poland in 2020, President Andrzej Duda, running for reelection, declared that "LGBT is not people, it's an ideology." He claimed that queer people were a greater threat to the nation than communism. Emboldened by this monstrifying language, some local authorities declared their districts "LGBT-free zones."[9] Poland currently also has a near-total ban on abortion, yet some 70 percent of the population support making abortion easier to access.[10] From Brazil to the Vatican, from Uganda to Taiwan, narratives scapegoating LGBTQIA+ people, blaming them for social, political, and economic woes, have become widespread.[11]

Being poor has become framed as a monstrosity too—a threat to society, a pathology, the problem of individuals choosing not to work or eating avocado toast instead of saving for a mortgage. The equivalent of nineteenth-century "ugly laws" that charged people with smelling too bad or causing a public nuisance by putting their poverty on display are reappearing (read, existing on the same earth as people who aren't homeless). In 2023 the (now former) British home secretary Suella Braverman called being homeless a "lifestyle choice," ignoring the austerity measures that the Tory-led government had inflicted on the United Kingdom for over a decade and the rising levels of inequality that contribute to homelessness.[12]

At the same time, billionaires who became rich on the backs of minimum-wage workers and the sale of our data are rushing to buy and build "apocalypse-proof real estate," bunkers and compounds everywhere from Hawaii to New Zealand.[13] Corporations want to mine both our data and our wallets and monstrify us out of society. During the early COVID-19 pandemic, the CEO of a company selling self-parking technology, Anuja Sonalker, explained the rising interest in contactless technology this way: "Humans are biohazards, machines are not."[14] These strategies have the effect of monstrifying all of us: they alienate the value we create through our minds and lives, value that accrues to corporations and their shareholders. By divesting themselves of our collective fate, bunker-building billionaires monstrify the rest of us and the earth itself: in their eyes "normal" excludes us.

Monster-making is contagious. Centuries-old narratives about who does or doesn't belong in a community or a nation and about who is monstrous because they threaten the imagined unity and distinctiveness of the whole have a habit of inspiring new monstrifying narratives. The Nazis explicitly studied, adapted, and expanded to a terrifying degree European formulations of racial hierarchy and colonial European and American justifications for expanding their geographic frontiers, segregationist policies, and the practice of eugenics—all at the expense of Jewish, disabled, Roma, Sinti, Black, Indigenous, and Brown people.[15]

Even the targets of monster-making—the victims of harrowing abuse, discrimination, and genocide—can become monster-makers, spinners of new narratives that monstrify people who are more vulnerable. In the final months of writing this book, nowhere has this been more apparent, more horrific, and more volatile than the Israel-Hamas War, which began in October 2023. The language of monster-making has been everywhere. Within days of Hamas's breach of the Gaza-Israel border and the attack by some 1,500 militants on Israeli communities, Israeli ministers were calling Palestinians "human animals."[16] Months into the conflict, the Israeli government's justification of civilian deaths expanded from destroying Hamas's underground tunnels to the claims that there are no Palestinian civilians, that every Palestinian aged four and up is a terrorist or potential terrorist; and that Palestinians do not exist as a people but are merely wanderers, Arabs from elsewhere.

Trying to make sense of the present war is to experience vertigo. Time contracts to a single day of horror, in which some 1,400 people, most of them Israelis, were murdered, more than 200 were taken hostage, hundreds were wounded and physically assaulted in unspeakable ways, and millions were traumatized, in and around Israel. In the next moment, time and space expand, as if October 7 were a star going supernova and ejecting psychic memory matter, old ghosts, into the universe in pulsing waves, into the past and the future.

Waves settle around Arab-Israeli wars since Israel's founding seventy-five years ago and the beginning of the period that Palestinians call the Nakba, or the catastrophe. Other waves coalesce in Europe in the 1930s and 1940s, around the unspeakable horrors of Nazi Germany and the death squads, deportations, and concentration camps that blighted the continent. Two thousand years of expulsions and persecution in Europe and the Middle East culminated in the Holocaust, genocide magnified in part by the countries that refused entry to so many Jewish refugees on the basis that they supposedly had no room. This was a compelling justification for a Jewish ethnostate. There was little precedent for believing that Jews could be safe from annihilation in the absence of a state that wasn't Jewish.

As I write, some forty thousand Palestinians have died, and more are dying, and not just at the hands of Israeli soldiers firing US-funded weapons. They are also dying because of the monstrification that Europe and especially Nazi Germany enacted on Jewish people in living memory. But that cycle too goes back in time. One of the ways that both Nazis and Stalinists built support for their murderous causes was by declaring that the woes of workers were the fault not of capitalism or feudalism but of rich Jews.[17] The twentieth-century

Jewish exodus to what became the state of Israel is in part the aftershock of those atrocities. This type of strategy—of monstrifying minority groups and blaming them for a nation's ills—is still the Far Right's election playbook, currently unfolding everywhere from Brazil to India, from the United Kingdom to China, from France to the United States. Black and Brown people; Indigenous people dispossessed by settler-colonialism; ethnic and religious minorities; and LGBTQIA+ communities are their regular targets. Acts against vulnerable populations can be both horrific and distinct from one another. That doesn't negate the wrongs done to any particular group. "Oppression Olympics" will fix nothing. Instead, it gives the billionaire class and the Far Right a wedge with which to pry apart solidarities across race, gender, religion, sexual orientation, education level, industry, and (even) politics. Instead of monstrifying other groups who are also poor, marginalized, or vulnerable, we might instead acknowledge everyone's humanity.

Naming and classification are monster-making acts. A library's worth of such acts sits in the foundations of the contemporary world, ready to be pulled out and used for thinking with at a moment's notice. Nations legislate against their chosen, invented monsters and thereby define the boundaries of their own identities. Nation and race are both local and global biopolitical lenses on human variety, bringing into being categories and category-disrupting communities. From the myth of Manifest Destiny to the myth of Greater Russia, stories told about geography, race, and nation justify land grabs and genocide. By looking across time at how people have monstrified communities at their nation's geographic boundaries and have monstrified groups whom they frame as their opposite, we can see how these ideas operate and intersect and then work to diminish their power. There are no monsters: there are only stories that monstrify people, systems that fail people, and assumptions that dehumanize people. It's time for new stories, better systems, and evidence and ethics in place of monstrifying assumptions.

I write this at a moment not just of geopolitical disaster but of climate and ecological catastrophe. From rising sea levels to cancer-causing chemicals in cookies, the consequences of acting as if humans and ecology are separate have a knock-on effect on humanity itself. The nature/culture divide of the modern West has become increasingly untenable as the planet speaks back to humanity through extreme weather events.[18] Numerous species have seen their numbers tumble from pesticide exposure.[19] Human beings are also changing in response to artificial chemicals, making humans subtly but fundamentally different over time, changes that will shape future generations.

Human sperm counts have been dropping. Sometimes deep change is hidden for years, even decades: radiation works on life at the cellular level, only manifesting its handiwork when it is too late to undo it. Are we turning ourselves from one sort of species into another, passing through some in-between, monstrous phase?

In *An Immense World* science writer Ed Yong argues that each animal species lives in a different sensory world or bubble—a different *Umwelt*—depending on what parts of their environment their senses can detect. Thus the perceptual world of, for example, elephants, who can sense sonic frequencies far lower than the lowest frequencies we can, is very different. Elephants experience a different planet from us, because their senses reveal a different planet. I think it is possible to expand this argument, in relation to human societies in particular. We possess not just a perceptual *Umwelt* but an ontological one. The systems that people devise by combining their experiences (sensory or otherwise) with their values, assumptions, and cultural baggage constitute the world they perceive through their senses into beings (monstrous or otherwise) and into packets of meaning (poison, staple food, delicacy, never-eating-that). Change the cultural baggage—change the story—and we can imagine a different way of engaging the real challenges of the present, of climate crisis, of income inequality, of intolerance that begets violence and tragedy.

Solving challenges like this requires that we expand the category of who counts as human in the story. People living in the Global North, especially those who are more affluent, are responsible for most of the fossil fuel burning that has elevated, and continues to elevate, average global temperatures. Yet it is people in the Global South and poor people in the Global North (who cannot, for example, afford air-conditioning in homes or who work outdoors) who have, to date, suffered the most from its effects. When societies, governments, and nongovernmental organizations make decisions about whose suffering is going to prompt them to act (or not), they are in effect making statements about whose humanity they fully recognize.

Climate justice would involve, among other things, polluters paying for their impact on their environment. Companies and individuals made multi-billion-dollar profits by burning fossil fuels for manufacturing, creating pesticide waste, underpaying workers who mine rare materials in dangerous conditions, and shipping their products (more fuel emissions and perhaps oceanic pollution)—the list goes on. People wonder what major pathogen will emerge next from ecosystems under pressure from humans, be it yet another SARS coronavirus or an anthrax epidemic caused by decades-old infected reindeer carcasses revealed by the melting of permafrost. If ecologically vital species like bees disappear, it could trigger a cascade reaction of extinction. How societies imagine the relationship between natural and human spheres of activity will shape environmental legislation and disaster management in the decades to come.

Today many of us live and work in places where laws and infrastructure bind us into an unsustainable relationship with ecology. Structures and practices that accelerated during the Industrial Revolution, notably the burning of fossil fuels, serve some people in the short term but harm people and damage ecologies around the world in the medium and long term. Attending to the blurry, connected space between humans and ecology highlights why it is worth seeking nonpolluting, environmentally sustainable approaches to life on earth—rather than remaining dependent on our fossil fuel–consuming, pollution-generating hacks. By ceasing to draw a sharp line between where human supposedly ends and ecology begins, societies would be better able to make environmental decisions that preserve or improve people's lives while also safeguarding the environment for future lives in all forms.[20] Our minds, bodies, and futures don't end at our skin.

As I write, the news cycle is also reverberating with AI stories. OpenAI consumes large amounts of water and energy and depends on very poorly paid labor in the Global South to train their product. How societies define terms like "profit," "success," and "wealth" help to create legal fictions that enable, justify, expand, and compound historical inequalities. Not only is this a human rights issue centered on the mistreatment of workers and degradation of the planet. This is also a case of trampling the privacy and intellectual property of individuals. In the new horrors in which I write this, WordPress and Tumblr announced that they will sell users' data (essentially their writing and art) for generative AI. We are at a hinge point in human history, where we could make choices and laws that turn back the tide of rising inequality and allow all of us to flourish, instead of allowing a few to harvest our minds and the data of our lives. Either we help one another out of this maze of monstrifying mirrors, or we'll be stuck here bashing our fists against our reflections until we melt in a planetary cauldron of our own making.[21]

Someone looking at the world through the lens of Indigenous cosmologies would likely understand beings as interconnected and interdependent. Our alien exobiologists, studying human societies in their ecologies, might agree. But modern Western thought has alienated humanity from the earth and some billionaires fund plans to leave the planet rather than to save it. Instead, why don't we lean into what we are: imperfect, mortal humans who are infinitely creative and capable of communicating and working together, even when it is hard. And we could lean into *where* we are: the only habitable and inhabited world we know of, full of so many forms of life that we haven't even named them all. Surely that's worth working to preserve rather than to escape or to abandon.

Monsters are portals.

Monsters are us.

Let's get to work.

ACKNOWLEDGMENTS

It's hard to believe that a book came out of my fingers again. It's a thrill and a pleasure to acknowledge the many friends, colleagues, and interlocutors who helped bring this about. I give grateful thanks to everyone who read chapters at various stages and provided so much valuable food for thought. With particular awe and affection I thank Carrie Frye, who munched her way through everything twice and was the book's biggest cheerleader and fairy godmother. Carrie was a genius at showing me how to spot and dodge the lectern-speak that spurted from my keyboard and to own my inner Muppet. For reading the entire monster, I thank Leah Redmond Chang, Sebastian Falk, Asa Simon Mittman, Caroline Dodds Pennock, Tamara J. Walker, and Suze Zijlstra and the anonymous peer reviewers for the University of California Press. For reading multiple chapters, I'm grateful to Charlotte Coffin, Caroline Duroselle-Melish, Hannah Murphy, Ricardo Padrón, and Sadiah Qureshi.

My agent, Roz Foster, saw the potential for this book in that first seat-of-the-pants book proposal. Signing with Roz during the first COVID-19 lockdown and having the excitement of a new adventure with an enthusiastic supporter, when the physical world seemed barely bigger than my apartment, helped me survive 2020 with my skin intact. At the University of California Press, I give special thanks to my editor Eric Schmidt for believing so strongly in this project and to Jyoti Arvey and LeKeisha Hughes for so patiently managing queries and logistics. I'm grateful to the Faculty Editorial Committee for invaluable suggestions. Stephanie Summerhays managed the production process wonderfully. Susan Silver's lynx-eyed, patient, indefatigable copyediting added touches of forensic precision while reenchanting me with the tiniest details of the book. Lia Tjandra designed the phenomenal cover. I thank Shannon Li for devising the index.

The research for this book has taken me to numerous libraries, archives, and museums in the United States, the United Kingdom, and continental Europe during the latter, COVID-vaccinated segment of the research and writing and in the course of earlier projects in which monsters and categories played a large part. I am immensely grateful to all the staff who make these institutions and their collections accessible in person and online. Special thanks go to Gabriela Hennebichler of the Austrian National Library's Map Department and Globe Museum for coordinating my recent in-person study of Sancho Gutiérrez's 1551 world map, an escapade that involved a vault, a basement, and a ladder.

Book projects have serendipitous beginnings and long, winding lives. Support for earlier projects also provided access to original source materials, scholarly conversations, and community that cemented the foundations of this one. I thank the American Historical Association, the American Philosophical Society, the Folger Shakespeare Library, the John Carter Brown Library, and the Library of Congress for grants and fellowships. Without their support this book would have been very different. For fellowships supporting this book and my ongoing adventuring in the history of monsters, I'm deeply grateful to the Linda Hall Library of Science, Engineering, and Technology and to the William L. Clements Library.

Morphing from academic to full-time authorpreneur has been a long and ongoing process. Many friends and mentors offered valuable advice and conversation over the years. They include Philip Ball, Marcia Chatelain, Ania Cieslik, Andrew S. Curran, Bathsheba Demuth, Lindsey Fitzharris, Catherine Fletcher, Deborah Harkness, Martha S. Jones, Marika Leino, Allison Levy, Peter C. Mancall, Brooke N. Newman, Julie Phillips, Claire Potter, Matthew Restall, and Brandy Schillace.

So much inspiration and camaraderie during the writing of this book came via the Republic of Emails and its neighbor, the Zoomiverse. Heartfelt thanks go to my three trade-list writing-accountability buddies, Leah Redmond Chang, Carrie E. Gibson, and Tamara J. Walker. Our weekly email or Zoom check-ins have taught me so much. What an amazing journey we're on together. Many friends have listened to me talk at length about monsters and have offered in-person and virtual conversations and hospitality over the years, including Ralph Bauer, Farah Bazzi, Charlotte Coffin, Amanda Crompton, Grace Crussiah, James Frost, Stephanie Koscak, Hal Langfur, Iris Montero Sobrevilla, Marcy Norton, Kerry Reynolds, Neil Safier, Alison Sandman, and Jessica Wolfe.

Numerous friends, mentors, colleagues, and monster enthusiasts weighed in with suggestions in response to direct queries and frenetic crowd-sourcing, including Ana-Lucia Araujo, Monica Azzolini, Francisco Bethencourt, Erin Blake, Allison Caplan, Jeffrey Jerome Cohen, Ananda Cohen-Aponte, Mackenzie Cooley, Eli Cumings, Nandini Das, Whitney Dirks, Joanna Ebenstein, Peter Erickson, David Fernández, Erika Gaffney, Karl Galle, Malick W. Ghachem, Touba Ghadessi, Jessica Goethals, Benjamin Gross, Christopher Heaney, Alexa Alice Joubin, Anna Kłosowska, Heather Miyano Kopelson, Sherry Maday Lindquist, Kathleen Long, Bertie Mandelblatt, Hannah Marcus, Dániel Margócsy, Kathleen McDermott, Asa

Simon Mittman (who, among other things, shared the final draft of the extraordinary *Cartographies of Exclusion* with me), Katrina Olds, Sara E.S. Orning, Teresa Inès Padrón, Zoë Padrón, Carol Pal, Jaya Remond, Anne Nellis Richter, Kirsty Rolfe, Sandra Sáenz-López Pérez, Claudia Swan, Miguel Valerio, and Leanne Wiberg. This book is for all my friends.

NOTES

INTRODUCTION

1. The feminist scholar of science and technology Donna Haraway calls monsters "boundary creatures." See *Simians, Cyborgs, and Women*, 2. For references to the copious scholarly literature on the histories of monsters, see, for example, Mittman, *Ashgate Research Companion*; Davies, *Renaissance Ethnography*; Hoquet, *Presques-Humains*; Asma, *On Monsters*; and Smith, *Making Monsters*.

2. These demons are the subject of Canales, *Bedeviled*.

3. I adapt here Patrick Geary's formulation of the scope of his book on the depiction of women in origin myths: "I pursue not the idol but the idolaters." *Women at the Beginning*, 9–10.

4. Yong, *Immense World*, 355.

I. ON THE ECOLOGY OF MONSTERS

1. Sousa, *Woman Who Turned*, 19.

2. Durán, *Book of the Gods*, 68. Some of the surviving Indigenous American codices have been digitized and made available online. Many have been published in facsimile editions, sometimes with translations. A beautifully illustrated, captivatingly accessible introduction by one of the premier experts in the visual culture of codices is Boone, *Descendants of Aztec Pictography*. See also Boone, *Cycles of Time*. Spanish missionaries, naturalists, and administrators wrote treatises about the Indigenous peoples among whom they lived and worked. A number exist in modern editions and translations.

3. López Austin, "Cosmovision," 32; Gruzinski, *Painting the Conquest*, 61. Accessible scholarly overviews of classical Mesoamerican culture include Townsend, *Fifth Sun*; and Restall, *Maya World*.

4. Ruiz de Alarcón, *Heathen Superstitions*, 3, 7. This edition comprises an English translation of the original Spanish and Nahuatl in the copy of the manuscript

in the Museo Nacional de Antropología, Mexico City, together with a standard-form edition of the Nahuatl text. The edition is prefaced by an extensive account of its editorial procedures and of the limits of Ruiz de Alarcón's hostile treatise as an account of actual Indigenous practices.

5. Ruiz de Alarcón, *Heathen Superstitions*, 7, 20 (for the importance of the devil in Catholicism), 43–48, 132.

6. For Europe and the Americas, see Norton, *Tame and the Wild*.

7. Davies, *Renaissance Ethnography*, 30–31; Céard, *Nature et les prodiges*, 3–20.

8. Ancient Greece and the Roman Empire were part of a culturally intercon-nected region that cut across three continents. I call this region Afro-Eurasia (roughly, Africa north of the Sahara Desert, much of the Middle East, and those parts of Europe that fell under Roman imperial control). Scientific ideas across this region cross-fertilized one another from antiquity onward. "Western" science and medicine before 1500 were deeply influenced by practitioners in what is now North Africa and the Middle East and, to a lesser extent, by knowledge from farther afield. For ancient Greek and Roman understandings of the effect of the world on the body, see Kaufman, "Race and Science."

9. The humoral mode of thinking about food and health had parallels elsewhere. Indian medical practices also understood that you are what you eat, for example, and included the categories of hot and cold foods. Ancient medical treatises like *Airs, Waters, Places*, attributed to the fifth-century BCE physician Hippocrates, outlined how environmental conditions influenced the humors. See, for example, Sutter, "Tropics," 180.

10. For the persistence of humoral thinking through the eighteenth century, see Seth, *Difference and Disease*, 283, 286.

11. For these tidbits, see Pliny the Elder, *Natural History* 4.1.2, 4.1.4, 5.8.72, 5.21.59–60. Books 4–6 are about peoples.

12. Relaño, *Shaping of Africa*, 33; Davies, *Renaissance Ethnography*, 30–31.

13. Pliny the Elder, *Natural History* 4.12.89, 5.8.45.

14. The sizes, shapes, and locations of places in relation to place-names that persist today vary. Names such as "Ethiopia" and "India" were fungible in the terms like "Far East" or "Oceania" and do not refer to an exact and unvarying space on the map today.

15. Pliny the Elder, *Natural History* 6.35.187, 7.2.21, 3.1.5. In the Harvard edition cited here, Europe is the "nurse" of Europeans.

16. Northern Europe was also associated by Mediterranean and western Asian thinkers with monstrous peoples, by dint of its cold climate and less urban polities.

17. For an accessible account of how scientists devise hypotheses about extrater-restrial life, see Kershenbaum, *Zoologist's Guide*. For a scholarly treatment, see Dick, *Impact of Discovering Life*.

18. Wey Gómez, *Tropics of Empire*, 74–86; Siraisi, *Early Renaissance Medicine*, 102–6.

19. For humor-balancing actions, see Earle, *Body of the Conquistador*, 33.

20. Davies, *Renaissance Ethnography*, 31.

21. For the consequences for European ideas about the human, see Davies, *Renaissance Ethnography*, esp. chaps. 1 and 5.

22. Ruiz de Alarcón, *Heathen Superstitions*, 7.

23. Norton, *Tame and the Wild*, 195–96.

24. Sousa, *Woman Who Turned*, 21.

25. "Codex Telleriano-Remensis," Département des Manuscrits, Bibliothèque Nationale de France, fols. 22r, 22v.

26. See, for example, Fausto, *Warfare and Shamanism*; Kohn, *How Forests Think*; and Norton, *Tame and the Wild*.

27. Norton, "Chicken or the *Iegue*"; Norton, *Tame and the Wild*, 4–5.

28. Norton, *Tame and the Wild*.

29. For Beringian thinking about this energy cycle, see Demuth, *Floating Coast*, 2–9, 327n5.

30. For the longer account of the Skywoman story that I summarize here, see Kimmerer, *Braiding Sweetgrass*, 3–10.

31. For additional examples of such worldviews, see Kimmerer, *Braiding Sweetgrass* (original peoples around the Great Lakes of North America), Viveiros de Castro, *Enemy's Point of View*, and Descola, *Society of Nature* (Greater Amazonia); and Glacken, *Rhodian Shore* (Europe up to 1800).

32. For this point, see Kimmerer, *Braiding Sweetgrass*.

33. A classic theoretical work that addresses culinary taboos and fears is Douglas, *Purity and Danger*. Readers looking for a cultural history of a consumable that crossed Indigenous spiritual and Western scientific commercial worlds may consult Jay, *Mescaline*. An in-depth analysis of the clash of Indigenous and colonial beliefs and culture over half a millennium is Sarreal, *Yerba Mate*. For a compelling account of two Aztec consumables in pre-Hispanic and colonial eras, see Norton, *Sacred Gifts*.

34. Lewis, *Lion*, 37.

35. Tolkien, *Lord of the Rings*.

36. That said, if anyone could magic the silk purse of a trophy out of this cow's-ear situation, it would be Rafa.

37. Alexander, *New Jim Crow*, contains a vivid discussion of the strategic criminalization of marijuana to target young progressives and African Americans. Lawmakers introduced more punitive punishments for using crack (a cocaine compound marketed to African Americans in the 1980s) than for cocaine (the choice of richer, whiter people in the United States); see 49–54, 90–93, 105–6, 112–14. For the opioid epidemic in the United States, see Macy, *Dopesick*. For a powerful fictional account of life in communities ravaged by the opioid epidemic, see Kingsolver, *Demon Copperhead*.

38. Nakamura, *Monstrous Bodies*, 15.

39. Dickens, *Bleak House*, 5.

40. Langston, "New Chemical Bodies," 259.

41. Langston, "New Chemical Bodies," 259–61, 262–66.

42. Mitchell, Russell, and Stoianoff, "Franken Foods."

43. My account is a summary of the example in Langston, *Toxic Bodies*, vii–viii.

44. Langston, *Toxic Bodies*, 1–2.

45. Carson, *Silent Spring*, 152.

46. *The Hulk* first appeared in 1962, the creation of Stan Lee and Jack Kirby. For a recent biography that reveals the collaborative nature of comic-book and movie creations and the artists and writers with whom Lee worked, see Riesman, *True Believer*.

47. For an accessible account of the molecular studies of evolution, see Quammen, *Tangled Tree*.

48. Science writer Ed Yong's *Immense World* is a richly textured journey of the world through animal senses and experiences, drawing from extensive interviews and on-site visits with scientists. In *Are We Smart Enough*, primatologist Frans de Waal argues that the intelligence of an animal species begins to become visible to us only when we look at the world from their experiences and priorities.

2. HUMAN OR ANIMAL?

1. The stylized tulip roots resemble the French royal lily oriented upside-down.

2. "Tavole acquerellate," Bologna University Library, fol. 132r: "Mulier viginti annorum hirsuto capite simiam imitante reliquo corpore glabro." Following Renaissance scholar Touba Ghadessi, I have chosen the French form of Antoinette's name, since she was born in and spent her earliest years in France. Antoinette's surname is variously spelled Gonsalvus, Gonzales, and González in the original sources and later commentary.

3. For an engaging biography of the Gonsalvus family, see Wiesner-Hanks, *Marvelous Hairy Girls*.

4. See, for example, Bleichmar, *Visual Voyages*, chaps. 1–2.

5. Wiesner-Hanks, *Marvelous Hairy Girls*, 3–7, 29.

6. Hoefnagel, "Ignis," National Gallery of Art. Digitized images of the whole volume may be accessed on the NGA website. For an account of Hoefnagel's albums and the world in which he worked, see Bass, *Insect Artifice*.

7. Hoefnagel, "Ignis," National Gallery of Art, fol. 2; for the miniatures, see Wiesner-Hanks, *Marvelous Hairy Girls*, 148–55.

8. Aiello, "Five Years." I have written in more detail about this example in Davies, *Renaissance Ethnography*, 148–49.

9. For people's denial of their animal natures, see especially Challenger, *How to Be Animal*.

10. For examples of this sort of thinking, see Ghadessi, *Portraits of Human Monsters*, 104–7.

11. This caption appears on the portrait in the Château de Blois, France, and is translated in Wiesner-Hanks, *Marvelous Hairy Girls*, 4–5. The plate in this book is of the version of the painting in a private collection.

12. Ghadessi, *Portraits of Human Monsters*, 108–11.

13. Wiesner-Hanks, *Marvelous Hairy Girls*, 3.

14. Molineux, *Faces of Perfect Ebony*, chap. 1; Walker, *Exquisite Slaves*.

15. There are, for instance, numerous reports preserved in the Royal Society in London and viewable online, as well as the Evanion Collection of pamphlets, largely digitized, at the British Library.

16. Hernández, *Obras completas*, 4:323, cited in Mason, *Ulisse Aldrovandi*, 124. Hernández's observation appears in his translation and commentary on Pliny the Elder's *Natural History*, in his commentary to book 7 (on wondrous accounts of peoples), chap. 16.

17. For the translation of Platter's words, published in his *Observationes*, or collection of medical cases, see Wiesner-Hanks, *Marvelous Hairy Girls*, 184.

18. Translated in Wiesner-Hanks, *Marvelous Hairy Girls*, 3.

19. For high-definition images of the portraits, see the Kunsthistorisches Museum Vienna website, with Petrus Gonsalvus's portrait here: "Haarmensch."

20. Hoefnagel, "Ignis," National Gallery of Art, fol. 1. The translation is from Bass, *Insect Artifice*, 239.

21. For the Japanese folktale *The Tale of the Clam*, see Kimbrough and Shirane, *Monsters*, 371–84.

22. Kimbrough and Shirane, *Monsters*, 306, 448–49; a version of the tale is on 449–70.

23. Kimbrough and Shirane, *Monsters*, 275; Meyer, "Ashura."

24. For a translation and notes on this tale, see Kimbrough and Shirane, *Monsters*, 275–93.

25. For the dialect, see Kimbrough and Shirane, *Monsters*, 275.

26. Heng, *Invention of Race*, 27. Heng defines race as the use of traits "that are selectively essentialized as absolute and fundamental" to justify uneven access to power.

27. Janson, *Apes and Ape Lore*, 73–74.

28. Janson, *Apes and Ape Lore*, 74.

29. Janson, *Apes and Ape Lore*, 29.

30. Janson, *Apes and Ape Lore*, 74.

31. Huguccio of Pisa, *Magnae derivationes*, Vat. Reg. Lat. 1627, fol. 144: "Et dicitur sic quasi monstruosa quia qui eam movit et induitur in ferarum habitum transformatur. Unde mastrucatus . . . mastruca indutus." This is cited and translated in Friedman, *Monstrous Races*, 32.

32. Janson, *Apes and Ape Lore*, 86, 94.

33. See, for example, Ndiaye, "Come Aloft."

34. For the entangled histories of race, human anatomy, and primatology, see, for example, Hoquet, *Presques-Humains*, 85–120.

35. Pepys, *Diary of Samuel Pepys*, p. 160, no. 24.

36. Tyson, *Orang-outang*, dedication, figs. 1, 2. The figures are front and rear views of the animal that Tyson dissected, albeit imagined as it appeared before death. For the origin of the animal, see Tyson, "Philological Essay," 31. This essay is bound after the 108-page orangutan treatise.

37. Tyson, *Orang-outang*, 91.

38. Tyson, *Orang-outang*, 92, 94. For the comparison, see 92–94; for the list, see 94–95.

39. Tyson could not have known that he was dissecting an animal that was still growing; infant and adult chimpanzees differ in their anatomical proportions, as do infant and adult humans. For this point, see Ashley-Montagu, *Edward Tyson*, 306.

40. Tyson, "Philological Essay," title page. This treatise is bound in the same volume as his *Ourang-outang*.

41. Tyson, "Philological Essay," 2.

42. Norton, *Tame and the Wild*, 13–14.

43. Linnaeus, *Systema naturae*, 1:1758–59.

44. For a history of feral children in Europe, see Newton, *Savage Girls*.

45. Linnaeus, *General System of Nature*, 9.

46. Challenger, *How to Be Animal*, 35–36.

47. The literature on Darwin and his landmark *On the Origin of Species* (first published in 1859) is copious. For a recent overview of the history of genetics and Darwin's place in it, see Mukherjee, *Gene*, esp. 28–55.

48. The idea of monsters being nature's jokes is a tradition going back to classical antiquity. For the continuation of this tradition in the early modern period, see Findlen, "Jokes of Nature."

49. For some of Darwin's predecessors and contemporaries, "human" was an umbrella term for beings who looked vaguely the same but had in fact been created separately. According to this theory of polygenesis, humanity's origins were multiple and separate. For others races came about through degeneration. See, for example, Curran, *Anatomy of Blackness*, 80–86, 124–28, 141–46; and Fernández-Armesto, *So You Think You're Human?*, 63–65, 83–89.

50. Denisovans also interbred with *Homo sapiens*; see Massilani et al., "Denisovan Ancestry."

51. I am grateful to Lisa Onaga for bringing this to my attention.

52. The rhesus factor is a protein: if individuals are rhesus positive, they have the protein; if they are rhesus negative, they don't.

53. Challenger, *How to Be Animal*, 134–35; Schillace, *Mr. Humble*.

54. Lu et al., "Human-Animal Chimeras."

55. Sonnenfeld, *Men in Black*.

56. Singer, *X-Men*.

57. For Indigenous ontologies, see Kimmerer, *Braiding Sweetgrass*.

58. Robinson, "Crafting with Ursula."

59. Robinson, "Crafting with Ursula." For an introduction to climate fiction or cli-fi, see Bell, "Climate Fictions."

3. RACE-NATIONS

1. Quoted in Earle, *Body of the Conquistador*, 8. Now a derogatory term, *mulata* referred to someone with one Black parent and one white parent.

2. For food and the body in colonial Spanish America, see Earle, *Body of the Conquistador*; and Norton, *Sacred Gifts*.

3. Gerald of Wales, *Invectiones*, circa 1200, cited in Cohen, *Hybridity, Identity, and Monstrosity*, 26.

4. I adopt the term "racecraft" from Fields and Fields, *Racecraft*. The literature on the constructed nature of race is extensive; for a recent example, see A. Fuentes, *Race*.

5. Heng, *Invention of Race*, 19–20.

6. Isabel Wilkerson, for instance, uses "caste" as an umbrella term to refer to systems of human hierarchy and considers the economic consequences of hierarchy—the creation of economic castes—as the overarching frame. See *Caste*.

7. For an entryway into the scholarly literature, see the six-volume series, *The Cultural History of Race*, edited by Marius Turda, spanning the history of race from antiquity to the present. Each volume covers a different era and contains nine chapters on set themes: definitions of race; race, environment, and culture; race and religion; race and science; race and politics; race and ethnicity; race and gender; race and the body; and race and anti-race (rejections of race-thinking).

8. Heng, *Invention of Race*, 27.

9. Appiah, *Lies That Bind*, chap. 3.

10. Rampell, "How the Government Can Keep 'Alternative Facts' Out of the Census."

11. For this point, see Lalami, *Conditional Citizens*.

12. Shelley, *Frankenstein*.

13. Anderson, *Imagined Communities*, 6, citing Gellner, *Thought and Change*, 168, with Anderson's added emphasis.

14. Sutter, "Tropics," 180.

15. Davies, *Renaissance Ethnography*, 39–40.

16. Pagden, *Fall of Natural Man*, 15–24.

17. Davies, *Renaissance Ethnography*, 41.

18. Davies, *Renaissance Ethnography*, 25–27.

19. Pagden, *Fall of Natural Man*, 16–19.

20. For this anecdote, see Morris, *Cursor mundi*, 466–69, lines 8072–8132. This edition prints four versions of the manuscript on facing pages. For the quotations, see version 2 (second column), 466 and 468, lines 8072 ("sarasinis"), 8076 ("misshapen creatures"), 8120 ("als milk"), 8121 ("fre blode" and "hew"), 8122 ("shap was turned new"). See also Steel, "Centaurs, Satyrs, and Cynocephali," 264.

21. Heng, *Invention of Race*, 15; Mittman, *Cartographies of Exclusion*.

22. See, for example, Mittman, *Cartographies of Exclusion*, xx, 48–52 (badges in England); 52 (living constraints in England); 103–4 (Fourth Lateran Council). See also Teter, *Blood Libel*, 18–27.

23. See Strickland, *Saracens, Demons, and Jews*; Lipton, *Dark Mirror*. For depictions of Jews on English medieval maps, see Mittman, *Cartographies of Exclusion*.

24. Heng, *Invention of Race*, 22–24.

25. Such questions are the subject of, for example, Cohen, *Hybridity, Identity, and Monstrosity*; and Heng, *Invention of Race*.

26. Khanmohamadi, *Light of Another's Word*, 37.

27. Gerald of Wales, *History and Topography*, 101–2; Gerald of Wales, *Topographia Hibernica*, 150–53.

28. See, for example, Panxhi, "Rewriting the Werewolf." For an accessible introduction to werewolves in Western thought and literature, including an extensive bibliography of works of fiction that contain werewolves, see Frost, *Essential Guide*.

29. Cohen, *Hybridity, Identity, and Monstrosity*, 1.

30. Appiah, *Lies That Bind*; Hirsch, *Brit(ish)*, chaps. 1, 5.

31. Cooley, *Perfection of Nature*.

32. Nirenberg, "Race"; K. Burns, "Unfixing Race."

33. Nirenberg, *Anti-Judaism*, chap. 6.

34. Leitch, *Mapping Ethnography*, 41–53.

35. For an overview, see Bartra, *Wild Men*.

36. Leitch, *Mapping Ethnography*, chap. 3.

37. Mittman, *Maps and Monsters*.

38. Hartnell, *Medieval Bodies*, 94.

39. Meserve, *Empires of Islam*.

40. Wintroub, *Savage Mirror*, chap. 1 and 40–84.

41. Tacitus, *Germania*, 135–36.

42. Krebs, *Most Dangerous Book*, 21, 182, 218.

43. For German readings of Tacitus over the past half millennium, see Krebs, *Most Dangerous Book*, including, for Nazi interpretations of the *Germania*, 17–22 and chap. 8.

4. RACE-NATIONS II

1. See, for example, Chaplin, *Subject Matter*.

2. Braude, "Sons of Noah."

3. For medieval mapping, see Edson, *World Map*; and Mittman, *Maps and Monsters*.

4. The quoted inscription is transcribed and translated in Westrem, *Hereford Map*, 69 (labeled Asia-Level 3), 141. See also Sáenz-López Pérez, *Mapas*, 47, 59, 158, 199, 249, 256.

5. Lewis and Wigen, *Myth of Continents*.

6. Bethencourt, *Racisms*.

7. Roberts, *Mediterranean World*, 9, 36–42, 75–78.

8. Davies, *Renaissance Ethnography*, 2–7, 167.

9. Heng, *Invention of Race*, 34.

10. Davies, *Renaissance Ethnography*.

11. Davies, *Renaissance Ethnography*.

12. Cañizares-Esguerra, "Patriotic Astrology."

13. Yellow fever was commonly the cause.

14. Seth, *Difference and Disease*, chap. 3.

15. Sutter, "Tropics," 180.

16. For the Spanish case, see Wheat, *Atlantic Africa*. For English colonies, see Rugemer, "Development of Mastery." For the French *Code noir*, see Curran, *Anatomy of Blackness*, 56–58.

17. Rugemer, *Slave Law*, 17–18. For my overview of Barbadian laws, I have drawn from the extensive analysis in Rugemer, "Development of Mastery," which was the basis of parts of Rugemer, *Slave Law*, chaps. 1 and 2. For Indigenous slavery, see, for example, Reséndez, *Other Slavery*. For the overlapping categories of slavery and servitude in early modern England, see Chakravarty, *Fictions of Consent*.

18. Rugemer, "Development of Mastery," 436–38, 440.

19. Rugemer, *Slave Law*, 33; Rugemer, "Development of Mastery," 442, 439. The Barbados Act of 1661 was titled "An Act for the Better Ordering and Governing of Negroes"; it is printed in Engerman, Drescher, and Paquette, *Slavery*, 105–13; see 105 for the slippage from "Negroes" to "Slaves." The act stands in contrast to "An Act for the Good Governing of Servants, and Ordering the Rights between Masters and Servants," in *Acts of Assembly*, 22–29, cited in Rugemer, "Development of Mastery," 431, 438, 439.

20. Rugemer, "Development of Mastery," 437–38. For the sugar forfeit and for "brutish" slaves, see the Barbados Act of 1661, in Engerman, Drescher, and Paquette, *Slavery*, 107.

21. For laws about mixed-race descendants of enslaved persons, see Morgan, "Partus sequitur ventrem."

22. Alexander, *New Jim Crow*, 28, 31–32, 35; Wilkerson, *Caste*, 111.

23. Alexander, *New Jim Crow*, 28–31, 2.

24. Alexander, *New Jim Crow*, 6–7.

25. For essays on the cultural history of the play, see Hulme and Sherman, *"Tempest" and Its Travels*.

26. Shakespeare, *Tempest* 1.2.389–90, in Shakespeare, *William Shakespeare*, 15.

27. Single women, especially of independent means, were often the target of such accusations. Ironically, Prospero is himself a magician, but the witch craze was initially directed against popular vernacular magic, such as that of midwives and women healers, rather than against educated elites. See also chapter 7 in this book.

28. Davies, *Renaissance Ethnography*, 97, 68, 97–98, 40.

29. Shakespeare, *Tempest*, 1.2.409–10, 426, in Shakespeare, *William Shakespeare*, 16.

30. Seth, *Difference and Disease*; Delbourgo, *Collecting the World*; Harrison, *Climates and Constitutions*.

31. Gray, *Good Speed to Virginia*, sigs. C.2r, C.3v–4r. This and the following two examples, along with others, are quoted and discussed in Hulme, *Colonial Encounters*, 157–73.

32. Purchas, *Hakluytus Posthumus*, 231 (pt. 2, bk. 9, chap. 20).

33. Waterhouse, *Declaration of the State*, 24.

34. The film was inspired by Pierre Boulle's novel, *Planète de singes*.

35. For a detailed study, see Greene, *Planet of the Apes*.

36. Schaffner, *Planet of the Apes*.

37. Peele, *Us*.

38. For a classic and, alas, still salient critique of the dehumanization of labor under global capitalism, see Klein, *No Logo*.

39. Miéville, *City and the City*, 62, 64.

40. This famous formulation appears in the title of Lévi-Strauss's *Raw and the Cooked*. The Ferengi make occasional appearances in *Star Trek: The Next Generation* but appear in a sustained fashion, as fully rounded, regular characters with their own story arcs only in *Star Trek: Deep Space Nine*. A classic theoretical work on culinary fears and taboos is Douglas, *Purity and Danger*.

41. Pagden, *Fall of Natural Man*, 27–56; Davies, *Renaissance Ethnography*, 219–21.

42. Davies, *Renaissance Ethnography*, 25–38, 178–79.

43. Earle, *Body of the Conquistador*, 5–8.

44. Norton, *Sacred Gifts*, chap. 6; Earle, *Body of the Conquistador*, 47.

45. Earle, *Body of the Conquistador*, 48–51, 57–58, 61–67; Cooley, *Perfection of Nature*, 51, 251.

46. In October 2022, for instance, when Just Stop Oil protesters blocked the Dartford Tunnel and access between the counties of Kent and Essex, UK home secretary Suella Braverman blamed the disruption on people she called "Guardian-reading, tofu-eating wokerati," dismissing readers of a particular newspaper, eaters of tofu, African Americans' alertness to the discrimination and racism they face, and people working against racism.

47. In the Spanish Empire, "the Indies" was a transpacific geographic space; see Padrón, *Setting Sun*.

48. Davies, *Renaissance Ethnography*, 220–21.

49. Van Deusen, *Global Indios*.

50. Rappaport, *Disappearing Mestizo*.

51. I refer here to social psychologist Amy Cuddy's 2012 TED Talk on how power poses shape people's bodies and self-image; see "Your Body Language."

52. Vinson, *Before Mestizaje*, 64–67, 161–62.

53. *Casta* paintings also emerged in Peru and Nueva Granada (the region of present-day Colombia, Ecuador, and Venezuela).

54. For race and modernity in Latin America, see, for example, Earle, *Return of the Native*; O'Hara, *History of the Future*; and Weinstein, *Color of Modernity*.

55. For hierarchy in the US, Nazi Germany, and India, see Wilkerson, *Caste*.

56. These and similar statistics appear regularly in the social media posts and Substack newsletters of the UC Berkeley professor and former secretary of labor Robert Reich and in the media more generally. See, for example, Reich, "Paid What You're Worth" (federal minimum wage, ballooning CEO salaries); and Alund, "World's Richest People" (gains for the wealthiest five hundred people).

57. For the chlordecone scandal, see Toto, "Chlordecone Health"; for an overview of the Windrush scandal, see "Windrush Scandal."

58. Caro, "Robert Caro."

59. McDaniel and Moore, "Lynching."

5. GENDER, SEX, AND MONSTROUS BIRTHS

1. Du Plessis, "Prodigious and Monstrous Births," Department of Manuscripts, British Library. The earliest anecdote in the volume is dated 1664. Du Plessis notes that he saw a "Negro Prince" in 1690 and again in 1725 (fol. 11v). The first page of the manuscript bears Du Plessis's name; the date, 1730; a price, "1-1-0" (presumably a guinea, or one pound and one shilling); and, in a different hand, "colector of thise boocke 1733," probably the date when Du Plessis sold the book to Sir Hans Sloane. The examples in the text appear on folios 6r–8v.

2. Huet, *Monstrous Imagination*, chap. 4.

3. Du Plessis, "Prodigious and Monstrous Births," Department of Manuscripts, British Library, fol. 5r.

4. Aristotle, *Generation of Animals* 2.3, 4.3–4. See also Huet, *Monstrous Imagination*.

5. Davies, *Renaissance Ethnography*, 30–31.

6. Sousa, *Woman Who Turned*, 21.

7. Du Plessis, "Prodigious and Monstrous Births," Department of Manuscripts, British Library, fol. 13v.

8. Du Plessis, "Prodigious and Monstrous Births," Department of Manuscripts, British Library, fols. 13r–v.

9. See, for example, Milanich, *Paternity*.

10. Many examples appear in Spinks, *Monstrous Births*.

11. See, for example, Paré, *Monstres et prodiges*.

12. "Collection of Advertisements," Department of Rare Books, British Library, item 15. I discuss another handbill about this person in chapter 6.

13. Peucer, *Commentarius de praecipius generibus*, fols. 42v–43v (translation from Daston and Park, *Wonders and the Order*, 193).

14. Bulwer, *Anthropometamorphosis*, 255, and, with minor typographical variations, in the expanded and copiously illustrated 1653 edition, 469.

15. Gates and Curran, *Who's Black and Why?*, ix, 68–69.

16. Nakamura, *Monstrous Bodies*.

17. Schillace, "Forgotten History." Schillace's book on the subject of this article is forthcoming.

18. Koerber, *From Hysteria to Hormones*.

19. My discussion in this section is based on Knox, *First Blast*, and on Wiesner-Hanks, *Marvelous Hairy Girls*, chap. 3.

20. Redmond Chang, *Young Queens*, 251–55; Knox, *First Blast*, fols. 2r, 17r, 19r.

21. Knox, *First Blast*, fols. 27r–v, 28r.

22. Boaistuau, "Histoires prodigieuses," Wellcome Collection, [fol. 29v]. This text appears in print in numerous editions and translations; see Boaistuau, *Histoires prodigieuses*, 27–28.

23. Knox, *First Blast*, fols. 27r, 32v–33r, 52v, 53v.

24. A. Fuentes, *Race*.

25. Vicente, "Transgender."

26. Sousa, *Woman Who Turned*, 4, 11, 20, 21.

27. For this subsection I have drawn on the definitive recent work DeVun, *Shape of Sex*. See 17–18, 21, 30, 53, 177; for citations to literature in this vein, see 214n5.

28. For these traditions, see DeVun, *Shape of Sex*, 19–22.

29. For this summary of medieval scholarly thought, I have drawn on DeVun, *Shape of Sex*.

30. Surgical interventions on intersex children at birth continue today.

31. Mittman, *Cartographies of Exclusion*, 153.

32. For eunuchs at the Ottoman court and the transmission of knowledge about them to Europe, I have drawn on Arvas, "Early Modern Eunuchs."

33. Arvas, "Early Modern Eunuchs."

34. For an extensive look at the intersection of gender, sexuality, and archival language and categories in colonial New Spain, see Tortorici, *Sins against Nature*.

35. A copious body of recent scholarship was inspired by Spillers, "Mama's Baby." See, for example, M. Fuentes, *Dispossessed Lives*; J. Johnson, *Wicked Flesh*; and Morgan, *Reckoning with Slavery*.

36. Morgan, *Reckoning with Slavery*, 5.

6. MONSTROUS PERFORMANCE AND DISPLAY

1. For the concept of enfreakment, see Garland-Thomson, *Extraordinary Bodies*, 17, 58–59.

2. For the display of distant peoples, see, for example, Durbach, *Spectacle of Deformity*; and Qureshi, *Peoples on Parade*.

3. For transcriptions of the Portuguese and translations into French, see Little and Vidal, *Mascarade nuptiale*, 14–17. I am grateful to Francisco Bethencourt for bringing this painting to my attention.

4. For eighteenth-century debates about what Black albinos and Black individuals with vitiligo revealed about human origins and race, see Curran, *Anatomy of Blackness*, 87–105.

5. Little and Vidal, *Mascarade nuptiale*, 10.

6. These boxes are labeled with the shelf marks EPH 499, EPH 499A, EPH 499B, EPH 499C, and EPH 499D. Individual items are labeled in the format "EPH 499A:1" with a number following the colon. Occasionally, as in the item "EPH 499:58B," there is a letter appended to the number. The boxes' disturbing titles in the online catalog are in the format "Freak Shows Ephemera: Box" followed by a number, 1–5.

7. For the widespread use of the terms "freaks" and "freak shows" by impresarios, advertising, the general public, and even by performers about themselves into the 1930s, see Bogdan, "Social Construction of Freaks," 35.

8. For handbills advertising the Bunkers' Pall Mall appearances, see "Ephemera" folder SC/GL/ENT/001–049, London Metropolitan Archives. In the Wellcome Collection, ephemera on Chang and Eng Bunker include "Freak Shows Ephemera: Box 2": EPH 499A:37 and EPH 499A:40.

9. "Freak Shows Ephemera: Box 2," EPH 449A:3, Wellcome Collection.

10. Several edited collections offer case studies of monstrosity and performance. An influential early example is Garland-Thomson, *Freakery*. For case studies from the eighteenth to the twentieth centuries, see Kérchy and Zittlau, *Exploring the Cultural History*.

11. Many of these cases can be consulted online. See, for example, the Johnstone Collection at the University of Oxford and the Evanion Collection at the British Library in London. Further examples, some digitized, are held by the London Metropolitan Archives (some of these collections were formerly at the Guildhall Library in London). For the idea of monsters in early modern European thinking about disability, see especially Bearden, *Monstrous Kinds*.

12. Newspaper or handbill cutting about the "Bosjemans" or "Bush people" exhibited at the Egyptian Hall, June 19, 1847, "Ephemera" folder SC/GL/ENT/001–049, London Metropolitan Archives.

13. Du Plessis, "Prodigious and Monstrous Births," Department of Manuscripts, British Library, fols. 11r–v.

14. Du Plessis, "Prodigious and Monstrous Births," Department of Manuscripts, British Library, fols. 11r–v, 53r–v.

15. Chaplin, *Subject Matter*, 202–3, 220–21.

16. Du Plessis, "Prodigious and Monstrous Births," Department of Manuscripts, British Library, fols. 6r–7r.

17. "Freak Shows Ephemera: Box 2," EPH 449A:8, "Freak Shows Ephemera: Box 3," EPH 499:58B; "Freak Shows Ephemera: Box 5," EPH 499D:77, Wellcome Collection. "Freak Shows Ephemera: Box 3": EPH 499B:19 comprises a pamphlet about O'Brien and his wife and child.

18. "Letter Book," November 1664, LBO 28/2, Royal Society ("containing an account of a monstrous Birth at Salisbury"); Douglas, "Account of a Hermaphrodite," Hunterian Collection, University of Glasgow Library, [fol. 1v]. A note on the first page of the discussion reads, "Feb. 16 1714/5."

19. "Letter Book," March 15, 1667–68, LBO 2/67, Royal Society ("discussing a monstrous birth at Framlington in Suffolk").

20. Ritvo, *Platypus and the Mermaid*, 150.

21. Ritvo, *Platypus and the Mermaid*, 150. For additional examples of "giants" and "dwarfs" who performed at fairs and of individuals objectified as monstrous curiosities, see pp. 131–74.

22. "Statement on the Skeleton."

23. "Freak Shows Ephemera: Box 5," EPH 499D:24, Wellcome Collection.

24. Newspaper or handbill cuttings, one from the *Globe*, August 26, 1887, "Ephemera" folder SC/GL/END/100–149, London Metropolitan Archives.

25. "Freak Shows Ephemera: Box 5," EPH 499D, Wellcome Collection.

26. Du Plessis, "Continuation," Department of Manuscripts, British Library, fol. 2r.

27. Mary Toft's confession, December 7, 1726; Fair copy, December 7, 1726; Mary Toft's confession, December 12, 1726, Hunterian Collection, University of Glasgow Library. For a detailed account of this imposture, see "Curious Case."

28. One account, which appeared in the *Whitehall Evening Post* on December 29, 1726, was, uncannily, "Printed for Tom Lowry at the three [*sic*] Rabbits near Lincoln's Inn [in London]." See "Transcribed Extract," Hunterian Collection, University of Glasgow Library.

29. Shakespeare, *Tempest* 2:2.24–28, in Shakespeare, *William Shakespeare*, 27.

30. Altick, *Shows of London*, 35–36. See also Semonin, "Monsters in the Market-place," 76–77.

31. Wordsworth, *Prelude*, 262, 264.

32. Garland-Thomson, *Extraordinary Bodies*, 59.

33. "Freak Shows Ephemera: Box 5," EPH 499D:54, Wellcome Collection. "St David's Streights" refers to the Davis Strait between Greenland and Baffin Island in Nunavut, Canada. The next item, EPH 499D:55, contains an illustration with a canoe in the background, a typical motif in European images of peoples in the region since the late sixteenth century.

34. "Freak Shows Ephemera: Box 5," EPH 499D:97, Wellcome Collection.

35. Du Plessis, "Prodigious and Monstrous Births." Department of Manuscripts, British Library, fol. 34r.

36. Semonin, "Monsters in the Marketplace," 69–81, 70; Altick, *Shows of London*, 36–37.

37. A page labeled "Plate VI," item 115, cut from a book, "Ephemera" folder SC/GL/NOB/C/026/5-026/51, item C.26.51. T. c. 1750, London Metropolitan Archives.

38. For examples of the marketing of human exhibitions to both learned and general audiences, see Qureshi, *Peoples on Parade*.

39. Qureshi, *Peoples on Parade*.

40. Locke, "Exhibitions and Collectors," 83. For the high and low culture appeals of Bartola and Maximo, see Durbach, *Spectacle of Deformity*, 117; for an extended account of the siblings' repeated appearances on the British show scene between the 1850s and the 1890s, see Durbach, *Spectacle of Deformity*, chap. 4.

41. "Freak Shows Ephemera: Box 2," EPH 499A:18, Wellcome Collection. For another copy of the flyer, see "Human Curiosity Prints," 108v, Harvard Theatre Collection, Houghton Library, Harvard University.

42. For this argument, see Durbach, *Spectacle of Deformity*, 115–22; for anthropological speculation about Bartola and Maximo's supposed racial hybridity, see pp. 135–43.

43. *Last Week in Philadelphia*, pamphlet, in "Human Curiosity Prints," Harvard Theatre Collection, 108r. The pair's ages are listed here.

44. For the capture, see Keane, "Krao," 246. For an in-depth discussion of how Krao featured in debates about evolution, imperialism, primitivism, and wild sexuality, see Durbach, *Spectacle of Deformity*, chap. 3.

45. "Freak Shows Ephemera: Box 2," EPH 499A:104, Wellcome Collection.

46. "Human Curiosity Prints," Harvard Theater Collection, Houghton Library, 129, verso of the two flyers in this folder; Keane, "Krao."

47. Durbach, *Spectacle of Deformity*, 103, 113.

48. There are also medical examples. When Henrietta Lacks was treated for cancer in the mid-twentieth century, Dr. George Gey at Johns Hopkins Hospital collected some of her cancerous cells; Gey and other scientists used them for foundational cancer research for decades, without Lacks's or her family's knowledge or consent. See "Legacy of Henrietta Lacks." In "The Tuskegee Study of Untreated Syphilis in the Negro Male," which ran from 1932 to 1972, the US Public Health Service recruited, as subjects in a supposed study on "bad blood," 600 poor Black men in Alabama, promising them free medical exams, meals, and burial insurance. A total of 399 had syphilis. Doctors neither informed the men of their condition nor treated them for it; rather, doctors intentionally followed the progression of the disease. See "Tuskegee Syphilis Experiment." But the fairground instances were embedded in people's recreational lives, not merely the activities of scientists and medical practitioners.

49. For the prodigy tradition, see Spinks, *Monstrous Births*; and Daston and Park, *Wonders and the Order*, 48–60.

50. See the extensive literature on color-conscious casting and lighting and on how white bodies have historically been seen as the default for a range of theatrical possibilities, in the work of, among others, Karim-Cooper, *Cosmetics*; and Thompson, "Josephine Waters Bennett Lecture."

51. Drewal, "Beauteous Beast," 77, 81.

52. For destruction of codices, see Boone, *Cycles of Time*, 5; for collecting and curiosity cabinets, see Davies, "Catalogical Encounters"; Marcaida López, *Arte y ciencia*, 45–71; Pennock, *On Savage Shores*, 220–24.

53. For the looting of the Benin bronzes, see Hicks, *Brutish Museums*, 135–51.

54. See, for example, the case of African sculpture in Paris, the subject of Monroe, *Metropolitan Fetish*.

55. Murray, "Rarities"; Galerie Flak, "Ferocious Poetry."

56. Rarey, *Insignificant Things*, 33.

57. For a scene-by-scene listening guide and description of the choreography, see Moore, *Rite of Spring*, chap. 6.

58. For this point, see Fauser, "Sacre du printemps," 83–87.

59. Fauser, "Sacre du printemps," 83.

60. Chap. 4 of Moore, *Rite of Spring*, details a number of vivid episodes and recounts the words of those present.

61. For Villa-Lobos's interleaving of Brazilian popular music in his orchestral works, see Dudeque, *Bachianas Brasileiras*, chap. 3.

62. This quotation, and the details of the historical overview of the ballet's reception, are drawn from Thomas, "Stravinsky."

63. Higa, "Don't Punish Simone Biles for Being the Best."

64. Morris, "Serena Williams's Final Run"; Rankine, *Citizen*, 26–32.

65. I have chosen not to reproduce this disturbing and offensive cartoon.

66. Barron, "Biles Finds Beauty in Beastly Athleticism." I am grateful to Melissa Murray for bringing this example to my attention by sharing it on Twitter.

67. For stereotypes of Black athletes in film, see Sheppard, *Sporting Blackness*.

68. Semenya, *Race to Be Myself*, 124–40, 140–47, 173, 179.

69. Semenya, *Race to Be Myself*, 183–88, 235–39.

70. Semenya, *Race to Be Myself*, 267–68, 271, 289.

71. For a recent critique of binary hormonal thinking in relation to sports, see J. Butler, *Who's Afraid of Gender?*, 190–94.

72. Semenya, *Race to Be Myself*, 251–52.

73. J. Butler, *Who's Afraid of Gender?*, 191.

7. GODS, MAGIC, AND THE SUPERNATURAL

1. Felton, "Embracing the Monstrous," 107; Mittman and Hensel, *Primary Sources on Monsters*, 4; Ziolkowski, "Gilgamesh," 313. For the history of the texts' discovery and the surviving tablets, see George, "Epic of Gilgamesh," 1–6.

2. For the Mesopotamian and Near Eastern roots of Greek thought, see, for example, West, *East Face of Helicon*.

3. The translation I have used is Lombardo and Beckman, *Epic of Gilgamesh*.

4. The material in this overview is drawn from Felton, "Embracing the Monstrous," 105–7.

5. López Austin, "Natural World," 141.

6. Miller and Taube, *Gods and Symbols*, 30, 68–69.

7. Miller and Taube, *Gods and Symbols*, 30, 70.

8. Locke, "Gods of Life," 172; López Austin, "Natural World," 142.

9. Restall, Sousa, and Terreciano, *Mesoamerican Voices*, 177–79.

10. McKeever Furst, *Natural History*, 10–13.

11. López Austin, "Cosmovision," 30–31.

12. Matos Moctezuma and Solis Olguín, *Aztecs*, 14; Yetman, "Cactus Metaphor." For the bird example, see Durán, *Aztecs*, 31.

13. For Mesoamerican origin myths and related gods predating Spanish contact, see Graulich, "Creation Myths"; and Graulich, "Creator Deities." For a highly readable and magnificently illustrated account of encounters between the Mexica and the Spaniards, see Gruzinski, *Painting the Conquest*.

14. Mittman, *Cartographies of Exclusion*, chap. 5, explores this conflation.

15. Bernus-Taylor, *L' Étrange et le Merveilleux*, 54.

16. Bernus-Taylor, *L' Étrange et le Merveilleux*, 34–36; for illuminated manuscript illustrations and commentary, see pp. 40–63.

17. For an English translation of the earliest (circa eleventh- to fourteenth-century) Persian retelling of the story of Alexander, in which Alexander is a Muslim Persian king and prophet, see Venetis, *Persian Alexander*.

18. For a discussion of this manuscript and the story of Alexander, the wall, and the tribes of Gog and Magog, see Bernus-Taylor, *L'Étrange et le Merveilleux*, 54–55.

19. Owen, *Chinese Literature*, 518. For early Chinese literary tellings of shamanic journeys through the heavens and shamanic rituals that bring the souls of the dead back to the material world, see pp. 176–214.

20. For the senses of the Aztec soul, see McKeever Furst, *Natural History*, 3–4.

21. Durán, *Book of the Gods*, 68n15.

22. A number are defined briefly in López Austin, "Términos," 15–17.

23. Sahagún, "Florentine Codex," Biblioteca Medicea Laurenziana, bk. 10, fol. 21v, translated in García Garagarza, "Tecolotl and the Chiquatli," 476n15. This website contains a digitized version of the manuscript, along with transcriptions of the codex's Nahuatl and Spanish texts and translations into English. For a published English translation of the Nahuatl texts, see Sahagún, *Florentine Codex*.

24. García Garagarza, "Tecolotl and the Chiquatli," 457.

25. Hagler, "Exhuming the Nahualli," 197–200.

26. Sousa, *Woman Who Turned*, 26, 23.

27. For an illustration, see Sahagún, "Florentine Codex," Biblioteca Medicea Laurenziana, bk. 6, fol. 209v; and Sousa, *Woman Who Turned*, 22–23.

28. For late medieval ideas about the afterlife, see Bernstein, "Heaven, Hell and Purgatory."

29. Cohen Suarez, *Everything in Between*, 52. This book takes as its subject mural painting in the colonial Andes. For monsters in images of hell, see also the works of Hieronymus Bosch in, for example, Silva Maroto, *Bosch*.

30. "Tripod Cylinder Vase."

31. Norton, *Tame and the Wild*, 122.

32. For medieval French and English coronation ceremonies, see Brogan, *Royal Touch*, chap. 1. The classic work on the binary ontology of crowned kings is Kantorowicz, *King's Two Bodies*.

33. For the processes by which sufferers were identified by the king's surgeons and admitted to the ceremony, see Brogan, *Royal Touch*, 3.

34. Stephen Brogan observes that monarchs who performed the royal touch "took on the role of religious leaders"; see *Royal Touch*, 4.

35. Few, *Evil Lives*, 54.

36. For an accessible cultural history of relics (particularly those of premodern Europe) and for how origin and discovery stories and reliquaries bring relics into being, see Hahn, *Reliquary Effect*.

37. For the materiality of relics, see Hahn, *Reliquary Effect*, chap. 1. All of Christ's body was believed to have ascended to heaven, apart from, perhaps, some of the blood he shed on earth, which the faithful believed to be preserved in relics of the Holy Blood; see Hahn, *Passion Relics*, 75–79.

38. Gershon, "The Incorruptible Body of Francis Xavier."

39. For the relic as a social category, see Geary, *Furta Sacra*, 3; Hahn, *Passion Relics*, 5; and Hahn, *Reliquary Effect*, 12–13.

40. Gregory, "Martyrs and Saints," 455.

41. Cornelius Gemma, *De naturae divinis characterismis*, 75–76, quoted in W. Williams, *Monsters and Their Meanings*, 315.

42. Kosiba, *Sacred Matter*; Fromont, "Paper."

43. López Austin, "Cosmovision," 32.

44. For Mesoamerican beverages, including chocolate and pulque, and the customs and effects of their use, see, for example, Carrasco, *Mesoamerican Cultures*, 1:85–89.

45. Gómez, *Experiential Caribbean*.

46. Few, *Evil Lives*, 54–55.

47. Restall, Sousa, and Terreciano, *Mesoamerican Voices*, 186. In the sixteenth century, Spanish missionaries and Indigenous scholars, converts, and interlocutors transliterated Nahuatl sounds using the Latin alphabet.

48. The standard work on ritual substances in Mesoamerica and the Spanish colonial world is Norton, *Sacred Gifts*. Rich in examples from original texts and visual sources, the book documents the anxieties of colonial authorities concerning the continuing consumption of what they called diabolical substances, as well as the proliferation of their use among European settlers, and argues that chocolate and tobacco effectively colonized early modern Europe.

49. Few, *Evil Lives*, 54–55.

50. Earle, *Body of the Conquistador*.

51. Norton, *Sacred Gifts*.

52. *Hammer of Witches* was titled *Malleus maleficarum* in the original Latin. An inquisitor was a prosecutor who operated in ecclesiastical—that is, church—courts to try religious crimes.

53. Levack, *Witchcraft Sourcebook*, 57–58. The quotations are taken from the translated extracts on pp. 58–68.

54. The scholarly literature on witchcraft and the witch hunt in late medieval and early modern Europe is copious. For an overview of how people viewed unorthodox beliefs on the eve of the Reformation, see Cameron, "Dissent and Heresy." For a comprehensive recent account of the phenomenon, see Goodare, *European Witch-Hunt*, which includes a chapter on scholarly trends and perspectives in the study of the history of the witch hunt. Levack's *Witchcraft Sourcebook* contains extracts from a wide variety of documents: ancient works on witchcraft, theological and legal works, extracts from trials, accounts of demonic possession, and even witchcraft in drama. For an introduction to beliefs about witchcraft, witch trials, and themes in scholarship on the history of witchcraft, in Europe and in the colonial Americas, see Levack, *Oxford Handbook*. For visual imagery of witchcraft, see Zika, *Appearance of Witchcraft*.

55. For the intellectual foundations of the witch hunt, see Levack, *Witch-Hunt*, chap. 2.

56. For older women's envy as a suspected motive for witchcraft, see Roper, "Fantasies," 112.

57. For accusations around fertility, see Roper, "Fantasies," 112.

58. For ways in which religious reformation in early modern Europe reconfigured gender relationships, see Rublack, *Gender*.

59. Zika, *Appearance of Witchcraft*, 27–29.

60. Few, *Evil Lives*, 29–30.

61. For the social functions of storytelling in the European witch hunt, see Lindemann, "Gender Tales," 134–35.

62. For this and other examples of accusations of children as witches, see Roper, "Evil Imaginings."

63. See, for example, the trial document extracts in Levack, *Witchcraft Sourcebook*, pt. 5. Jurists described the use of torture in their witch-hunting guides; see, for example, Bodin, *Démonomanie*, 4, chaps. 1–3.

64. Zika, *Appearance of Witchcraft*, 11–13.

65. For ways of working with inquisition documents and other sources hostile to or skeptical of those whose lives and testimonies they record, the classic essay is Ginzburg, "Inquisitor as Anthropologist." See also reflections by Davis, *Fiction in the Archives*; and, more recently, Hartman, *Wayward Lives*.

66. For my account of the trial and the quoted translations, I have drawn on Levack, *Witchcraft Sourcebook*, doc. 39.

67. Braham, *From Amazons to Zombies*, 154.

68. See, for example, Dillon, "Zombie Biopolitics."

69. For a holistic account of African diasporic health and healing, see Gómez, *Experiential Caribbean*. For an overview of West African medicine between the sixteenth and mid-nineteenth centuries, including the part played by spirits in health, see Kananoja, *Healing Knowledge*.

70. For an extensive study, see Fromont, "Paper." For the inquisition, see Bethencourt, *Inquisition*. For an overview of inquisition scholarship of the second half of the twentieth century and pithy summaries of the Spanish, Roman, and Portuguese Inquisition offices, see Monter, "Inquisition."

71. Telling histories of Africa and of Indigenous peoples in regions that experienced settler-colonialism is often hampered by the uneven survival of written sources: colonizers told stories in their own words and sometimes burned—and certainly neglected to archive—voices of the colonized. In other cases, where histories were primarily passed on through oral traditions, Western institutions that have prioritized the written word have erased non-Western modes of knowing and recording. For a critique of anthropology, see, for example, Trouillot et al., *Trouillot Remixed*.

72. Braham, *From Amazons to Zombies*, 155.

73. Morgan, *Reckoning with Slavery*.

74. Braham, *From Amazons to Zombies*, 155–57. Latin American literature and film explore an array of monsters and are the subject of this book.

75. For an introduction, see Komatsu, *Introduction to Yōkai Culture*. This tripartite typology of yōkai is described on pp. 13–18. The classic recent work in English on yōkai is Foster, *Book of Yōkai*. See also Foster's *Pandemonium and Parade*.

76. See Canales, *Bedeviled*, x.

77. Davies, "Unlucky," 50; Felton, "Embracing the Monstrous," 128.

78. The classic work on prints as propaganda in the German Reformation is Scribner, *Simple Folk*. For a detailed study of images of monstrous births and prodigies in the German Reformation, see Spinks, *Monstrous Births*; see also Scribner, *Simple Folk*, 127–36, 232–34.

79. Buck, *Roman Monster*, 8–11.

80. For discussions of this pamphlet, see, for example, Scribner, *Simple Folk*, 129–32, 135–36, 139, 180; and Spinks, *Monstrous Births*, 64–72. For a forensically detailed analysis of Melanchthon's Papal Ass pamphlet, see Buck, *Roman Monster*, chap. 4.

81. For a variety of case studies, see Bown, Burdett, and Thurschwell, *Victorian Supernatural*.

82. O'Hearn, "The Strange Fate of Pillaged Mummies."

83. Luckhurst, *Mummy's Curse*.

8. MACHINES

1. In practice automation has often led to some communities losing jobs and livelihoods entirely. The much-feted benefits of automation make societies more unequal unless legislation is in place to make opportunities available to those who have been denied them, as we shall see later.

2. For income inequality in the United States, see Desmond, *Poverty in America*; and Reich, *System*.

3. Barber, "Generative AI Copyright Fight."

4. Rowe, "'It's Destroyed Me Completely.'"

5. Pasquale, *New Laws of Robotics*, chap. 2.

6. For the automaton as an imaginative tool for thinking about the limits of humanity in European culture, see Kang, *Sublime Dreams*.

7. Darling, "New Breed."

8. Or, as classics scholar Adrienne Mayor puts it, robots are "made, not born." Mayor, *Gods and Robots*, 1.

9. Vint, *Science Fiction*, 76.

10. Since Cylons, the synthetic beings in *Battlestar Galactica* we'll meet later in this chapter, were not born as organic beings but engineered to contain organic and machine parts from scratch, you could say that they are neither androids nor cyborgs.

11. Mayor, *Gods and Robots*, 3.

12. Rabelais, *Vie tres horrificque*, chap. 24, fol. 72r: "petits engins automates— c'est a dire, soy mouvens eulx memes." This example appears in Truitt, *Medieval Robots*, 2–3.

13. See especially Mayor, *Gods and Robots*. On classical archetypes in science fiction, see Rogers and Stevens, *Classical Traditions*. The work engages examples of hybrid creatures, robots, gods, and monsters.

14. Minsoo Kang has argued that the automaton "is a central idea in the Western imagination." See *Sublime Dreams*, 5. This book includes numerous examples of robots in Western literature and thought. For automata in ancient Greece and Rome, see *Sublime Dreams*, chap. 1.

15. Bedingfield, "Problems."

16. These issues are admirably explained in Noble, *Algorithms of Oppression;* and O'Neil, *Weapons of Math Destruction.*

17. Mayor, *Gods and Robots*, 145–46; Truitt, *Medieval Robots*, 3. Further examples of ancient Greek, Egyptian, and central Eurasian automata appear on pp. 3–5.

18. Voskuhl, *Androids in the Enlightenment*, 206–10.

19. Edmund Wilson, "Poetry of Drouth," 616, cited in Palattella, "But If It Ends," 6.

20. Čapek and Čapek, *R. U. R.*

21. For robots and racialized labor in science fiction, see Vint, *Science Fiction*, 79–80.

22. Klein, *No Logo;* Desmond, *Poverty in America.*

23. For examples of robots speaking to questions of labor and dehumanization in Japanese anime, see Bolton, "Mecha's Blind Spot."

24. For Taylorism, see Kang, *Sublime Dreams*, 170.

25. Tegmark, *Life 3.0.*

26. Nelson, "Society after Pandemic," cited in Pasquale, *New Laws of Robotics,* 28.

27. Asimov, *I, Robot*, 30–52.

28. Pasquale, *New Laws of Robotics*, 3.

29. Pasquale, *New Laws of Robotics*, 3–12.

30. Darling, *New Breed*, 94.

31. Darling, *New Breed*, 101.

32. Jentsch was referring his readers to a character in in the German writer Ernst Theodor Amadeus Hoffmann's 1817 short but convoluted horror story, "The Sandman," which involves a legendary creature who steals the eyes of children who won't go to sleep and a metallurgist who makes eyeless faces.

33. Mori, "Uncanny Valley."

34. Nyholm, *Humans and Robots*, 1–3.

35. Scheerer, "Measure of a Man," *Star Trek.*

36. Wachowski and Wachowski, *Matrix.*

37. On terms-of-service agreements, see Mejias and Couldry, *Data Grab*, 11–14.

38. The sixteenth-century barber-surgeon Ambroise Paré wrote treatises on monsters and on battlefield surgery and prosthetic limbs.

39. Christian, "If A.I. Models Are Wrong."

40. D. Williams, "Bias Optimizers"; Christian, "A.I. Models Are Wrong."

41. "Cishet" refers to people who are cisgender and heterosexual. See also Heffernan, "Disturbing Resurrection."

42. O'Neil, *Weapons of Math Destruction.*

43. O'Brian, Fingerhut, and Associated Press, "A.I. Tools Fueled." Shaolei Ren's research team at UC Riverside will be publishing an article on the environmental impact of generative AI tools.

44. Naughton, "Sure, Google's AI Overviews Could Be Useful"; Naughton, "Mushroom Pickers Urged to Avoid Foraging Books."

45. For a sustained discussion of the problem of human beings as data, see O'Neil, *Weapons of Math Destruction*; and Mejias and Couldry, *Data Grab*.

46. For critiques of systemic exploitation and inequality, see, for example, Klein, *No Logo;* Reich, *Supercapitalism*; Blakeley, *Vulture Capitalism*.

9. EXTRATERRESTRIALS

1. Davies, *Renaissance Ethnography*, 25–29.

2. Das et al., *Keywords of Identity*, 20.

3. For the quotation and context, see Pepys, *Diary of Samuel Pepys*, 9:123. Among the duchess's published works are a biography of her husband, Willam Cavendish, the Lord Newcastle. In his critique Pepys noted that he was reading the book for the sake of his eyes (it was "a fair print"), and he had a copy only because someone had sent it to his wife. Pepys's epithet for Lady Cavendish is quoted in Leslie, *Renaissance Utopias*, 120.

4. Spielberg, *E.T.*

5. Scott, *Alien*. For an introduction to *Alien* and its sources, innovations, and cultural influence, see Luckhurst, *Alien*.

6. Blomkamp, *District 9*.

7. Quammen, *Tangled Tree*.

8. Livingston, *Star Trek*, "Homefront."

9. Helfrich, "Pope Scope," 48.

10. "Mount Graham"; Helfrich, "Pope Scope," 49.

11. "Mount Graham."

12. Brandt, "Dzil Nchaa Si An"; Krol, "Mount Graham"; Helfrich, "Pope Scope."

13. Helfrich, "Pope Scope," 61.

10. MONSTROFUTURISM

1. The information in this summary is drawn from Headley, *Beowulf.* Headley's interview on the *Between the Covers* podcast offers an illuminating discussion; see "Crafting with Ursula."

2. Headley, *Beowulf,* xvi.

3. Headley, *Beowulf,* xxiii, 56, lines 1255–58.

4. Headley, *Beowulf,* xxvi, xxvii, xxv. For the 1922 glossary appearances of *aglaeca* and *aglaec-wif,* see *Beowulf and the Fight,* 298. Klaeber opens his entry on *aglaeca* with "wretch, monster, demon, fiend" by noting that it is "used chiefly of Grendel and the dragon" before giving the translation "hero" in the case of "Beowulf and the dragon."

5. Gardner, *Grendel,* 6.

6. Gardner, *Grendel,* 26–28.

7. Morrison, "Grendel and His Mother," 256.

8. Morrison, "Grendel and His Mother," 257, 258.

9. Wilson, "Found in Translation."

10. Emily Wilson, "First Woman to Translate."

11. Hartman, "Venus in Two Acts," 3–4.

12. Ginzburg, "Inquisitor as Anthropologist."

13. Roper, *Witch Craze,* 52–54.

14. Levack, *Witchcraft Sourcebook,* 185–87.

15. Jones, *Vanguard,* 81.

16. hooks, *Ain't I a Woman,* 3–9; Jones, *Vanguard,* 23.

17. Crenshaw, "Mapping the Margins."

18. "Freak Shows Ephemera: Box 2," EPH 499A:104, Wellcome Collection.

19. Jones, *Vanguard,* 82–83.

20. Mbembe, *Critique of Black Reason,* 151.

21. Dery, "Black to the Future," 179–80. For more on the Tuskegee experiment, see, in the present volume, chapter 6, note 48.

22. Dery, "Black to the Future," 180.

23. Lavender, *Afrofuturism Rising,* 1–2.

24. Lavender, *Afrofuturism Rising,* 2.

25. My outline of this case summarizes parts of the account in De Souza, "Elenx de Céspedes."

26. De Souza, "Elenx de Céspedes," 47–49.

27. De Souza, "Elenx de Céspedes," 47.

28. De Souza, "Elenx de Céspedes," 47–48.

29. De Souza, "Elenx de Céspedes," 49–50.

30. De Souza, "Elenx de Céspedes," 42.

31. LaFleur, Raskolnikov, and Kłosowska, *Trans Historical,* 9, 2, 4.

32. De Souza, "Elenx de Céspedes," 42.

33. Heyam, *Before We Were Trans,* 220, 221.

34. Le Guin, "National Book Award," 57. For Le Guin's reflections, see the epigraph at the beginning of this chapter.

35. Docter, Silverman, and Unkrich, *Monsters, Inc.*

EPILOGUE

1. Lyons, "Black History."

2. Mystal, "Alabama's IVF Ruling."

3. Lenharo, "Is IVF at Risk?"

4. For the ongoing fight over new anti-IVF measures, see, for example, Mystal, "Alabama's IVF Ruling."

5. Bouie, "Samuel Alito Opened the Door to Reproductive Hell."

6. See, for example, J. Butler, *Who's Afraid of Gender?*, 96–97, 102–6.

7. Early reporters assumed that Benedict used "they" pronouns, but they did not speak with trans people in Benedict's community or establish the pronouns Benedict used. See McMenamin, "Nex Benedict."

8. J. Butler, *Who's Afraid of Gender?*, 143–43, 155–59, and, more generally, chap. 5.

9. Duda's party, reelected in 2020, lost power in 2023, raising some cause for optimism; see Dunin-Wąsowicz, "In Poland, the Home of 'LGBT-Freezones.'" As this book goes to press, proposed amendments to ease these restrictions are in discussion in parliament.

10. Both liberal and illiberal shifts are on the table as I write; see Kassam, "'Try Harder!'"

11. J. Butler, *Who's Afraid of Gender?* Chaps. 1 and 2 survey some examples from around the world.

12. Otte, "Suella Braverman Says Rough Sleeping Is 'Lifestyle Choice.'"

13. See, for example, Scrimgeour, "Top-Secret Hawaii Compound"; and Pollan, "Why Billionaires Are Obsessed," in which he reviews Rushkoff's *Survival of the Richest*.

14. Quoted in Klein, *Doppelganger*, 147–48.

15. For an overview, see Klein, *Doppelganger*, chaps. 13, 14.

16. Makdisi, "Things in Palestine."

17. Klein, *Doppelganger*, 285–88.

18. See, for example, Ghosh, *Nutmeg's Curse*.

19. Langston, "New Chemical Bodies," 271–72.

20. See, for example, Mbembe, *Necropolitics*; Graeber, *Debt*; and Thunberg, *Climate Book*.

21. For a compelling account of propaganda narratives that catalyze people into fighting false threats and prevent them from working together to solve real problems, see Klein, *Doppelganger*, a book whose theme (doppelgangers, theories, and nations) offers many parallels to monsters.

BIBLIOGRAPHY

MANUSCRIPT AND ARCHIVAL SOURCES

Bologna

Bologna University Library

"Tavole acquerellate di U. Aldrovandi." Circa 1560–1610. 10 vols. 001–2 Animali. Fondo Ulisse Aldrovandi. Accessed June 21, 2024. http://aldrovandi.dfc .unibo.it/pinakesweb/UlisseAldrovandi_tavoleacquerellate4.asp?objtypeid= all&macrofamilyid=10&comptypeid=102&language=it.

Cambridge, MA

Harvard Theatre Collection, Houghton Library, Harvard University

"Human Curiosity Prints, Playbills, Broadsides, and Other Printed Material, 1697–1937." MS Thr 736.

Florence

Biblioteca Medicea Laurenziana

Sahagún, Bernadino de. "Florentine Codex." 3 vols. Med. Palat. 218–20, 1577. Digital "Florentine Codex." Accessed June 21, 2024. https://florentinecodex .getty.edu/.

Glasgow

Hunterian Collection, University of Glasgow Library

Douglas, James. "Account of a Hermaphrodite. By J. D." 17—. GB 247 MS Hunter DF60/1–3.

Hunterian Collection (*continued*)

Fair copy of Mary Toft's confession. December 7, 1726. GB 247 MS Hunter D325.

Mary Toft's confession. December 12, 1726. GB 247 MS Hunter D328.

Mary Toft's confession. December 7, 1726. GB 247 MS Hunter D324.

"Transcribed Extract regarding Mary Toft from Whitehall *Evening Post*, 29 Dec. 1726." GB 247 MS Hunter D332.

London

Department of Manuscripts, British Library

Desceliers, Pierre. "Mappemonde." 1550. Add. MS. 24065.

Du Plessis, James Paris. "Continuation [of Prodigious and Monstrous Births]." Circa 1736. Sloane MS 3253.

———. "A Short History of Human Prodigious and Monstrous Births, of Dwarfs, Sleepers, Giants, Strong Men, Hermaphrodites, Numerous Births, and Extream Old Age Etc." Circa 1730–33. Add MS 5246. Formerly Sloane MS 5246.

Psalter World Map. Circa 1265. Add. MS. 28681.

Department of Rare Books, British Library

"Collection of Advertisements." BL N.Tab.2026/25.

Evanion Collection of Ephemera.

London Metropolitan Archives

"Ephemera" folders: SC/GL/ENT/001–049; SC/GL/END/100–149; SC/GL /NOB/C/026/5-026/51. Item C.26.51. T. c. 1750.

Royal Society

"Letter Book of the Royal Society: 'Original' Copies." 1664–68. LBO 2/67; LBO 28/2.

Wellcome Collection

Boaistuau, Pierre. "Histoires prodigieuses." 1559. MS 136.

"Ephemera" folders: EPH 449A:3; EPH 449A:8; EPH 499A:18; EPH 499A:37; EPH 499A:40; EPH 449A:76; EPH 499A:104; EPH 499B:19; EPH 499:58B; EPH 499D:19; EPH 499D:24; EPH 499D:54; EPH 499D:55; EPH 499D:77; EPH 499D:97.

Paris

Département des Manuscrits, Bibliothèque Nationale de France

"Codex Telleriano-Remensis." Mid-sixteenth century. Mexicain 385. Accessed June 27, 2024. https://gallica.bnf.fr/ark:/12148/btv1b8458267s.

Vienna

Austrian National Library

Gutiérrez, Sancho. *Esta carta general en plano hizo Sancho Gutierrez cosmographo.* 1551. K I 99.416.

Vincennes

Service Historique de la Défense, Bibliothèque Vincennes

Le Testu, Guillaume. "Cosmographie universelle selon les navigateurs, tant ancien que moderns." 1555 [1556 n.s.]. D.2.z.14.

Washington, DC

National Gallery of Art

Hoefnagel, Joris. "Ignis: Animalia rationalia et insecta." Circa 1577. 1897.20.8. Accessed June 7, 2024. www.nga.gov/collection/art-object-page.69668.html.

BOOKS, ARTICLES, AND ESSAYS

Acts of Assembly Passed in the Island of Barbadoes, from 1648 to 1718. London, 1721.
Aiello, Leslie. "Five Years of 'Homo Floresiensis.'" *American Journal of Physical Anthropology* 142 (2010): 167–79.
Alexander, Michelle. *The New Jim Crow: Mass Incarceration in the Age of Colourblindness.* London: Penguin, 2019.
Altick, Richard D. *The Shows of London.* Cambridge, MA: Belknap Press of Harvard University Press, 1978.
Alund, Natalie Neysa. "World's Richest People Have Become $852 Billion Wealthier in 2023, Led by Musk, Bezos: Bloomberg." *USA Today,* July 5, 2023.
Anderson, Benedict. *Imagined Communities: Reflections on the Origin and Spread of Nationalism.* London: Verso, 1991.
Andrews (Bitterroot Salish), Tarren. "Indigenous Futures and Medieval Pasts: An Introduction." *English Language Notes* 58, no. 2 (October 2020): 1–17.
Appiah, Kwame Anthony. *The Lies That Bind: Rethinking Identity.* London: Profile Books, 2018.
Aristotle. *Generation of Animals.* Translated by Arthur Leslie Peck. Cambridge, MA: Harvard University Press, 1963.
———. *The Nicomachean Ethics.* Translated by Harris Rackham. Cambridge, MA: Harvard University Press, 1926.
———. *On the Soul.* Translated by Walter Stanley Hett. Cambridge, MA: Harvard University Press, 1957.

———. *Politics*. Translated by Harris Rackham. Cambridge, MA: Harvard University Press, 1932.

Arvas, Abdulhamit. "Early Modern Eunuchs and the Transing of Gender and Race." *Journal for Early Modern Cultural Studies* 19, no. 4 (Fall 2019): 116–36.

Ashley-Montagu, Montague Francis. *Edward Tyson, M.D., F.R.S., 1650–1708, and the Rise of Human and Comparative Anatomy in England*. Philadelphia: American Philosophical Society, 1943.

Asimov, Isaac. *I, Robot*. 1950. Reprint, London: Harper Voyager, 2018.

Asma, Stephen T. *On Monsters: An Unnatural History of Our Worst Fears*. Oxford: Oxford University Press, 2011.

Atran, Scott, and Douglas L. Medin. *The Native Mind and the Cultural Construction of Nature*. Cambridge, MA: MIT Press, 2008.

Bakhtin, Mikhael M. *Rabelais and His World*. Translated by Hélène Iswolski. Cambridge, MA: MIT Press, 1968.

Ball, Philip. *The Book of Minds: Understanding Ourselves and Other Beings from Animals to Aliens*. London: Picador, 2023.

Barber, Gregory. "The Generative AI Copyright Fight Is Just Getting Started." *Wired*, December 7, 2023.

Barraclough, Eleanor Rosamund, Danielle Marie Cudmore, and Stefan Donecker, eds. *Imagining the Supernatural North*. Edmonton: University of Alberta Press, 2016.

Barron, David. "Biles Finds Beauty in Beastly Athleticism." *Houston Chronicle*, July 21, 2021, sec. C, p. 1.

Bartra, Roger. *Wild Men in the Looking Glass: The Mythic Origins of European Otherness*. Translated by Carl T. Berrisford. Ann Arbor: University of Michigan Press, 1994.

Bass, Marisa Anne. *Insect Artifice: Nature and Art in the Dutch Revolt*. Princeton, NJ: Princeton University Press, 2019.

Bassett, Molly H. *The Fate of Earthly Things: Aztec Gods and God-Bodies*. Austin: University of Texas Press, 2015.

Bearden, Elizabeth. *Monstrous Kinds: Body, Space, and Narrative in Renaissance Representations of Disability*. Minneapolis: University of Minnesota, 2019.

Bedingfield, Will. "The Problems Lurking in Hollywood's Historic AI Deal." *Wired*, November 27, 2023.

Beezley, William H., ed. *A Companion to Mexican History and Culture*. Chichester, UK: Wiley-Blackwell, 2011.

Bell, Matt. "Climate Fictions: Future-Making Technologies." In *The Cambridge Companion to Environmental Humanities*, edited by Jeffrey Cohen and Stephanie Foote, 100–113. Cambridge: Cambridge University Press, 2021.

Bernstein, Alan E. "Heaven, Hell and Purgatory: 1100–1500." In *The Cambridge History of Christianity: Christianity in Western Europe, c. 1100–1500*, edited by Miri Rubin and Walter Simons, 200–216. Cambridge: Cambridge University Press, 2009.

Bernus-Taylor, Marthe. *L'Étrange et le Merveilleux en terres d'Islam: Catalogue d'exposition, Paris, Musée du Louvre, 23 avril–23 juillet 2001*. Paris: Réunion des Musées Nationaux, 2001.

Betancourt, Roland. *Byzantine Intersectionality: Sexuality, Gender, and Race in the Middle Ages*. Princeton, NJ: Princeton University Press, 2020.

Bethencourt, Francisco. *The Inquisition: A Global History*. Cambridge: Cambridge University Press, 2010.

———. *Racisms: From the Crusades to the Twentieth Century*. Princeton, NJ: Princeton University Press, 2014.

Blakeley, Grace. *Vulture Capitalism: Corporate Crimes, Backdoor Bailouts and the Death of Freedom*. London: Bloomsbury, 2024.

Bleichmar, Daniela. *Visible Empire: Botanical Expeditions and Visual Culture in the Hispanic Enlightenment*. Chicago: University of Chicago Press, 2012.

———. *Visual Voyages: Images of Latin American Nature from Columbus to Darwin*. New Haven, CT: Yale University Press, 2017.

Boaistuau, Pierre. *Histoires prodigieuses*. Edited by Stephen Bamforth and Jean Céard. Geneva: Droz, 2010.

Bodin, Jean. *De la démonomanie des sorciers*. Edited by Virginia Krause, Christian Martin, and Eric MacPhail. Geneva: Droz, 2016.

Bogdan, Robert. "Social Construction of Freaks." In Garland-Thomson, *Freakery*, 23–37.

Bolton, Christopher. "Mecha's Blind Spot." *Science Fiction Studies* 29, no. 3 (November 2002). www.depauw.edu/sfs/backissues/88/bolton.html.

Boone, Elizabeth Hill. *Cycles of Time and Meaning in the Mexican Books of Fate*. Austin: University of Texas Press, 2007.

———. *Descendants of Aztec Pictography: The Cultural Encyclopedias of Sixteenth-Century Mexico*. Austin: University of Texas Press, 2021.

Bouie, Jamelle. "Samuel Alito Opened the Door to Reproductive Hell." *New York Times*, February 23, 2024. www.nytimes.com/2024/02/23/opinion/alabama-embroyo-dobbs-reproductive-freedom.html?smid=nytcore-ios-share&referringSource=articleShare&sgrp=c-cb.

Boulle, Pierre. *La planète de singes*. Paris: Juillard, 1963.

Bown, Nicola, Carolyn Burdett, and Pamela Thurschwell. *The Victorian Supernatural*. Cambridge: Cambridge University Press, 2004.

Braham, Persephone. *From Amazons to Zombies: Monsters in Latin America*. London: Bucknell University Press, 2015.

Brandt, Elizabeth. "The Fight for Dzil Nchaa Si An, Mt. Graham: Apaches and Astrophysical Development in Arizona." *Cultural Survival Quarterly*, 2010. www.culturalsurvival.org/publications/cultural-survival-quarterly/fight-dzil-nchaa-si-mt-graham-apaches-and-astrophysical.

Braude, Benjamin. "The Sons of Noah and the Construction of Ethnic and Geographical Identities in the Medieval and Early Modern Periods." *William and Mary Quarterly* 54, no. 1 (1997): 103–42.

Breen, Benjamin. *The Age of Intoxication: Origins of the Global Drug Trade*. Philadelphia: University of Pennsylvania Press, 2019.

Brogan, Stephen. *The Royal Touch in Early Modern England: Politics, Medicine and Sin*. Woodbridge: Boydell, 2015.

Buck, Lawrence P. *The Roman Monster: An Icon of the Papal Antichrist in Reformation Polemics*. State Park: Pennsylvania State University Press, 2014.

Bulwer, John. *Anthropometamorphosis: Man Transform'd, or The Artificial Changeling*. 2nd ed. London, 1653.

———. *Anthropometamorphosis: Man Transform'd, or The Artificial Changeling*. London, 1650.

Burnett, Mark Thornton. *Constructing "Monsters" in Shakespearean Drama and Early Modern Culture*. Basingstoke, UK: Palgrave, 2002.

Burns, Kathryn. "Unfixing Race." In Greer, Mignolo, and Quillian, *Rereading the Black Legend*, 188–202.

Burns, William E. "The King's Two Monstrous Bodies: John Bulwer and the English Revolution." In *Wonders, Marvels, and Monsters in Early Modern Culture*, edited by Peter G. Platt, 187–202. Newark: University of Delaware Press/East Brunswick, NJ: Associated University Presses, 1999.

Butler, Judith. *Who's Afraid of Gender?* New York: Farrar, Straus and Giroux, 2024.

Butler, Octavia E. *Kindred*. New York: Doubleday, 1979.

———. *Parable of the Sower*. New York: Four Walls Eight Windows, 1993.

Bychowski, Gabrielle M. W., Howard Chiang, Jack Halberstam, Jacob Lau, Kathleen Long, Marcia Ochoa, and C. Riley Snorton. "'Trans*historicities': A Roundtable Discussion." *TSQ: Transgender Studies Quarterly* 5, no. 4 (November 2018): 658–85.

Bynum, Caroline Walker. *Wonderful Blood: Theology and Practice in Late Medieval Northern Germany and Beyond*. Philadelphia: University of Pennsylvania Press, 2007.

Cameron, Euan. "Dissent and Heresy." In Hsia, *Reformation World*, 3–21.

Campbell, Mary Baine. *Wonder and Science: Imagining Worlds in Early Modern Europe*. Ithaca, NY: Cornell University Press, 1999.

Canales, Jimena. *Bedeviled: A Shadow History of Demons in Science*. Princeton, NJ: Princeton University Press, 2020.

Canguilhem, Georges. "La monstruosité et le monstrueux." *Diogène* 40 (1962): 29–43.

Cañizares-Esguerra, Jorge. *How to Write the History of the New World: Historiographies, Epistemologies, and Identities in the Eighteenth-Century Atlantic World*. Stanford, CA: Stanford University Press, 2001.

———. "New World, New Stars: Patriotic Astrology and the Invention of Indian and Creole Bodies in Colonial Spanish America, 1600–1650." *American Historical Review* 104, no. 1 (1999): 33–68.

Čapek, Josef, and Karel Čapek. *R. U. R. and the Insect Play*. 1923. Reprint, Oxford: Oxford University Press, 1975.

Čapek, Karel. "*R. U. R. (Rossum's Universal Robots):* A Play in Three Acts and an Epilogue." In Čapek and Čapek, *R. U. R.*, 1–104.

Carrasco, Davíd. *The Imagination of Matter: Religion and Ecology in Mesoamerican Traditions*. Oxford: B. A. R. International Series, 1989.

———, ed. *The Oxford Encyclopedia of Mesoamerican Cultures*. 3 vols. Oxford: Oxford University Press, 2001.

Carroll, Lewis. *Alice's Adventures in Wonderland*. London: Macmillan, 1865.

Carson, Rachel. *Silent Spring*. London: Hamilton, 1962.

Céard, Jean. *La nature et les prodiges: l'insolite au XVIe siècle en France*. Geneva: Librairie Droz, 1977.

Chakravarty, Urvashi. *Fictions of Consent: Slavery, Servitude, and Free Service in Early Modern England*. Philadelphia: University of Pennsylvania Press, 2022.

Challenger, Melanie. *How to Be Animal*. Edinburgh: Canongate Books, 2021.

Chaplin, Joyce. *Subject Matter: Technology, the Body, and Science on the Anglo-American Frontier, 1500–1676*. Cambridge, MA: Harvard University Press, 2001.

Chiang, Ted. *Exhalation*. London: Picador, 2019.

Cohen, Jeffrey Jerome. "Green Children from Another World, or The Archipelago in England." In *Cultural Diversity in the British Middle Ages: Archipelago, Island, England*, edited by Jeffrey Jerome Cohen, 75–94. New York: Palgrave Macmillan, 2008.

———. *Hybridity, Identity, and Monstrosity in Medieval Britain: On Difficult Middles*. New York: Palgrave Macmillan, 2006.

———, ed. *Monster Theory: Reading Culture*. Minneapolis: University of Minnesota Press, 1996.

———. *Of Giants: Sex, Monsters, and the Middle Ages*. Minneapolis: University of Minnesota Press, 1999.

Cohen Suarez, Ananda. *Heaven, Hell, and Everything in Between: Murals of the Colonial Andes*. Austin: University of Texas Press, 2016.

Cooley, Mackenzie. *The Perfection of Nature: Animals, Breeding, and Race in the Renaissance*. Chicago: University of Chicago Press, 2022.

Crawford, Julie. *Marvelous Protestantism: Monstrous Births in Post-Reformation England*. Baltimore: Johns Hopkins University Press, 2005.

Crenshaw, Kimberlé. "Mapping the Margins: Intersectionality, Identity Politics, and Violence against Women of Color." *Stanford Law Review* 43, no. 6 (July 1991): 1241–99.

"The Curious Case of Mary Toft." University of Glasgow Library. August 2009. www.gla.ac.uk/myglasgow/library/files/special/exhibns/month/aug2009.html.

Curran, Andrew S. *The Anatomy of Blackness: Science and Slavery in an Age of Enlightenment*. Baltimore: Johns Hopkins University Press, 2011.

Darling, Kate. *The New Breed: How to Think about Robots*. London: Lane, 2021.

Darnton, Robert. *The Great Cat Massacre and Other Episodes in French Cultural History*. Harmondsworth, UK: Penguin, 1984.

Darwin, Charles. *On the Origin of Species by Means of Natural Selection, or The Preservation of Favoured Races in the Struggle for Life*. London: Murray, 1859.

Das, Nandini, João Vicente Melo, Haig Smith, and Lauren Working. *Keywords of Identity, Race, and Human Mobility in Early Modern England*. Amsterdam: Amsterdam University Press, 2021.

Daston, Lorraine, and Katharine Park. *Wonders and the Order of Nature, 1150–1750.* New York: Zone Books, 1998.

Davies, Surekha. "Catalogical Encounters: Worldmaking in Early Modern Cabinets of Curiosities." In *Early Modern Things: Objects and Their Histories, 1500–1800,* edited by Paula Findlen, 227–54. 2nd ed. London: Routledge, 2021.

———. *Renaissance Ethnography and the Invention of the Human: New Worlds, Maps and Monsters.* Cambridge: Cambridge University Press, 2016.

———. "The Unlucky, the Bad and the Ugly: Categories of Monstrosity from the Renaissance to the Enlightenment." In Mittman, *Ashgate Research Companion,* 49–75.

Davis, Natalie Zemon. *Fiction in the Archives: Pardon Tales and Their Tellers in Sixteenth-Century France.* Stanford, CA: Stanford University Press, 1987.

Dean, Carolyn. *A Culture of Stone.* Durham, NC: Duke University Press, 2010.

Delbourgo, James. *Collecting the World: Hans Sloane and the Origins of the British Museum.* Cambridge, MA: Harvard University Press, 2017.

Demuth, Bathsheba. *Floating Coast: An Environmental History of the Bering Strait.* New York: Norton, 2019.

Denecke, Wiebke, and Ilaria L. E. Ramelli, eds. *Third Millennium BCE to 600 CE.* Vol. 1 of *A Companion to World Literature.* 6 vols. Hoboken, NJ: Wiley-Blackwell, 2020.

Denis, Ferdinand. *Une fête brésilienne célébrée à Rouen en 1550.* Paris: Techener, 1850.

Dery, Mark. "Black to the Future: Interviews with Samuel R. Delany, Greg Tate, and Tricia Rose." In *Flame Wars: The Discourse of Cyberculture,* edited by Mark Dery and Tricia Rose, 179–222. Durham, NC: Duke University Press, 1994.

Descola, Philippe. *Beyond Nature and Culture.* Translated by Janet Lloyd. Chicago: University of Chicago Press, 2013.

———. *In the Society of Nature: A Native Ecology in Amazonia.* Translated by Nora Scott. Cambridge: Cambridge University Press, 1994.

Desmond, Matthew. *Poverty in America.* London: Lane, 2023.

De Souza, Igor H. "Elenx de Céspedes." In LaFleur, Raskolnikov, and Kłosowska, *Trans Historical,* 42–67.

DeVun, Leah. *The Shape of Sex: Nonbinary Gender from Genesis to the Renaissance.* New York: Columbia University Press, 2021.

Dick, Stephen J., ed. *The Impact of Discovering Life beyond Earth.* Cambridge: Cambridge University Press, 2015.

Dickens, Charles. *Bleak House.* Edited by George Ford and Sylvère Monod. New York: Norton, 1977.

Dillon, Elizabeth Maddock. "Zombie Biopolitics." *American Quarterly* 71, no. 3 (2019): 625–52.

Douglas, Mary. *Purity and Danger: An Analysis of Concepts of Pollution and Taboo.* London: Routledge and Kegan Paul, 1966.

Drewal, Henry John. "Beauteous Beast: The Water Deity Mami Wata in Africa." In Mittman, *Ashgate Research Companion,* 77–101.

Dudeque, Norton. *Heitor Villa-Lobos' "Bachianas Brasileiras": Intertextuality and Stylization.* Abingdon, UK: Routledge, 2022.

Dunin-Wąsowicz, Roch. "In Poland, the Home of 'LGBT-Freezones,' There Is Hope at Last for the Queer Community." *Guardian,* November 1, 2023. www.theguardian.com/commentisfree/2023/nov/01/poland-lgbtq-new-government-law-and-justice-equality.

Durán, Diego. *The Aztecs: The History of the Indies of New Spain.* Translated by Doris Heyden and Fernando Horcasitas. London: Cassell, 1964.

———. *Book of the Gods and Rites and the Ancient Calendar.* Norman: University of Oklahoma Press, 1971.

———. *Historia de las Indias de Nueva España e islas de la tierra firme.* 1570. Edited by Ángel Ma. Garibay K. 2 vols. Mexico City: Porrua, 1967.

Durbach, Nadja. *The Spectacle of Deformity: Freak Shows and Modern British Culture.* Berkeley: University of California Press, 2010.

Earle, Rebecca. *The Body of the Conquistador: Food, Race and the Colonial Experience in Spanish America.* Cambridge: Cambridge University Press, 2012.

———. *The Return of the Native: Indians and Myth-Making in Spanish America, 1810–1930.* Durham, NC: Duke University Press, 2007.

Edson, Evelyn. *The World Map, 1300–1492.* Baltimore: Johns Hopkins University Press, 2007.

Einhard. *Vita et gesta Karoli Magni.* Cologne, 1521.

Eire, Carlos M. N. *War against the Idols: The Reformation of Worship from Erasmus to Calvin.* Cambridge: Cambridge University Press, 1986.

Engerman, Stanley, Seymour Drescher, and Robert Paquette, eds. *Slavery.* Oxford: Oxford University Press, 2001.

Falen, Douglas J. *African Science: Witchcraft, Vodun, and Healing in Southern Benin.* Madison: University of Wisconsin Press, 2018.

Fauser, Annegret. "Le sacre du printemps: A Ballet for Paris." In *The Rite of Spring at 100,* edited by John Reef, Neff Severine, Maureen Carr, and Gretchen Horlacher, 84–97. Bloomington: Indiana University Press, 2017.

Fausto, Carlos. *Warfare and Shamanism in Amazonia.* Cambridge: Cambridge University Press, 2012.

Felton, Debbie. "Rejecting and Embracing the Monstrous in Ancient Greece and Rome." In Mittman, *Ashgate Research Companion,* 103–31.

Ferdowsi, Abolqasem. *Shahnameh: The Persian Book of Kings.* Translated by Dick Davis. New York: Penguin Books, 2007.

Fernández-Armesto, Felipe. *Out of Our Minds: What We Think and How We Came to Think It.* Oakland: University of California Press, 2019.

———. *So You Think You're Human?* Oxford: Oxford University Press, 2004.

Few, Martha. *Women Who Live Evil Lives: Gender, Religion, and the Politics of Power in Colonial Guatemala.* Austin: University of Texas Press, 2002.

Fields, Karen E., and Barbara J. Fields. *Racecraft: The Soul of Inequality in American Life.* London: Verso, 2014.

Findlen, Paula. "Jokes of Nature, Jokes of Knowledge: The Playfulness of Scientific Discourse in Early Modern Europe." *American Historical Review* 43, no. 2 (Summer 1990): 292–331.

Foster, Michael Dylan. *The Book of Yōkai: Mysterious Creatures of Japanese Folklore.* Oakland: University of California Press, 2015.

———. *Pandemonium and Parade: Japanese Monsters and the Culture of Yōkai.* Oakland: University of California Press, 2009.

Foucault, Michel. *The Order of Things.* 1966. Reprint, London: Taylor and Francis, 2005.

Friedman, John Block. *The Monstrous Races in Medieval Art and Thought.* Syracuse, NY: Syracuse University Press, 2000.

Fromont, Cécile. "Paper, Ink, Vodun, and the Inquisition: Tracing Power, Slavery, and Witchcraft in the Early Modern Atlantic." *Journal of the American Academy of Religion* 88, no. 2 (June 2020): 460–504.

Frost, Brian J. *The Essential Guide to Werewolf Literature.* Madison: University of Wisconsin Press, 2003.

Fuentes, Agustín. *Race, Monogamy, and Other Lies They Told You: Busting Myths about Human Nature.* 2nd ed. Oakland: University of California Press, 2022.

Fuentes, Marisa J. *Dispossessed Lives: Enslaved Women, Violence, and the Archive.* Philadelphia: University of Pennsylvania Press, 2016.

Galerie Flak. "Ferocious Poetry: Ancient Arts of New Ireland." Advertisement. *Apollo: The International Art Magazine,* July–August 2019, 50.

García Garagarza, León. "The Tecolotl and the Chiquatli: Omens of Death and Transspecies Dialogues in the Aztec World." *Ethnohistory* 67, no 3 (July 2020): 455–79.

Gardner, John. *Grendel.* New York: Knopf, 1976.

Garland-Thomson, Rosemarie. *Extraordinary Bodies: Figuring Physical Disability in American Literature and Culture.* New York: Columbia University Press, 2017.

———, ed. *Freakery: Cultural Spectacles of the Extraordinary Body.* New York: New York University Press, 1996.

Gates, Henry Louis, Jr., and Andrew S. Curran, eds. *Who's Black and Why? A Hidden Chapter from the Eighteenth-Century Invention of Race.* Cambridge, MA: Harvard University Press, 2022.

Geary, Patrick J. *Furta Sacra: Thefts of Relics in the Central Middle Ages.* Princeton, NJ: Princeton University Press, 1978.

———. *Women at the Beginning: Origin Myths from the Amazons to the Virgin Mary.* Princeton, NJ: Princeton University Press, 2006.

Gellner, Ernest. *Thought and Change.* London: Weidenfeld and Nicolson, 1964.

George, Andrew R. "The Epic of Gilgamesh." In *The Cambridge Companion to the Epic,* edited by Catherine Bates, 1–12. Cambridge: Cambridge University Press, 2010.

Gerald of Wales. *De invectionibus lib iv. de menevensi ecclesia dialogus: Vita S. David.* Vol. 3 of *Giraldi Cambrensis opera.* Edited by J. S. Brewer, James F. Dimock, and George F. Warner. Cambridge: Cambridge University Press, 2012.

———. *The History and Topography of Ireland.* Translated by John O'Meara. 1951. Reprint, London: Penguin, 1982.

———. *The Journey through Wales and the Description of Wales.* Translated by Lewis Thorpe. 1978. Reprint, London: Penguin, 2004.

———. *Topographia Hibernica, et expugnatio Hibernica.* Vol. 5 of *Giraldi Cambrensis opera.* Edited by J. S. Brewer, James F. Dimock, and George F. Warner. Cambridge: Cambridge University Press, 2012.

Gershon, Livia. "The Incorruptible Body of Francis Xavier." *JSTOR Daily,* June 20, 2023. https://daily.jstor.org/the-incorruptible-body-of-francis-xavier/.

Ghadessi, Touba. "Inventoried Monsters: Dwarves and Hirsutes at Court." *Journal of the History of Collections* 23, no. 2 (2011): 267–81.

———. *Portraits of Human Monsters in the Renaissance: Dwarves, Hirsutes, and Castrati as Idealized Anatomical Anomalies.* Kalamazoo, MI: Medieval Institute, 2018.

Ghosh, Amitav. *The Nutmeg's Curse: Parables for a Planet in Crisis.* London: Murray, 2021.

Ginzburg, Carlo. *Clues, Myths, and the Historical Method.* Baltimore: Johns Hopkins University Press, 1989.

———. *History, Rhetoric, and Proof.* Hanover, NH: University Press of New England, 1999.

———. "The Inquisitor as Anthropologist." In Ginzburg, *Historical Method,* 156–64.

Glacken, Clarence J. *Traces on the Rhodian Shore: Nature and Culture in Western Thought from Ancient Times to the End of the Eighteenth Century.* Berkeley: University of California Press, 1967.

Gómez, Pablo F. *The Experiential Caribbean: Creating Knowledge and Healing in the Early Modern Atlantic.* Chapel Hill: University of North Carolina Press, 2017.

Goodare, Julian. *The European Witch-Hunt.* London: Routledge, 2016.

Graeber, David. *Debt: The First 5,000 Years.* New York: Melville House, 2021.

Graulich, Michel. "Creation Myths." In Carrasco, *Mesoamerican Cultures,* 1:280–84.

———. "Creator Deities." In Carrasco, *Mesoamerican Cultures,* 1:284–86.

Gray, Robert. *A Good Speed to Virginia.* 1609. Reprint, Amsterdam: Theatrum Orbis Terrarum/Da Capo, 1970.

Greene, Eric. *Planet of the Apes as American Myth: Race, Politics, and Popular Culture.* Jefferson, NC: McFarland, 2006.

Greer, Margaret T., Walter D. Mignolo, and Maureen Quillian, eds. *Rereading the Black Legend: The Discourses of Religious and Racial Difference in the Renaissance Empires.* Chicago: University of Chicago Press, 2007.

Gregory, Brad S. "Martyrs and Saints." In Hsia, *Reformation World,* 455–70.

Gruzinski, Serge. *Painting the Conquest: The Mexican Indians and the European Renaissance.* Paris: Flammarion, 1992.

"Haarmensch, Haarmann, Petrus Gonsalvus (geboren 1556), Pedro Gonsales, Pedro Gonsalez." Kunst Historisches Museum Wien. Accessed May 14, 2024. www.khm.at/de/object/5529/.

Hagler, Anderson. "Exhuming the Nahualli: Shapeshifting, Idolatry, and Orthodoxy in Colonial Mexico." *Americas* 78, no. 2 (April 2021): 197–228.

Hahn, Cynthia. *Passion Relics and the Medieval Imagination: Art, Architecture, and Society.* Oakland: University of California Press, 2020.

———. *The Reliquary Effect: Enshrining the Sacred Object.* London: Reaktion Books, 2017.

Haraway, Donna. *Primate Visions: Gender, Race, and Nature in Modern Science.* London: Routledge, 1989.

———. *Simians, Cyborgs, and Women: The Re-invention of Nature.* New York: Routledge, 1991.

Harrison, Mark. *Climates and Constitutions: Health, Race, Environment and British Imperialism in India.* Delhi: Oxford University Press, 2002.

———. *Medicine in an Age of Commerce and Empire: Britain and Its Tropical Colonies, 1660–1830.* New York: Oxford University Press, 2010.

Hartman, Saidiya. *Lose Your Mother: A Journey along the Atlantic Slave Route.* London: Profile Books, 2021.

———. "Venus in Two Acts." *Small Axe* 26 (June 2008): 1–14.

———. *Wayward Lives, Beautiful Experiments: Intimate Histories of Riotous Black Girls, Troublesome Women and Queer Radicals.* London: Profile Books, 2021.

Hartnell, Jack. *Medieval Bodies: Life, Death and Art in the Middle Ages.* London: Profile Books, 2019.

Headley, Maria Dahvana, ed. *Beowulf: A New Translation.* New York: Farrar, Straus and Giroux, 2020.

Heffernan, Virginia. "The History—and Disturbing Resurrection—of Black Androids." *Wired*, February 18, 2022. www.wired.com/story/history-disturbing-resurrection-black-androids/.

Helfrich, Joel. "The 'Pope Scope.'" *Wicazo Sa Review* 41, no. 1 (Spring 2019): 48–80.

Heng, Geraldine. *The Invention of Race in the European Middle Ages.* Cambridge: Cambridge University Press, 2018.

Hernández, Francisco. *Obras completas.* 7 vols. Mexico City: Universidad Nacional de México, 1959.

Heyam, Kit. *Before We Were Trans: A New History of Gender.* New York: Seal, 2022.

Hicks, Dan. *The Brutish Museums: The Benin Bronzes, Colonial Violence and Cultural Restitution.* London: Pluto, 2020.

Higa, Liriel. "Don't Punish Simone Biles for Being the Best." *New York Times*, October 9, 2019. https://www.nytimes.com/2019/10/09/opinion/simone-biles-gymnastics-beam.html.

Hirsch, Afua. *Brit(ish): On Race, Identity and Belonging.* London: Vintage, 2018.

Hoffmann, Ernst Theodor Amadeus. "The Sandman." 1817. In *Tales of Hoffmann*, translated by Reginald John Hollingdale, 85–125. London: Penguin, 2012.

Homer. *The Odyssey*. Translated by Robert Fagles. New York: Viking, 1996.

hooks, bell. *Ain't I a Woman: Black Women and Feminism*. London: Pluto, 1982.

Hoquet, Thierry. *Les Presques-Humains: mutants, cyborgs, robots, zombies . . . et nous*. Paris: Seuil, 2021.

Hsia, Ronnie Po-chia, ed. *A Companion to the Reformation World*. Maldon, MA: Blackwell, 2006.

Huet, Marie-Hélène. *Monstrous Imagination*. Cambridge, MA: Harvard University Press, 1993.

———. "Monstrous Medicine." In *Monstrous Bodies/Political Monstrosities in Early Modern Europe*, edited by Laura Lunger Knoppers and Joan B. Landes, 127–47. Ithaca, NY: Cornell University Press, 2004.

Hulme, Peter. *Colonial Encounters: Europe and the Native Caribbean, 1492–1797*. London: Methuen, 1986.

Hulme, Peter, and William H. Sherman, eds. *"The Tempest" and Its Travels*. London: Reaktion, 2000.

Ibbotson, Eva. *The Dragonfly Pool*. London: Macmillan, 2008.

Isenberg, Andrew C., ed. *The Oxford Handbook of Environmental History*. Oxford: Oxford University Press, 2017.

Ishiguro, Hiroshi. *How Human Is Human? The View from Robotics Research*. Tokyo: Japan Publishing Industry Foundation for Culture, 2020.

Ishiguro, Kazuo. *Klara and the Sun*. London: Faber and Faber, 2021.

Janson, Horst W. *Apes and Ape Lore in the Middle Ages and the Renaissance*. London: Warburg Institute, 1952.

Jay, Mike. *Mescaline: A Global History of the First Psychedelic*. New Haven, CT: Yale University Press, 2019.

Jentsch, Ernst. "On the Psychology of the 'Uncanny.'" In *Uncanny Modernity: Cultural Theories, Modern Anxieties*, edited by Jo Collins and John Jervis, translated by Roy Sellars, 216–28. Basingstoke: Palgrave Macmillan, 2008.

Johnson, Carina L. *Cultural Hierarchy in Sixteenth-Century Europe: The Ottomans and Mexicans*. New York: Cambridge University Press, 2011.

Johnson, Jessica Marie. *Wicked Flesh: Black Women, Intimacy, and Freedom in the Atlantic World*. Philadelphia: University of Pennsylvania Press, 2020.

Jones, Martha S. *Vanguard: How Black Women Broke Barriers, Won the Vote, and Insisted on Equality for All*. New York: Basic Books, 2020.

Jones-Davies, Marie-Thérèse, ed. *Monstres et prodiges au temps de la Renaissance*. Paris: Diffusion Touzot, 1980.

Kananoja, Kalle. *Healing Knowledge in Atlantic Africa: Medical Encounters, 1500–1850*. Cambridge: Cambridge University Press, 2021.

Kang, Minsoo. *Sublime Dreams of Living Machines: The Automaton in the European Imagination*. Cambridge, MA: Harvard University Press, 2011.

Kantorowicz, Ernst. *The King's Two Bodies*. Princeton, NJ: Princeton University Press, 1957.

Karim-Cooper, Farah. *Cosmetics in Shakespearean and Renaissance Drama*. Rev. ed. Edinburgh: Edinburgh University Press, 2019.

Kassam, Ashifa. "'Try Harder!': Poland's Women Demand Tusk Act over Abortion Promises." *Guardian*, February 6, 2024. www.theguardian.com/world/2024 /feb/06/poland-women-donald-tusk-abortion-promises.

Katzew, Ilona. *Casta Painting*. New Haven, CT: Yale University Press, 2004.

Kaufman, David. "Race and Science." In *A Cultural History of Race in Antiquity*, edited by Denise Eileen McCoskey, 67–82. London: Bloomsbury Academic, 2021.

Keane, Augustus Henry. "Krao, the 'Human Monkey.'" *Nature* 27 (1886): 245–46.

Kérchy, Anna, and Andrea Zittlau, eds. *Exploring the Cultural History of Central European Freak Shows and "Enfreakment."* Newcastle upon Tyne, UK: Cambridge Scholars, 2012.

Kershenbaum, Arik. *The Zoologist's Guide to the Galaxy: What Animals on Earth Reveal about Aliens—and Ourselves*. London: Penguin, 2021.

Khanmohamadi, Shirin A. *In Light of Another's Word: European Ethnography in the Middle Ages*. Philadelphia: University of Pennsylvania Press, 2013.

Kimbrough, Keller, and Haruo Shirane, eds. *Monsters, Animals, and Other Worlds: A Collection of Short Medieval Japanese Tales*. New York: Columbia University Press, 2018.

Kimmerer, Robin Wall. *Braiding Sweetgrass: Indigenous Wisdom, Scientific Knowledge and the Teaching of Plants*. London: Penguin, 2020.

Kingsolver, Barbara. *Demon Copperhead*. New York: Harper, 2022.

Klaeber, Friedrich. *Beowulf and the Fight at Finnsburg*. 3rd ed. Lexington, MA: Heath, 1950.

Klein, Naomi. *Doppelganger: A Trip into the Mirror World*. London: Lane, 2023.

———. *No Logo: Taking Aim at the Brand Bullies*. London: Flamingo, 2000.

Knox, John. *The First Blast of the Trumpet against the Monstrous Regiment of Women*. Geneva, 1558.

Koerber, Amy. *From Hysteria to Hormones: A Rhetorical History*. State Park: Pennsylvania State University Press, 2018.

Kohn, Eduardo. *How Forests Think: Toward an Anthropology beyond the Human*. Berkeley: University of California Press, 2013.

Komatsu Kazuhiko. *Introduction to Yōkai Culture: Monsters, Ghosts, and Outsiders in Japanese History*. Translated by Hiroko Yoda and Matt Alt. Tokyo: Japan Publishing Industry Foundation for Culture, 2017.

Kosiba, Steven, John Wayne Janusek, and Thomas Cummings, eds. *Sacred Matter: Animacy and Authority in the Americas*. Washington, DC: Dumbarton Oaks, 2020.

Krebs, Christopher. *A Most Dangerous Book: Tacitus's Germania from the Roman Empire to the Third Reich*. New York: Norton, 2011.

Krol, Debra Utacia. "Mount Graham: Apaches Say a Sacred Place Was First Stolen, Then Defiled." *Arizona Republic*, August 20, 2021. https://eu.azcentral.com /in-depth/news/local/arizona/2021/08/20/mount-graham-sacred-space-apaches-stolen-defiled/7903881002/.

LaFleur, Greta, Masha Raskolnikov, and Anna Kłosowska, eds. *Trans Historical: Gender Pluralities before the Modern.* Ithaca, NY: Cornell University Press, 2021.

Lalami, Laila. *Conditional Citizens: On Belonging in America.* New York: Pantheon Books, 2020.

Langston, Nancy. "New Chemical Bodies: Synthetic Chemicals, Regulation, and Human Health." In Isenberg, *Environmental History*, 259–81.

———. *Toxic Bodies: Hormone Disruptors and the Legacy of DES.* New Haven, CT: Yale University Press, 2010.

Lavender, Isiah, III. *Afrofuturism Rising: The Literary Prehistory of a Movement.* Columbus: Ohio State University Press, 2019.

"The Legacy of Henrietta Lacks." Johns Hopkins University. Accessed June 26, 2024. www.hopkinsmedicine.org/henrietta-lacks.

Le Guin, Ursula K. *The Language of the Night.* New York: Putnam, 1979.

———. *The Left Hand of Darkness.* New York: ACE, 1969.

———. "National Book Award Acceptance Speech." 1973. In *Language of the Night*, by Ursula K. Le Guin, 57–58.

Leitch, Stephanie. *Mapping Ethnography in Early Modern Germany: New Worlds in Print Culture.* New York: Palgrave Macmillan, 2010.

Lenharo, Mariana. "Is IVF at Risk in the US? Scientists Fear for the Fertility Treatment's Future." *Nature* 628 (2024): 241–42.

León-Portilla, Miguel. *The Aztec Image of Self and Society: An Introduction to Nahua Culture.* Edited by J. Jorge Klor de Alva. Salt Lake City: University of Utah Press, 1992.

Leslie, Marina. *Renaissance Utopias and the Problem of History.* Ithaca, NY: Cornell University Press, 2019.

Levack, Brian P., ed. *The Oxford Handbook of Witchcraft in Early Modern Europe and Colonial America.* Oxford: Oxford University Press, 2013.

———. *The Witchcraft Sourcebook.* New York: Routledge, 2004.

———. *The Witch-Hunt in Early Modern Europe.* 4th ed. Abingdon, UK: Routledge, 2016.

Lévi-Strauss, Claude. *The Raw and the Cooked.* Translated by John Weightman and Doreen Weightman. New York: Harper and Row, 1969.

Levitsky, Steven, and Daniel Ziblatt. *How Democracies Die.* New York: Crown, 2018.

Lewis, C. S. *The Chronicles of Narnia.* London: Collins, 1980.

———. *The Lion, the Witch and the Wardrobe.* London: Collins, 1980.

Lewis, Martin W., and Kären E. Wigen. *The Myth of Continents: A Critique of Metageography.* Berkeley: University of California Press, 1997.

Lindemann, Mary. "Gender Tales: The Multiple Identities of Maiden Heinrich, Hamburg, 1700." In Rublack, *Early Modern German History*, 131–51.

Lindfors, Bernth. "Ethnological Show Business: Footlighting the Dark Continent." In Garland-Thomson, *Freakery*, 207–18.

Linnaeus, Carl. *A General System of Nature, through the Three Grand Kingdoms of Animals, Vegetables, and Minerals.* Translated by William Turton. London: Lackington Allen, 1806.

———. *Systema naturae, sive regna tria naturae systematice proposita per classes, ordines, genera, et species.* Leiden, 1735.

———. *Systema naturae, sive regna tria naturae systematice proposita per classes, ordines, genera, et species.* 2 vols. Leiden, 1758–59.

Lipton, Sara. *Dark Mirror: The Medieval Origins of Anti-Jewish Iconography.* New York: Metropolitan Books, 2014.

Little, Roger, and Laurent Vidal. *Mascarade nuptiale.* La Rochelle, France: Musée d'Art et d'Histoire de La Rochelle, 2011.

Locke, Adrian. "Exhibitions and Collectors of Pre-Hispanic Mexican Artefacts in Britain." In Matos Moctezuma and Solis Olguín, *Aztecs,* 80–91.

———. "Gods of Life." In Matos Moctezuma and Solis Olguín, *Aztecs,* 171–203.

Lombardo, Stanley, and Gary Beckman, eds. *The Epic of Gilgamesh.* New York: Hackett, 2019.

Long, Kathleen P., ed. *Gender and Scientific Discourse in Early Modern Culture.* Aldershot, UK: Ashgate, 2010.

———. *Hermaphrodites in Renaissance Europe.* Aldershot, UK: Ashgate, 2006.

López Austin, Alfredo. "Cosmovision, Religion and the Calendar of the Aztecs." In Matos Moctezuma and Solis Olguín, *Aztecs,* 30–37.

———. *The Human Body and Ideology: Concepts of the Ancient Nahuas.* Translated by Thelma Ortiz de Montellano and Bernard Ortiz de Montellano. Salt Lake City: University of Utah Press, 1988.

———. "The Natural World." In Matos Moctezuma and Solis Olguín, *Aztecs,* 141–69.

———. "Términos del nahuallatolli." *Historia Mexicana* 17, no. 1 (1967): 1–36.

Lu, Yingfei, Yu Zhou, Rong Ju, and Jianquan Chen. "Human-Animal Chimeras for Autologous Organ Transplantation: Technological Advances and Future Perspectives." *Annals of Translational Medicine* 7, no. 20 (October 2019). www.ncbi.nlm.nih.gov/pmc/articles/PMC6861770/.

Luckhurst, Roger. *Alien.* Basingstoke, UK: Palgrave Macmillan, 2014.

———. *The Mummy's Curse: The True History of a Dark Fantasy.* Oxford: Oxford University Press, 2012.

Lyons, Sierra. "Black History You Probably Won't Be Taught in States That Ban Critical Race Theory." *Teen Vogue,* February 6, 2024. www.teenvogue.com/story/black-history-you-probably-wont-be-taught-in-states-that-ban-critical-race-theory.

Macy, Beth. *Dopesick: Dealers, Doctors, and the Drug Company That Addicted America.* New York: Little, Brown, 2018.

Magnus, Albertus. *Albertus Magnus on Animals: A Medieval Summa Zoologica.* Edited by Kenneth F. Kitchell Jr. and Irven Michael Resnick. Baltimore: Johns Hopkins University Press, 1999.

Makdisi, Saree. "Things in Palestine May Never Be the Same Again." *Nation,* October 12, 2023. www.thenation.com/article/world/gaza-israel-conflict-future/.

Manget, Jean-Jacques. *Traité de la peste.* Geneva, 1721.

Marcaida López, José Ramón. *Arte y ciencia en el Barroco español.* Madrid: Marcial Pons, 2014.

Marrone, Steven P. *A History of Science, Magic and Belief from Medieval to Early Modern Europe*. London: Palgrave, 2015.

Mason, Peter. *Ulisse Aldrovandi: Naturalist and Collector*. London: Reaktion, 2023.

Massilani, Diyendo, Laurits Skov, Mateja Hajdinjak, Byambaa Gunchinsuren, Damdinsuren Tseveendorj, Seonbok Yi, Jungeun Lee, et al. "Denisovan Ancestry and Population History of Early East Asians." *Science* 370 (2020): 579–83.

Matos Moctezuma, Eduardo, and Felipe Solis Olguín, eds. *Aztecs*. London: Royal Academy of Arts, 2002.

Mayor, Adrienne. *Gods and Robots: Myths, Machines, and Ancient Dreams of Technology*. Princeton, NJ: Princeton University Press, 2018.

Mbembe, Achille. *Critique of Black Reason*. Translated by Laurent Dubois. Durham, NC: Duke University Press, 2017.

———. *Necropolitics*. Durham, NC: Duke University Press, 2019.

McDaniel, Eric, and Elena Moore. "Lynching Is Now a Federal Hate Crime after a Century of Blocked Efforts." *NPR News*. March 29, 2022. www.npr .org/2022/03/29/1086720579/lynching-is-now-a-federal-hate-crime-after-a-century -of-blocked-efforts.

McKeever Furst, Jill Leslie. *The Natural History of the Soul in Ancient Mexico*. New Haven, CT: Yale University Press, 1995.

McMenamin, Lex. "Nex Benedict: Everything We Know about 16-Year-Old Oklahoma Student's Death." *Teen Vogue*, February 21, 2024. www.teenvogue.com /story/nex-benedict-everything-we-know-about-16-year-old-oklahoma-students- death.

Mejias, Ulises A., and Nick Couldry. *Data Grab: The New Colonialism of Big Tech (and How to Fight Back)*. London: Penguin Random House/Allen, 2024.

Meserve, Margaret. *Empires of Islam in Renaissance Historical Thought*. Cambridge, MA: Harvard University Press, 2008.

Meyer, Matthew. "Ashura." *Yokai.com: The Online Database of Japanese Folklore*. Accessed June 7, 2024. https://yokai.com/ashura/.

Miéville, China. *The City and the City*. London: Macmillan, 2009.

Milanich, Nara B. *Paternity: The Elusive Quest for the Father*. Cambridge, MA: Harvard University Press, 2019.

Miller, Dean Arthur. "Bridge Essay: Superhuman Humans, Heroes and Heroines." In Denecke and Ramelli, *Third Millennium*, 307–12.

Miller, Joseph C. *The Princeton Companion to Atlantic History*. Princeton, NJ: Princeton University Press, 2015.

Miller, Mary, and Karl Taube. *The Gods and Symbols of Ancient Mexico and the Maya: An Illustrated Dictionary of Mesoamerican Religion*. London: Thames and Hudson, 1992.

Mitchell, Glenn, Wendy Russell, and Natalie Stoianoff. "Franken Foods or Smart Foods? A New Language for Biotechnology?" *Nature Agbiotech* 17, no. 46 (1999). https://doi.org/10.1038/70417.

Mittman, Asa Simon, ed. *Ashgate Research Companion to Monsters and the Monstrous*. With Peter Dendle. Farnham, VT: Ashgate, 2012.

———. *Cartographies of Exclusion: Christian Mapping of Jews in the Age of the English Expulsion.* University Park: Pennsylvania State University Press, 2024.

———. *Maps and Monsters in Medieval England.* New York: Routledge, 2006.

Mittman, Asa Simon, and Richard H. Godden, eds. *Monstrosity, Disability, and the Posthuman in the Medieval and Early Modern World.* Cham, Switzerland: Palgrave Macmillan, 2019.

Mittman, Asa Simon, and Marcus Hensel, eds. *Primary Sources on Monsters.* Vol. 2. of *Demonstrare.* Leeds: ARC Humanities, 2018.

Molineux, Catherine. *Faces of Perfect Ebony: Encountering Atlantic Slavery in Imperial Britain.* Cambridge, MA: Harvard University Press, 2012.

Monroe, John Warne. *Metropolitan Fetish: African Sculpture and the Imperial French Invention of Primitive Art.* Ithaca, NY: Cornell University Press, 2019.

Monter, William. "The Inquisition." In Hsia, *Reformation World,* 255–71.

Moore, Gillian. *The Rite of Spring.* London: Head of Zeus, 2019.

Morgan, Jennifer L. "Partus sequitur ventrem: Law, Race, and Reproduction in Colonial Slavery." *Small Axe* 55 (March 2018): 1–17.

———. *Reckoning with Slavery: Gender, Kinship, and Capitalism in the Early Black Atlantic.* Durham, NC: Duke University Press, 2021.

Mori, Masahiro. "The Uncanny Valley." Translated by Karl F. MacDorman and Norri Kageki. *IEEE Robotics and Automation* 19, no. 2 (2012): 98–100. Original work published in 1970.

Morris, Richard, ed. *Cursor Mundi: A Northumbrian Poem of the XIVth Century in Four Versions.* 7 vols. London: Kegan Paul, 1875.

Morrison, Toni. "Grendel and His Mother." In *The Source of Self-Regard: Selected Essays, Speeches, and Meditations,* 255–62. New York: Knopf, 2019.

"Mount Graham: Science and Apache Religion." Native American Net Roots. April 18, 2010. http://nativeamericannetroots.net/diary/471.

Mukherjee, Siddhartha. *The Gene: An Intimate History.* London: Vintage, 2017.

Murgia, Madhumita. *Code Dependent: Living in the Shadow of AI.* New York: Holt, 2024.

Murray, Thomas. "Rarities from the Himalayas to Polynesia." Advertisement. *Apollo: The International Art Magazine,* July–August 2019, 48.

Mystal, Elie. "Alabama's IVF Ruling Is Christian Theology Masquerading as Law." *Nation,* February 23, 2024. www.thenation.com/article/society/alabama-ivf-ruling/.

Nakamura, Miri. *Monstrous Bodies: The Rise of the Uncanny in Modern Japan.* Cambridge, MA: Harvard University Press, 2015.

Naughton, John. "Mushroom Pickers Urged to Avoid Foraging Books on Amazon That Appear to Be Written by AI." *Guardian,* September 1, 2023.

———. "Sure, Google's AI Overviews Could Be Useful—If You Like Eating Rocks." *Guardian,* June 1, 2024.

Ndiaye, Noémie. "'Come Aloft, Jack-Little-Ape!' Race and Dance in *The Spanish Gypsie.*" *English Literary Renaissance* 51, no. 1 (2020): 121–51.

Nelson, Alondra. "Society after Pandemic." *Items: Insights from the Social Sciences.* April 23, 2020. https://items.ssrc.org/covid-19-and-the-social-sciences/society -after-pandemic/.

Newton, Michael. *Savage Girls and Wild Boys: A History of Feral Children.* New York: St. Martin's Press, 2002.

Ng, Su Fang. *Alexander the Great from Britain to Southeast Asia: Peripheral Empires in the Global Renaissance.* Oxford: Oxford University Press, 2019.

Nirenberg, David. *Anti-Judaism: The Western Tradition.* New York: Norton, 2013.

———. "Race and the Middle Ages: The Case of Spain and Its Jews." In Greer, Mignolo, and Quillian, *Rereading the Black Legend,* 71–87.

Noah, Trevor. *Born a Crime: Stories from a South African Childhood.* New York: Spiegel and Grau, 2016.

Noble, Safiya. *Algorithms of Oppression: How Search Engines Reinforce Racism.* New York: New York University Press, 2018.

Norton, Marcy. "The Chicken or the *Iegue:* Human-Animal Relationships and the Columbian Exchange." *American Historical Review* 120, no. 1 (February 2015): 28–60.

———. *Sacred Gifts, Profane Pleasures: A History of Tobacco and Chocolate in the Atlantic World.* Ithaca, NY: Cornell University Press, 2008.

———. "Subaltern Technologies and Early Modernity in the Atlantic World." *Colonial Latin American Review* 26, no. 1 (2017): 18–38.

———. *The Tame and the Wild: People and Animals after 1492.* Cambridge, MA: Harvard University Press, 2024.

Nyholm, Sven. *Humans and Robots: Ethics, Agency, and Anthropomorphism.* London: Roman and Littlefield, 2020.

O'Brian, Matt, Hannah Fingerhut, and Associated Press. "A.I. Tools Fueled a 34% Spike in Microsoft's Water Consumption, and One City with Its Data Centers Is Concerned about the Effect on Residential Supply." *Fortune,* September 9, 2023. https://fortune.com/2023/09/09/ai-chatgpt-usage-fuels-spike-in-microsoft-water -consumption/.

O'Hara, Matthew. *The History of the Future in Colonial Mexico.* New Haven, CT: Yale University Press, 2018.

O'Hearn, Megan. "The Strange Fates of Pillaged Mummies." *JSTOR Daily,* October 17, 2018. https://about.jstor.org/blog/the-strange-fates-of-pillaged-mummies/.

O'Neil, Cathy. *Weapons of Math Destruction: How Big Data Increases Inequality and Threatens Democracy.* New York: Penguin, 2017.

Otte, Jedidajah. "Suella Braverman Says Rough Sleeping Is 'Lifestyle Choice.'" *Guardian,* November 4, 2023. www.theguardian.com/society/2023/nov/04 /suella-braverman-says-rough-sleeping-is-lifestyle-choice.

Owen, Stephen, ed. *An Anthology of Chinese Literature: Beginnings to 1911.* New York: Norton, 1996.

Padrón, Ricardo. *The Indies of the Setting Sun: How Early Modern Spain Mapped the Far East as the Transpacific West.* Chicago: University of Chicago Press, 2020.

Pagden, Anthony. *The Fall of Natural Man: The American Indian and the Origins of Comparative Ethnology*. Cambridge: Cambridge University Press, 1986.

Palattella, John. "But If It Ends the Start Is Begun: 'Spring and All,' Americanism, and Postwar Apocalypse." *William Carlos Williams Review* 21, no. 1 (1995): 1–21.

Paré, Ambroise. *Des monstres et prodiges*. Edited by Jean Céard. 1573. Reprint, Geneva: Droz, 1971.

———. *Les oeuvres d'Ambroise Paré*. Paris, 1579.

———. "On Monsters and Marvels." Translated by Janis L. Pallister. 1573. Reprint, Chicago: University of Chicago Press, 1982.

Pasquale, Frank. *New Laws of Robotics: Defending Human Expertise in the Age of AI*. Cambridge, MA: Harvard University Press, 2020.

Pennock, Caroline Dodds. *On Savage Shores: How Indigenous Americans Discovered Europe*. London: Weidenfeld and Nicolson, 2023.

Pepys, Samuel. *The Diary of Samuel Pepys: A New and Complete Transcription*. Edited by Robert Latham and William Matthews. 11 vols. London: Bell, 1970.

Peucer, Caspar. *Commentarius de praecipius generibus divinationum*. Wittenberg, Germany, 1560.

Phillips, William J., Jr. *Slavery in Medieval and Early Modern Iberia*. Philadelphia: University of Pennsylvania Press, 2014.

Pimentel, Juan. *Fantásmos de la ciencia española*. Madrid: Pons, 2020.

———. *The Rhinoceros and the Megatherium: An Essay in Natural History*. Translated by Peter Mason. Cambridge, MA: Harvard University Press, 2017.

Pliny the Elder. *Natural History*. Translated by Harris Rackham. Cambridge, MA: Harvard University Press, 1969.

Pollan, Jared Marcel. "Why Billionaires Are Obsessed with the Apocalypse." *Nation*, February 14, 2024. www.thenation.com/article/culture/douglas -rushkoff-survival-richest/.

Purchas, Samuel. *Hakluytus Posthumus, or Purchas His Pilgrimes: Containing a History of the World in Sea Voyages and Lande Travells by Englishmen and Others*. Glasgow: Maclehose, 1905–7.

Quammen, David. *The Tangled Tree: A Radical New History of Life*. London: Collins, 2019.

Quiñones Keber, Eloise. *Codex Telleriano-Remensis: Ritual, Divination, and History in a Pictorial Aztec Manuscript*. Austin: University of Texas Press, 1995.

Qureshi, Sadiah. *Peoples on Parade: Exhibitions, Empire, and Anthropology in Nineteenth-Century Britain*. Chicago: University of Chicago Press, 2011.

Rabelais, François. *La vie tres horrificque du Grand Gargantua*. Lyon, 1542.

Rampell, Catherine. "How the Government Can Keep 'Alternative Facts' Out of the Census." *Washington Post*, January 25, 2021. www.washingtonpost.com/opinions /how-the-government-can-keep-alternative-facts-out-of-the-census/2021/01/25 /fab56eb8–5e7d-11eb-9430-e7c77b5b0297_story.html.

Rankine, Claudia. *Citizen: An American Lyric*. New York: Penguin, 2015.

Rappaport, Joanne. *The Disappearing Mestizo: Configuring Difference in the Colonial New Kingdom of Granada*. Durham, NC: Duke University Press, 2014.

Rarey, Matthew Francis. *Insignificant Things: Amulets and the Art of Survival in the Early Black Atlantic*. Durham, NC: Duke University Press, 2023.

Redmond Chang, Leah. *Young Queens: Three Renaissance Women and the Price of Power*. London: Bloomsbury, 2023.

Reich, Robert B. "The 'Paid What You're Worth' Myth." Substack. June 20, 2023. https://robertreich.substack.com/p/the-paid-what-youre-worth-myth.

———. *Supercapitalism: The Transformation of Business, Democracy, and Everyday Life*. New York: Knopf, 2007.

———. *The System: Who Rigged It, and How to Fix It*. New York: Penguin Random House, 2021.

Reider, Noriko. *Tales of the Supernatural in Early Modern Japan: Kaidan, Akinari, Ugetsu Monogatari*. Lewiston, NY: Mellen, 2002.

Relaño, Francesc. *The Shaping of Africa: Cosmographic Discourse and Cartographic Science in Late Medieval and Early Modern Europe*. Aldershot, UK: Ashgate, 2002.

Reséndez, Andrés. *The Other Slavery: The Uncovered Story of Indian Enslavement in America*. New York: Houghton Mifflin Harcourt, 2016.

Restall, Matthew. *The Maya World: Yucatec Culture and Society, 1550–1850*. Stanford, CA: Stanford University Press, 1997.

Restall, Matthew, Lisa Sousa, and Kevin Terreciano, eds. *Mesoamerican Voices: Native-Language Writings from Colonial Mexico, Oaxaca, Yucatan, and Guatemala*. Cambridge: Cambridge University Press, 2005.

Riesman, Abraham. *True Believer: The Rise and Fall of Stan Lee*. New York: Penguin Random House, 2022.

Ritvo, Harriet. *The Platypus and the Mermaid and Other Figments of the Classifying Imagination*. Cambridge, MA: Harvard University Press, 1997.

Roberts, Sean. *Printing a Mediterranean World: Florence, Constantinople, and the Renaissance of Geography*. Cambridge, MA: Harvard University Press, 2013.

Rogers, Brett M., and Benjamin Eldon Stevens, eds. *Classical Traditions in Science Fiction*. Oxford: Oxford University Press, 2015.

Roper, Lyndal. "'Evil Imaginings and Fantasies': Child Witches and the End of the Witch Craze." In Rublack, *Early Modern German History*, 102–30.

———. "'Fantasies': Child-Witches and the End of the Witch Craze." *Past and Present* 167 (May 2000): 107–39.

———. *The Witch Craze: Terror and Fantasy in Baroque Germany*. New Haven, CT: Yale University Press, 2004.

Rowe, Niamh. "'It's Destroyed Me Completely': Kenyan Moderators Decry Toll of Training of AI Models." *Guardian*, August 2, 2023. www.theguardian.com /technology/2023/aug/02/ai-chatbot-training-human-toll-content-moderator -meta-openai.

Rublack, Ulinka. *Gender in Early Modern German History*. Cambridge: Cambridge University Press, 2002.

Rugemer, Edward B. "The Development of Mastery and Race in the Comprehensive Slave Codes of the Greater Caribbean in the Seventeenth Century." *William and Mary Quarterly* 70, no. 3 (2013): 429–58.

————. *Slave Law and the Politics of Resistance in the Early Atlantic World*. Cambridge, MA: Harvard University Press, 2018.

Ruiz de Alarcón, Hernando. *Treatise on the Heathen Superstitions and Customs That Today Live among the Indians Native to This New Spain, 1629*. Edited by James Richard Andrews and Ross Hassig. Norman: University of Oklahoma Press, 1984.

Rushkoff, Douglas. *Survival of the Richest: Escape Fantasies of the Tech Billionaires*. New York: Norton, 2023.

Sáenz-López Pérez, Sandra. *Los mapas de los beatos: La revelación del mundo en la Edad Media*. Burgos, Spain: Siloé, 2014.

Sahagún, Fray Bernardino de. *Florentine Codex: General History of the Things of New Spain*. Translated by Arthur J. O. Anderson and Charles E. Dibble. Vol. 13. Santa Fe, NM: School of American Research/Salt Lake City: University of Utah Press, 1950.

Sarreal, Julia J. S. *Yerba Mate: The Drink That Shaped a Nation*. Oakland: University of California Press, 2022.

Schikore, Jutta. *About Method: Experimenters, Snake Venom, and the History of Writing Scientifically*. Chicago: University of Chicago Press, 2017.

Schillace, Brandy. "The Forgotten History of the World's First Trans Clinic." *Scientific American*, May 10, 2021. www.scientificamerican.com/article/the-forgotten-history-of-the-worlds-first-trans-clinic/.

————. *Mr. Humble and Dr. Butcher: A Monkey's Head, the Pope's Neuroscientists, and the Quest to Transplant the Soul*. New York: Simon and Schuster, 2021.

Scribner, Robert W. *For the Sake of Simple Folk: Popular Propaganda for the German Reformation*. Cambridge: Cambridge University Press, 1981.

Scrimgeour, Guthrie. "Inside Mark Zuckerberg's Top-Secret Hawaii Compound." *Wired*, December 4, 2023. www.wired.com/story/mark-zuckerberg-inside-hawaii-compound/.

Semenya, Caster. *The Race to Be Myself*. London: Penguin Random House, 2023.

Semonin, Paul. "Monsters in the Marketplace: The Exhibition of Human Oddities in Early Modern England." In Garland-Thomson, *Freakery*, 69–81.

Seth, Suman. *Difference and Disease: Medicine, Race, and the Eighteenth-Century British Empire*. Cambridge: Cambridge University Press, 2018.

Shakespeare, William. *William Shakespeare: Complete Works*. Edited by Jonathan Bate and Eric Rasmussen. Basingstoke, UK: Macmillan, 2007.

Shelley, Mary. *Frankenstein, or The Modern Prometheus*. 3 vols. London, 1818.

Sheppard, Samantha N. *Sporting Blackness: Race, Embodiment, and Critical Muscle Memory on Screen*. Oakland: University of California Press, 2020.

Silva Maroto, Pilar, ed. *Bosch: The 5th Centenary Exhibition*. London: Thames and Hudson, 2017.

Siraisi, Nancy G. *Medieval and Early Renaissance Medicine: An Introduction to Knowledge and Practice*. Chicago: University of Chicago Press, 1990.

Smith, David Livingstone. *Making Monsters: The Uncanny Power of Dehumanization*. Cambridge, MA: Harvard University Press, 2021.

Sousa, Lisa. *The Woman Who Turned into a Jaguar and Other Narratives of Native Women in Archives of Colonial Mexico*. Redwood City, CA: Stanford University Press, 2017.

Spillers, Hortense J. "Mama's Baby, Papa's Maybe: An American Grammar Book." *Diacritics* (Summer 1987): 65–81.

Spinks, Jennifer. *Monstrous Births and Visual Culture in Sixteenth-Century Germany*. London: Pickering and Chatto, 2009.

Spinks, Jennifer, and Dagmar Eichberger, eds. *Religion, the Supernatural, and Visual Culture in Early Modern Europe: An Album Amicorum for Charles Zika*. Leiden: Brill, 2015.

"Statement on the Skeleton." Hunterian Museum. January 11, 2023. https://hunterianmuseum.org/news/statement-on-the-skeleton-of-charles-byrne-from-the-board-of-trustees-of-the-hunterian-collection.

Steel, Karl. "Centaurs, Satyrs, and Cynocephali: Medieval Scholarly Teratology and the Question of the Human." In Mittman, *Ashgate Research Companion*, 257–74.

Stevenson, Robert Louis. *Dr. Jekyll and Mr. Hyde: With "The Merry Men" and Other Stories*. London: Wordworth, 1999.

Strahan, Jonathan, ed. *Made to Order: Robots and Revolution*. Oxford: Solaris, 2020.

Strickland, Debra Higgs. *Saracens, Demons, and Jews: Making Monsters in Medieval Art*. Princeton, NJ: Princeton University Press, 2003.

Sturtevant, William C. "La 'Tupinambisation' des Indiens d'Amérique du Nord." In *Figures de l'Indien*, edited by Gilles Thérien, 345–61. Montreal: Université du Québec à Montréal, 1995.

Sutter, Paul S. "The Tropics: A Brief History of an Environmental Imaginary." In Isenberg, *Environmental History*, 178–204.

Tacitus. *Germania*. In *Agricola, Germania, and Dialogue on Orators*, translated by Maurice Hutton and William Peterson, 128–215. Loeb Classical Library 35. Cambridge, MA: Harvard University Press, 1914.

TallBear, Kim. *Native American DNA: Tribal Belonging and the False Promise of Genetic Science*. Minneapolis: University of Minnesota Press, 2013.

Taube, Karl A. "Beverages." In Carrasco, *Mesoamerican Cultures*, 1:85–88.

Tegmark, Max. *Life 3.0: Being Human in the Age of Artificial Intelligence*. New York: Penguin, 2018.

Teter, Magda. *Blood Libel: On the Trail of an Antisemitic Myth*. Cambridge, MA: Harvard University Press, 2020.

Thomas, Michael Tilson. "Stravinsky: The Rite of Spring." With the San Francisco Symphony Orchestra. *Keeping Score*. PBS. November 9, 2006.

Thompson, Ayanna. "The 2021 Josephine Waters Bennett Lecture: On Protean Acting; Race and Virtuosity." *Renaissance Quarterly* 75, no. 4 (2023): 1127–43.

———. *The Cambridge Companion to Shakespeare and Race*. Cambridge: Cambridge University Press, 2021.

Thunberg, Greta, ed. *The Climate Book*. London: Penguin, 2022.

Tolkien, John Ronald Reuel. *The Lord of the Rings*. 3 vols. London: HarperCollins, 2012.

Tortorici, Zeb. *Sins against Nature: Sex and Archives in Colonial New Spain*. Durham, NC: Duke University Press, 2018.

Toto, Elodie. "The Chlordecone Health and Racism Scandal in the French Antilles: Case Dismissed, but the Fight Goes On." *Equal Times*, January 15, 2024. www .equaltimes.org/the-chlordecone-health-and-racism.

Townsend, Camilla. *Fifth Sun: A New History of the Aztecs*. Oxford: Oxford University Press, 2021.

"Tripod Cylinder Vase." Museum of Fine Arts, Boston. Accessed June 18, 2024. https://collections.mfa.org/objects/437204.

Trouillot, Michel-Rolph, Yarimar Bonilla, Gregg Beckett, and Mayanthi L. Fernando. *Trouillot Remixed: The Michel-Rolph Trouillot Reader*. Durham, NC: Duke University Press, 2021.

Truitt, Elly R. *Medieval Robots: Mechanism, Magic, Nature, and Art*. Philadelphia: University of Pennsylvania Press, 2015.

Turda, Marius, ed. *A Cultural History of Race*. 6 vols. London: Bloomsbury Academic, 2021.

"Tuskegee Syphilis Experiment." Equal Justice Initiative. Accessed June 26, 2024. https://eji.org/news/history-racial-injustice-tuskegee-syphilis-experiment/.

Tyson, Edward. *Orang-outang, Sive Homo Sylvestri, or The Anatomy of a Pygmie Compared with That of a Monkey, an Ape, and a Man*. London, 1699.

———. "Philological Essay." In Tyson, *Orang-outang*, 1–58.

Van Deusen, Nancy E. *Global Indios: The Indigenous Struggle for Justice in Sixteenth-Century Spain*. Durham, NC: Duke University Press, 2015.

———. "Seeing *Indios* in Sixteenth-Century Castile." *William and Mary Quarterly* 69, no. 2 (2012): 205–34.

Venetis, Evangelos, ed. *The Persian Alexander: The First Complete English Translation of the Iskandarnāma*. London: Tauris, 2018.

Vicente, Marta V. "Transgender: A Useful Category? Or How the Historical Study of 'Transsexual' and 'Transvestite' Can Help Us Rethink 'Transgender' as a Category." *TSQ: Transgender Studies Quarterly* 8, no. 4 (November 2021): 426–42.

Vinson, Ben, III. *Before Mestizaje: The Frontiers of Race and Caste in Colonial Mexico*. Cambridge: Cambridge University Press, 2017.

Vint, Sherryl. *Science Fiction*. Cambridge, MA: MIT Press, 2021.

Viveiros de Castro, Eduardo. *From the Enemy's Point of View: Humanity and Divinity in an Amazonian Society*. Translated by Catherine V. Howard. Chicago: University of Chicago Press, 1992.

Voskuhl, Adelheid. *Androids in the Enlightenment: Mechanics, Artisans, and Cultures of the Self*. Chicago: University of Chicago Press, 2013.

Waal, Frans de. *Are We Smart Enough to Know How Smart Animals Are?* London: Granta Books, 2017.

Walker, Tamara J. *Exquisite Slaves: Race, Clothing, and Status in Colonial Lima.* Cambridge: Cambridge University Press, 2017.

Waterhouse, Edward. *A Declaration of the State of the Colony in Virginia.* 1622. Reprint, Amsterdam: Theatrum Orbis Terrarum/Da Capo, 1970.

Weinstein, Barbara. *The Color of Modernity: São Paulo and the Making of Race and Nation in Brazil.* Durham, NC: Duke University Press, 2015.

Wekker, Gloria. *White Innocence: Paradoxes of Colonialism and Race.* Durham, NC: Duke University Press, 2016.

West, Martin L. *The East Face of Helicon: Western Asiatic Elements in Greek Poetry and Myth.* Oxford: Clarendon, 1997.

Westrem, Scott D. *The Hereford Map: A Transcription and Translation of the Legends and Commentary.* Turnhout, Belgium: Brepols, 2001.

Wey Gómez, Nicolás. *The Tropics of Empire: Why Columbus Sailed South to the Indies.* Cambridge, MA: MIT Press, 2008.

Wheat, David. *Atlantic Africa and the Spanish Caribbean, 1570–1640.* Chapel Hill: University of North Carolina Press, 2016.

Wiesner-Hanks, Merry. *The Marvelous Hairy Girls: The Gonzales Sisters and Their Worlds.* New Haven, CT: Yale University Press, 2009.

Wilkerson, Isabel. *Caste: The Origins of Our Discontents.* New York: Random House, 2020.

Williams, Damien Patrick. "Bias Optimizers." *American Scientist* 111, no. 4 (2023): 204–7.

Williams, Wes. *Monsters and Their Meanings in Early Modern Culture: Mighty Magic.* Oxford: Oxford University Press, 2011.

Wilson, Edmund. "The Poetry of Drouth." *Dial* 717 (1922): 611–16.

Wilson, Emily. "First Woman to Translate Homer's Odyssey into English: How Modern Bias Is Projected onto Antiquity." *Time*, November 6, 2017. https://time.com/5008920/odyssey-translation-gender-history/.

———. "Found in Translation: How Women Are Making the Classics Their Own." *Guardian*, July 7, 2017. www.theguardian.com/books/2017/jul/07/women-classics-translation-female-scholars-translators.

"The Windrush Scandal in a Transnational and Commonwealth Context." Arts and Humanities Research Council. Accessed June 25, 2024. https://windrushscandal.org/.

Wintroub, Michael. *A Savage Mirror: Power, Identity and Knowledge in Early Modern France.* Stanford, CA: Stanford University Press, 2006.

Wordsworth, William. *The Prelude.* Edited by Jonathan Wordsworth, Meyer Howard Abrams, and Stephen Gill. New York: Norton, 1979.

Yetman, David. "The Cactus Metaphor." In Beezley, *Companion to Mexican History*, 131–42.

Yong, Ed. *I Contain Multitudes: The Microbes within Us and a Grander View of Life.* London: Vintage, 2017.

———. *An Immense World: How Animal Senses Reveal the Hidden Realms around Us.* London: Vintage, 2023.

Zachary Panxhi, Lindsey. "Rewriting the Werewolf and Rehabilitating the Irish in the Topographica Hibernica of Gerald of Wales." *Viator: Medieval and Renaissance Studies* 46, no. 3 (2015): 21–40.

Zika, Charles. *The Appearance of Witchcraft: Print and Visual Culture in Sixteenth-Century Europe.* Abingdon, UK: Routledge, 2007.

Ziolkowski, Theodore. "Gilgamesh: A Cultural Seismograph." In Denecke and Ramelli, *Third Millennium*, 313–24.

FILM AND TELEVISION

Blomkamp, Neill, dir. *District 9.* Los Angeles: QED International, 2009.

Cameron, James, dir. *The Terminator.* Los Angeles: Hemdale, 1984.

Docter, Pete, David Silverman, and Lee Unkrich, dirs. *Monsters, Inc.* Emeryville, CA: Pixar Animation Studios, 2001.

Kolbe, Winrich, dir. *Star Trek: The Next Generation.* Season 5, episode 2, "Darmok." Hollywood: Paramount Domestic Television, 1991.

Larson, Glen A. *Battlestar Galactica.* Universal City, CA: NBC Universal Television Studio; Universal Media Studios; and Universal Cable Productions, 2003–9.

Livingston, David, dir. *Star Trek: Deep Space Nine.* Season 4, episode 10, "Homefront." Hollywood: Paramount Domestic Television, 1996.

Peele, Jordan, dir. *Us.* Los Angeles: Monkeypaw Productions, 2019.

Romero, George A., dir. *Night of the Living Dead.* Evans City, PA: Image Ten, 1968.

Schaffner, Franklin J., dir. *Planet of the Apes.* Beverly Hills, CA: APJAC Productions, 1968.

Scheerer, Robert, dir. *Star Trek: The Next Generation.* Season 2, episode 9, "Measure of a Man." Hollywood: Paramount Domestic Television, 1989.

Scott, Ridley, dir. *Alien.* Los Angeles: Twentieth-Century Fox, 1979.

———, dir. *Blade Runner.* Hollywood: Ladd Company, 1982.

Singer, Bryan, dir. *X-Men.* Los Angeles: Twentieth-Century Fox, 2000.

Sonnenfeld, Barry, dir. *Men in Black.* Culver City, CA: Columbia Pictures, 1997.

Spielberg, Steven, dir. *E.T.: The Extra-Terrestrial.* Universal City, CA: Universal Studios, 1982.

———, dir. *The Terminal.* Universal City, CA: Dreamworks Pictures, 2004.

Stanton, Andrew, *Wall-E.* Emeryville, CA: Pixar Animation Studios, 2008.

Wachowski, Lana, and Lilly Wachowski, dirs. *The Matrix.* Burbank. CA: Warner Bros, 1999.

PODCASTS AND VIDEOS

Caro, Robert A. "Robert Caro on How He Does It." Interview by Pamela Paul. *New York Times Book Review Podcast.* April 19, 2019. www.nytimes.com/2019/04/19/books/review/podcast-robert-caro-working.html.

Christian, Brian. "If 'A.I. Models Are Wrong,' Why Do We Give Them So Much Power?" *Ezra Klein Show.* June 4, 2021. www.nytimes.com/2021/06/04/opinion/ezra-klein-podcast-brian-christian.html.

Cuddy, Amy. "Your Body Language May Shape Who You Are." TED Talk. June 2012. www.ted.com/talks/amy_cuddy_your_body_language_may_shape_who_you_are.

Darling, Kate. "The New Breed: What Our Animal History Reveals For Our Robotic Future." Long Now Foundation. August 10, 2021. https://longnow.org/seminars/02021/aug/10/new-breed-what-our-animal-history-reveals-our-robotic-future/.

Headley, Maria Dahvana. "Crafting with Ursula: Maria Dahvana Headley on Feminist Translation and Classical Retellings." Interview by David Naimon. *Between the Covers.* October 11, 2022. https://tinhouse.com/podcast/crafting-with-ursula-maria-dahvana-headley-on-feminist-translation-classical-retellings/.

Morris, Wesley. "Serena Williams's Final Run." Interview by Natalie Kitroeff. *Daily,* September 12, 2022. www.nytimes.com/2022/09/12/podcasts/the-daily/serena-williams-tennis-retirement.html.

Robinson, Kim Stanley. "Crafting with Ursula: Kim Stanley Robinson on Ambiguous Utopias." Interview by David Naimon. *Between the Covers.* June 10, 2022. https://tinhouse.com/podcast/crafting-with-ursula-kim-stanley-robinson-on-ambiguous-utopias/.

INDEX

Note: Page numbers followed by *fig.* indicate figures. Color plates are indicated as *pl. 1, pl. 2*, and so on.

Catherine of Aragon, Queen of England, 111
Catherine de Medici, Queen Mother of France, 111
Catholic Church: and extraterrestrials, 218–20; *vs.* Indigenous beliefs, 9–10, 16, 175–77, 219; *vs.* Protestants, 111, 174, 184–86; relics, 173–74. *See also* Christians and Christian theology
cave dwellers, 13
Cavendish, Margaret, Duchess of Newcastle, 272n3; *The Blazing World*, 213–14
censorship, 238
centaurs, 41, 41*fig.*, 133
Céspedes, Elenx de, 233–34, 235
Cest la déduction du sumptueux ordre, 72*fig.*
Charlemagne, Holy Roman Emperor, 71, 71*fig.*, 170, 173
Charles V, Holy Roman Emperor, 71*fig.*
ChatGPT, 191, 209
chattel slavery, 82, 83, 210
chemical toxins, 24–26
child prodigy label, 144–45
childbirth and pregnancy, 3, 103, 105–6, 108, 125, 136, 178, 239. *See also* monstrous births; reproduction
childishness, 94, 133, 156
chimeras, 51–52
chimpanzees, 44–46, 45*fig.*, 50
Chinese folklore, 38
chocolate, consumption of, 92, 175, 176–77, 268n48
cholera epidemics, 23
Christ, 170, 172, 173, 174, 267n37
Christians and Christian theology: afterlife in, 167–69, 168*fig.*, 169*fig.*, 171*fig.*, pl. 9, pl. 10; biblical interpretation applied to gender, 116–18, 119–20; biblical interpretation applied to geography, 74–77; creation story, 16, 116–18; divine ordination of rulers, 170–72; and evolutionary theory, 48–49, 50; faith and community boundaries, 65–66, 68–69, 174–75; human-animal hybrids in morality tales, 41–42; *vs.* Indigenous beliefs and conversion, 9–10, 16, 91–92, 93–94, 116, 175–77, 219; Protestants *vs.* Catholics, 111, 174, 184–86; relics, 173–74, 267n37; souls, 38, 167; witch hunts, 177–78

Chrysoloras, Manuel, 77
Church of San Pedro Apóstol de Andahuaylillas (Peru), 169, 169*fig.*, 171*fig.*, pl. 10
circuses, 131. *See also* spectacularization
citizenship: definitions of, 57; legal administrative *vs.* cultural idea of, 60–62; and race, 61, 95–96, 97, 98, 99–100; of robots, 203
civility and civilization, discourse on: and art, 148–50; *vs.* barbarism, 63–65, 70–71, 74; and colonialism, 35, 36, 74, 88, 91, 133, 148; in fiction, 89; and spectacularization, 129, 142
classical antiquity worldviews: on gender, 110, 116–18, 120; geographical location, 252n8; on group identity and divisions, 63–65; on monstrous persons, 11–16, 12*fig.*, 63, 65, 104–5, 110, 164, 213; mythology, 6, 7*fig.*, 40–41, 41*fig.*, 85, 131, 162, 195; on souls, 166; and translation, 225–27
classification. *See* categorization
Claudius, Roman Emperor, 66
climate. *See* environment
climate change, 242–44
coca, 21, 177
Code noir (black code), 82–84
Codex Telleriano-Remensis, *9*
Cohen, Jeffrey Jerome, 68
colonialism: and civility and civilization, discourse on, 35, 36, 74, 88, 91, 133, 148; colonist *vs.* Indigenous worldviews/practices, 8–10, 16, 92, 93–94, 115–16, 175–77, 182, 268n48; and exhibition practices, 129, 130, 138–39; and human susceptibility to environment, 80–81, 87, 91–92; intergalactic, 54; and nationalism, 60; unequal rights, 97; written *vs.* oral sources, 269n71. *See also* slavery
commodification, 107
complexion, 15. *See also* humoral theory
con artists, 136
conjoined twins, 131, 133–34
Consolmagno, Guy, 218–20
Constantinople, 75, 77
Constitution, US, 83–84
contagion theory, 21–23, 22*fig.*

Du Plessis, James Paris, "A Short History of Human Prodigious and Monstrous Births," 101–4, 102*fig.*, 105–6, 107, 132–33, 136, 138, 261n1

Duda, Andrzej, 239, 274n9

Durán, Diego, 8; *Historia de las Indias,* 164*fig.*, 172*fig.*

Dürer, Albrecht, *Witch Riding Backwards on a Goat,* 179, 180*ofig.*

dwarfs, 35, 36, 127–29, 128*fig.*, 131, 133, 135, *pl. 4, pl. 7*

E.T. (film), 199, 215

eagles, 17, 163, 164*fig.*

Earle, Rebecca, 92

early modern worldviews: on gender, 111–14, 123–24, 233–34; on group identity and divisions, 69–72, 174–75; on health and disease, 23; on the supernatural, 177–83, 184–86. *See also* colonialism

ecology: defined, 8; in evolutionary time, 27–28; humans as distinct and separate from, 16, 19, 24–25; humans as interconnected with, 8–9, 10, 16–19, 46, 166–67; intergalactic, 54; intergenerational relationships to, 26; and public health, 23–24, 25; *vs.* virtual reality, 54. *See also* environment

economic inequality, 89–90, 96–97, 189, 240

Egyptian artifacts, 148, 150, 186–87

Egyptian Hall (London, United Kingdom), 131, 132

Einhard, *Vita et gesta Karoli Magni,* 71*fig.*

El Salvador, 139

Elenx de Céspedes, 233–34, 235

Eliot, T. S., *The Waste Land,* 196

Elizabeth I, Queen of England, 113

Elliott (fictional character, *E.T.*), 215

Emmett Till Antilynching Act (US, 2022), 98

emotion, excessive, 110

empathy: for atypically embodied persons, 37–38, 132, 144; for the dispossessed, 90; ethics of care, 227; for extraterrestrials, 215, 217; for machines, 196, 198–200, 200*ofig.*, 201*fig.*, 203–4; at the national level, 100

endocrine-disruptor pollution, 25–26

enfreakment, process of, 127, 137

England, 111–12. *See also* United Kingdom; Welsh Marches

engravings, 70*fig.*, 71*fig.*, 72*fig.*, 179, 180*ofig.*

Enkidu (epic figure), 161

Enlightenment. *See* early modern worldviews

enslaved persons: atypically embodied persons treated as, 33, 129, 132, 141; hierarchies of, 123; and literacy, 227, 230. *See also* slavery

entertainment. *See* spectacularization

environment: and AI water consumption, 209, 244; and climate change, 242–44; extreme *vs.* temperate, 13–15, 63, 65, 69–70, 77, 80–81, 105; human bodies as susceptible to, 11, 13, 15, 47, 80–81, 87, 91–92, 252n9; pollution of, 24–27, 53, 97. *See also* cartography; ecology

Epic of Gilgamesh, The, 160–61, 211

equatorial zone, 14

ethics of care, 227

Ethiopia, 13, 252n14

Ethiopians, trope of washing off blackness of, 156

ethnicity and ethnic groups, 40, 62, 66–68, 72, 98, 99, 158, 242. *See also* race

Eucharist, 174

eugenics, 22

eunuchs, 122–24

Europe, in geographic thought, 75, 76*fig.*, 77

Eve (biblical figure), 116–18

Evelyn, John, 138

evolution, 27–28, 32, 48–50, 256n49

exceptionalism, human, 16, 19

exhibitions. *See* spectacularization

exoticism, 149

extraterrestrials: and alternate dimensions, 214; connection with, 215–17; and divinity, 217–18; and religious exclusion, 218–20

eyeglasses, 144

factory work, 196

Fagles, Robert, 226

Fairfax, Nathanial, 134

medieval worldviews: on gender, 116–17, 119–22, 234–35; on group identity and divisions, 65–69, 74–75, 99, 165; on hierarchies of beings, 42–43; on human-animal hybrids, 41–42; on machines, 193–94; on monarchy, 170–72; on relics, 173–74

Mediterranean Sea, 77

Melanchthon, Philipp, 184–86

Mello e Castro, Martinho de, 128*fig.*, 129, *pl. 7*

men: anxieties about paternity, 106, 110, 125; anxieties about witches' power over, 177, 181; masculinity, 147–48. *See also* gender and sexuality; women

Men in Black (film), 52

mental illness, 110

Merkel, Angela, 203

mermaids, 146

Mesoamerica. *See entries at Indigenous*

Mesopotamia, 160–61

mestizo/a label, 56

Mexica persons (Aztecs), 8–10, 9*fig.*, 16, 17, 148, 163, 164*fig.*, 166–67, 175, 176, *pl. 1*

Mexico: Indigenous worldviews/practices in, 8–10, 16, 17, 115, 124, 148, 163, 176; mixed-race persons in, 55, 94

miasma, 22*fig.*, 23

microcephaly, 139

microorganisms, 52–53

Microsoft, 209

Middle Ages. *See* medieval worldviews

midget label, 133

midrashic tradition, 117

midwives, 3, 105, 136, 176, 178, 259n27

Miéville, China, *The City and the City,* 90

mimicry/imitation, 43

mind-altering substances, 10, 21, 92, 167, 175, 176–77

Minnelli, Liza, 221

Minotaur (mythical figure), 6, 7*fig.*, 85

mixed-race/heritage persons: *casta* classification, 94–95, 95*fig., pl. 6;* as category-breakers/problems, 36, 56, 57, 59, 87, 94; and degeneration, 139; and demigods, 162; legislation on, 61, 83, 99, 124–25; "one-drop" rule and hypodescent, 61, 83. *See also* black codes

monarchy: divine ordination of, 170–72; queens, monstrousness of, 111–14

Mongol Empire, 194

Monk Calf, 184–86, 185*fig.*

monster-making/monstrification, as concept, 2, 3–4. *See also* empathy; environment; gender and sexuality; humans; nationalism and national identity; race; religion and cosmology; spectacularization

monsters: definitions of, 2–3; humans defined in relation to, 6–7. *See also* extraterrestrials; machines; monstrous births; *specific beings*

Monsters, Inc. (film), 236–37

monstrofuturism, 236–37

monstrous births: as accidents of nature, 11, 104, 105, 107; anxieties about, overview, 104; as divine warnings/punishment, 11, 104, 105, 107–8, 184–86; and parental resemblance, 110; as result of extreme environments, 13–15, 63, 65, 69–70, 77, 105; as result of mother's behavior, 103, 105–7, 108; specimenization of, 107, 134

morality and sin, 42, 74–75, 92, 116, 118

Mori, Masahiro, 200–201

Morris, Wesley, 155

Morrison, Toni, "Grendel and His Mother," 225

Mount Graham International Observatory (Arizona), 219–20

Mozambique, 129

Mozart, Anna Maria, 145

Mozart, Wolfgang Amadeus, 145

mulato/a label, 55, 256n1

multicultural individuals. *See* mixed-race/ heritage persons

mummies, 186–87

Muppet Show, The (TV series), 38, 214, 221–22

murals, 168–69, 169*fig.*

Murray, Thomas, 149

Musée du Nouveau Monde (La Rochelle, France), 127–28, 128*fig.*

Museum of Fine Arts (Boston, Massachusetts), 170

museums, collection and display practices in, 34–35, 35*fig.*, 37, 127, 134–35, 141–43, 148, *pl. 4*

intersectionality, 229–31; legislation based on, 81–85, 96, 99, 124–25; and maternal imagination, 108; and musical culture, 153; and racism, origins of, 58–59; and religion, 65–66, 68–69, 91, 93–94; and spectacularization, 127–30, 128*fig.*, 130*fig.*, 132, 133, 139–41, 140*fig.*, *pl. 7;* and sports, 154–57; and unequal rights, 83–84, 96–97. *See also* ethnicity and ethnic groups; mixed-race/heritage persons; *specific groups*

race-nation, as concept, 62

race-thinking/racecraft, 58, 257n4

racism, origins of, 58–59

radioactivity, 26–27

Rambaldi, Carlo, 216

Rankine, Claudia, 155

rarity label, 149

Raskolnikov, Masha, 235

raza term, 68

reason: and humanity, 42; women stereotyped as irrational, 110

rebellions, slave, 183

recreational substances, 21, 253n37

Reeve, Christopher, 221–22

Reformation, Protestant, 111, 174, 184–86

reincarnation, 38, 40, 166

relics, 173–74, 267n37

religion and cosmology: afterlife, understandings of, 167–69, 168*fig.*, 169*fig.*, *pl. 9, pl. 10;* end of time, understandings of, 163–65; and race, 65–66, 68–69, 91, 93–94; souls, understandings of, 38–40, 165–66, 167, 169–70, 182, 183, 204. *See also* god(s); supernatural, the; *specific religions/worldviews*

Ren, Shaolei, 209

Renaissance. *See* early modern worldviews

renarrativizing, 70–73

reproduction: and eugenics, 23; of extraterrestrials, 216; interracial/interspecies (*see* mixed-race/heritage persons); as mysterious, 105, 178; and nationalism, 23, 110; and pollution, 25; pregnancy and childbirth, 3, 103, 105–6, 108, 125, 136, 178, 239; "pro-life" movement, 239; and soul-shifting, 40. *See also* monstrous births

resurrection theology, 119–20

rhesus proteins, 51, 256n52

Rings of Power, The (TV series), 146

Ripley, Ellen (fictional character, *Alien*), 216

Rite of Spring, The (Stravinsky), 150–53, 151*fig.*

ritual calendars, 9*fig.*, 17, *pl. 1*

ritual practices, 10, 92, 115, 162–63, 170, 175–77, 182

ritual specialists, 166–67, 182

Robinson, Kim Stanley, 54

Robinson, Marius and Emily, 230

robots. *See* machines

Roddenberry, Gene, 146–47, 211

Roerich, Nicholas, 152

Roma persons, 96, 110

Roman worldviews. *See* classical antiquity worldviews

Romero, George A., 85

Roombas, 192, 200

Ross, Diana, 221

Rothschild Canticles, 43

Royal Aquarium (London, United Kingdom), 141–43

Royal College of Surgeons (London, United Kingdom), 133

Royal Society (London, United Kingdom), 103, 133–34, 138, 214

royal touch, 172

Roza, Dona, 128–29, 128*fig.*, *pl. 7*

Roza, José Conrado, *La mascarade nuptiale,* 127–30, 128*fig.*, 129*fig.*, *pl. 7*

Ruiz de Alarcén, Hernando, 9–10; *Treatise on the Heathen Superstitions and Customs That Today Live among the Indians Native to This New Spain,* 10, 16

rulers. *See* monarchy

Russian folk traditions, 150–53

sacrifices, human, 150, 163–64

Sampras, Pete, 154

Santiago de Compostela (Spain), 173

SARS epidemic (2003), 144

satyrs, 42, 46

Saudi Arabia, 203

Saunders, Charles, 231

Schloss Ambras, 34–36, 35*fig.*, *pl. 4*

Schongauer, Martin, *Shield with Stag Held by Wild Man,* 70*fig.*
Schwarzenegger, Arnold, 193
sciapods, 43
science fiction, and Afrofuturism, 231–32. *See also* fiction
sciences. *See specific fields*
Scotland, 111–12. *See also* United Kingdom
Scott, Ridley, 201, 215
scriptural interpretation, 74–77, 116–18, 119–20
scrofula, 172
Seabrook, William, *The Magic Island,* 183
Semenya, Caster, 157, 158
sensationalism. *See* spectacularization
Sepulveda, Ginés de, 93
servitude *vs.* slavery, 82–83
settler-colonialism. *See* colonialism
sexuality. *See* gender and sexuality
Shakespeare, William, 124; *The Tempest,* 85–88, 86*fig.*, 136–37
shamans, 166–67, 182
shape-shifters, 8–9, 10, 16–18, 21, 37–38, 163, 166–67, 170, 218
Sharapova, Maria, 145
Shatner, William, 147
Shelley, Mary, *Frankenstein,* 6, 28, 62, 186, 194
Siamese (conjoined) twins, 131, 133–34
sickness. *See* health and disease
sin and morality, 42, 74–75, 92, 116, 118
Sinti persons, 96, 110
sirens, 41, 41*fig.*, 42
Siriaco (dwarf), 128*fig.*, 129–30, *pl. 7*
Skywoman, 18
slam dunk (basketball technique), 154
Slave and Servant Acts (for Barbados, 1661), 83
slavery: abolition of, 127, 229; and Afrofuturism, 231–32; chattel, 82, 83, 210; as institution, 182–83; legislation on, 81–84, 124–25; and origins of racism, 58; and rebellion, 183. *See also* enslaved persons
Sloane, Hans, 103, 107, 138
soccer (football), 156
socioeconomic inequality, 89–90, 96–97, 189, 240

socioeconomic status, hierarchies of, 40
sodomy label, 116, 124, 233, 234–35
Sonalker, Anuja, 240
Sophia (android), 203
souls, 38–40, 165–66, 167, 169–70, 182, 183, 204
South Africa, 99, 157, 216–17
Southeast Asia, 141, 149, 186
Sow, Osmane, 127
Spain, 68–69, 173
Spanish colonies, 8, 9–10, 16, 35, 55, 91–92, 93–94, 124, 148, 175–77, 233–34
Spartans, 64–65
species. *See* Darwin, Charles; hierarchies of beings: classification of species; *entries at Homo*
specimenization, 34, 107, 134–36, 138, 141–43
spectacularization: advertisements, 107, 131, 132, 133, 135–36, 137–38, 139–41, 140*fig.*, 142*fig.*, 143*fig.*; and civility and civilization, discourse on, 129, 133; coercion *vs.* agency, 33, 129, 132, 133–36, 139; and colonialism, 129, 130, 138–39; and curiosity cabinets, 34–35, 35*fig.*, 130, *pl. 4;* entertainment venues, 131–32, 136–38; as phenomenon, 127–28; and specimenization, 34, 107, 134–36, 138, 141–43. *See also* performance
sphinxes, 46
Spielberg, Steven, 81
spirituality. *See* religion and cosmology
sports: and gender, 125–26, 157–59; and prodigious talent, 145, 155; and race, 154–57
Star Trek (TV series), 1, 146–47, 211, 222
Star Trek: Deep Space Nine (TV series), 91, 217–18
Star Trek: The Next Generation (TV series), 193, 202–4, 206, 218
Star Wars (film series), 192, 193
Stevenson, Robert Louis, *Dr. Jekyll and Mr. Hyde,* 20
stochastic terrorism, 239
Stoker, Bram, *Dracula,* 6, 35, 85, *pl. 4*
Strabo, 63
Stravinsky, Igor, *The Rite of Spring,* 150–53, 151*fig.*

Founded in 1893,
UNIVERSITY OF CALIFORNIA PRESS
publishes bold, progressive books and journals
on topics in the arts, humanities, social sciences,
and natural sciences—with a focus on social
justice issues—that inspire thought and action
among readers worldwide.

The UC PRESS FOUNDATION
raises funds to uphold the press's vital role
as an independent, nonprofit publisher, and
receives philanthropic support from a wide
range of individuals and institutions—and from
committed readers like you. To learn more, visit
ucpress.edu/supportus.